La Bonne Table

LA BONNE TABLE

~ *Ludwig Bemelmans* ~

❖

SELECTED AND EDITED BY DONALD AND ELEANOR FRIEDE

DAVID R. GODINE, PUBLISHER
Boston

This is a NONPAREIL BOOK, first published in 1989 by
DAVID R. GODINE, *Publisher*
Post Office Box 450
Jaffrey, New Hampshire, 03452
www.godine.com

Permissions continued on page 447.

Library of Congress Cataloging-in-Publication Data:
Bemelmans, Ludwig, 1898–1962
La bonne table / Ludwig Bemelmans;
selected and edited by Donald and Eleanor Friede.
p.   cm.
Reprint. Originally published: New York: Simon and Schuster, 1964.
Includes bibliographic references and index.
ISBN: 0-87923-808-9 (softcover: alk. paper)
1. Gastronomy. 2. Dinners and dining. 3. Bemelmans, Ludwig,
1898–1962. I. Friede, Donald. II. Friede, Eleanor. III. Title.
TX631 .B4 2001   641'.01'3—dc21
89-45382   2001040947

Third printing, 2016
Manufactured in the United States of America

CONTENTS

Introduction by *Donald and Eleanor Friede*   11

1. *Behind the Scenes*   19

ADIEU TO THE OLD RITZ   21
MONSIEUR VICTOR   32
"THE PROBLEM OF SEATING PEOPLE . . ."   37
GRAPES FOR MONSIEUR CAPE   38
HERR OTTO BRAUHAUS   43
BEAU MAXIME   50
THE EDUCATION OF A WAITER   53
DINNER OUT   59
OLD LUCHOW   64
ART AT THE HOTEL SPLENDIDE   65
THE BRAVE COMMIS   73
"THE ARMY IS LIKE A MOTHER . . ."   78
THE BUTTERMACHINE   79
NO TROUBLE AT ALL   83

AFFAIR	92
"ALL MAÎTRES D'HÔTEL LOVE TO EAT . . ."	104
COMING OUT	106
"MY FIRST VISIT TO PARIS . . ."	119
THEODORE AND "THE BLUE DANUBE"	120
"MOST SWINDLES IN AUSTRIA . . ."	124
THE KITCHEN OF THE GOLDEN BASKET	125
LADY MENDL'S CHEF	130
THE SURVIVORS	131
MONSIEUR ALBERT OF MAXIM'S	133
ON INNKEEPING	134
THE CHEF I ALMOST HIRED	140
MONSIEUR DUMAINE	142
MONSIEUR SOULÉ	143

II. At Table 145

DOWN WHERE THE WÜRZBURGER FLOWS 147
GRANDFATHER AND THE *Zipperl* 150
"AMONG THE BIRDS THAT MAKE GOOD EATING . . ." 152
FILET DE SOLE COLBERT 153
THE S.S. *Mesias* 155
THE DAY WITH HUNGER 163
APPLES 168
VACATION 169
YOU SHALL HAVE MUSIC 176
"WHAT HAS HAPPENED TO THE FAMOUS VINTAGES . . ." 185
LES SAUCISSONS D'ARLES 186
BAKED CLAMS CHEZ GEORGES 191
THE TREASURED CLIENT 192
TO BE A GOURMET 194
"PRINCES, GENERALS, DEEP-SEA CAPTAINS . . ." 198
THE SPAGHETTI TRAIN 199
POULETS DE BRESSE 201
LADY MENDL'S DINING ROOM 203
LUNCH WITH BOSY 205
LUCHOW'S 207
"LADY MENDL LIKED DOGS AND PEOPLE SLIM . . ." 210
AMONG THE ARABS 211
CAVIAR 213
AT THE MÉDITERRANÉE 225
RECIPE FOR COCKLES OR CLAMS 226
TEXAS LEGEND 227
"SECOND DOOR TO YOUR RIGHT . . ." 230
THE BEST WAY TO SEE CUBA 231
CHEZ RENE 234
THE BEST WAY TO SEE RIO 235
SHIPOWNER 240
THE ISLAND OF PORQUEROLLES 243
TONI AND ROCCO 244
THE SOUL OF AUSTRIA 245
HOW I TOOK THE CURE 249
LETTER TO A RESTAURATEUR 265

The French Train 266

Hotel de Paris, Monte Carlo 269

L'Oustau de Baumanière 270

The First Cherries 274

Menus— 275
> Le Pavillon, Maxim's, Grand Véfour, Lapérouse,
> Lucas Carton, Larue, Chapon Fin, La Pyramide,
> l'Oustau de Baumanière, Münchner Hofbrauhaus,
> Luchow's

III. Fancies 291

The Elephant Cutlet 293

Christmas in Tyrol 295

Glow Wine 310

About Clouds and Lebkuchen 311

Wedding in Tyrol 314

Schweinerei 317

Tales of the South American General 319

Pepito 339

Germiny à l'Oseille 340

Romanoff's for Lunch 343

Romanoff's—Two Views 352

The Commissary 353

Servant Trouble 360

Snowy Night in Malibu 363

Come Rain, Come Shine 371

Mocambo 374

Hunger Dream 379

Guten Appetit 380

Twelve Little Girls 388

Madame l'Ambassadrice 389

The International 399

The Woman of My Life 400

Wedding Breakfast 409

Of Pigs and Truffles 410

Perfect Service 414

Heavenly Soup 423

The Tour d'Argent   424
When You Lunch with the Emperor   441
   Attributions   443

Introduction

Everything in this book has something to do with eating. And all of it is from Ludwig Bemelmans' own writings and drawings. The yield is astonishingly abundant and diverse, for the subject of food and drink, of restaurants and hotels and those who serve and are served in them, came naturally and often into everything Bemelmans wrote. It appeared in letters, tales of true adventures, articles, novels, and even in his books for children. Next to the people he loved and his work, the art of dining well, and the whole world of activity surrounding it, was probably his major concern. It was certainly his first thought, for example, when he went to France in the spring of 1962, and began a letter . . .

Just got through ordering my first dinner in Paris. They called me up and said, at the Méditerrannée, we want to celebrate your return on the third day of Easter—and because the markets close we have to shop—and Papa who is in Nice told me to call you—would it make you happy to have a poulet aux morilles à la crème—we got the idea looking at your favorite menus—and then wild asparagus—and perhaps to start a truite à la nage. Yes, yes, yes. So that is settled.

We were working then with him on the final stages of his last novel, *The Street Where the Heart Lies*, but only with the prospect of a fine meal in view could this truly civilized person concern himself with the details of proofs and queries. First things first. "Then, there is the problem of the cheese in 'Perfect Service,'" the letter continued, "and I hasten to settle that too . . ." This is a chapter in which an American professor in Paris describes a classic dinner to a *clochard* he has befriended. The scene takes place, quite logically, under a bridge on the bank of the Seine. And the problem was that Ludwig had left out the cheese course. Now this was perhaps the one course in the lavish meal to which the French hobo, who remembered the neighborhood restaurant of his bourgeois days, could fully relate his own experience. We agreed there had to be cheese. The evolution of the final menu involved meetings, telephone calls, letters, and ultimately, a few cables, but "Perfect Service" does finish with "a fine Brie." It is included in Part III of this book, complete in itself as a story with only the merest deletion of unrelated material, as is the case, fortunately, with much of Bemelmans' fiction.

The editors of this book were privileged—and it is an unforgettable privilege to have known and loved such a man—to be close to Ludwig Bemelmans during, roughly, the last five years of his life. Donald Friede was his editor on his last two novels, *Are You Hungry Are You Cold* and *The Street Where the Heart Lies;* Eleanor, working in the same publishing house, was in charge of advertising, publicity, and promotion. The three of us worked together in a penthouse on the Ile St. Louis in Paris, in the huge studio of a Gramercy Park duplex, in a house atop the high dunes of East Hampton, and in fine restaurants on both sides of the Atlantic. We drank his favorite Dom Perignon champagne with him (there was always a chilled bottle awaiting us) and we witnessed his special artistry at table. For him the preparing and serving of food was an art he knew and appreciated, and he was sad to watch the deepening evidence of its neglect. In his black moods he was convinced that the next generation would either have to settle for a lifetime diet of hamburgers or learn to cook, and he had little hope for the latter. About dining he was himself the true *amateur*—to use the word without its pejorative sense. "I like pudding, I like wine, roast goose, Virginia ham, shepherd's pie, and lobster stew. I am hungry and thirsty a good deal of the time, which accounts for the fact that I have acquired a reputation as a connoisseur of wines and as a gourmet," he wrote with typical understatement in *To the One I Love the Best*, his book about his friendship with Elsie Mendl. In the same book he summed up Lady Mendl's definition of Good Taste, in its overall sense, as Simplicity-Suitability-Proportion. Certainly Good

Uncle's Hotel in KLOBENSTEIN TIROL

Taste—Lady Mendl's version and the cook's—characterized the meals we shared with Ludwig, at home or in his favorite restaurants. As an instance, after a dinner in the Oak Room of the Plaza in New York, he wrote a thank-you note that was both an apology to the chef and a credo, and the foods are both simple and suitable.

Thank you so much for your hospitality last night. I did not order ham and Bibb lettuce out of lack of faith dans la cuisine du Plaza, but because I was still on European mealtime, and in such cases I always eat ham which is a kind of tranquilizer for me. Ham and eggs, incidentally, or the ham at Fouquet's with epinards either creamed or en branche are as good a thing as I ask for. It is incidentally very limited, the list of things in the kitchen that one can really like, especially if you are given to sane living with knife and fork.

It was inevitable, from his earliest moments, that Ludwig Bemelmans be "given to sane living with knife and fork." He was born on April 27, 1898, in a hotel in Tyrol, and spent the first years of his life in a beer garden. "An old maître d'hôtel was my nurse, and the chef himself made up my formula," he wrote in an early book called *Life Class* (1938). As a boy he was apprenticed in the hotels owned by his uncle, and flopped magnificently. It has been said that he shot a headwaiter, and was given the choice of going to reform school or America. And so in 1914 he began his association with New York hotels—as bus boy, commis de rang, waiter, and ultimately assistant banquet manager at the Ritz Carlton—and acquired the inside knowledge for the stories and articles in Part I of this book. Here the viewpoint is from "Behind the Scenes," as the section is titled. Except for the first selection, in which L. B. bids an affectionate adieu to the old Ritz—a fitting preface to the accounts of hotel life that follow—the arrangement is generally chronological within each of the three parts of the book. And so, when the hero of "The Brave Commis" joins the Army, so, soon after, did Bemelmans: two excerpts from his wartime experiences as told in his first adult book, *My War with the United States*, therefore came next. Bemelmans returned to the Ritz after the war, and it was then that he worked in the banquet department; here we have the classic stories of parties on a grand scale in "Affair," "Coming Out," and "No Trouble at All."

The Bemelmans of Part II, "At Table," is an exceptional guest who observes the scene about him—the menu, the fare, the other diners, and those who serve—with the unique awareness of the ex-waiter turned artist and writer. Here the point of view of the selections is from out front, on stage, from the participant. But certainly few have sat at table with such special knowledge. Toward the end of this section are several pieces from a journal Ludwig Bemelmans kept on his last trip to France in April, May, and June of 1962. He died on October 1 of that year. He obviously planned to expand these notes into articles and stories at a future date, but a few, without any rewriting beyond punctuation and minor deletion, happily met the requirements for this book. That is, they concerned food or restaurants and they made sense on their own, whether a brief anecdote or longer description. In these notes there is perhaps the perfect illustration of the lifelong blend of the "behind the scenes"

Bemelmans "at table." It is the short piece titled "Hotel de Paris, Monte Carlo," and in it Ludwig shows a young *piccolo* (and all of us) the correct way for a bus boy to serve bread with a spoon and a fork.

The third and final part of this book, following a collection of menus from some of Bemelmans' favorite restaurants, is for the most part fiction and is entitled "Fancies." There are, of course, stories in Part I that were published as fiction, but they are about "behind the scenes" people and they belong there. Just as it was impossible to categorize Ludwig Bemelmans, so it is impossible to put any neat labels on his work. He took a fact, a happening, something he saw, and embroidered it. His fiction stemmed from experience, of course, but some of the pieces spill over so that fact and fiction are indistinguishable, as they were most of all to the author himself. He lived and created in a world he made up to live in, day by day. And in this section of the book are some of the mad and wonderful people with whom he filled his world, as well as some very bitter social satire about those he couldn't keep out.

To our best count, Bemelmans wrote thirty-nine books of which seventeen were written for children and seven were novels. He also wrote hundreds of stories and articles for magazines, some introductions to others' books, a ballet libretto, motion picture and stage musical scripts. He kept a journal, and he wrote a phenomenal num-

ber of letters. And constantly he painted and drew—canvases, many of them huge, illustrations, sketches, and sketches for sketches on whatever scrap of paper was handy. We have seen all of these things. The unpublished material and very many unpublished drawings and sketches were made available to us by Ludwig's widow, Madeleine Bemelmans, and their daughter, Barbara, and the book is richer for them. It should be said that everything that Bemelmans wrote about food is not in this book: some very good material just couldn't be drawn out of context.

There were many times during the months we were preparing this book—reading the journals and letters, re-reading all of the published writings, looking at pictures, remembering—that we had the feeling that the pieces were coming together to form almost an autobiography. His natural habitat was hotels and restaurants, and it is all by his own hand. At the same time we knew that if Bemelmans had written his autobiography as such, it would undoubtedly have been a revelation of yet another side of this remarkable man. And we can say this with some assurance. For there came a moment, quite early in our friendship, when we needed his approval of a paragraph or so of biographical material to appear in connection with one of his books. He rejected all the usual and unusual adjectives we could devise and wrote his own evaluation of himself, which, for some reason, was never used.

The description of my versatility can be very sick-making, like any slight of hand. But I don't mind at all saying it without fanfare. Just say then: a curious, complicated being who is driven by an excess of energy which he tries to discipline, but since it is like wild horses it runs away with him. He works with fury, and lives as if it were his last day on earth. He is overly kind, overly generous—and hides it under a cloak of arrogance. He paints or writes the night through, is never where he says he will be, changes his plans constantly, drinks, smokes, eats to excess, but fortunately has the constitution of an ox.

What a great autobiography his would have been.

DONALD AND ELEANOR FRIEDE

June 1964

Those for whom *La Bonne Table* may serve as a clarion call for "More Bemelmans!"—food or no—will find at the end of the book a list of Attributions leading them to the sources from which these selections have been made.

I · *Behind the Scenes*

*The early years were the years of train-
ing, of apprenticeship. The kitchen and
the pantry were the starting points, and
then the restaurant itself became the field
of play—but with the folded-napkin
badge of the one who stands and waits.*

When L. B. wrote this nostalgic memorial in 1950, he confirmed in print for the first time what the cognoscente *had guessed and smiled at for years. Hotel Splendide, Hotel Bemelmans, even the fabulous Cocofinger Palace were really the "Old Ritz" as one man saw it. In some of the stories that follow—*Monsieur Victor, Grapes for Monsieur Cape, Herr Otto Brauhaus, No Trouble at All, *and* Affair, *to name a few—those who knew the Ritz-Carlton Hotel, which filled the block from Forty-seventh to Forty-eighth Streets on New York's Madison Avenue, will have little trouble recalling its atmosphere and may even recognize the backstage personalities identified by their real names for the first time here.*

Adieu to the old Ritz

Bemelmans

Everybody has a favorite hotel,
and the greatest of them all, I am told,
is the Cocofinger Palace in Switzerland.
It is so vast that the chef has to use
a motorboat to put the noodles
in the soup. Personally, I am partial
to smaller hotels. For me,
the old Ritz-Carlton in New York
was the ideal hotel. I knew it well.

I came to the Ritz soon after landing in New York. I was sent there to learn the hotel business as practiced in America. I started in the wine-women-and-song department at the age of eighteen. I learned how to press a duck, open a bottle, and push a chair under a lady.

The president of the corporation
which operated the hotel then
was a Mr. Harris, who had
started out in life
as an accountant. He came
once a year from London
to look over the accounts
and to inspect the hotel.
Mr. Harris had a great feeling
for the employees.

One of the outstanding members
of the backstage family was
Monsieur Bonafou, the baker.
He weighed
two hundred and sixty-eight pounds,
and on that account he entered and left
the hotel via the sidewalk elevator.
It took him straight from the door
of his tiled bakery in the third basement
to the sidewalk, where his arrival
was announced by the loud ringing
of a warning bell.

Interesting as the hotel was, my ambition
was to paint. I used to make
my first sketches on the walls
of the bakery. The brush slid like a skate
over the smooth tile. This arrangement
was very helpful, for it gave me
a carefully divided surface to work on,
and with a wet rag it was all washed away
and the wall ready to be used again.
The most exciting scenes were always
in the kitchen at the rush hour,
where the frequent clashes of the cooks
dressed in white with the waiters
dressed in black provided
not only interesting contrasts
but constant action.

The one who brought order
into the chaos
was the chef, Monsieur Louis Diat,
a very quiet and distinguished Frenchman,
the creator of vichyssoise
and many other dishes.
He never raised his voice,
he never lost his temper.

M. Loui's Diat

The opposite
of Monsieur Diat
in temperament was
Mr. Albert Keller,
a German from
the Palatinate who weighed more
than Monsieur Bonafou and was
known among the backstairs family
as "Cheeses Greisd," which was his
most frequent expression.
He sometimes varied it with
"Gotdemn, Cheeses Greisd."
He was my patron, and I owe him
a great deal. He extended me such
tolerance and generosity as only
the most fortunate of artists
have enjoyed. We see him here
running on his way to give somebody
a "boiling out." Loud and fearful
as he was, he never could get himself
to fire anybody.

Cheeses GReisd

*By applying myself thoroughly
to the study of kitchen
and cellar . . .*

*. . . and by carefully following
the example of my superiors
and trying to be like them . . .*

. . . my talents were soon recognized. I was promoted to a position to which a large income and little responsibility were attached, as well as the most luxurious mode of living.

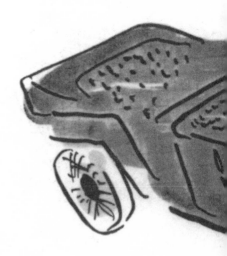

I had good quarters, wine, food,
and laundry free.
It was the time when even the rich
could buy themselves something,
and I became the owner of a Hispano-Suiza.

The Hispano

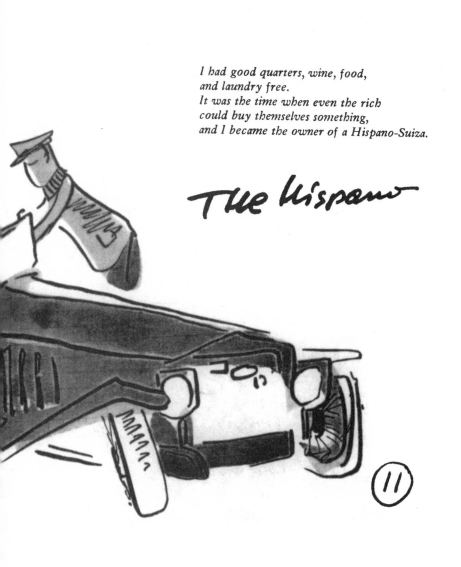

(11)

Amadou's Den

One of the backstairs family was a Senegalese porter named Amadou, who lived in a tent made of unused rugs under the stairs of the Crystal Room. There he looked through L'Illustration and made himself a powerful drink, pouring the leftovers from the various glasses that were removed from banquet tables into a pitcher and seasoning the mixture with lemon and sugar. It was Amadou's ambition to become a doorman or a chauffeur. He went to the Russian tailor who took care of the uniforms of our doormen and had him make a uniform and I employed him as a part-time companion.

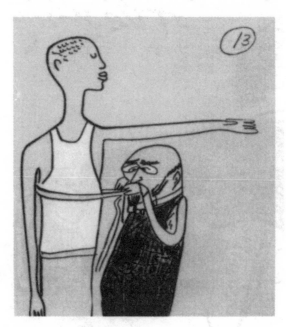

I forgot to say that I also had a secretary.

Miss Cutting

In the summer,
business slackened, and
my department was very quiet.
I arranged a studio for myself
in one of the smaller ballrooms,
put up a model stand,
and painted when the light
was best.

Because this was a French hotel,
everybody had a French name,
and I was known as Monsieur Louis.
One day I entered the office,
and there was a green slip
in the typewriter.

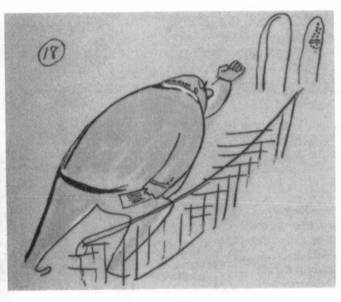

Although there was no business,
my efficient secretary sent
a daily report to Mr. Keller.
She was out of the office, the report
was almost finished, I read:
Date, department, etc., no parties,
no inquiries, etc., and then—
"Monsieur Louis came down
from his room at ten-thirty.
Monsieur Louis telephoned for his Hispano.
Monsieur Louis had his breakfast
in the Japanese garden. Monsieur Louis
took the houseman, Amadou, with him.
Monsieur Louis said he would be back
at three." I sat down at the typewriter
and finished the note, writing:
"Monsieur Louis came back at three.
Monsieur Louis read this note.
Monsieur Louis went to the châlet de nécessité
and while there Monsieur reflected what a bitch he had for a secretary."
I thought Miss Cutting would find the note and that it would teach her
a lesson. Unfortunately she did not read my postcript
but signed the report and sent it to Mr. Keller.

He stormed up the stairs
the next day at eleven,
the note in his hand.
He bellowed
like a wounded bull.
On such occasions he was
to be avoided.
I took the Hispano—and
drove around the country.
Amadou sat in the back,
for he did not know
how to drive.
It always took three days
for Mr. Keller's anger
to evaporate.
When I got back, he came up
to the studio on a routine
inspection. He saw the model
and the drawing.
"Gotdemn, Cheeses Greisd!"
he said.
"What sort of business
are you making
out of this place?"

All that was a long time ago and in a softer mood.
This is my obituary and now Monsieur Charles
and Monsieur François make their last bow—
to the old house that has been so good to us all.

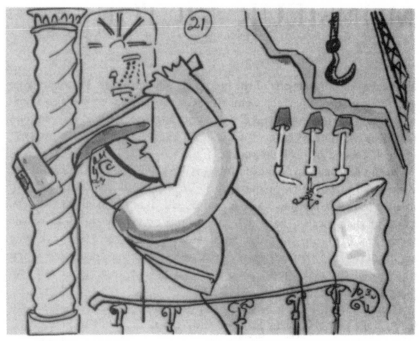

O.K., boys—take it away!

MONSIEUR VICTOR

Monsieur Victor was one of the best in his difficult trade. He knew wine and food; he had a perfect memory for names and faces. He also knew who was in Society, who was almost in Society and, what is most important, who was not. With such facts in his head, he guarded the interests of the hotel and of his own pocket.

During luncheon and dinner Monsieur Victor stands at the head of the wide stairs that lead from the Jade Lounge up into the restaurant. He usually leans on his desk, a maître d'hôtel's desk, with eight drawers, seven of them neatly marked from the top down for the days of the week: *Lundi, Mardi, Mercredi, Jeudi, Vendredi, Samedi, Dimanche*. The eighth drawer is for special parties and reservations far ahead, and in the top part of the desk, under a lid that lifts up, are reservation lists and place cards and signs marked "Reserved."

Monsieur Victor has a secretary in a tight hole-in-the-wall office, and his first assistant, Monsieur Serafini, takes people from his hand and, following Victor's instructions, pilots them to the table whose number is whispered to him in French. At that table a chef de rang takes their order.

On a balcony overhanging Victor's desk is a small orchestra, the leader of which is a very good Hungarian violinist. He plays an eternally unchanging repertoire of dinner music and, like Victor, he looks out over the Jade Lounge as the guests arrive. While Victor is chiefly concerned with the social position of the arrivals and, first of all, when they are still distant, looks at their faces, the Hungarian violinist fastens his eyes on the women's legs and turns around to look at the rest of them only as they pass by him into the restaurant. Thus a person entering at the far side of the Jade Lounge is watched advancing to the stairs by many eyes: by all the guests who sit in the Jade Lounge and on the balcony, by Victor and his assistants, who stand to the right of him, by the violinist, and also by all the other musicians. They never have to read their notes; they have played these same pieces of hotel music so often that they have become part of the dining room, like the tables, the chairs, and the salt and pepper shakers.

Victor's assistant holds a list of reservations in his hand. The best tables are for Society; close by them sit celebrities, actresses, publishers. In a wider circle are the people who are photographed much and appear in the rotogravure sections, who are found at the Atlantic Beach Club, in Miami, and occasionally murdered or mixed up in fashionable messes; also Italian aristocracy, young men who give morning concerts or dancing lessons, and movie stars. Beyond these come the tables of the untouchables. Victor's salary from the hotel is not large, only $350 a month, plus his food, a dressing room, linen, and a valet; but his income in a good year is about $40,000.

Society contributes little of that, and they treat him badly, but no matter when they arrive and in what mood or unexpected numbers, he will bow deeply, address them loudly by name, so that all the other waiting guests may be properly impressed, and seat them immediately. He is very careful not to address one of their women by her last year's name. Their complaints are immediately attended to, and when they leave they are again bowed out with a compliment that would cost other people at least twenty dollars. All that because, without them, the restaurant is through and would be closed in a short while.

But other guests, too, may receive good tables, after they have stuck a little folded bill into Monsieur Victor's hand. When he is not certain from experience of the size of the bill, he always hears an imaginary telephone bell ringing and rushes into his office. Attached to the wall at the level of his hand is a mirror. In it Victor can see whether there is five or ten dollars printed on the corner of the bill and, around Christmas time, whether it is twenty, fifty or a hundred. During the five hasty steps that take him back to the door, he has performed a lightning-quick

33

calculation, an exercise in the nice adjustment of many factors: the available table, the time of the day, the day of the week and the amount of the banknote. The assistant hears a softly pronounced table number, and the guests are led to a table. If they are delighted or make faces, the little mirror in the office knows why.

But such people have no hope whatever if they don't pay. They will join the outermost circle of untouchables, who fill out the noisy, drafty corners, sit close to service tables, and are squeezed against mirrors and the edges of the balcony stairs—women in bad copies of the latest fashion, mousy little couturières with French names written on the windows of their side-street shops, Westchester housewives in gray squirrel coats and galoshes on rainy days. They order an œuf Bénédict and a glass of milk before going to a matinee. There are, besides, a lot of innocent people who just walked in off the street, thinking that this was a restaurant. A description of Victor's behavior to them may well serve as a manual for his trade.

Entering the Jade Lounge, they are far away from him and below him, which is to their disadvantage. They have to cross the wide hall and climb up the stairs, and there they are met by the music, by Victor, and by his moping assistants, one of them with a seating diagram and the large list of reservations in his hand.

As these intruders stand in front of him, Victor looks them over with a slow, deliberate inventory of shoes, trousers, hands. He stops at the necktie; the face he has seen below, when it came in through the door at the end of the Jade Lounge. Victor has his heels together; he stands straight, then leans forward a little and turns his head in a listening gesture. The guest in front of him is by now ill at ease and wishes he had not come; he is a plain, well-dressed and respectable-looking person.

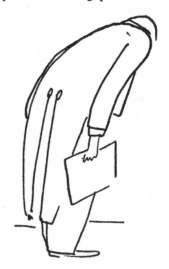

"Your name?" asks Victor. The man now has his hand to his tie, at which Victor has been looking all the while.

Victor repeats the name to his assistant, lisping it slowly. The assistant looks at the list and finds no such name.

"You have no reservation?" says Victor now, with the tone in which he might say, "Where did you steal that watch?"

"Reservation?" says the man.

"Yes, reservation," answers Victor. He turns to his assistant and says, "*Il n'a pas de réservation.*"

"Oh!" says the assistant, regretting this on behalf of Victor. Victor, who has never once looked at the good wife of the man, though she has been standing beside her husband all this while, says, if he likes the looks of the man, in French and to his fingernails: "Find him a table somewhere." If he doesn't like him, then suddenly and with finality he looks at the man's face and tells him, "Sorry, I have no table for you," turns on his heel and walks into the dining room, to bow and smile left and right to the good guests at the first tables.

Sometimes people will balk at this treatment; a brave and corpulent businessman will try to shake off Victor. An invisible wrestling match starts, the man pushing back the lapels of his coat, putting his hands in all of his pockets and taking them out again, looking into the faces of bystanders for support and pointing at empty tables inside the room. In such cases Victor takes the list of reservations from his assistant, drums on the edge of it with the end of his golden pencil and looks past the man's ear into faraway space.

The man usually says, "I called up this morning at nine o'clock. I was there when my secretary made the call. It was a few minutes past nine. She asked for a table for two at one-fifteen; now it's ten minutes

after one and you say haven't got a table. Look at your list there, and see if you haven't go the name, Stanley Cohan, C-o——"

"I've told you, Mr. Cohan, that I have no reservation in your name," says Victor.

"I called up this morning," the man starts again.

"Yes, I know, Mr. Cohan. I have a very careless secretary."

Victor leaves him and takes someone else personally into the room, or just turns again to smile and nod at seated guests. The assistants fight out the rest.

This sometimes ends in a man running after Victor with a threat of a punch in the nose, or, in case of Westerners, with an offer to buy the whole hotel just to fire Victor.

There is also the address to the wife: "Come on, Vi, let's get out of here, let's go some other place. You know there are places in this town where they know how to take care of people. Why, I wouldn't eat here if they paid me. Come on."

The orchestra plays a selection from *Naughty Marietta,* and they climb down the stairs and are gone.

Monsieur Victor and his assistants look after them without anger, with the detachment of a bullfighter who has done his routine work and waits until the horses have dragged the animal out, ready to start on the next. With folded arms they look at the chandelier, then into the room, tapping the tempo of the music with their pencils. In a few seconds it starts all over again.

Occasionally Victor meets his match, a man who will not be thrown out, one who is quite capable of taking Victor by the collar of his coat, shaking him, or pushing him out of the way. Victor is very sensitive in feeling out such people; they are seated.

The technique—looking at the tie and shoes and not the face, the voice, the faraway look—all this Victor has taken over from his most important clients, from Society.

*T*he problem of seating people properly in a fashionable restaurant in
a large city is a bigger headache to the management than running the
kitchen and wine cellar combined. Because of crowded interiors and
the problems of architecture, most restaurants have their "good" and
"bad" locations—a situation that could be avoided only by the installation
of a revolving floor, on which each table in turn would be "good" and
"bad."

As it is, there is much heartbreak and frustration attached to where
one is seated—it has even led to divorce. A lady who came regularly to
one of the fashionable restaurants was always kept waiting and always
badly seated—when with her husband. One day she went to the place
with another man and immediately was placed at the best table. The
consequences were awful for everybody concerned.

Everyone in the hotel was saying, "Monsieur Cape is coming, Monsieur Cape is coming from England." There was much cleaning up and shining, and everybody seemed to be afraid of Monsieur Cape. For Monsieur Cape was the president of our company. His offices were in London, and from there he always went on his rounds, first to Paris, where the company had another big hotel, then across to Rio de Janeiro and Havana, where the company also had restaurants, and finally to the Splendide.

Serafini told me that from Thursday on I would be on duty every morning at seven, with clean collar, brushed hair, shined shoes, and fingernails in shape, to serve Monsieur Cape's breakfast; and that, he added, was "a great honor."

At last the great man arrived, was received with much bowing and scraping, and was installed in the Adam Suite, one of the private apartments, our most palatial accommodations. It was a completely isolated duplex home with its own salon, dining room, staircase and back service entrance. Up the latter, every morning, I brought breakfast to him and his niece. For he had brought a very beautiful niece with him, a girl with blue eyes and ash-blond hair. He had many nieces, the chambermaid told me; this was the fifth one, and always a different one came with him from England, and the maid closed one eye when she said that.

In bed Mr. Cape was very small and not much bigger when he got up. He had a red face with a small beard at the bottom, which made it look like a radish upside down. He talked very little and walked back and forth, playing with the keys in his pocket and looking at the floor, like Uncle Hans. One of the first things he did whenever he came from England was to go to the coatroom of the restaurant, where there was a beautiful Irish girl, take her arm, go behind a sea-green drapery with her, and there whisper a joke into her ear. Unlike the nieces, it was always the same joke.

For his breakfast I had to go down into the kitchen and first of all order a basket of fruit from an old Frenchman in charge of them. The fruit was kept in the innermost and coldest refrigerator of a series of three, one inside the other. I gave the old Frenchman a slip on which I had written: "*Un Panier de Fruit*" and under this, underscored with two thick lines: "*Pour Monsieur Cape*."

It always took a lot of time. The old man searched for the keys, unlocked each refrigerator in turn, skewered the slip on a long bent needle that hung over his desk, and said to himself several times, "*Un panier de fruit, pour Monsieur Cape.*" When we were inside, he held

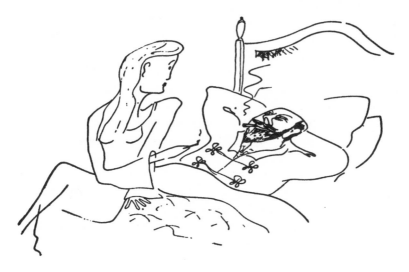

the fruit up to his eyes, placed it in the basket and rearranged it several times to get the right Fruit Basket feeling.

When all was built up to his satisfaction, he placed a bunch of grapes on top, a big beautiful Belgian hothouse bunch with fat grapes that were so closely pressed together that some of them had square sides. These grapes came six bunches to a box, in a bed of ground cork and soft tissue paper. Then, in the open spaces around the grapes, the old Frenchman put a few more figs and plums, and finally he straightened out and said: "*Voilà, mon petit, un panier de fruit pour Monsieur Cape.*"

I carried the basket of fruit carefully upstairs. In the warm air outside of the icebox a film of water in tiny beads set on all the fruit; the plums were most beautiful that way. Fruit should always be served so, from out of the cold.

On my first trip up I also took with me a fingerbowl, a pair of silver shears for the grapes, and the linen. Then I went down again, by the private staircase, through the reception room of the apartment, out the door to the hotel corridor, down with the service elevator, across the pantry, and down into the kitchen. On the second trip up I brought the orange juice for the niece, the porridge and the tea. For everything I had to write slips with "Pour Monsieur Cape" underlined.

After I had carried all this upstairs, I sat in the salon and waited until Monsieur Cape rang. The little alcohol flames burned under the silver kettle—he made his own tea—and under the porridge, which stood in a dish of hot water. For the toast I had to run down a third time while Monsieur Cape ate his fruit. It was a job nobody liked.

It took a long time for him to wake up. I started with the basket of fruit at seven-thirty and busied myself with this breakfast until about nine-thirty, because, while I was there, no one could call me away for any other duty. On the desk in the salon were the accounts of the hotel. I read them every morning; much was in red ink; it did not seem to be a very profitable hotel. Uncle Hans's hotels were much better paying. After I had read the accounts and the English funny papers, there was nothing to do.

I started on the first day to eat a few of the grapes on the Belgian hothouse bunch. The bunch got to look bad on one side, so I turned it around. But still Monsieur Cape did not ring, and I ate more on the good side. Then the bunch was altogether bad-looking; it was impossible to serve it to anyone, and so I finished it and put some figs in its place. From then on I ate a bunch of grapes every morning.

Soon after I had eaten the grapes, a door would open and I would hear a little swish of nightgown and soft steps. That was the niece going to her own bedroom. Then another door would open and close and soon the little bell would ring and Monsieur Cape got his breakfast. The niece would come in and say "Good morning" to me and to the uncle, and then she would sit on the side of the bed and help him prepare his tea. When I bent over, I could smell her hair and see that she was very young and firm and beautiful.

When I took the dishes down and brought the basket back to the icebox, it was about nine-thirty and the first chef was in his office, through the window of which he could see me pass and hand the basket back to the old man.

The first chef was, of course, also a Frenchman, but he was tall and, unlike most cooks and most Frenchmen, very quiet and self-controlled. One had to stand close to him to hear what he said, for he never raised his voice, not even in the greatest luncheon rush, when dishes clattered and the cooks were red in the face and excited and everybody ran and shouted. He was very saving for the hotel and he knew the contents of all his iceboxes. He also knew about the fruit and the basket for Mr. Cape and, of course, about the grapes.

When I came back with the basket, he always stepped to the door and looked at it, and said quietly: "They are costly, these grapes of Belgium." I wrote out a slip then, for *"Une grappe de raisin de Belgique,"* and for whatever other fruit had been used up, and the old man took it in exchange for the slip I had given him before for the whole basket. The first slip was torn up, and the slip for the grapes was collected by the accounting department with all the others and billed, but of course the president of the company had everything free and never received a bill.

All this went along very nicely for weeks. In the morning I served Monsieur Cape and in the evening worked in the wind-swept roof garden, overlooking the city from the thirty-second floor. There was a foyer on it with little tables and a large buffet that was made of tin containers filled with ice and with a little fountain in its center.

About six o'clock I had to be up there and help arrange cold dishes

on the ice: large salmons in parsley and lemons, glacéd pheasants, poussins in aspic, cold bœuf à la mode, galantines of capon, hors d'œuvres,
saucissons d'Arles, sauce verte, mayonnaise, beautifully decorated salads,
strawberry tarts with whipped cream, compotes—many fine, good things.
The first chef supervised all this and watched out that nothing disappeared.

On a very hot evening Monsieur Cape and his niece came and waited
for their dinner guests in the chairs in front of the buffet. In a little
while Monsieur Cape was walking back and forth, with his hands in
his pockets, playing with his keys. The chef had not seen Monsieur
Cape since his arrival and he bowed and smiled. The guests were arriving
now and engaging Monsieur Cape in conversation as they walked away
from the buffet, and I thought everything was going to turn out all
right. But the chef walked in front of them, and Monsieur Cape shook
hands with him and introduced him to his guests. The air became thick,
and though the chef spoke so quietly, I could hear him say: "Monsieur
Cape loves the Belgian hothouse grapes I send up every morning, yes?"

"What Belgian hothouse grapes?" asked Monsieur Cape.

I did not hear any more because I went out quickly with some plates.

The chef sent for me, he held my arm so tight it hurt, and he said
quietly: "*Sacré voleur!* It is shameful, such a young man of good
family as you are! You will never be allowed to serve Monsieur Cape
again."

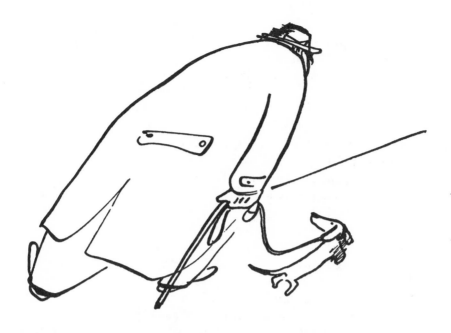

HERR OTTO BRAUHAUS

RARELY DOES ONE FIND in America a hotel manager who has survived the winds of complaint, the climate of worry, and the floods of people, and of whom one can still say that, besides being short or tall, thin or fat, he has this or that kind of a personality. Such a one, a real person, honest, always himself with a unique character, was Otto Brauhaus, manager of the Hotel Splendide.

Otto Brauhaus was an immense stout man; he had to bend down to pass under the tall doorways of his hotel. Big as his feet, which gave him much trouble, telegraphing their sorrows to his ever-worried face, was his heart. For despite his conception of himself as a stern executive and strict disciplinarian, he could not conceal his kindness. He liked to laugh with guests and employees alike, and the result was that his countenance was the scene of an unending emotional conflict.

He was a German, from the soft-speaking Palatinate. For all his years in America, he had somehow never been able to improve his accent.

Too genuine a person to learn the affected English of Monsieur Victor, who was a fellow-countryman, Brauhaus spoke a thick dialect that sometimes sounded like a vaudeville comedian trying for effect. He was, in any case, inarticulate, and hated to talk. Two expressions recurred in his speech like commas; without them he seemed hardly able to speak: "Cheeses Greisd!" and "Gotdemn it!"

His friends were all solid men like himself. Most of them seemed to be brewers, and they would have occasional dinners together, small beer fests, up in the top-floor suite. There they drank enormous quantities of beer and ate canvasback ducks with wild rice. They held little speeches afterward and ate again at midnight. They spoke mostly about how proud they were of being brewers. Almost weeping with sentiment and pounding on the table with his fist, one of them would always get up and say: "My father was a brewer. So was my grandfather, and his father was a brewer before him. I feel beer flowing in my veins."

Then Herr Brauhaus usually summed up their feelings by rising to say, "My friends, we are all here together around this table because we are friends. I am demn glad to see all my friends here." They would all nod and applaud and drink again.

But things had not been going too well with Brauhaus's friends, these elderly men who ate and drank too well. In one week Mr. Brauhaus went to two funerals. He came back very gloomy from the second, saying, "Gotdemn it, Cheeses Greisd, every time I see a friend of mine, he's dead."

Beautiful was it also when he described his art gallery. Of the Rubens sketch he owned, he often said, "If something happens to me, Anna still has the Rubens," and of his primitives he said, "Sometimes when I'm alone, I look at them, and they look at me, so brimidif, like this," and he would look sideways out of his face, just like his primitives.

Brauhaus's goodness of heart, his reliance on the decency of his people, his unwillingness to face them when they had caused trouble, meant that he was always being taken advantage of by the smooth, tricky, much-traveled people who were his employees. "Why doesn't everybody do his duty? Why do I have to bawl them out all the time?" he pleaded with them.

But when someone went too far, then Otto Brauhaus exploded. His big face turned red, his voice keeled over, he yelled and threatened murder. The culprit's head somewhere on a level with Brauhaus's watch

chain, the storm and thunder of the big man's wrath would tower and sweep over him. Brauhaus's fists would be raised up at the ceiling, pounding the air; the crystals on the chandelier would dance at the sound of his voice: "I'll drow you oud, I'll kill you, Gotdemn it, Cheeses Greisd, ged oud of here!"

Fifteen minutes later, he enters his office and finds waiting for him the man he has been shouting at. Brauhaus looks miserable, stares at the floor like a little boy. He puts his hand on the man's shoulder and squeezes out a few embarrassed sentences. First he says, "Ah-ah-ah," then comes a small prayer: "You know I am a very pusy man. I have a lot of worries. I get excited and then I say things I don't mean. You have been here a long time with me, and I know you work very hard, and that you are a nice feller." Finally a few more "Ah-ah-ahs," and then he turns away. To any man with a spark of decency, all this hurts; almost there are tears in one's eyes and one's loyalty to Otto Brauhaus is sewn doubly strong with the big stitches of affection.

Since he could not fire anyone, someone else had to get rid of the altogether impossible people, and then an elaborate guard had to be thrown around Brauhaus to keep the discharged employees from reaching him in person or by telephone. Once a man got by this guard, all the firing was for nothing.

One night it was announced that Mr. Brauhaus was leaving on his vacation. Such information seeps through the hotel immediately, as in a prison. The trunks were sent on ahead, and late that night Mr. Brauhaus took a cab to the station. But he missed his train, and, since the hotel was not far from the station, he decided to walk back. With his little Tyrolese hat, his heavy cane and his dachshund, which he took with him on trips, he came marching into his hotel. Outside he found no carriage man, no doorman; inside no one to turn the revolving door, no night clerk, also no bellboy and no elevator man. The lobby was quite deserted; only from the cashier's cage came happy voices and much laughter.

Mr. Brauhaus stormed back there and exploded: "What is diss? Gotdemn it! Cheeses Greisd! You have a birdtay zelepration here?"

They made themselves scarce and rushed for their posts. Only the bottles of beer were left, as the revolving door was turned, without guests in it, the elevator starter slipped on his gloves, and the night-clerk vaulted behind the counter and began to write. "You are fired, all fired, everyone here is fired, Gotdemn it!" screamed Herr Brauhaus. "Everyone here is fired, you hear, *raus*, every one, you and you and you." He growled on: "*Lumpenpack, Tagediebe, Schweinebande!*" He had never heard or seen anything like this.

The men very slowly started to leave. "No, not now, come back, tomorrow you are fired," Brauhaus shouted at them.

He was so angry he could not think of going to sleep, and, as always on the occasions when he was upset, he walked all the way around the hotel and back to the main entrance. There the doorman got hold of him. With sad eyes, he intercepted Mr. Brauhaus, mumbled something about the twelve years he had been with the hotel, that only tonight, for the first time, had he failed in his duty, that he had a sick child and a little house in Flatbush and that his life would be ruined.

"All right," said Brauhaus. "You stay, John. All the others, Gotdemn it, are fired."

But there was no one to protect him that night. Inside he heard the same story, with changes as to the particular family misfortunes and the location of the little houses. They had all been with the Splendide since the hotel was built; the bellboy had gray hair and was fifty-six years old. Mr. Brauhaus walked out again and around the block. When he came back, he called them all together. He delivered them what was for him a long lecture on discipline, banging the floor with his stick, while the dachshund smelled the doorman's pants.

"I am a zdrikt disziblinarian," he said. They would all have to work together; this hotel was not a Gotdemn joke, Cheeses Greisd. It was hard enough to manage it when everyone did his duty, Gotdemn it. "And now get back to work."

A late guest arrived. He was swung through the door, saluted, wished a good-night, expressed up to his room with a morning paper and a passkey in the hands of the gray-haired bellboy. No guest had ever been so well and quickly served. "That's good, that's how it should be all the time," said Otto Brauhaus. "Why isn't it like this all the time?" Then he went to bed.

Besides all of Mr. Brauhaus's other troubles, there was the World War, and his hotel was filled in front with guests, and staffed in the rear with employees, of every warring nation. Whenever this problem arose, he always shouted: "We are all neudral here, Gotdemn it, and friendts!"

One Thursday afternon, about five-thirty, I had been sent to the kitchen to get some small sandwiches for some tea guests. The man who makes these sandwiches is called the *garde-manger*. Instead of ovens, this cook has only large iceboxes, in which he keeps caviar, pâté de foie gras, herrings, pickles, salmon, sturgeon, all the various hams, cold turkeys, partridges, tongues, the cold sauces, mayonnaise. Next to him is the oysterman, so that all the cold things are together.

In spite of being in a cool place instead of, as most cooks are all day, in front of a hot stove, this man was as nervous and excitable as any cook. Also I came at the worst possible time to ask anything of a cook —that is, while he was eating. He sat all the way in the back of his department, and before him were a plate of warm soup on a marble-topped table and a copy of the *Courrier des Etats Unis*, which announced in thick headlines a big French victory on the western front.

To order the sandwiches, the commis had first to write out a little slip, announce the order aloud, go to the coffeeman at the other end of the kitchen for the bread, and finally bring the bread to the garde-manger to be spread with butter, covered and cut into little squares.

47

The garde-manger was still eating, but since the guest was in a hurry, I repeated the order to him. "Go away," the cook said angrily. "Can't you see I'm eating? Come back later."

I insisted he make the sandwiches now. "Go away!" he repeated. "*Sale Boche!*"

I called him a French pig. Near him was a box of little iceflakes to put under cold dishes; he reached into this box, came forward and threw a handful of ice in my face. On the stone counter next to me stood a tower of heavy silver platters, oval, thick, and each large enough to hold six lobsters on ice; I took one of these platters, swung and let it fly. It wabbled through the air, struck him at the side of the head between the eye and ear, and then fell on the tiled floor with a loud clatter. A woman who was scrubbing a table close by screamed.

Her scream brought the cooks from all the departments as well as the cooks who were eating—my old Frenchman of the fruit baskets and the first chef. Four of them carried the garde-manger to the open space in front of the ranges. There he kicked and turned up his eyes; blood ran from the side of his face, and skin hung down under a wide gash. They poured water on him, shouted for the police, and everybody ran around in circles.

It was then I put into practice the Splendide maxim I had already learned: Get to Mr. Brauhaus first. I ran up the stairs and found him as usual worrying in his office under the sign: "Don't worry, it won't last, nothing does." I told him my story as quickly as I could. "What did he call you?" said Mr. Brauhaus, getting up. "A *Boche*, a *sale Boche?*

Come with me." He took me by the hand and we went down to the kitchen.

On one side of the garde-manger stood all the cooks; on the other, the waiters, most of whom were Germans. But the French and the Italian waiters were also with them, for all waiters hate all cooks and all cooks hate all waiters. In the forefront of the waiters was Monsieur Victor; in the van of the cooks stood the first chef.

One side was dressed in white, the other in black. The cooks fiddled around in the air with knives and big ladles and the waiters with napkins. They insulted each other and each other's countries; even the calm first chef was red in the face. The garde-manger lay on the floor, no longer kicking; sometimes he gulped and his lips fluttered. I thought he was going to die while we waited for an ambulance.

Everyone made room for Mr. Brauhaus. He waved them all back to work and went into the office with the first chef and me. "You hear me, Chef," he said, "I don't want no Gotdemn badriodism in this Gotdemn hotel, only good cooking and good service is what I want, Cheeses Greisd!" If the cook had done his work, he said, and not called me a "sale Boche," he would not have had his head knocked in; he got what he deserved and he, Brauhaus, wasn't sorry for him. "This little poy is not to blame, it's your Gotdemn dumm cooks," he shouted.

When the garde-manger came out of the hospital after some days, he waited for me on the service stairs of the hotel. "Hsst!" he said and pointed to his head, turbaned in bandages. "You know," he went on, "perhaps I should not have insulted you. I am sorry and here is my hand." I shook his hand. "But," he said, pointing again to his head, "it would be very dear for you, my friend, if I should make you pay for the pain. But let us forget that. I will ask you to pay only for the doctor and the hospital. Here is the bill. It is seventy-five dollars."

I did not have that much money, of course, but Monsieur Serafini lent it to me out of his pocket after I had signed a note promising to pay it back in weekly installments of five dollars.

BEAU MAXIME

I WAS A COMMIS DE RANG in Monsieur Victor's domain for several months, during which I met some remarkable people, but none more remarkable than the maître d'hôtel whom the others sometimes called "Beau Maxime" because he was so ugly, and sometimes "Useless." Maxime was a bankrupt hotelkeeper from Paris. His ugliness was almost decorative; he had arthritis and could hardly see out over the two cocoa-colored hammocks of wrinkles that hung under his smeary eyes. He had his station on the dining-room balcony, where he could walk up and down with his cane and his beard and see himself reflected in the mirror.

He was a great trouble to the chefs de rang, the commis and the kitchen because he took the guests' orders down wrong, forgot things, dictated orders upside down. His hand was too shaky to write; he held the menu up against his face and read it through a lorgnette.

When guests had eaten, smoked and talked, and there was still no sign of a tip for him, a kind of hysteria would come over Beau Maxime. He became part of the table then. With heavy breath, he moved glasses about, took away a sugar bowl, dusted off a few bread crumbs with the edge of his menu. Then he would leave for a while, but not for long, and the chicanery would start all over again. Again he moved the glasses back to where they were before; his eyelids twitched as he looked at the people; he brought a clean napkin to cover up a little coffee stain, took away a vacant chair. If still nothing had happened, he bent to the guest's ear and asked if everything had been all right.

He mumbled as the guests started to leave, and watched them in the mirror and outside of it with a kind of despair in his face and hands, as if in a minute it would be too late to keep something terrible from happening. He kept behind them, pulled out their chairs, and bowed, and if again nothing happened, then he played his last card. He hung his stick on the banister, the service table, or over the back of a chair, and ran after them. He had a glove in his pocket, which he kept for just such purposes; he pulled this glove out and, in the center of the Jade Lounge, asked if they had forgotten it. Sometimes this worked; they would say no, but give him his dollar, and then he climbed back to the restaurant and up to his balcony.

He ate unbelievable amounts of food. The maîtres d'hôtel had luncheon and dinner before the guests, a very bad arrangement. They should be fed afterward; a man who has just filled himself cannot recommend things well, he is asleep on his feet and makes unpleasant noises. But, as a matter of fact, they did also eat afterward.

On the stations where the chefs and commis had their service tables, which contained extra plates, silver, napkins, vinegar, oil, ketchup bottles and mustard pots, there were also electric heaters. On these heaters the commis put all the food that was left over after his chef had served the guests. After the guests had left, the commis took the food down to the employees' dining room, where the chef de rang and his commis, sitting across from each other, shared it. With these meals they usually had a bottle of wine, bought underhand, and since the portions were liberal, and the food excellent, and too much of everything was ordered, the men ate very well and of the best—that is, all of them did except the chefs and commis on Beau Maxime's station.

For after each serving he visited all the service tables on his station,

of which there were three, and carefully lifted the covers of the casseroles, stirred around in them with a fork, fished out wings of capons,
little tender foie gras dumplings, pieces of truffle, cocks' combs. Then
he sent a commis for soup plates and, while the poor chef and the
commis stared at him, he filled one of the plates with the very best of
their left-overs. He grunted while he did this, his eyes shone and almost
fell into the pots. For his second soup plate he would take a lobster claw,
tilt the casserole to get the fine sauce for it, add some rice. In the third
plate might go a little curry. When he had enough, one of the commis
whom he had robbed, a pale little French boy, had to take the plate
upstairs to the captains' dining room. (On the stairway, when no one
could see him, the commis carefully spat into all three plates.) Beau
Maxime followed, a long French bread under his arm as if it were an
umbrella.

Up there, he ate slowly, then moved his chair over to the window.
From this third-floor window one could see over the curtains and into
the fitting room of a corsetière on the second floor of the building
across the street, where, in the afternoon, fat women undressed to try
on corsets. Beau Maxime took off his shoes and put his feet on a pile of
used napkins that were put there to be counted later. He watched the
scene for an hour and then fell asleep. A bus boy cleared away the dishes
and reset the table for the dinner of the maître d'hôtel, which was
served at five-thirty. Maxime woke up in time for that, put on his shoes
and turned around, to eat.

THE

EDUCATION

OF A WAITER

My job was to stand in a white apron and help fix up a buffet, to wheel around curries and learn to slice ham and to cut up ducks, chickens and turkeys. I thus became acquainted with a little Bohemian waiter stationed 'way in the back of this room. His name was Wladimir Slezack, but since no one could pronounce it, it had gradually become Mr. Sigsag. He was the smallest man in the restaurant, and because he worked very hard and was very fast on his feet, he was a favorite of Victor.

Every waiter in a hotel has a "side job." A side job is extra work, other than serving, that he must perform before or after meals: most of it is done in the morning. One man is in charge of filling and collecting all the salt and pepper and paprika shakers and seeing that they are kept clean. Others must get the clean linen from the linen room every morning and check it at night; others collect the dirty linens. Two who write a good hand get out of unpleasant work by writing little menus for special parties and keeping various accounts. Another has to keep the stock of sauces and pickles, make the French and Russian salad dressing, keep clean the oil and vinegar bottles and the mustard pots. This side job is called the "drugstore," and it was assigned to Mr. Sigsag.

Mr. Sigsag lived in a little room on the East Side, where he read the works, in many volumes bound in limp green leather with gold stamping, of a man who called himself the "Sage of East Aurora." These concerned trips to the homes of great men, but the biggest book was one entitled

Elbert Hubbard's Scrapbook (that was the name of the Sage). With these books and included in their total price had come candlesticks, jars of honey, maple-sugar candies and other souvenirs, all in the one package with the volumes. When I visited him he was expecting some new volumes from East Aurora, this time with bookends included to hold his little library together.

Mr. Sigsag studied these books earnestly and drew the lessons from them that he should. They filled him with respect for a life of work and success. He was also a student by correspondence of the La Salle University and had subscribed to several courses, but he told me that what was most important in life was not knowledge or hard work but the right connections, also the ability to "sell" oneself, to call guests by their correct names and to remember their faces.

From his library, now lying one volume on top of another, he took a book of which he was very fond, a waiter's bible. After his working hours at the Bristol in Vienna, he had attended a school which the hoteliers of Vienna maintained for the training of new waiters. He graduated from it with high honors. A diploma, a colored lithograph, decorated like a menu with pheasants, geese, wine bottles and grapes, surrounded his name printed in the center. It was signed by the dean of the school and the president of the Society of Hoteliers, Restaurateurs, Cafetiers and Innkeepers of Vienna and by the city's burgomaster, and hung in a frame over Mr. Sigsag's desk. So well had he been liked at the school that the maître d'hôtel principal had had him pose for the photographs that illustrated the manual of the waiter's art, which was learnedly entitled *Ein Leitfaden der Servierkunde mit besonderer Berücksichtigung des Küchenwesens* ("An Introduction to the Science of Serving, with Special Reference to Culinary Matters").

The photographs showed Mr. Sigsag, a little waiter in a tailcoat, standing in the proper positions for receiving a guest and for recommending dishes from the menu, and also standing incorrectly while doing this. They showed him handing a newspaper to a guest, carrying a tray, lighting a diner's cigar, and demonstrating how to carry the side towel, as well as various ways of how not to carry it. There was a list of books at the end of the book, for further study, among them the *Almanach de Gotha* and various cookbooks, and there were color charts of sleeve stripes and collar stars showing the various grades of army and naval officers. One whole chapter was given over to the art of folding napkins into the shapes of swans, windmills, boats and fans.

Mr. Sigsag spent his free time puttering on a secondhand motorboat which he kept up near Dyckman Street; he asked me to visit him there sometimes. He seemed to have influence. We got days off, with mysterious ease, to work on the boat. These were lovely days. As the lights grew stronger in the little portholes and were reflected on the sides of the boats next to them, and the gramophones started to play, and the smell of food came out of imitation funnels, we stopped work and sat in the cabin while Mr. Sigsag told me of his youth.

Wladimir Slezack, the eleventh son of a Bohemian blacksmith, was born in a village two hours out of Przemysl. When he was old enough, though still a child, his father paid to have him apprenticed as piccolo

at the great Hotel King Wenceslaus in Przemysl. Here he served part of his apprenticeship and then went on to Vienna, where, his recommendations being of the best, he got a job in a small hotel.

The child piccolo is an institution in all European restaurants. His head barely reaches above the table; his ears are red and stand out, because everybody pulls them. And when he is a man, he will still pull his head quickly to one side if anyone close to him suddenly moves, because he always did that to soften the blows that rained on him from the proprietor down to the last chambermaid; they hit him mostly out of habit.

For the rest, the boy learned to wash glasses, to fold newspapers into the bamboo holders and hang them on the wall, to learn the grade of an officer by the stars on his collar, to bow, to chase flies from the tables without upsetting the glasses, to carry water and coffee without spilling, and to know the fifty-one varieties of coffee that are served in Viennese restaurants, starting with the "mélange," which is a pale mixture of coffee and cream served in a glass with whipped cream on top, down to the "capuchin," which is a tiny demitasse of black coffee served with nothing but two pieces of sugar on a little silver saucer.

He studied how to make up and write the bill of fare, let the awnings up and down over the sidewalk in the summer, and scatter ashes out on the ice on winter mornings. He also cleaned ashtrays and matchstands, and one could still see his right thumb bent sideways from polishing two hundred of these every day; they were made of a light-colored, very sensitive brass, and the cigarettes burned deep stains into them that were hard to get out.

The boys started to work at six in the morning; they ate standing up and got to bed at eleven at night. A free day was not provided for, since on Sundays and holidays the restaurant was busier than on other days, serving happy people. The piccolos slept in the restaurant, and Wladi, who was the smallest of them, slept in a kitchen drawer under the pastry cook's noodle board, where it was warm. The others had to sleep in the dining room on cold benches under which their dirty pillows and covers were stowed away in a drawer during the day.

Little Wladi was fortunate not only in his sleeping quarters, in which he was at least warm, but also in his parentage. So many of the other boys were the chance sons of a chambermaid and a transient guest or waiter, or at best a soldier loved on a bench when the trees were in bloom and all was beautiful on the Prater.

A restaurant in the morning, before it is aired and swept and the guests enter, is an unhappy place. The stale smells of tobacco smoke, of empty beer and wineglasses and of spilled food and coffee stay on and hang about the draperies and furniture. It is no place for a growing child; this life eventually draws on the faces of these little boys two lines from their nostrils to the corners of their young lips and it makes them pale and brings out the thin veins at their temples. They get to look tired and high-bred; in later years this pallor and nervousness will give them just the right touch of grand-hotel elegance they will need for their parts. The boys also learn to repeat the smut they hear from the guests, and to smoke, and to drink themselves to sleep.

Nevertheless, the piccolo was looked upon with envy by the apprentices of plumbers and cobblers; they had the red ears, too, but not enough to eat, and no cigarettes, no drinks, no tips. The piccolo could at least save money. It was the custom in Austria for guests to leave three separate tips. The biggest was for the *Zahlkellner*, the captain to whom one paid the bill and who had taken the order; the next was for *the Speisenträger*, or *Saalkellner*, the ordinary waiter who actually served one; and the third, a little stack of coppers, was for the piccolo. These three tips had to be left in clearly defined heaps and far enough apart from each other; for the restaurant law was that all the coins that the first waiter could get within the reach of his outstretched thumb and index finger were his. That is why, in old Viennese restaurants, the three tips were always left very far apart from one another, almost on the edges of the small marble tables.

Despite the big hands of the headwaiters, the piccolo was often able to earn and put aside a good sum of money; he had little chance to spend it. His dress coat, a child's garment, he had made by a cheap tailor, or bought it secondhand from another piccolo. His trousers could be dark blue or gray, for in the bad light of the restaurants no one could see below the levels of the tables. Finally there was a waistcoat. Under the latter the piccolo need not wear a shirt; a celluloid plastron, like a bosom cut out of an evening shirt, was attached by a button to his celluloid collar, and a tie held the arrangement together. Save for his shoes and socks, the dickey and cuffs, which were stuck in his coat sleeves, the piccolo stood naked in his trousers and frock coat. His hair was plastered down with brilliantine and kept in order with a greasy comb that he carried in his waistcoat pocket.

He knew all about love and women, and had never played. He

looked most unhappy when in the spring he brought ice cream out to the restaurant garden for some well-dressed child with its father and mother, who smiled at him when the music played and the large-grained sand was hard to walk on. And when one sees somewhere in a cheap restaurant—say in a beer hall in Coney Island—one of those old waiters who are known as "hashers" leaning on a chair, with ugly, lightless eyes and a dead face that is filled with misery and meanness, one is seeing that little boy grown old, with flat crippled feet, on which he has dragged almost to the end of his useless life his dead childhood.

But little Wladimir was made of stronger material. He survived, he went to school, he saved his money and paid his father back what had been spent to make him a piccolo, and he went to France and England and finally to America. Now he had a job as chef de rang in the best hotel in New York, in the Grill Room of the Splendide, and the maître d'hôtel was his friend. When looked at from Przemysl, this was as great and brave a success as any recorded in the high tales Mr. Sigsag read in the honey-and-candlestick books of Elbert Hubbard.

DINNER OUT

ONLY ONCE did I go out to dine with Mr. Sigsag, and I never would again. One night we had no party at the hotel, and he said, "Come on, I'll take you down to Luchow's. You'll like it there."

This restaurant was in the center of a block on Fourteenth Street, close to the German theater on Irving Place. It was bathed in cigar smoke and beer smells, as such a restaurant should be and always is in Hamburg or Bremen. Antlers hung on the walls, and on its upper level, behind a mahogany banister, an orchestra—a piano, two violins and a cello—played German restaurant pieces.

A red-faced captain, who had been in this restaurant for thirty years, leaned up against the banister with his hands folded over his stomach. He was very kind but beautifully ugly, and had a mouth and throat like an old toad. His eyes were half asleep, and when some of the guests smiled and waved at him and made faces, he would stick his fat tongue out at them, which made him look all the more like an old toad catching

flies. Then he would wipe his hand over his face, smile, greet them with a bill of fare, which was much too big for comfortable reading, and go away for a little while only to return to the banister and lean against it again.

We came as the orchestra was playing an elaborate "Liebestraum." Especially remarkable among the musicians was the pianist. As would a great virtuoso, he leaned back until he almost fell off the piano stool, with his eyes closed and his hair hanging down. Then he brought his nose down to the keys, close over his fingers, which walked along the high keys in a calm passage. He sat sideways to reach the lower keys, pounded them, and looked up. For an encore he gave the "March of the Wooden Soldiers." Mr. Sigsag applauded both pieces.

Mr. Sigsag could not sit still; he twitched and turned, looking at what other people were ordering. In a little while he was out at the bar, where he found the manager, introduced himself and brought him to our table. With critical eyes he went over the menu, looked at the prices, criticized the arrangement of it. When the waiter came, Mr. Sigsag told him who we were: "I'm Monsieur Wladimir of the Splendide, and this is Monsieur Louis, and we want a little special attention here."

The waiter got the captain, and Mr. Sigsag started to order. The table d'hôte dinner allowed a choice of either fish or meat, but Mr. Sigsag took hold of the captain's sleeve and, with his red, yellow and blue silver pencil, pointed at the card and said: "Now you go out and tell the chef that it's for us, for Monsieur Louis here and for myself, and we want a little special attention. Now listen, instead of having one fish and one meat, we'll have one portion of each divided. First bring the fish for both of us, one portion, you know what I mean, and then the meat, also one portion served for two."

"Well," said the captain, "that's easy. The waiter will bring one portion and two plates and then you divide it yourself."

Mr. Sigsag was not in the habit of having his orders changed. "Bring me the headwaiter," he said, and then to me: "I'm sorry about this, but we'll get service here in just a minute now."

The headwaiter came and everything was all right. We received two full portions of fish and two of duckling. Then came a salad. On the dinner a plain lettuce salad was included, but under the salad list on the à la carte side of the menu Mr. Sigsag had noticed a celery-root salad,

of which he knew I was very fond. He called the headwaiter again and said, "Could we have some celery-root salad instead of the plain lettuce? Because my friend Monsieur Louis, here, and I are very fond of it."

"Yes, yes," said the headwaiter and wrote out a slip. The captain sneered and the waiter was disgusted. The salad and the dessert eaten, Mr. Sigsag called for the headwaiter again. Now he wanted to see the kitchen, and I had to come along.

Out there he asked a thousand questions and talked hotel memories to the chef. He went into the iceboxes and tried sauces and soups. He made comments about everything, honestly and sincerely, and also suggestions: that a little shelf here would help, that the waiters should come in from that side and not from the other, that an attachment to pull kitchen smells out from over the service door would be better than their own arrangement. Now the chef was also mad; no chef likes his kitchen talked about.

At last I thought it was over and that we might get to the theater, for which we had two very good seats in the second row. But no. As we came out into the dining room, Mr. Sigsag saw seated about a large table some Jewish Wedding friends, people whose daughter had been married in the Splendide. They greeted him like a long-lost son. The mother almost kissed him. He had to sit by her side, and I got a seat on the other side of the table. We had to drink a glass of wine with them. "Have you eaten? Eat with us. Order anything you want."

Now the evening was completely ruined. Mr. Sigsag talked wedding, for they had another daughter; besides, they were going to send some friends. Although the last wedding was so very recent, Mr. Sigsag asked whether any happy events were in sight, and of course there were, in April.

He asked after Grandpa, after Grandma, as if they were his own grandparents, and all this time his eyes wandered about the room. "Excuse me a minute," he said, but not to go to the washroom; he had seen a customer trying to attract the attention of a waiter with motions of the hand and by saying "Psst." The waiter, with folded arms, stood talking to another waiter.

"Come on, come on, you, wake up," Sigsag said to him, "Customer there wants to see you," and the man went. If he hadn't, Sigsag would have upset the whole restaurant. He was eternally in business, and every hotel and restaurant in the world was his worry.

We finally left for the theater and arrived in the middle of the play. When we were seated, Sigsag turned to me. "You know what they should have?" he asked.

"What?"

"They should have the pantry in front of the kitchen on the right, less cooking smell and the waiters don't run into each other, one door marked 'in' and the other 'out,' like this."

And here in the second row, under Walter Hampden's nose, he designed the whole thing with his three-colored pencil on the menu which he always took along from every restaurant, as well as the wine card. He did not hear a word of *Cyrano*, but the next day he told everybody that we had seen a wonderful show.

*T*he captain told me about the founder, old Luchow. He was very strict with his men, but also very decent to them and provident of their old age. He had certain pet ideas. One was that his employees could drink all the domestic beer they wanted but never imported beer. He saw to it that they were well fed, but he did not like to have them steal food to eat, something that is, of course, done in every restaurant. His office was upstairs, and he had mirrors so arranged all through the rooms that with their aid he could look into every corner of the restaurant from his window.

He had a Kellermeister, old John, who was with him for many years and who was very fond of strawberry shortcake. He once swiped a big slice of it and began to eat it in a corner, but Luchow, who had observed him in his mirrors, came down. John tried to swallow as much as he could and threw the rest of it into a linen basket.

"John," Luchow said to him, "that was an expensive strawberry shortcake you had just now. It would not have been so expensive if you had eaten it all, but to throw it away into the linen basket here, that's not right; it's wasting things, and besides it's trying to make a fool of me. This strawberry shortcake will cost you five thousand dollars." And when Luchow died, the Kellermeister received a legacy, and it was five thousand dollars short of what the others got. Another employee, a waiter, paid two thousand dollars for an imported Würzburger beer.

ART
AT THE
HOTEL SPLENDIDE

"From now on," lisped Monsieur Victor, as if he were pinning on me the Grand Cross of the Legion of Honor, "you will be a waiter."

It was about a year after I had gone to work at the Splendide as Mespoulets' bus boy and only a month or two after I had been promoted to commis. A commis feels more self-satisfied than a bus boy and has a better life all around, but to become a waiter is to make a really worthwhile progress.

The cause of my promotion was a waiters' mutiny. On a rainy afternoon several of the waiters had suddenly thrown down their napkins and aprons and walked out. One had punched the chief bus boy in the nose and another had upset a tray filled with Spode demitasse cups. They wanted ten dollars a week instead of six; they wanted to do away with certain penalties that were imposed on them, such as a fine of fifty cents for using a serving napkin to clean an ashtray; and they wanted a full day off instead of having to come back on their free day to serve dinner, which was the custom at the Splendide, as at most other New York hotels. The good waiters did not go on strike. A few idealists spoke too loudly and got fired, and a lot of bad waiters, who had mediocre stations, left.

After my promotion I was stationed at the far end of the room, on the "undesirables'" balcony, and my two tables were next to Mespoulets'.

It rained all that first day and all the next, and there were no guests on the bad balcony. With nothing to do, Mespoulets and I stood and looked at the ceiling, talked, or sat on overturned linen baskets out in the pantry and yawned. I drew some pictures on my order pad—small sketches of a pantryman, a row of glasses, a stack of silver trays, a bus boy counting napkins. Mespoulets had a rubber band which, with two fingers of each hand, he stretched into various geometric shapes. He was impressed by my drawings.

The second night the dining room was half full, but not a single guest sat at our tables. Mespoulets pulled at my serving napkin and whispered, "If I were you, if I had your talent, that is what I would do," and then he waved his napkin toward the center of the room.

There a small group of the best guests of the Splendide sat at dinner. He waved his napkin at Table No. 18, where a man was sitting with a very beautiful woman. Mespoulets explained to me that this gentleman was a famous cartoonist, that he drew pictures of a big and a little man. The big man always hit the little man on the head. In this simple fashion the creator of those two figures made a lot of money.

We left our tables to go down and look at him. While I stood off to one side, Mespoulets circled around the table and cleaned the cartoonist's ashtray so that he could see whether or not the lady's jewelry was genuine. "Yes, that's what I would do if I had your talent. Why do you want to be an actor? It's almost as bad as being a waiter," he said when we returned to our station. We walked down again later on. This time Mespoulets spoke to the waiter who served Table No. 18, a Frenchman named Herriot, and asked what kind of guest the cartoonist was. Was he liberal?

"*Ah*," said Serriot, "*c'ui là? Ah, oui alors! C'est un très bon client, extrêmement généreux. C'est un gentleman par excellence.*" And in English he added, "He's A-1, that one. If only they were all like him! Never looks at the bill, never complains—and so full of jokes! It is a pleasure to serve him. *C'est un chic type.*"

After the famous cartoonist got his change, Herriot stood by waiting for the tip, and Mespoulets cruised around the table. Herriot quickly snatched up the tip; both waiters examined it, and then Mespoulets climbed back to the balcony. "*Magnifique*," he said to me. "You are an idiot if you do not become a cartoonist. I am an old man—I have sixty years. All my children are dead, all except my daughter Mélanie, and for me it is too late for anything. I will always be a waiter. But you— you are young, you are a boy, you have talent. We shall see what can be done with it."

Mespoulets investigated the famous cartoonist as if he were going to make him a loan or marry his daughter off to him. He interviewed chambermaids, telephone operators and room waiters. "I hear the same thing from the rest of the hotel," he reported on the third rainy day. "He lives here at the hotel, he has a suite, he is married to a countess, he owns a Rolls-Royce. He gives wonderful parties, eats grouse out of season, drinks vintage champagne at ten in the morning. He spends half the year in Paris and has a place in the south of France. When the accounting department is stuck with a charge they've forgotten to put on somebody's bill they just put it on his. He never looks at them."

"Break it up, break it up. Sh-h-h. Quiet," said Monsieur Maxim, the maître d'hôtel on our station. Mespoulets and I retired to the pantry, where we could talk more freely.

"It's a very agreeable life, this cartoonist life," Mespoulets continued, stretching his rubber band. "I would never counsel you to be an actor

67

or an artist-painter. But a cartoonist—that is different. Think what fun you can have. All you do is think of amusing things, make pictures with pen and ink, have a big man hit a little man on the head, and write a few words over it. And I know you can do this easily. You are made for it."

That afternoon, between luncheon and dinner, we went out to find a place where cartooning was taught. As we marched along Madison Avenue, Mespoulets noticed a man walking in front of us. He had flat feet and he walked painfully, like a skier going uphill.

Mespoulets said "Pst," and the man turned around. They recognized each other and promptly said, "*Ah, bonjour.*"

"You see?" Mespoulets said to me when we had turned into a side street. "A waiter. A dog. Call 'Pst,' click your tongue, snap your fingers, and they turn around even when they are out for a walk and say, 'Yes sir, no sir, *bonjour, Monsieur-dame.*' Trained poodles! For God's sakes, don't stay a waiter! If you can't be a cartoonist, be a streetcleaner, a dishwasher, anything. But don't be an actor or a waiter. It's the most awful occupation in the world. The abuse I have taken, the long hours, the smoke and dust in my lungs and eyes, and the complaints—*ah, c'est la barbe, ce métier.* My boy, profit by my experience. Take it very seriously, this cartooning."

For months one does not meet anybody on the street with his neck in an aluminum-and-leather collar such as is worn in cases of ambulatory cervical fractures, and then in a single day one sees three of them. Or one hears Mount Chimborazo mentioned five times. This day was a flat-foot day. Mespoulets, like the waiter we met on Madison Avenue, had flat feet. And so did the teacher in the Andrea del Sarto Art Academy. Before this man had finished interviewing me, Mespoulets whispered in my ear, "Looks and talks like a waiter. Let's get out of here."

On our way back to the hotel we bought a book on cartooning, a drawing board, pens and a penholder, and several soft pencils. On the first page of the book we read that before one could cartoon or make caricatures, one must be able to draw a face—a man, a woman—from nature. That was very simple, said Mespoulets. We had lots of time and the Splendide was filled with models. Two days later he bought another book on art and we visited the Metropolitan Museum. We bought all the newspapers that had comic strips. And the next week Mespoulets looked around and everywhere among the guests he saw funny people. He continued to read to me from the book on how to become a cartoonist.

The book said keep a number of sharpened, very soft pencils handy for your work. I did, and for a while I was almost the only waiter who had a pencil when a guest asked for one. "And remember," said the book, "you can never be expert in caricaturing people unless you shake off the fear of drawing people." I tried to shake off the fear. "Most people like to have their own pictures drawn," Mespoulets read solemnly. "Regular-featured people should be avoided, as they are too simple to draw. Your attention should be concentrated on the faces with unique features."

The most "unique" faces at the Splendide belonged to Monsieur and Madame Lawrance Potter Dreyspool. Madame Dreyspool was very rich; her husband was not. He traveled with her as a sort of companion-butler, pulling her chair, helping her to get up, carrying books, flasks, dog leashes, small purchases and opera glasses. He was also like the attendant at a sideshow, for Madame was a monstrosity and everyone stared at her. They were both very fat, but she was enormous. It was said that she got her clothes from a couturier specializing in costumes for women who were *enceinte*, and that to pull everything in shape and get into her dresses she had to lie down on the floor. She was fond of light pastel-colored fabrics and her ensembles had the colors of pigeons, hyacinths and boudoir upholstery. Her coat covered her shoes and a wide fur piece her neck, and even in the middle of winter she wore immense garden hats that were as elaborate as wedding cakes.

Monsieur and Madame Dreyspool were the terror of maîtres d'hôtel all over the world. Wherever they stayed they had the table nearest the entrance to the dining room. This table was reserved for them at the Splendide in New York, at Claridge's in London, at the Ritz in Paris, and in various restaurants on the luxurious boats on which they crossed. Like the first snowflakes, Monsieur and Madame Dreyspool always appeared in the Splendide at the beginning of the season. They left for Palm Beach at the first sign of its end.

Their entrance into the dining room was spectacular. First Madame waddled in, then Monsieur with a Pekingese, one of the few dogs allowed in the main dining room. Madame answered with one painful nod Monsieur Victor's deep bow, climbed up the two steps to the balcony on the right, where their table was, and elaborately sat down. Everyone in society knew them and nodded, coming in and going out. Monsieur and Madame thanked them briefly from the throne. They never spoke to each other and they never smiled.

Monsieur Dreyspool had consoled himself with whisky so many years

that his face was purple. The gossip in the couriers' dining room, where the valets and maids and chauffeurs ate, was that he also consoled himself with Susanne, Madame's personal maid. He did not seem so fat when he was alone, but when he and Madame were sitting together at their table on the good balcony, they looked like two old toads on a lily leaf.

The maître d'hôtel who took care of them was a Belgian and had come from the Hôtel de Londres in Antwerp. He never took his eyes off their table and raced to it whenever Monsieur Dreyspool turned his head. Monsieur and Madame were waited upon by a patient old Italian waiter named Giuseppe. Because he never lost his temper and never made mistakes, he got all the terrible guests, most of whom paid him badly. Madame Dreyspool was not allowed any sugar. Her vegetables had to be cooked in a special fashion. A long letter of instruction about her various peculiarities hung in the offices of the chefs and maîtres d'hôtel of all the hotels she went to. It was mailed ahead to the various managers by Monsieur.

The exit of Monsieur and Madame Dreyspool was as festive as the entrance. When they were ready to leave, the maître d'hôtel pulled Monsieur's chair out. Monsieur pulled out Madame's chair. Madame produced the dog from her generous lap—it had slept there under a fold of the tablecloth while she ate—and gave the dog to Monsieur, who placed it on the carpet. Then the maître d'hôtel, taking steps as small as Madame's, escorted her out, walking on her left side and talking to her solicitously, his face close to hers. Monsieur followed about six feet behind, with a big Belinda Fancy Tales cigar between his teeth, his hands in his pockets and the leash of the dog slipped over one wrist. From where Mespoulets and I stood on the bad balcony, she looked like several pieces of comfortable furniture piled together under a velvet cover and being slowly pushed along on little wheels.

Mespoulets was convinced that Madame Dreyspool was the very best possible model for me to begin drawing. The book said not to be afraid. "Take a piece of paper," it said, "draw a line down the center, divide this line, and draw another from left to right so that the paper is divided into four equal parts." I took an old menu and stood on the good balcony between a screen and a marble column. It was possible there to observe and sketch Madame Dreyspool unnoticed. I divided the back of the menu into four equal parts. Once I started to draw, I saw that Madame's left half-face extended farther out from the nose than her right and that one eye was always half closed. When someone she knew came in, the eyelid went up over the rim of the pupil in greeting and the corners of the lips gave a short upward jump and then sank down again into a steady mask of disgust.

Monsieur and Madame were easy to draw; they hardly moved. They sat and stared—stared, ate, stared, stirred their coffee. Only their eyes moved, when Giuseppe brought the cheese or the pastry tray. Quickly, shiftily, they glanced over it, as one looks at something distasteful or dubious. Always the same sideways glance at the check, at Giuseppe when he

took the tip, at the Belgian maître d'hôtel, and at Monsieur Victor as they left.

I took my sketches back to Mespoulets, who had been studying the book on art in the linen closet. "It shows effort and talent," he said. "It is not very good, but it is not bad. It is too stiff—looks too much like pigs, and while there is much pig at that table, it is marvelously complicated pig." He considered the book a moment and then slapped it shut. "I think," he said, "I understand the gist of art without reading any more of this. Try and be free of the helping lines. Tomorrow, when they come again, think of the kidney trouble, of the thousand pâtés and sauces they have eaten. Imagine those knees, the knees of Madame under the table—they must be so fat that faces are on each knee, two faces, one on each knee, laughing and frowning as she walks along. All that must be in the portrait. And the ankles that spill over her shoes—this must be evident in your drawing of her face."

Monsieur and Madame came again the next day, and I stood under a palm and drew them on the back of another menu. Mespoulets came and watched me, broke a roll in half and kneaded the soft part of the bread into an eraser. "Much better," he said. "Try and try again. Don't give up. Remember the thousand fat sauces, the ankles. The eyes already are wonderful. Go ahead."

He went back to his station and soon after I heard "Tsk, tsk, tsk, tsk!" over my shoulder. It was the Belgian maître d'hôtel and he was terror-stricken. He took the menu out of my hand and disappeared with it.

When I came to work the next noon I was told to report to the office of Monsieur Victor. I went to Monsieur Victor's desk. Slowly, precisely, without looking up from his list of reservations, he said, "Ah, the *Wunderkind*." Then, in the manner in which he discharged people, he continued, "You are a talented young man. If I were you, I would most certainly become an artist. I think you should give all your time to it." He looked up, lifted the top of his desk and took out the portrait of Monsieur and Madame Lawrance Potter Dreyspool. "As your first client, I would like to order four of these from you," he said. "Nicely done, like this one, but on good paper. If possible with some color—green and blue and purple. And don't forget Monsieur's nose—the strawberry effect, the little blue veins—or the bags under the eyes. That will be very nice. A souvenir for my colleagues in London, Paris, Nice, and one for the maître d'hôtel on the *Mauretania*. You can have the rest of the day off to start on them."

THE BRAVE COMMIS

IN THE LOCKER next to mine in the waiters' dressing room hung the clothes of a young French commis who worked in Monsieur Victor's restaurant. This young man had a dream; for every waiter, like every prisoner, has a dream. With the older ones it is about a chicken farm, or becoming rich through an invention, or various small businesses, or a return home to a little house and peace; with relatively few it is a hotel or a restaurant—of this they say: "*Sale métier*, filthy profession." But the young ones have more daring dreams: becoming an aviator, a detective, a movie actor, an orchestra leader, or a dancer; and because the French champion prize fighter is visiting America, a certain young blond commis de rang is going to lead a very healthy life and become a boxer.

He has the boxer's picture pasted up on the inside of his locker door; he does not eat stews and dishes that are made with sauces; when he comes down with his chef to the employees' dining room, he brings that man's food, but runs up again for plain vegetables, cheese and a cutlet for himself; he drinks no wine and empties a quart of milk into himself at every meal. He arrives at the hotel in a trot, his fists at the sides of his chest; he has come all the way down Fifth Avenue this way after a short run through the park. In the locker room he makes a few boxing motions—*l'uppercut, le knockout*—dancing and twisting his head and then with a loud "Ah, brrr, bhuff" and "*Ça, c'est bon,*" he takes a cold shower. He has immaculate linen, fine muscles, and he brings his chest out of the shower as if it were a glass case full of jewels. He takes a shower after all meals, rubs himself down afterward, and then sits in his undershirt in the employees' barbershop, reading books on boxing and arguing with Frank, the American engineer, about who knocked out whom, when and where.

Up in the restaurant he looks fine, first because he is tall and handsome, secondly because he stands straight and the mess jacket and the long apron look good on him, and thirdly because he is always clean. Victor likes him because he is always smiling and is as quick as lightning.

He takes the stairs up from and down to the kitchen—thirty iron steps, of which every other man complains—as if they were built for him to train on. He makes the run up in two seconds flat, pushing four steps at a time from under him and flying past the heavily loaded older men so that he almost upsets their trays. They stop and curse him, but he laughs back over his shoulder, takes a stack of hot plates out of the heater, and worms his way to his station through the crowded dining room with an elegant twist. To reward him, when the visiting French champion comes to the restaurant with his friends, he is seated at the young commis's station and gets service such as no one else receives.

Victor has also promised the young man a future: he will make him a chef de rang at the next opportunity, then in a little while maître d'hôtel. Men so engaging, so fine-looking, who, moreover, know their business well and are quick-thinking and intelligent, are few. And he is a Frenchman, and so does not underestimate the value of such a future and the advice of Victor. He is, besides, very sober in his estimate of the boxing profession. He will try it while he keeps one foot in the Splendide. If all goes well, if he should be another champion, fine. For lesser rewards, no. Meanwhile, he will have had fun and acquired a well-trained body, which is a good possession, especially since most maîtres d'hôtel and managers are fat, bald, pale and flat-footed. For one so youthful he shows much good sense in his planning.

He asked me once to go to the Young Men's Christian Association with him. This institution seemed to me far from a benevolent undertaking. The commis had a miserable cell for a room and paid well for it; the walls were covered with invitations to various pleasures and benefits to mind and body, always with the prices clearly marked. The quarters were crammed and so were the pools and gymnasiums. The walls needed painting and the runners were shaggy and worn. The guests were nice clean-cut earnest boys who wished to get ahead, but the atmosphere of the place, I thought, was commercial, unhospitable and false.

The commis introduced me to the gym instructors with the casualness of an old habitué, and for my benefit he put on a little boxing show with one of them and with a ball suspended from a parquet board, which to me, who understood little, seemed very good. When it was time to get back to the hotel to set the tables for dinner, he took another shower and we arrived at the Splendide in a hurry. I was out of wind and perspiring, but he took his shoulders out of his narrow athletic undershirt and asked me in loud French to tell those others what I had seen this afternoon in the way of "*le boxe*."

The brave commis did finally become a chef de rang with a good station, being jumped over the heads of several older men. He made very good money, but more of it went into boxing, and he became stronger and stronger. Because he was such a good, swift, smiling waiter, he received some of the most difficult guests, and one day during a rush he had to serve a man who was generally feared, for he had had many men dismissed. Mr. Mistbeck, a blanket manufacturer, lived in the hotel. He should never have been allowed in the hotel at all, but he had millions. He was on some kind of diet, and everything had to be cooked for him without salt or sugar; a long list of how his food was to be prepared hung down in the kitchen. Also he had his own wines and his own mustard; he mixed his own salads; and all this, in the middle of a rush, was always difficult. The cooks cursed; there was sometimes delay.

Mr. Mistbeck then became abusive. He knocked on his glass, shouted, "Hey" or "Hey, you," said, "Tsk, tchk, tchk" or "Psst," and pulled his waiter by the apron or the napkin at luncheon or by the tailcoat at dinner. His wife, a little frowsy, scared but kindly woman, would try to calm him. That only made him madder; he spoke so loud that the people at the tables around him looked up in surprise; his face turned red and blue, and a vein on his forehead stood out; he moved the silver and glasses, bunched the napkin into a ball, pounded on the table and sometimes got up and walked to the door, his napkin in his hand, to complain to Victor.

His complaints always started "I have been coming here for the last five years, and, goddamn it, these idiots don't know yet what I want, you charge enough in this lousy dump!" Or it would go "Listen, you"—he held the waiter while he said that—"listen, you old fool, one of these days I'll buy this goddamn joint and fire every one of you swine and get some people that know how to wait on table; now get going!" With that he would push the man loose. During these embarrassing moments his poor wife would turn red and look down on her plate and behave as if she were not there. When the waiter was gone, Mr. Mistbeck would continue to shout at her, as if she too had kept him waiting or brought him something he did not like.

One of the dreadful things about the hotel business is that it offers no defense against such people. The old waiters who have families just mumble, "Yes, sir. No, sir. Right away, sir. I'm sorry, sir." They insult

the guest outside the room, on the stairway down to the kitchen; that is why one sees these poor fellows talking so much to themselves—they are delivering a long repartee and threatening to throw out some imaginary customer and telling him what they think of him. Sometimes an incident will rankle for days afterward, and they will continue to mumble tremblingly at a pillar, a chair, or through a window out into the street. One can tell from their faces what they are saying, and it usually comes to an end with the swish of a napkin or the quick folding of arms. It is also then that they don't see an upraised hand or hear a call.

Mr. Mistbeck sat at the station of the new waiter, the former brave commis. He was for some reason even unusually abusive, nothing suited him, and finally he pushed back his chair, threw away his napkin and, getting up, took hold of the young man's lapels to deliver his usual speech. Now the brave commis could not stand being touched; his hands leaped up in fists. In a second, Mr. Mistbeck had *l'uppercut* and *le knockout*, and had fallen into his chair with his arms hanging down, his face on his fork and his toupee on the floor.

That ended the Splendide career of the brave commis. Downstairs he was congratulated by all the waiters; in the barbershop he had to show Frank the engineer just how he had done it; and Victor gave him a good recommendation. But in a week the brave commis came back—in uniform. He had enlisted in the American Army.

All the men looked at him with great envy; for a waiter it was so wonderful to be brave, and to be where there were no guests.

FORT ONTARIO the Kitchen of the Isolation HOSPITAL

The Army is like a mother; one cannot go hungry or without a bed. It is my home.

Assigned to the kitchen of the field hospital, we can order eggs, steaks, chops, vegetables, rice, noodles, sugar, flour and many more things, even dried fruit and chocolate. In that foolish language which Beardsley and I talk, concocted of distorted words, elaborate gestures, Ohs and Ahs, the raising of eyebrows, and deep nods, we decide after the patients are asleep that we are more hungry than they and need building up ourselves and that they can be kept without harm on a liquid diet for another week or so.

Beardsley is a fine cook. Many of the seasonings that he needs are missing, but he does well with what he has. The groceries and meats arrive promptly when ordered, the baskets are left on the porch, and we stand around the oven and fry and broil and stew ourselves into a contented after-dinner state twice every day, and have besides thick ham and eggs for breakfast. No wine, but cigars—Beardsley bought a box of them before we came.

THE

BUTTERMACHINE

THERE ARE two Doyles here—one a sergeant, the other a lieutenant. The sergeant is efficient and thin; the lieutenant is fat, with the face of an old lady and little eyes that easily turn hard with offense. He always looks past my face when he speaks to me. The soldiers have invented a very right and beautiful name for him—his trousers have given them this idea—they call him "Satchel Ass." A "satchel" is a portmanteau and "ass" is a donkey but in this case it is the Army word for *derrière* —it fits well. When he walks, it looks as if this portmanteau were constantly opened and closed, and when he sits down it flows over the chair. When he has been around, they do not say, "Lieutenant Doyle was here"; they say, "Doyle was here." Question: "Which one?" Answer: "Satchel Ass Doyle."

Lieutenant Doyle is the glee-club leader and mess officer. He complains all day long about the flies, looks into the ice machine and the iceboxes, and his pet is the buttermachine. He looks at it twice a day with affection. He bought it himself and he shows all the other officers or some friends of his that come visiting how it works. "That's a great little piece of machinery there," he says to them.

The buttermachine has been here ten days. Before that we cut the butter with a small square frame over which a row of thin sharp wires were stretched, making about sixteen squares. These wires run from left to right and up and down. One man and a tub of water with ice is all that is needed to cut all the butter for the men, the patients and even the officers' mess; and all this takes is at the most ten minutes.

Now we have to first rinse the buttermachine with hot water, fill it with ice, then trim the blocks of butter, because as they are they do not fit the round cylinder inside the ice. The cylinder is long and round; the blocks of butter are square and short. One and a half of them, after they are trimmed, fit into the machine. When they are in there, a tight cover is attached, the heavy lid clamped down, and then the work begins.

A man has to stand in front of the machine and work a little lever from left to right and back again to the left; and every time these two motions are completed, one little square of butter falls out of the machine.

I have told Lieutenant Doyle that it is a waste of time, that the butter was cut in ten minutes before and now it takes two hours to do it, and twice a day; it is ridiculuous. But he says, "That buttermachine is all right."

I have detailed Mulvey, who is the laziest of the K.P.s, to this work, and he is now in the dining room and sings his awful song in there and makes these little butterpieces. Mulvey soon finds out that, with making a little fuss, he can stretch his work so that he has nothing else to do, and when Lieutenant Doyle comes in and sees him cleaning the machine very carefully, he stops and smiles and he tells me, "Mulvey is a good man." But I will fix that.

We have one mess table that has a broken leg. After midday meal, when the dishes are washed, would be a good time to do this, but then there are too many people and I think such things should always be done alone with no one around for confusion when somebody asks questions later on.

Sunday is the best day; then all is very quiet, everyone is out. On the next Sunday, when I am not invited out until late in the evening, I move the table with the broken leg over to the door and change it for the one on which the buttermachine sits. This one has good legs. There is a corner of the table which meets the door when it is opened—soldiers rush into rooms—and on that corner is the machine. It is very heavy, about one hundred and fifty pounds.

After this is arranged, I go up to my quarters. There was a crash as soon as I got up there, but I dressed and left, because it was time to meet Doris's car.

The next day when I am back in the mess hall, the cook says, "Somebody busted the buttermachine. Lieutenant Doyle is wild and wants to see everybody who works here."

The best thing is to go right over to headquarters and look surprised and make a face that asks, "Who could have done this? Let me think."

THE MESS HALL IN FORT PORTER
BUFFALO

Mulvey is there already answering questions. The buttermachine is also there, but I am afraid that it can be repaired; one of the pig-iron legs is broken off, and the machinery under the cylinder, where the lever goes back and forth and the butter comes out, seems mangled, but it looks good otherwise.

Lieutenant Doyle has no suspicions; he points at the machine and says, "What do you think of that?" but he asks no more. Mulvey has told him when he saw the machine last and another man how he found it. Whoever opened the door and broke it is not to be determined because he would not report himself and no one has seen anybody else.

All questions and answers are filled out on a long printed statement which the Army issues for all things that break or are lost or worn out. Mulvey is back washing dishes and we cut the butter the old way for some weeks. Then Lieutenant Doyle comes and takes Mulvey away from the dishwashing. He comes back with a small table with very strong legs. Lieutenant Doyle has picked out a corner where to put it; near this corner are no doors. Outside is a truck, with a new buttermachine.

ability to remember names & faces

3 LANGUAGES

Tact and DIPLOMACY

DETAIL AND EXECUTIVE ABILITY

Knowledge of FOOD & VINTAGES

Anticipation

Discipline

NO TROUBLE AT ALL

THE WORLD IS FULL of maîtres d'hôtel, many of whom are able, well-informed men. But only one in a hundred thousand is blessed with that rarest, most priceless of qualities so generously evident in Gabriel, the Maître of the Cocofinger Palace Hotel in New York.

We see this peculiar talent in the profile above, behind the ear, under "Detail and Executive Ability." It is the faculty of "Anticipation," an astral clairvoyance with which to sense catastrophe, anywhere in the wide realm of his authority. Not only to feel it ahead, but to prepare for it and minimize the effect thereof.

One more look at the graph, and it is evident to anyone why, with such talents, Gabriel has come up, up, up, from the position of third piccolo at the humble King Wenceslaus in Przemysl, through the pantries and over the red carpets of Madame Sacher's, the Negresco, Shepheard's, the Meurice, Claridge's, up to the golden doors of the restaurant of the hotel of hotels—the Cocofinger Palace Hotel in New York.

Gabriel smokes Dimitrinos, he has ten dozen shirts, Lobb makes his boots, he is driven in a Minerva, thinks in French, his hats come from Habig in Vienna, and both Noel Coward and Cole Porter have asked him who builds his fine tailcoats.

To his many subordinates, he speaks through his assistant, one Hector de Malherbes, who at one time worked for Max Reinhardt. (This temperamental aesthetic experience has fitted Malherbes most admirably for his present position.) Between the Maître and Malherbes is perfect, wordless understanding.

Never was proof positive of Gabriel's great talents and of the mute felicity of Malherbes more clearly demonstrated than on the night and day of February the twenty-fifth, 1937.

On that Thursday at three-fifteen in the afternoon, when the last luncheon guest had left, Gabriel leaned on his desk with its seven drawers, one for each day of the week, and nodded gently to Malherbes. Malherbes bent down to the drawer *Jeudi*—because it was Thursday— and took from it a salmon-colored folder with a sulphur label, on which was written, "Birthday Party, February 25, 1937, Mrs. George Washington Kelly."

Gabriel carried the folder up to his room; Malherbes bowed and left. In his room, Gabriel took off his fine tailcoat, which was rounded from much bowing, hung it up, sat on his bed and carefully unfolded the bills that five-, ten- and one-dollar patrons had pressed into his hand. He added them up and entered into a little crimson book, "February 25, *Déjeuner*, $56." Then he took off his boots, leaned back into the pillows, stretched his toes in the sheer, black Sulka silk socks, and opened the salmon-colored folder.

Madame George Washington Kelly was a difficult and exacting client.

The Italian waiters called her *bestia*, the French *canaille* and the Germans *die alte Sau*. She had a desperate countenance, partly concealed by a veil; behind this, her face shone the color of indigo. Her skin had the texture of volcanic rock seen from the air, with dirty snow swept into the crevices.

She dressed with complete immunity to fashion, except for the Beaux Arts Ball. On the night of that elaborate *affaire*, she had come with her friend, the "Spirit of the Midnight Sun," and together they had engaged the rooms and made the preliminary plans for this birthday party, of which Malherbes had said to Gabriel in *sotto voce* French, "It is not a birthday party—it is a centennial celebration." Gabriel had stared him into silence.

After many more visits and consultations with architects, stage designers and florists, Madame had decided to build, at one end of the ballroom, a replica of her Miami retreat, O Sole Mio, in its original noble dimensions. This was to be set among hibiscus, poinciana and orange trees in bloom, surrounded by forty-foot royal palm trees and fronted

by wide terraces. Cutting through the center of the room, from the terraces on the north to a magnificent flight of stairs on the south, ran the lagoon, filled with real water, and in this water was to float the genuine gondola which Mr. George Washington Kelly had brought as a souvenir from Venice and taken all the way to Miami. The stairs on the north end rose to a balcony; from there, a birthday cake was to be carried down, placed on the gondola and rowed across to Sole Mio, where Mrs. Kelly's own "darkies" would bring it to her table to be cut.

The gondola was in Miami, also the royal palms, also the four white-haired Negroes, brothers named Morandus. The Fire Department had sent a captain to study the position of the hydrants and windows, to connect a pumping truck and fill the lagoon, which, it was estimated, would take fourteen hours.

To do all this properly, the complete entertaining facilities of the hotel had been rented for the three days preceding the party and for an additional two following it, to clear away the debris.

Since Monday morning, the house was filled with drafts from open doors and windows, tall ladders and empty smilax crates. Careless carpenters, careless stagehands, careless plumbers and florists ruined the peace and the carpets of the hotel with hammering, riveting and soldering together of the two-hundred-foot tank. Following on the heels of the plumbers came the painters, who painted the sides of the lagoon emerald-green and a pattern of underwater scenery on its bottom. An eminent artist from Coral Gables supervised this.

The menu for this party was dictated by Madame herself, without benefit of Gabriel's advice. It was in the tradition of her entertainments and composed itself—at twelve dollars a cover for four hundred guests—of the following: Caviar aux Blinis, Borsch, Homard Sole Mio, Faisan Miami, Purée de Marrons, Pommes Soufflées, Salade Georges et Marthe, Bombe Washington, Café.

For the one thousand five hundred additional guests for supper, she had chosen an equally unfortunate repast. This, at five dollars a cover, consisted of Velouté Marthe aux Croûtons, Poussin en Cocotte Washington, Nouilles Polonaise, Petits Pois Parisienne, Bombe Sole Mio aux Fraises Cardinal, Gâteaux Georges, Café.

Breakfast was to be served from four o'clock on, at one dollar and fifty cents per person. Provision was also made for eighty musicians' suppers, suppers for chauffeurs, maids, the secretaries at the door, and the announcer and detectives, at one dollar per person.

Cocktails were to be served during the reception: a fantastic, violent drink of Madame's own invention, named "High Diddle," the secret formula for which Madame fortunately gave to no one. Closely guarded, her trusty "darkies"—the Morandi—were to mix this, bringing most of the ingredients themselves.

After Gabriel had read the papers and made several notes, he rose, looked into a mirror and took a loose smoking jacket from his closet. He slipped on a pair of white gloves and walked below. Malherbes was waiting for him. It was six o'clock.

Gabriel nodded, and his assistant followed him with a silver pencil and a morocco portfolio.

They walked through the kitchen, where the cooks fished red lobsters

out of steaming casseroles and chopped them in half. From there they went on to the cellar. Here, men broke open cases of *co.don rouge* 1921, at eleven dollars a bottle, put them away in tubs and stood them on top of one another. From here, they walked up to the ballroom proper. The tables, seating eight guests each, were set to the left and right of the lagoon. Sole Mio was finished, and on the lower terraces in front of it—as indicated on the plan—was the crescent-shaped table, facing the room. Here, Monsieur and Madame George Washington Kelly and their son, George Washington Kelly, Jr., as well as their most intimate friends, were to sit.

Two painters were busy pouring and stirring fifty gallons of turquoise ink into the lagoon, to give it the precise color of the waters in Miami. The Coral Gables artist had left with them a sample of that shade on a piece of water-color paper, and, from time to time, they compared this and then added more ink. Up on the balcony of Sole Mio two electricians were focusing spotlights across the room, up to the magenta curtain on the other side.

From the street could be heard the last "*Poooommmph,*" "*Puuuuuuu-mph,*" "*Poomph*" of the Fire Department pumping truck. The lagoon was filled.

Gabriel, walking into the hall, saw the last of twenty royal palms—in tubs, with their leaves carefully bandaged—being carried upstairs, and below from the street appeared the neck of the Venetian gondola.

The great Maître nodded to Malherbes. Malherbes ran down to the door and told the men, "Watch out for the paint, you." Later on, in the office, Malherbes made certain that a gondolier had been engaged. Yes, he had. He was to report at the ballroom in costume, with a knowledge of how to row a gondola and ability to sing "*O Sole Mio.*"

Gabriel went back to his room, lit a cigarette, and rested in his bath for half an hour. Then he dressed.

As on every evening, so now he received the dinner guests of the hotel at the door of the restaurant.

Madame George Washington Kelly's party over in the ballroom was in the able hands of his third assistant, Monsieur Rudi, a withered, one-time stable boy of Prince Esterházy.

At regular intervals a courier crossed from the ballroom and whispered to Malherbes, "The guests are arriving." Then again, "The cocktails are being passed." After this, "The guests are entering the ballroom." Then, "Madame George Washington Kelly is very pleased," and on to "The guests are sitting down," and "The soup is being served." These bulletins were translated into French by Malherbes and whispered on to Gabriel, who nodded.

Dinner was almost over in the restaurant when Gabriel went into a little side room, where, on a table behind a screen, a plain meal was prepared for him. It consisted of some cold pheasant, cut from the bones, field salad with lemon dressing, and a plain compote of black cherries cooked without sugar. In ice under the table was his favorite wine, an elegant, slim bottle of Steinberger Kabinett, Preussische Staatsdomäne, 1921.

In the middle of his meal, before he had touched the great wine, Gabriel rose abruptly and quickly walked across the restaurant. Malherbes, who had eaten out in the second little room, swallowed quickly and followed him. Almost running, they crossed the entrance hall of the ballroom and went up the staircase, to the third palm.

Gabriel stopped and beside him, as always, stopped Hector de Malherbes. The dessert had just been served, the remnants of the Bombe Washington were being carried from the room by the waiters, and, as set forth in the sheet of instructions, the lights were lowered.

Two heralds sounded the *Aïda* theme as a command to silence and attention.

The heavy magenta curtains sailed back, and high above the audience appeared the birthday cake. It was magnificent, of generous proportions, and truly beautiful. The masterpiece of Brillat Bonafou, *Chef Pâtissier* of the Cocofinger Palace Hotel, twice the winner of the Médaille d'Or de la Société Culinaire de Paris, Founder and President of the Institut des Chefs Pâtissiers de France. In weeks of patient, sensitive, loving labor, he had built a monument of sugar, tier upon tier, ten feet high, of raisin and almond cake. Of classic simplicity, yet covered with innumerable ornaments that depicted scenes from a happy sporting life. Up and down the sides of the cake, dozens of cherubim were busy carrying ribbons; these—Bordeaux and emerald—represented the racing colors of the G. W. K. stables.

But the most wonderful part of the wonderful cake was its top. There,

complete in all details, stood a miniature replica of O Sole Mio, correct as to palms, orange trees, the lagoon, the gondola. Under the portico, an inch high, smiling, hand in hand, stood Monsieur and Madame George Washington Kelly—Madame with a bouquet of roses, Monsieur with his ever-present cigar, an Hoyo de Monterrey, at the end of which was a microscopic tuft of cotton.

That was, however, not all. Over the miniature Sole Mio hovered a brace of doves. In their beaks, most artfully held, were electric wires, so arranged that flashing on and off they spelled first "George" and then "Martha." "George" in green, "Martha" in red. Five lady midgets, dressed as the Quintuplets, carried the cake downstairs in the light of the amber spotlights.

The Hawaiians played "Happy Birthday to You, Happy Birthday to You." Everyone sang, and all eyes were moist.

The gondolier started to punt down the lagoon to receive the cake.

At that moment, with all eyes upon them, one of the Quintuplets, Yvonne, stepped on an olive pit and turned her ankle. The cake trembled, swayed and fell into the lagoon, taking the midgets with it. *"Ffsssssss-hss"* went the electric wires.

But where was Gabriel?

He stood under the royal palm and nodded quietly to Malherbes. Malherbes lifted one finger and looked up at the man with the spotlight.

The amber light left the lagoon and raced up the stairs. Out came the trumpeteers again and sounded the *Aïda* theme, the curtain swung open once more, again the Hawaiians played "Happy Birthday to You, Happy Birthday to You."

As if the last dreadful minutes had never been on the watches of the world, there appeared to the unbelieving eyes of Monsieur and Madame George Washington Kelly and their guests and friends—THE CAKE again, unharmed, made with equal devotion, again the work of Brillat Bonafou, identically perfect and complete, with the scenes of the happy life, the cherubim, cigar and smoke, lagoon and gondola, doves, lights flashing the names in green and red, and carried on the shoulders of a new set of Quintuplets.

The miserable first set of midgets swam to the shore of the lagoon, scrambled out and tried to leave the ballroom in the shade of the tables.

Gabriel hissed *"Imbéciles!"* to Malherbes. Malherbes hissed *"Imbéciles!"* down to the midgets.

The new cake was rowed across, besung, carried to the table, cut and served. Not until then did the great maître d'hôtel leave the protecting shadow of the royal palm. Now he walked quietly, unseen, to his room, for, in spite of possessing every talent, and besides the gift of "Anticipation," Gabriel was a very modest man.

AFFAIR

Jewish weddings were an important and very remunerative part of the Splendide's banqueting business. They took place in the relatively quiet months, and much money was spent on them for food, wine and floral decorations. The menus were never less than seven dollars and fifty cents per person, and went up to as high as fifteen dollars. The floral decorations cost on an average a thousand dollars, and this did not include the bouquets for the bride and the bridesmaids. Wines came to about another thousand dollars, and an orchestra to play during the ceremony, the dinner and the dancing was again almost that much.

There was in addition a rental charge for the rooms of about three hundred dollars, about which most of them complained: "They don't charge that at Sherry's or any place else." For that Mr. Sigsag had learned a very cool answer, the only stiff words he ever used: "Madame, the Splendide competes with no one."

For such weddings, the Orchid Salon, the large staircase, the foyer of the ballrooms and the ballroom proper were used, to which were also added a suite in which the bride and groom could stay overnight and which was connected with the ballroom by a high-speed elevator, and a room for each set of parents.

The ceremony is staged in the Orchid Salon, and after the ceremony the upper landing of the staircase provides an excellent place to kiss the bride, the scene being reflected in the forty panels of high mirrored doors that lead to the oval restaurant. The Kissing of the Bride takes a long time, so long that for a while before the conversation of the up-coming guests drowns it, one thinks a baby is being smacked on the back-side. Then they climb up another beautiful staircase that swings left and right, to the ballroom level, where caviar and cocktails are served until everybody has come up and the music can start. The curtains are drawn back, revealing the high mirrored ballroom. The glasses, linen and china shine on the tables in the glow of the candles. The lights of the chan-deliers are reflected in the many mirrors; there are no columns to spoil the spacious effect. Public rooms should always be built like these to include several levels broken up by stairways, where women can stop, turn, go back again, up and down, and show their dresses.

The people who wished to have their daughter's wedding here were usually brought to the Splendide by a friend who had already given such a party. They came to the restaurant for luncheon, long before the date of the wedding. Mr. Sigsag went down with his date book, the day was chosen and booked, a deposit of several hundred dollars was paid, and the rooms were looked at. Mr. Sigsag had learned two phrases for these interviews which he thought very highly of and used very often. One was "the Affair," a word loved by the Jewish matrons: "We were to an Affair at the Plaza." The other he had fished out of the rotogravure sections of the Sunday newspapers—"the Bride-Elect." Therefore we had constantly recurring in these conversations: "We don't compete with anyone, Madame," "the Affair" and "the Bride-Elect."

There were many other visits after the first: plans were made and changed, menus worked over, wines selected, dishes tasted, music en-gaged, prices arrived at, cigars ordered. All this went into contracts and estimates. Then there were several rehearsals, at which some man who had made millions running a big business could be seen in all his awk-wardness: always starting off with the wrong foot, almost falling down the stairs, and becoming more helpless the more he was talked to. For these rehearsals Mr. Sigsag sang "La, la, la, la!" to the wedding march of *Lohengrin*. He upset tradition, too, by having the mothers of the bride and the groom march down in front of the procession a little ahead of the parade. They loved this.

When finally everything is settled and written down, all the details are gone over once more. The menu is most important and is discussed at length. The soup has to have something swimming in it. If it is a cream of asparagus, there must be little pieces of asparagus in it; it has to be thick and golden, so the spoon can almost be stood up in it. The fish is for the most part trout in butter with almonds, but of most concern is the squab, an individual squab chicken. They always anxiously come back to this, although the reputation of former weddings is great: "You won't forget, Mr. Wladi?"

They look deeply into his eyes when they talk or listen to him; he belongs to the family almost, and the father has slapped Mr. Sigsag on the back and told him to come to the store and he'll put a piece of goods on his back, the best in the place. "You won't forget, Mr. Wladi, the individual broilers, with lots of gravy, lots of gravy. An individual broiler for everybody. We want this Affair to be a big success."

"Yes, lots of gravy, Madame." It is underlined in our copy of the estimate, and the order that goes down to the chef reads: *"Poussins individuels, avec beaucoup de jus."*

The salad, covered with Russian dressing, is a mixture of endives, a slice of pineapple, and a little ball of cream cheese with chopped chives. "Mmm—oh, that's wonderful, Mr. Wladi." Mr. Wladi has some six such terrible combinations which he has cut out from an advertisement in a magazine, a double page in full colors with which the chef almost threw him out of the office.

After this, the dessert. With a silver pencil that writes in three colors—red, yellow and blue—Mr. Sigsag shows that "it's a dream, a little temple of ice cream, on a floating block of ice, in which is a little light. Inside the temple are a miniature bride and groom, and around the ice are crushed strawberries or nectarines in a cream sauce." For this all the lights will be lowered, and the music will play "Midsummer Night's Dream," and the waiters will march with all the little lights in their ice cream temples in a long row all around the room. The march is shown on the plan; that again is "wonderful."

While coffee is being served outside, the entire ballroom will be transformed in fifteen minutes; when the curtains are again drawn back, the musicians will have eaten, the tables and service will have been cleared away, and there will be a wide dance floor, with, at one end of the room, a large buffet containing a silver bowl of orangeade, drinks and cigars and cigarettes. Fauteuils will be distributed on strips of carpet all around

the room, in which the older people can sit while waiters pass them refreshments.

Another great moment follows this. The wedding cake is wheeled in. The bride, with a spotlight shining down on her from the balcony and to a roll of the drums, will make the first cut; the rest will be cut for her. Everybody will get a piece of wedding cake to eat and another piece to take home, wrapped in silver paper and put into a little box with gold initials and a silk ribbon.

The dancing starts; the bride will throw the bouquet from the balcony; and Mr. Sigsag will then take the newlyweds up to their apartment by way of a private passage and private elevator. As he explains this, their eyes hang on his face, like those of children on a Christmas tree; of all the people who come here, they are the only ones who are happy without being drunk.

"He's wonderful, that little Mr. Wladi," they say. "And this is the only place to have an Affair. They charge you for it, but it's worth it."

When the last interview is ended, Mama gets up first, pushes herself in the stomach, adjusts her bosom, and then goes with the back of her hands down her backside. The Bride-Elect, who has spoken very little, gets up and smiles, and the father shakes hands with Mr. Sigsag. They are great friends; the father admires the brevity, the business acumen, of Mr. Wladi. During the interview Mr. Sigsag has given several orders to assistants in bad French and German, and that has impressed them greatly; such a smart fellow, he has been called to the phone a dozen times and spoken to various people, having his information always ready in his mind. Besides, he looks tired and worried and is nervous, which is always a great asset in the eyes of a fellow businessman. They walk down the stairs, look into the ballroom once more, point to the place where the bride will be kissed, "and then we go up this way for the cocktails."

Finally they leave. Mama looks over her bosom down at the steps below and feels for them with her tight shoes. Halfway down the stairs, she stops once more, and for the last time the phrase is sent up: "And don't forget, Mr. Wladi, lots of gravy with the broilers." If it happens that they meet, coming through the door of the restaurant, friends who have the next appointment, then they stop briefly and sing, "Oh, you having an Affair here too?"

If then one wished to sell them something additional—a more elaborate menu, better wines, more musicians or flowers—it was necessary only to call them up and inform them during the conversation that their friends had ordered it. They would become angry that we hadn't suggested it in the first place. "Sure we want it. Now you just go ahead, Mr. Wladi. We want to do things right. Thirty-five musicians? Sure, I know the room is big."

On the day of the wedding the bride arrives about five o'clock and is immediately whisked upstairs. It is the first personal touch of the untiring Mr. Sigsag; he waits for her. But he has been here since nine o'clock in the morning, setting up and upsetting the room. He has, with the aid of the housemen, placed on the dais the table for the bride, the groom and their families, measuring everything himself, and also carrying legs for the tables and helping move the platforms. Then in the middle of the room, in front of the bride's table, he has built the young people's table in three sections, in the shape of a heart, with its center open for dancing. He has seen to it that the old people's table is placed where they will be comfortable, out of the draft, and near the wedding families; the other tables are placed and replaced, and pushed back and forth, to get everybody seated. He has shown the florists where to place a fountain and has arranged to cover up the lower edge of some old smilax from a previous party that has been sold over again, with a few fresh inches of greenery. When the tables are ready for setting with silver and glasses, and the bride is upstairs, Mr. Sigsag goes up to take a shower and dress.

Below, in the ballroom kitchen, Kalakobé the Senegalese is dragging the huge casseroles up out of the elevator with an iron hook; they have come from the main kitchen, where they have been partly prepared, and they are lifted onto steam tables, where the chefs arrange the food on silver platters and stow them away in hot compartments—hundreds of trout, the individual broilers with the gravy separate. In the pantries stand long tables and shelves on which the caviar, the salads, the dressing for the salads, bread and butter, celery and olive services and the services

for dessert and coffee are being prepared, as well as the rolling table for the wedding cake. Nothing must be forgotten.

As Mr. Sigsag goes up to dress, I come down dressed, and all the waiters are assembled in the ballroom. I have a list of them and give them their stations; each one gets eight people to wait on. The best, fastest, serve the bride's table and the family; slow, considerate and elderly men get the old people. We have one man who is almost blind; he has been with us since the hotel opened; he sometimes spills things and goes with his nose close to the plates to see them and also passes cigars to the ladies. He is teamed up with a young, quick man to help him and he gets the table next to the kitchen, where he does not have to walk far. The youngest men get the tables far away; they can run faster.

Then the other employees have to be checked: there has to be a door-man outside, a man in gala livery to turn the revolving door; coatroom attendants, maids, washroom boys; a man to show the guests down to the Orchid Salon for the ceremony; a man down there at the electric control of the lights; a man in the lobby with a counting machine so that we may know just how many guests have arrived. All the room decorations must be supervised, the décor of the Orchid Salon, which is that of a night club, is hidden with greenery, and in front of a fountain at its far end is placed the bower, filled with white roses, lilies and rows of white candles. The engineers are called to adjust the temperature; wines have to be opened.

When all this is checked, the ceremony can begin. The chairs, which are arranged as in a chapel, slowly fill with guests. The best man and the groom stand waiting behind the bower and the bride has been spirited upstairs. The rabbi arrives, the family comes and is seated in the first rows reserved for them, musicians and a singer are hidden behind palms, the fountain is turned low, everything has been rehearsed, and the wedding starts now!

First the lights are lowered while the singer sings "Oh, Promise Me." The rabbi goes to the post where he will stand during the ceremony. Mr. Sigsag lifts a little finger, and all the people turn around as a curtain is pulled back at the top of the stairs; the mothers of the bride and groom march down as, at a signal, the musicians play the Wedding March. Mr. Sigsag is upstairs counting one, two, three, four; they have started off on the wrong foot, but it doesn't matter. At the last moment Mr. Sigsag kneels on the floor behind the bride to arrange her train as widely and beautifully as possible before she descends into the salon, which is again brightly lit by the sparkling oval chandelier, to face the rabbi.

If Rabbi Stephen Wise is officiating, the service is brief. He comes in as if he were trying to step on two alternating cockroaches that run about a foot ahead of him; he faces the audience and rocks his tall form back and forth, looking up at the ceiling, with his hands folded in front of him. A heroic man with much dignity, his wide mouth is a straight line; sometimes he blows his nose loudly while waiting and blinks his eyes impatiently up the stairway. When the procession is in front of him, he hammers a sermon down on them that sounds as if someone were cracking cigar boxes by walking over them, a sermon designed for Madison Square Garden. At the end he reaches up over them, blesses them beautifully, and then the great man lopes out, stooping, holding both lapels of his coat in his hands. He never stays for dinner and seems to be glad when his part is over.

But heaven help us when, with the fidelity with which Jewish people cling to their friends and the people who were with them in their beginnings, they bring along a little orthodox rabbi, one from Far Rockaway or another such place, whose day of glory has come with

such a wedding. He speaks a very precise English, as if he were in a school of elocution; also he behaves with great condescension. He wishes to run the entire wedding and has to be subdued. He brings with him most of his congregation, to look on; they are placed out of the way up on a balcony, but before the party is over they are always invited to stay and join in. Since no provision has been made for them, this is upsetting; extra tables have to be carried in and a menu improvised.

Such a rabbi always brings a little imaginary ship with him; it is the ship of marriage, and he starts it on endless voyages. Whenever his sermon runs low, the little ship appears again. On board this ship the husband is the captain, the wife is the crew. The ship goes out into a storm and comes back again into the harbor; the captain cannot steer it alone, neither can the crew; both must steer it together. The little ship is new with fresh paint in youth, and old with mended sails in age, but there is a harbor, a beautiful harbor, waiting for it. This little ship travels about while the caviar gets warm and the soup thickens upstairs. We make signs to him and turn the fountain on full force to drown out his words, but he is not to be stopped. Finally he has exhausted all the uses of the ship, the chandelier lights are lowered, the mothers weep in loud sobbing rhythm, the fathers' mouths lose shape, the orchestra has put mutes on the fiddles, and while they play softly the Rockaway rabbi says an endless blessing over them. Bride and groom drink out of a silver cup; the groom crushes a glass with his foot. The orchestra plays the Mendelssohn Wedding March, all parade out to the reception, and the kissing begins—everything precisely as in the estimate.

Upstairs, on the wide balcony outside the ballroom, are little tables with large blocks of ice; on the ice are cans of caviar and in front of them are warmed Peek and Frean crackers. Ten waiters stand about with trays of cocktails, the favorite being Orange Blossoms, a mixture of gin and orange juice, undrinkably sweet. The reception lasts half an hour, until the last guest has kissed the bride.

We had among the waiters here an old fellow whose name was Gustav, Gustl for short. He was happiest at these weddings, and whereas we had to call the others to come from behind the curtain, where they talked politics, to pass the cocktails, he was always ready, tray in hand. The reason was that he suffered from a mild nervous disorder, which he confessed to me when I caught him red-handed indulging it. As he moved about in the crowd, serving cocktails, I once noticed that the back of his left hand, every now and then, brushed past the hips of some of the women. When I got to know him better, he told me that in the beginning he would have had more pleasure if he could have used the palm of his hand, but he found that too dangerous, so that now, after many years of adapting himself, he had developed quite as much sensitivity in the nerves on the back of his hand. He loved Jewish weddings, there was such wonderful material for his hobby; and since he did no one any harm, I always put him in the thick of it. At an Affair he would be radiant, and sometimes he would come back to me and point out some particularly fine specimen in the way of curve and resistance. For dinner I would give him stations with round women, and it was charming to see how he could not do enough for them, serving them with all possible dispatch and hovering over the backs of their chairs. Gustl was not so happy at coming-out parties, the young girls having hardly anything to offer him. Sometimes he would slip a little in technique and an astonished Jewish matron with her mouth full of canapés would turn around on the crowded balcony as if stung by an insect; but when she saw dear old Gustl with his white hair and the lackey's immobile face, she would look at her husband beside her with "Hey, hey, what's going on here?" eyes.

The eating at the wedding dinners was accomplished with noise and fat fingers, the individual broilers with plenty of gravy being cleaned to the bone. There was also a type of table talk which went exclusively with these wedding dinners. A wife would say loudly, "You know what happened last time, Sam. You'll get sick to your stomach. Remember how sick you was? You'll take a physic when I get you home." Then, while the orchestra played "Les Millions d'Arlequin," the conversation would become general and turn to the relative merits of various purges. Also they would exchange parts of chicken: "Here, take a taste of this."

After the dessert, which is carried in as promised, in the dark and to the accompaniment of music, there is usually some singing. The family poet has written the words—they are about the bride and the groom—and they are sung to a tune that everyone knows. The song has been printed, along with photographs showing the bride as a "tot," the groom and the scene of their meeting. The coffee is served and the cigars are passed around. The men take both the little and the big cigars, sometimes two of each, their wives encouraging them: "Take another, Sam; they have to pay for it anyway."

It is time for the photograph, and it is then that someone misses

Grandpa, who has disappeared during the meal. He arrived in a tailcoat and egg-colored shoes, with unkempt whiskers and the hollow, unhappy face of the Jewish immigrant. He has a drivelly nose, red eyelids and a little black skullcap, and he climbs all over the hotel like a baby. You can see him going down the stairs sideways, holding onto one railing with both hands. He walks into the ladies' washroom, into the outdoor garden, comes out of the elevator in the corridor of an upper floor, or appears in the kitchen, where the chef says, "*Qu'est-ce qu'il veut ici, ce phénomène?*" Finally Mr. Sigsag finds him, takes his arm and brings him back.

During the day, a photographer and his assistant, standing on a ladder, had concealed flashlights in white fireproof bags in the greenery overhead and had focused their camera on a tripod up on the balcony so that it overlooked the room. Now the waiters leave the room, having no desire to have their pictures taken, while the guests straighten their neckties and the women wiggle in their chairs and tilt their heads. Everyone is asked to smile and face the photographer, who then sets off the flashes. Mr. Sigsag is in every picture, standing at attention in a corner, on his face a devout smile; he is a sort of trade-mark in them, the guarantee that he has personally taken care of all the details of the wedding, and he has an album full of these pictures. And when people later show the photographs they will point to him and say, "And that's Mr. Sigsag, he's wonderful."

The bride throws her bouquet from the balcony and disappears with the groom. Mr. Sigsag takes them up in the private elevator, running it himself, wishes them "good night" and smiles coyly as he bows himself out. As the dancing begins downstairs, the mothers usually rush up for a last word with bride and groom—"Be nice to her"—and weep and embrace them.

Below, the ladies pluck at the centerpiece for flowers to take home with them. Mr. Sigsag sends for paper to wrap them up with. By midnight they are usually gone.

The father stays to the end. If the bill is ready he pays it then and there, and has the cash with him to leave a liberal sum, at least ten per cent of the bill, for the employees as tips, and a large gift of money for Mr. Sigsag. There are rarely squabbles of any kind; they leave with many thanks for the good service, shake hands with all the employees in sight, and say again and again that everything has been wonderful and to come to the store to get that wonderful suit.

*A*ll maîtres d'hôtel love to eat. They lean over sideboards, behind high screens, to stuff something quickly away. They are especially fond of little fried things which they can pick up from hot dishes as the commis bring them up from the kitchen, such easily disposed-of things as whitebait, oyster crabs, fried scallops, frogs' legs and fried potatoes. They have learned to eat so that their cheeks and jaws do not move; they can eat in the middle of the dining room and no one know it.

One of the maîtres d'hôtel in the Splendide, a very good-looking one, had a front tooth missing; it was being repaired. At one very busy luncheon he took a green olive from a tray behind the screen on one of his service tables. Just then he was called to a table; the publisher Frank Munsey wanted to order the rest of his luncheon while he waited for his soup to cool. Mr. Munsey looked over the card that was handed him and decided on some tête de veau en tortue. As the maître d'hôtel repeated this, with its many T's, the olive pit shot out through the hole in his teeth and landed in Mr. Munsey's soup.

Fortunately the publisher was bent over talking to someone at the next table and saw nothing. The maître d'hôtel nervously asked if he could

not take the soup back and get something hotter, but Mr. Munsey, a very much feared guest, said he had been waiting for it to cool; it was just about right now.

But there is a way out of such difficulties, a technique of upset and confusion, often employed in dangerous situations with hard clients. The maître d'hôtel first instructs the chef de rang and the commis; there is a small quick meeting—then excitement, noise, shouting, a waving in the face of bills of fare, some pushing, and one, two, three, the soup is gone. All this happens while the maître d'hôtel is a few tables away, so that the client can call him to complain. He comes, is surprised and calls the waiter names: "Specimen of an idiot, where is the soup of Monsieur Munsey?" "Ah, pardon—I thought—" "You should not think, stupid one! Ah, Monsieur Munsey, pardon, pardon." The soup is back on the table after the commis, behind the screen, has fished the olive pit out with his fingers. For the rest of the meal the guest has perfect service, and when he leaves the maître d'hôtel says once more, "So sorry about the soup," and for this he gets sometimes one, two or five dollars, but never from Mr. Munsey.

COMING OUT

THE LARGEST, the most elaborate parties given in a fashionable hotel are the debuts. They brought prestige to the Splendide, and in all the newspapers were published long accounts of the decorations, the menu and the number and names of the guests. Pictures of the debutante appeared in the fashionable magazines, and her debut at the Splendide was announced months ahead of, and described many times after, the party. The captions always read: "Miss So-and-So, who is coming out on December twelfth at the Splendide," and, for a year after: "Miss So-and-So, who came out on December twelfth at the Splendide."

Such a party is very costly, and only people with a great deal of money can afford it. There is a standard for food, decoration and music below which one cannot go, and the staff needed consists of about two hundred and fifty to three hundred men. The guests are in the neighborhood of two thousand.

There are, during a winter, twenty or thirty coming-out parties, and at the end of them all our men are half dead; even the girls who attend them look worn out. A succession of parties, each lasting from seven-thirty in the evening until four or five in the morning, and requiring an additional two hours to get things cleared, leave about three hours' sleep for everybody. The housemen and the Genomies sleep on rolled-up carpets and on the felt covers of the large tables, covering themselves with used tablecloths and making pillows of old napkins. So do many of the late waiters. After they wake up, it takes an hour for them to come out of their stupor. They have to drink to keep going. Hardest of all works Mr. Sigsag.

Von Kyling gets home a little earlier than the others: one man must keep a clear head to supervise, to see that no fatal mistakes in booking are made. He has a hard time these days restraining Mr. Sigsag, who is always taking on additional parties. On the Sunday on which we might have rested he has booked a little wedding of forty people on the first floor and a dance of the Brooklyn Consumptive Relief League for the afternoon. "It pays the overhead," he says. Also the moment there is a room free, as, for instance, after a coming-out dinner has been served in the Orchid Salon, he books it for the same night for a dance by a Hungarian society. It is then not only a strain to clear the room in half an hour of tables, carpets, silver, china, and to force drafts into it, to get the smoke out, but we must also calm down the Hungarian lady in charge of the dance who has arrived in the middle of the coming-out dinner and who will never believe that at the time at which the room will be hers it will be clean, fresh and properly arranged. During the rest of the evening it will also be hard to keep the Hungarians from running upstairs and trying to get into, or hanging on the edges of, the other party. But no matter how von Kyling cries, there is nothing to be done with Sigsag; he continues to throw everything out of gear and even to bring in morning concerts or lectures on busy days.

The most brilliant parties are managed by a very highborn, virtuous lady of ruined fortunes who runs a "social service" and blue-pencils the invitation lists for her clients. She receives a percentage from the hotel and a fee from the host and she comes several times before the party, bringing her hostess with her. Her general color scheme is that of a dairy —cream-colored dresses, lacy and negligee-like; yellowish-white hair; the ancient face powdered flat white; pale blue tile-colored eyes; a butter-hued fan. Her voice is a *précieux* alto that stabs through the ears up to the back of the head. To von Kyling she speaks with a perpetual umlaut: "Good uevenueng, von Kuehlueng." There is about her a cloud of perfume of a bitter musky scent, affected by many old ladies, and around her neck is tied a black velvet ribbon. When she calls during the day, she is dressed in a *trotteur* and wears a hat with a thousand cloth violets, a Queen Mary toque.

This lady also engages the announcer and a stern man with white gloves who stands next to the secretary at the door, beside a little green-covered table on which lie two pads and pencils. The people without invitations are turned back here. We also have to supply men at all the doors, at the elevators, at every possible entrance and exit, but some of the young men get in anyway. It is this secretary from the "social service" bureau who, after all the doors and rooms have been staffed, distributes the place cards on the dinner tables in the Orchid Salon. She has also removed the donors' cards from the hundred baskets of exquisite flowers hung around on the wall and has written on the backs of them the kind of flowers they came with so that the proper personal thanks may be sent.

The rooms engaged for a typical coming-out party—at a very high rental—include the entire public facilities of the hotel: the Orchid Salon for a dinner for the closer circle of friends, up to perhaps two hundred and fifty; the ballroom for the reception of the guests and for the dancing; the restaurant, the Jade Lounge, and the adjoining rooms for supper; and a little top-floor suite, connected with the ballroom by a high-speed elevator (usually employed for the bringing up of linen, ice and glasses, but now with its scratches covered by a silken curtain), to which the host may take his elderly guests and where, at the best parties, a Budapest string orchestra plays, card tables are laid out, champagne and supper are served and, if possible, the young people are kept out.

The rooms are rented for three days: one in which to build them up, another to finish them and have the party, and the third to tear them down again. For when the arrangements are made by an energetic hostess, she will often arrive with a squadron of orchestra leaders, architects, florists and stage designers and think nothing of asking us to move a wall or break down a few doors for such entertainments. Carpenters and plumbers hammer, florists run around. There is confusion and drafts through the house up to within three minutes of the party, and while the last painter and florist are being pushed out the back, the first guests are coming in through the front.

The hostesses try to outdo one another in decorations. For one party the suite will be clothed in soft silks and have not one sprig of greenery; for the next it will become a Southern plantation with old white-haired colored retainers in livery imported from Georgia. For the third party it will be transformed into a replica of an Italian villa. Many ideas are beautiful, more are mad, and some are laughable, as, for example, the interior of a tropical cabaret in the south of France, which one woman in despair imported, complete with primitive murals, bamboo tables and chairs, artificial banana trees, monkeys and an elephant-hide bar.

There were décors all in white, all in silver, all in gold. The famous palms of the late King Leopold of Belgium, every leaf carefully bandaged, were once brought in from Long Island, carried up the stairs by twenty men, and put into a Florida *mise-en-scène,* while forty florists worked for a day to wire oranges and blossoms into boxed trees.

In the restaurant the dinner for the ordinary hotel guests is still being served, while outside, in the pantries, a regiment of waiters is busy polishing glasses and silver and preparing everything so that it can be rushed at a moment's notice onto the tables of the coming-out supper. It is in the pantries too that the florists finish the centerpieces, and a half hour after the last restaurant guest has left, the room has been ventilated, the

tables completely set up anew and rearranged according to the seating plan specified, together with the Jade Lounge and adjoining rooms— ready to serve the two thousand for supper. And in between all this there is hardly time to change and put on a clean shirt.

The menus for the family dinners downstairs have usually been well selected and not too heavy, but the supper is and always will be a problem. The dancers are young and hungry and therefore need something fairly substantial; but they want to get back to the dance floor as soon as possible, and therefore the meal must be brief. Hence the monotony of the menu: the eternal consommé, the small breast of guinea hen on Virginia ham with mushrooms, the small plain salad and the dessert. There are hostesses who have tried to be original at supper and recklessly substituted such things as Boston baked beans or corned-beef hash. These only make the room smelly; such dishes belong in a tiled restaurant, in the daytime. However, supper is really not important; neither are the decorations. All that matters is the music and the dance floor, proper temperature in the ballroom, and the liquor. No one cares about the food except a few old people who have never forgotten their wonderful dinners of ten years ago. A ham sandwich would make the youngsters just as happy.

As for the liquor, it is under lock and key in the pantries, and the cases of champagne are broken open and iced under the watchful eyes of Pommer, the old German bartender, who directs the seeming confusion with sure, fast commands.

For the big parties there were usually three orchestras, of about sixty men each and of the best; a favorite one was frequently brought in from Washington. There was always a fight among the bands for the best side of the ballroom, and they also fought us for space. To satisfy them we would have to give them half the ballroom and leave no space for dancing. We therefore always first built their platforms flat against the walls and so steep that the musicians seemed almost to be sitting on top of one another. Then when they tearfully begged us for just a little more room, we would let them out a few inches and make them happy. The bands always tried to outplay one another, waging a musical warfare that would grow fiercer with the night, and at the end of the party the men would be so excited that it would be hard to stop hem.

These orchestras are efficient machines; their rhythms pound like the pistons of a precise engine while angry brasses yell the melody and violins sing a soft embroidery above them. There is a discipline and order here that is rare even in symphonic orchestras, a clean, mathematical rightness of musical ornament that is partly in the composition of the pieces but is mostly in the playing of them. I think it gives a clearer portrait of the "American" than anything else. It "clicks," it washes away all tiredness, it makes laughable any worry, it is a form of liberation. One cannot be in the center of this magnificent machine and be upset about anything except the fear that the drummer may drop his stick. In one of the best bands there was a drummer who made such naked faces as he crouched over his instruments, who was so completely given over to his playing, that one was embarrassed to watch the revelation of the savage animal let loose.

The conductor of this orchestra was untiring. He had a cheap face, with something of the ape in it, and an overfriendly smile. Also he wore the typical musician's overcoat, a paunchy bathrobe of material such as Teddy bears are made of, held together by a wide sash with no buckle, tied around him; a derby went with this costume. This man had worked his way to the top; the young people insisted on him, and a party was considered dead if he was not there. He pounded the podium with his feet like a madman, smashing the rhythms through its planks and almost breaking them. He worked his men angrily, but no one could get out of an orchestra the sure, high sensuous playing he did. Many of his musicians were from the Philharmonic, and I never could understand how, after one of these sessions, they could be any good at another tempo. They earned a great deal of money, and deserved it, for they worked very hard and enjoyed their work. They all spent freely and most of them wore overcoats like their leader's and owned wire-haired terriers and smoked big cigars. They liked to speak of their wives and mothers and of their homes on Mosholu Parkway, or the Grand Concourse, or Myrtle Avenue, or the numbered avenues of Astoria, or in some apartment house with a magnificent name in Jackson Heights. Their leader was said to be a millionaire.

He was disliked by his men, and more so by our waiters, because he would never quit. At half past three, and again at half past four, he would play quiet pieces, and just at the point when the hostess had to decide whether to keep him another hour, he would stamp out his wild favorites, shouting at his men, "Don't die on me, boys, don't die on me." During the soft pieces he had let some of his best musicians go out for a drink and a rest; at ten minutes to the hour they were back giving all they had in them. The party had meanwhile thinned, and there was more room to dance in, and now no one would go home. He always brought three shirts, collars and ties with him, and we gave him a room to change in. He never drank or smoked; he played; and at the end of every hour the maneuver was repeated, if possible until six or seven. At three o'clock we served breakfast, but a "good party" was one in which the guests went home in the daylight.

The supper was usually served at one. A half hour before that, Frank the engineer came up to prepare the opening of the doors of the restaurant, the two wings of which were each forty feet high and twenty-five feet wide and folded back like a screen of immense tall glass panels. When the supper march was played—sometimes thrillingly by a Highland troupe of tall, handsome bagpipers with leopard-skin aprons under their big drums—the dancers streamed down and overran the suites of rooms that had thus been thrown together. During the supper another orchestra played in the dining rooms while the dance musicians ate a supper, as good as the guests', down in the Grill Room. At the same time the chauffeurs and the maids who came as chaperones and who waited from eight in the evening, when their young charges came to dinner, until four or five the next morning, in the lobby or in some drafty entrance hall, with a French or German book, received sandwiches and coffee.

Upstairs the piano keys were being washed. They would be covered with a gray smear from the pianist's pounding, this sweaty soup reaching back between the black keys, and the board at the end of the keys was scratched from the scraping down of fingernails. A waiter walked around to look for forgotten fans, pocketbooks, gloves and heels—a job I often assigned to old Gustl because, among his other weaknesses, he confessed to one for ladies' heels, which he liked to feel in his pocket. The housemen swept the carpets and the floor, and the engineers drew out the smoke and pumped in cold air, but not too much because the cold air would run along the carpets of the ballroom balcony, and from there it poured down two wide circular stairways and into the dining room, where the candles flickered and the curtain, if closed, swung up into the room. All this had to be remembered and done right, down to the detail of one supper that had to be served to the social secretary in her corner, with a glass of wine and a smile. Mr. Sigsag took care of that; he appreciated the worth of the opinions of servants, butlers and secretaries, to the point of sending a certain one a little birthday box of flowers with the compliments of the hotel on every thirteenth of June.

Standing on the bridge of the balcony and looking down, one could see a scene of unmatched elegance. First there was the brilliant arrangement of the rooms, in three descending levels—ballroom, restaurant, Jade Lounge—with wide spaces between them; even the service facilities were well-nigh perfect, for the architect had consulted the chef and the maître d'hôtel as to the placing of doors, kitchens, elevators, stairways and pantries. The interiors, too, were not merely in good taste but also intelligently planned. The restaurant, oval in shape and large enough to seat four hundred people, yet had all the happy intimacy of design of that most beautiful of all rooms, the little silver-and-blue dining room of the Amalienburg in the gardens of Nymphenburg, outside Munich.

The blue smoke that hung over this scene, the sound of conversation, the hurry and the music, the shining glasses and the happiness in the very young girls' faces made an exciting picture. The young people, men and women, were better-looking, better built, more fortunate of face, than any other race in the world. Some of the older of these Americans also had fine powerful heads, but best of all were the girls, with their young ready figures, their slender ankles, their lovely bosoms, their free graces. The faces of the boys were young and clean. There was little snobbishness in their behavior, which showed the results of good kindergartens and schools. It was nice to see almost two thousand happy young

people gathered together.

There was often trouble, of course. It started later, after supper, and could not be avoided, for, as in every large group of people, there were always several fools present. It was usually started by one particularly bad egg who managed to gather a few of his kind, and together they were brave enough to behave so that they had to be thrown out. That was one of the results of prohibition, for, though the boys were given champagne, they also carried hip flasks, out of which they and the girls drank awful liquor behind bowers and palms and under the stairways. And then the boys sometimes engaged in pranks that could be outrageously nasty, as when one of them, in what he and his friends thought was fun, horribly humiliated the inoffensive little man who took care of the men's room, making him cry.

We had a way of dealing with such young guests. It would have been unfair to let our men do it. They were here to serve; they would stay in this business many years; and the young men who performed such messy antics would grow up and inherit money, and, since they and the employees moved in the same places, sooner or later when they were drunk again they would remember some humiliation at the hands of a servant and be in a position to pay it back. Luckily mostly nice people came to these dances, and among them were two young giants with big hands that hung down almost to their knees, icy bespectacled faces and coiffures that were almost German—hair cut short and then worked back so that the top of it looked like a tight black shoe brush. They played football, in spite of which they hung much around the bar; but they could drink. We had promised them a bottle any time they wished to come into the hotel, if they would do certain little jobs of this sort for us. They enjoyed the work.

When a fellow got out of hand, we called these two. They smiled, said, "Where?" and almost ran to their assignment. They would engage the troublemaker in conversation, hook their arms into his and, with many pleasantries and wide smiles, carry him off. He couldn't do anything about it, for he hung in the air between them. Then he had a little ride in the elevator down to the basement. There they pushed him in the chest so that he sat up against the wall, and if he persisted in being fresh, they twisted his nose and arms and might even give him, if he had been particularly vicious, a thrashing that was a joy to watch. Then, if he was not quiet about it, we took him out to Officer Casey, who patrolled the street in front of the hotel and who did a little night-stick poking on his arms and back and the soles of his feet. Finally the young man was sent home in a taxi, and he usually stayed away from the next few parties.

It was remarkable how well the young men knew the hotel, better than the architect who built it. They would eventually find their way to the top floor, to the Budapest string quartet and the private bar for the older people, by riding up to the roof in the front elevator, crossing over through the maids' dormitory, riding down the baggage elevator, climbing up an outside stairway under the air-cooling equipment, coming through a door beside the ventilating ducts of the ballroom, and thus entering through the pantry. All at once a young man and his friend would be standing in front of the bar, where he was not supposed to be. Then there would be two more of them, very polite, bowing to the old people, so that no one thought of throwing them out. Then there would be four more, then sixteen, and then they would get fresh.

Pommer, the old bartender, was a strong tough man; he had to be. He had under his bar table a big wooden mallet with which he opened wine and whiskey cases. This he would wave in the boys' faces and tell them to go away when they took glasses from the trays prepared for the older guests and held them in a ring in front of him. The young son of the host would be called and he would tell the bartender who he was and order him to serve them champagne. Pommer would answer that he didn't care who the young man was; he had orders not to serve him. Then he would lie about their age, deny that they were as young as they looked, all the while pushing about the bar and egging on the son. The boy would threaten to go get his father, saying that Pommer would be sorry. Pommer would just look up at the ceiling and down again and tell them, please, to go away.

Once they pushed too hard and one of them reached over the bar and got hold of a bottle while the others kept Pommer busy. There was behind the bar a mop for soaking up spilled wine, whisky and mineral water, and it was kept in a corner where the broken glass was pushed. Pommer was tired and nervous from the unbroken series of many parties; he grabbed the mop, swished it across the young men's shirt fronts and faces, then took up his mallet and said he'd break their skulls if one of them came near. He looked so wild that they stood away out of his reach. The son called me and demanded that I immediately discharge the man. He shouted that he would tell his father about this, and then we would see what we would see!

When he brought his father back with him, he pointed at old Pommer and said, "That's him, and there's the mop, and these fellows all saw it, and I asked to have him fired." The father spoke to Pommer, shook hands with him and gave him a twenty-dollar bill. The boys left.

Every morning, in the season, the house after such a party is strewn with wreckage, dirty dishes and empty bottles. The party usually ends at five in the morning, and the musicians drink up the rest of the orange juice, tilting up the silver punch bowl, as they talk and start to pack up their instruments.

So I told the boss, do me a favor, put my name down
Come on, you guys, break it up
Hey, I got a car downstairs waiting
I played for Whiteman, sure
Why is an old maid like a tomato
I know a better one
I paid six hundred bucks for it brand-new
She has one just like it
I gave mine away
I said to the old lady, what do you want to wear that
    one for, I'll get you a new one
Well, so long

Hey, coming, I got a car waiting
I'm going with him
Well, so long, if you want to stay all night.
Come on, come on
High class
She has a sister works for the Standard Oil
No, I sold mine at 53

The keys of the piano are again sweaty when the lid is finally put down on it. The bass fiddler goes up to put his instrument away in the locker which his union provides, along with an instrument, in every hotel, so that the musician need not carry the big fiddle around; and he takes the tape off his hands, for he seldom bows the strings for dance music, only plucking them. The lips of the brass players are split. Even after the men are gone, the music still seems to go on playing.

Mr. Sigsag is busy collecting leftovers. No matter how tired his men are, they must help him save all the junk that can be rescued: cheesecloth draperies used in decorations, the stumps of candles, fancy lamps, Christmas ornaments, lost gloves and fans, branches of silver-sprayed smilax, empty cigar and cigarette boxes and the tinfoil therefrom, champagne corks, flower baskets. Even the oranges that were wired to trees he collects at five-thirty in the morning. The cut flowers are placed in water in champagne tubs; the rest goes up to his museum, a room filled from floor to ceiling with boxes and shelves of junk.

When this is done, he leaves orders for the next day. The flowers in the champagne tubs are to be sent to friends, or given to the lady cashiers. In the middle of all this late work he sits down and writes out a rough draft of the bill and checks over stubs, his face the color of cold salmon. Under his desk, in a tub of ice, are some bottles filled with cocktails left over from dinner. He keeps them there for the scrubladies.

Officer Casey comes in to say good night—that is, to get a drink—his voice hoarse from his standing in the street. He is given a few packs of cigarettes, and he likes to go into the icebox with us when we get a little caviar for ourselves.

"Gee, look at that ham!"
"Gee, look at that turkey!"
"Gee, thanks."

He wraps an extra slice of roast beef in a piece of bread and puts the sandwich away while his night stick hangs on the uppermost left button of his coat. Then he takes a second drink and goes home.

The doorman is the last person from outside; he has locked the doors and turned off the lights on the marquee. He gets a drink too, half a glass of whisky straight; he is cold from standing all evening in the slush and rain, the snow, or just the cold wind.

When he is gone, the old scrubwomen come out of the elevator; they live in a dormitory on the top floor of the Splendide. Mr. Sigsag has fallen asleep, sprawled over his bills and the next day's orders. One of the scrubwomen knows where he keeps the drinks for them; she reaches down between his chair and the desk, careful not to wake him, and pulls the bottles out of the ice. Then they rub their brushes on brown bars of soap, tuck up their skirts, take another drink, stick into their hair flowers that have fallen off young dresses, and sing Irish melodies while they start to scrub the marble in the ladies' room.

My first visit to Paris depressed me. I hated it. I was then a bus boy in a New York hotel and my mortal enemies were waiters, waiter captains and headwaiters. I worked my way over on the old S.S. Rotterdam and dutifully made my way to Paris. It seemed filled with battalions of my enemies. I left after two days and swore never to return. (I even circled around it to get back to New York.) I fled to my native Tyrol, got into buckskin shorts and a green hat with the shaving brush. A photograph taken of me at that time is referred to by my daughter Barbara as the "Bing Crosby picture of Pappy." The buckskin pants have got too tight for me, the mood has changed. I have developed a tolerance for hotel personnel, and now my favorite city is Paris.

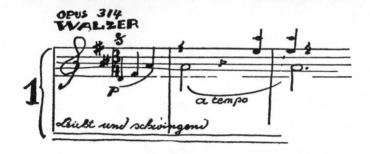

THEODORE AND "THE BLUE DANUBE"

DINNER WAS OVER, the room was filled with smoke and empty tables, the orchestra played "The Blue Danube" and a waiter cleared off the buffet.

"*Sale métier! Bande de voleurs!*" said Theodore Navarre *né* Navratil, the maître d'hôtel, and he thought of that dog Wenzel Swoboda, headwaiter many years back, at the restaurant in Vienna where he had served his apprenticeship.

The tip of Theodore's nose was white with anger; he crumpled the list of reservations, tore a table plan into small pieces and walked up to his dressing room. He counted the tips. Filthy money! Filthy profession! The end of "The Blue Danube" came up the stairs and he had to think again of that specimen of a dog, Wenzel Swoboda.

Theodore had been young then; he had wavy blond hair and his first slim tailcoat. It was spring in Vienna. The restaurant had a garden shaded with old chestnut trees that were in full bloom. Under one of them stood a buffet, a square table covered with a white cloth, and arranged on this were trays of pastry, peach, apricot, plum and apple tarts, and a bowl of whipped cream with fragrant wild strawberries.

Wenzel Swoboda was the maître d'hôtel and to this restaurant came every day the not altogether young but American Mrs. Griswold Katzenbach. She always asked for Theodore; he served her under a large yellow umbrella.

One Friday afternoon a dark cloud floated past the hotel and stopped over the chestnut tree, water came out of it, and together with the blossoms from the tree messed up the pastries, the tarts and the whipped cream with the strawberries.

Swoboda saw this and looked for Theodore; Theodore leaned over Madame Griswold Katzenbach and pointed to the scenery.

The dog Swoboda danced to the table and kicked Theodore in the heel; then he himself pointed to the scenery and smiled at Madame Katzenbach, and while she looked he hissed at Theodore in Bohemian, "Clear off the buffet—son of a swine," and he kicked him again with more power and higher up.

The orchestra played "The Blue Danube." Theodore attacked the buffet; he cleared it with the speed of an acrobat, stacking tarts and pastries all over himself. In one trip he made the kitchen—strawberries and all—without dropping anything.

Ever since then Theodore had suffered when he heard "The Blue Danube," saw a buffet, or came upon a chestnut tree in bloom. As for Madame Katzenbach, she lives upstairs in this very hotel where he sat on his bed in thought. She talks to him for hours in the dining room where he stands behind her chair. When she meets him on the street, she stares at a lamppost or looks into a shop window until he has passed, but then they were all alike—and besides, in two more weeks they could all go to the devil! In this hope Theodore mumbled a litany that went: "*Que le diable les emporte—j'en ai assez, moi—pique-assiette, pique-fourchette, je m'en vais, moi, je m'en fiche—foutez-moi la paix, bande de sauvages, salauds!*"

Every year Theodore Navarre went to Europe, first class in a modest cabin on one of the slow boats, because none of the hotel guests ever crossed on them. He took the Orient Express but would change to a slow train in Salzburg. It took him to a little village on the shore of a quiet lake and he walked to the Hotel Alpenrose, and there he took the cure for his soul.

As soon as he arrived at the Alpenrose he went up to his room— Number 5, with a balcony—waited for his trunks and came down a changed man.

He took a bath in esteem and respect, and this started in the morning when he appeared at the table for breakfast. Stefi, the waitress, with soft round arms and flaxen hair, wished him a loud and healthy "Good morning, Herr Direktor," and "How has the Herr Direktor slept?" and "What does the Herr Direktor want for breakfast?"

It would never do to live in this respectable hotel without a title. Everybody has one and Herr Theodore Navarre had written, where the register asked for his name, birthday, profession, domicile and national-

ity, *Navarre, Theodore, July 6, 1878, Direktor, New York, U. S. A.*

Dinner was at noon, at a round table. Most of the guests came here year after year and they were, from left to right:

> *Herr und Frau Generalkonsul von Kirchhoff, Vienna*
> *Herr und Frau Oberstaatsanwalt Zeppezauer, Vienna*
> *Herr und Frau Professor der alten Philologie Leichsenring, Graz*
> *Herr Direktor Theodore Navarre, New York*

Supper was at seven, the ladies dressed in crêpe de Chine and chiffons; afterward there were parties, once a week the peasant theater, quiet evenings at the hotel—Schubert *Lieder*, cards.

Herr Direktor Navarre was invited to play, to swim, to dance. Everyone listened to him, no one called him Theodore. He sat on a chair and important men took off their hats when they met him on the street and smiled and said, "Good morning, Herr Direktor," "Good afternoon, Herr Direktor," and "Good evening, Herr Direktor."

Herr Direktor had a good deal of trouble getting on and off his bicycle, but he stopped, even on a curve, for a few words with the gendarmes. They saluted and spoke to him with their heels together, their hands at the seams of their green trousers—it was good medicine.

On his birthday Stefi decorated the table with crocuses and Herr Direktor ordered twelve bottles of the young heady wine that was the best he could find in the cellar of the hotel.

The Alpenrose did itself proud with lake trout *au bleu*, Wiener Schnitzel with cucumber salad, and a pancake, big as a garden hat. The Generalkonsul made a speech, the bottles were emptied, and Herr Direktor Navarre sang.

After dinner it was decided to hire a car and go all together to the other side of the lake and take coffee there.

The automobile arrived and slowly turned the lake for them. Herr Professor Leichsenring, who sat next to the driver, pointed at a dark cloud, but the driver said that it hung too high and would pass.

On this other side of the lake a table had been set close to the water; two rowboats bobbed up and down. The restaurant "On the Lake" was elegant; it had a waiter.

Herr Direktor Navarre stared at a loose button hanging from the man's shiny dress coat while he ordered Cointreau for the ladies and drank brandy with the men. On a painted platform played a small orchestra, zither, guitar and fiddle. Frau Oberstaatsanwalt's cup was empty.

"Psst," more coffee—Direktor Navarre turned in his chair and looked for the waiter with the loose button.

He saw a large chestnut tree; under it stood a buffet, a square table covered with linen. Arranged on it were pastries, apricot, pear and plum tarts, Apfelstrudels, wild strawberries and a bowl of whipped cream.

The zither player plucked his strings.

The wind leaned into the tree, it swayed, the dark cloud hung over it, rain started to fall and with it the blossoms of the chestnut tree, like rose-tinted popcorn.

Without knowing it, Herr Direktor Navarre left his table and rushed to the buffet. He stacked cakes and pastries all over himself, took along the whipped cream, the wild strawberries, and disappeared into the kitchen.

The orchestra finished "The Blue Danube."

"Herr Direktor!" said Frau Generalkonsul. "Herr Direktor?" looked the others.

He left with the first train, the one that carries peasants to Salzburg, and he never came back.

*M*ost swindles in Austria have a quality of humor. One happened in a Vienna restaurant which I highly recommend. It is called Zur Linde. One evening a man and a small boy, apparently father and son, entered the restaurant. They were served by an old waiter named Herr Lehner, who had been there over fifty years. He brought them the best of everything, including two bottles of wine and French cognac for the man. After the coffee, the man disappeared in the direction of the washroom. Thirty minutes passed, then Herr Lehner approached the boy.

"Tell me, did your father leave?"

"He isn't my father," said the little boy. "He met me on the street and kindly invited me in to eat with him."

The boy was too small to be held responsible. The Linde could well afford the loss; the swindle made great publicity, and Herr Lehner had a new story to tell.

Viennese waiters are polite, even friendly, but not servile—and they say what they think. Herr Lehner is capable of fast repartee. A guest—a man who gave himself the air of a great gourmet—impatiently called him to the table and said, "You know, the service here—in fact the whole restaurant—has gone down frightfully. It's not at all as it was in the old days."

"Yoh yoh, you are right, Herr Baron," said the old waiter, "but if you excuse me, it has not gone down as badly as the clientele."

THE
KITCHEN
OF THE
GOLDEN BASKET

JAN'S FATHER is not only the proprietor of the Golden Basket but also its proud chef. A long life devoted to good cooking has slowly changed him into what a real cook should look like.

He stands all day long and far into the evening under a fragrant cloud that comes up from a wide stove full of good cooking.

His kitchen is connected with the dining room by a swinging door with glass panels. Monsieur ter Meulen wears a spotless white linen jacket with two rows of round covered buttons down the front and a napkin with a sailor knot for a necktie. Tied around his ample stomach is a big apron and on his head is always a newly starched chef's cap. Into the rim of the cap he sticks a pencil and into his apron, as in a belt, the wooden cooking spoon, the fork and the knife he uses most.

In front of him, toward the dining room, is a stout table with a top that is scrubbed three times a day. Behind him is the big stove. It is built of white tile and iron, ten feet long, and a nickel railing is attached to it, from which dangle heavy iron hooks, a shovel and a poker. Coal is used for the stove; it's the best heat to cook with.

The walls are covered with shining copper dishes, round and oval, deep and shallow. They have strong handles; some are made in the shape of a pudding or a fish. There is a clock and a stone jar with fresh parsley in it, lots of big and little knives, wooden spoons, beaters, mashers, cleavers, sieves and, on a shelf, long rows of jars that hold nutmeg, bay leaves, vanilla sticks, raisins, paprika, cinnamon and cloves. In large containers, flour, barley and rice are kept. In short, there is hardly room for Monsieur ter Meulen to turn around in.

When Celeste and Melisande came here to visit, they were very quiet and stood in one little corner, first of all because they were out of the way and secondly because beside them was an ice-packed container with frozen desserts in it and over them a cupboard with blancmange, candied fruit and raisin cakes; and while the chef had no time to talk to them, he often cut a slice of cake or spooned into the container for a plateful of ice cream. It tasted much better here, where it was made, than inside at the table.

Monsieur ter Meulen's face is red from looking into his many pots. He stirs soups and mixes sauces. He cooks with a watchful eye, with his nose and his heart; he dreams of it at night and is unhappy if anything goes wrong.

One finger of his right hand was dipped into all dishes. He tasted everything before it was allowed to leave his kitchen.

He could look at his clock, bend to open the oven door and watch a capon turn brown, drink a glass of water with a little red wine in it, cut a carrot with a big knife, "clop-clop-clop," into a row of little even disks and, besides, smile at the little girls, and with a large wooden paddle stir the soup in the big tureen—all alone, without cutting himself, with only two hands, and almost at one time. It was unbelievable.

No less busy and no less in a hurry was Monsieur Carnewal. His cheeks were apple red; he smiled half a smile like the chef to say, "Oh, you are here again—that's nice." The rest was haste and attention.

Guests are impatient and the good food must not get cold. It is very important in cooking that even the smallest beginnings are right; therefore one must learn, in a long and hard apprenticeship, how to cut a bird to pieces quickly and neatly, how to stir and season, even how to peel a potato.

Good things that are so earnestly cooked deserve fine names and they have them. When he ordered something from the chef, Monsieur Carnewal did it with proper form. He came into the kitchen and sang out in the best French, *"Un risotto de volaille à la Flamande,"* and Monsieur ter Meulen repeated, *"Un risotto de volaille à la Flamande."*

This is only an order for a humble chicken stew, cooked as the Flemish peasants make it.

Monsieur ter Meulen ladles a portion—not too much, not too little— of it into a round earthen dish. Quickly his finger is dipped in and tasted —it's good, but it needs a little more pepper. That added, a cover is placed on the pot, a small bunch of greenery next to it, a warm plate— "Take it away, Carnewal," and Monsieur Carnewal sails away with it, saying once more, "*Un risotto de volaille à la Flamande.*"

Many people order just anything and eat it in a hurry. For them nothing can be done and both Monsieur Carnewal and the chef are sorry for them.

There are, however, others, and such a one is the Mayor of Bruges, His Excellency the Honorable Camille Jacques Leopold van der Vichte, who looks not unlike Monsieur Carnewal. He is no taller but he has more hair, golden spectacles and several faces.

He has a sad face. He wears it at the City Hall, where he listens every morning and afternoon to much and every sort of trouble. A city is made of many houses. A lot happens in them, good things and bad. And for most of the bad, the citizens like to blame the government. They even blame him, says the Mayor, if it rains too long.

City streets have to be swept, watered in summer and cleared of snow in winter. Rubbish has to be taken away. The parks have to be raked, the swans fed in the canals, the grass cut along the banks, trees have to be trimmed and lampposts painted. In an historic city like Bruges there are besides many statues, ancient buildings and museums that have to be cleaned and repaired, and this goes on and on down to ink, blotters and buttons for the policemen.

It is plain that Monsieur van der Vichte, the Mayor, filled a difficult position which called for sound knowledge, much experience and a very strong character. That he had all these could be seen in some of the photographs that were hung on the wall behind his chair.

In the first picture he is the honor student of his school with a parchment diploma in his hands. On his shoulder rests the hand of the proud master.

In the second, he is shown as a lieutenant of Infantry. He has a small mustache, spurs on his boots, and a riding whip, but there is no horse in the photograph.

In the third, he has eyeglasses and receives the order of the Legion of Honor, whose little rosette he has worn in his buttonhole ever since.

There is one more, the largest, in front of a row of marble columns, with flags, music and little girls in starched dresses. Many people are listening to his speech. He stands on a platform. Behind him are a group of serious men who wear, like him, black coats, top hats and beards.

Although he should be very proud of all his honors and positions, he looks sad and tired when he is seated behind the desk in his high office.

But Monsieur van der Vichte also has a very happy face, and he wore it when he came to eat almost every day at his little table in a corner of the dining room where Celeste and Melisande could watch him. On a glass in front of his plate was a card with his name and title.

His Excellency was received at the door. Monsieur Carnewal watched for him and could see him hurry across the Grande Place. He lifted his hat many times, thanking everyone who greeted him, and he almost ran when he came near to the Golden Basket.

Monsieur Carnewal took his hat and coat and pulled out his chair with a deep bow. He handed the Mayor the menu while he flicked the table clean with his napkin, bent to put a slice of cork under one leg of the table—because all restaurant tables wobble and finally raised his eyebrows and waited.

Monsieur van der Vichte's face was buried in the large, handwritten card. It was alight with happiness and his lips silently formed the names of every dish. He asked questions about how this or that was prepared and nodded when Monsieur Carnewal told him.

He would have liked to order everything. After a while he took his little fork, held the card away from himself and made the face that says "yes and no." He slid the fork up and down the row of names and finally ordered.

Monsieur Carnewal hurried into the kitchen.

The Mayor sat back in his chair; now he noticed the other guests. He greeted them with a comfortable smile and a nod, broke his bread, brushed his beard and watched the door for Monsieur Carnewal.

On days when he had eaten very well, he walked out into the kitchen with his napkin tied around him and said to Monsieur ter Meulen: "The wild duck tonight, for example, my good friend—it was—" and in search of words he looked at the ceiling, took off his glasses with one hand, with the other put index finger and thumb together in a gesture which to all French-speaking people means—so, so very good that I cannot tell you.

The little girls awaited the coming of the Mayor every evening. They played with words on the menu as he did and went up and down and across the list with their small forks, mumbling and asking Monsieur Carnewal endless foolish questions about everything, mostly about the nicest part of the menu, down at the bottom where the sweets are grouped.

On Sunday evening their little forks wandered around there until after much yes and no they rested on the lemon soufflé. This is very hard to make but pleasant to eat. It needs much care. Almonds have to be cooked in carmel sugar and ground, the rind of two lemons, only the yellow part, grated, sugar and eggs must be stirred slowly with a wooden spoon, milk added. It has to be beaten with a whip in a wide copper drum and then slowly poured into a mold. It goes in the oven. Monsieur ter Meulen watches the clock—five, ten, fifteen, twenty minutes. On the dot he takes it out, powdered sugar is sprinkled on top, back into the oven it goes for half a minute under the fire, now it's golden brown and ready. "Take it away, Carnewal."

"The soufflé au citron," says Monsieur Carnewal with respect. He is already out of the door—he has to run; it is very frail, this soufflé—it will fall flat and look like a stupid pie if he doesn't hurry.

I shall always miss the table at Lady Mendl's houses and the cooking of Monsieur Fraise. What pleasure it was to go into his kitchen and talk to an honest chef, one of the few who did not tell you that he was a pupil of Escoffier! How neat his dishes were! How superb his simplest effort! I have never seen a chicken so well cooked and so cleanly sliced and put together again; you did not know it was carved when it came to the table. The rarest thing is a French chef who does not kill you with sauces and seasoning. The master of his trade, such as Monsieur Fraise is, knows how to season so that the suggestion is there, as the bouquet in wine.

THE SURVIVORS

THE FIRST FACT that came to my attention was that, of all people, the proprietors of luxury hotels, of the best restaurants and night clubs, weathered the war and political upheaval better than anyone else. Their faces are the least lined; they and their headwaiters and wine butlers are of the same weight, humor and philosophy as they were before.

The pleasures they dispense render these high priests of the good life and friends of the stomach immune to the persecution and the disasters that befall the ordinary citizen.

One of the most esteemed clients of the Paris Ritz before the war was Miss Barbara Hutton. She left to make room for Herr General von Brauchitsch, who appreciated a well-laid table also, celebrated his conquest with goose-liver paste and truffles, and discussed wines in the language of the fancier and expert. After he packed, the silver was polished again, the same pans went over the fire and the corks popped once more, now in celebration of the departure of the Herr General. And when the broken glass and the confetti of that glorious fiesta were swept up and the barracks air cleared from the rooms, the old suite was made ready again for Miss Hutton. *Bonjour, Mademoiselle. Guten Tag,* Herr General Brauchitsch. Welcome, General Eisenhower. *Bonjour Mademoiselle.*

In a white-and-gold, small temple of gastronomy whose blue-ribbon chef is also its proprietor, and who now carves his black-market hams and fine meats with his old skill, I was shown the table where Goering munched his caviar and smiled down at the quail and the other game of which he was so fond. "He sat over there," said the famous cook, pointing with his carving knife. "He brought his own provisions; we had everything he wanted. He made the iceboxes burst with Persian caviar, Polish geese, wild boar, Westphalian hams—everything he brought along. Enough to feed a whole battalion."

I asked him whether the Field Marshal ever became interested in his views or political opinions, or what he thought about the Wehrmacht and the Third Reich. "*Ah, non, alors,*" said the cook, who is as portly still as Goering was in his Paris days, "*Ah, non, Monsieur,* he was not so crazy as all that! Here in my restaurant he sat where I placed him, he spoke low, and the conversation was limited to praise of the cooking. And when he left he thanked me nicely."

Later on he said, "Now I remember—one of them touched on the subject, once. One of them, a general, once asked me what I thought of their efficiency, because, a few hours after they had marched in, the truck with provisions was at the back door of my establishment and also an adjutant at the front door who made the reservations and discussed the preferences of the High Command and arranged the menu.

"I told the general that I found it remarkable. Nothing wrong in that. I did not give praise, I only called it *remarquable.*

"The general said that in the last few months they had taken several capitals and everything had gone like clockwork. His aide-de-camp always reported to him an hour or so ahead of time, and he would say, 'Excellency, we are occupying So-and-so, according to plan, at exactly ten minutes past eleven,' or whatever time they had arranged to occupy the place. The aide would continue, 'We shall enter the city through this or that avenue, and over this route, and Your Excellency's quarters are rooms number so-and-so at the Hotel So-and-so.'

"The general said, 'When we got there, not a minute late, I always found the rooms ready and my luggage there.' The general laughed then, and turning to another officer, he said, smiling, 'You know what I am afraid of? I have a nightmarish fear that one day we shall take another capital, and my aide will come and tell me at what hotel I am staying and the numbers of my rooms, and when we get there the rooms will not be ready. And that, my friend, will be the disastrous moment after which the entire magnificent and minute organization of the Reichswehr will collapse.'

"They clicked their glasses then and laughed," said the cook, who was stirring the sauce for a lobster in a little pan over an alcohol lamp. "But you know, that is almost the way it happened," he continued. "They failed to reserve rooms at the Savoy in London, the Metropole in Moscow and the Waldorf-Astoria in New York."

L·B·

*T*he maître of maîtres d'hôtel—and the unquestioned First Headwaiter of France and perhaps of the world—is Monsieur Albert of Maxim's in Paris.

He seats the guest of his restaurant with a regard for protocol and politics as stiff as that of the Pope's Chamberlain.

He places a Balkan pretender no higher or lower than his present chances merit, he bows deeply to the Duchess of Windsor and puts Elsa Maxwell where he thinks she belongs, and he remembers those of the French aristocracy who have in the past remembered him.

Imprisoned both by the Germans and by the French, he was always returned quickly to the door of his establishment and in the hazardous years gained seventy pounds. He stared Goering into acquiescence, and today many a gourmet who goes to Maxim's, when offered the card, says, "Why a menu, when Albert is here to order for us?"

Albert has a share of the profits of Maxim's, which is owned by a British syndicate.

ON INNKEEPING

INNKEEPING is one of the most pleasant ways of earning a living. If you are lonesome, there is always company; if you are hungry, you have a chef and eight cooks who know exactly what you like; when you are thirsty, there is a wine cellar stocked with your favorite bottles.

If thirty guests show up for dinner when you expected only five, you simply pass the word along to the manager. Your tables have flowers freshly cut by your gardener. The cigars are properly kept in the humidor. You have a chauffeur—no, two chauffeurs—you have a valet, and most of these people are your friends. If you like to argue, you can engage in a dozen arguments a day. You never have time to be bored, for you are constantly alerted by complaints, by felicitations, abuse or pleas for reservations. If you are nervous and upset, you don't bother seeing a psychoanalyst—you simply go and watch the pastry cook make pies, the vegetable cook slice string beans, or the soup cook stir his broths; these observations calm you because each activity is a necessary and sensible thing.

Above all else, if you run an inn for the average person, you have constant proof that 95 per cent of the people in this world are nice. That is comforting to know, and helps you to sleep at night.

If, in spite of all that, you still can't sleep, you go down and sit in the bar or the dining room and listen awhile. Those places are always filled with stories; plots unwind before you as the characters talk. A thousand scenarios come at you in a steady stream. I am not given to profound thinking but, occasionally, I reflect that the life of an innkeeper is better than any other.

At intervals of several years this realization bothers me enough so that I put my paints away, cover up my typewriter and look for a door through which I can step back into my old profession, for I come from a long line of brewmasters and innkeepers.

Some years ago, together with some friends of like persuasion, I decorated an old house in Manhattan. We bought chairs and tables and a stove, we installed a wine cellar and we called the place "The Hapsburg House." It was an exercise in transplanting Austrian cooking, zither music and the candlelit Mozart mood of old Vienna to New York. That done, I went back to the easel and the typewriter. A while ago I heard the call again and this time I acquired a place which is a landmark—an institution and an inn in the modern American sense. I bought the White Turkey Inn, at Danbury, Connecticut. During the time that I owned it, it provided me with much entertainment. For example: there was a quaint, three-room building called The Honeymoon Cottage. Located a few hundred feet from the Inn itself, the Cottage was seldom unoccupied and it was always a source of entertainment. Take the modest little story that was enacted there on the fifth of that May.

The newlyweds arrived. They had a new car, new luggage, and they themselves were all newly decked out. Hand in hand they walked into the dining room, and with their dinner they ordered a bottle of champagne. (It is normally not good form to have the cork popped, but at an inn like the White Turkey it must be popped; the louder the report, the happier the guest.) After their dinner and champagne, the honeymooners strolled outdoors. The moon was shining and they decided to go for a drive around Candlewood Lake in their new convertible, with the top down. They asked that their car be brought to the door from the parking lot. They waited and waited, becoming noticeably nervous, but the car didn't come. This was because Joe, the parking-lot attendant, had taken advantage of a lull in business to pay a visit to his girl, who waited for him regularly under an old elm tree at the far end of a pond behind the Inn. Over the pond is a rustic bridge with widely spaced planking. Returning from his rendezvous, Joe stopped on the bridge to take a pack of cigarettes from the pocket of his jacket, and as he did so, the honeymooners' keys came out and dropped through a crack into the pond.

Unfortunately, the pond is the home of a pair of large swans, and the male is very jealous—he resents anyone's going into the water or any-where near his wife. Joe tried to wade into the water after the keys, but the big male bird furiously chased him away.

By this time, word had reached the anxious newlyweds that the precious keys to their car, the luggage and their new home were resting on the bottom of the pond. Along with some twenty other guests, they now stood at the bridge, anxiously watching.

The scene was illuminated by the moon, several flashlights and lanterns. The Inn's gardener, who feeds the swans and is known to them, was holding the enraged male bird, while Joe, who had donned swimming trunks, raked the bottom of the pond. After half an hour the keys were retrieved, a shout went up from the crowd on the shore, the young couple beamed, and everybody was happy.

The honeymooners will never forget the incident. It will be told over and over again to their children, who will possibly one day stand on the rustic bridge and be shown the scene of the story of the lost keys.

Episodes of this kind—small troubles with happy endings—are one part of the repertory; there is also another part, less amusing.

As the lion cage is the place to keep out of at the circus, so the kitchen of an inn is a place to avoid during busy hours; it is a place of tension, very much like a theater before the curtain goes up; often a quarrel in the kitchen will spill over into the dining room.

Here is a story of one July Fourth. People are running about, there's trouble in the kitchen. The heat near the oven is 125°. There has been a rush business all day, tempers are frayed, and over some misunderstanding a fight has started between the little sauce cook and the big roast cook.

At the end of a battery of ovens stands an immense stock pot in which the carcasses of turkeys and chickens simmer. It is a pot much like the ones in which missionaries are cooked in the pages of humorous magazines. The big cook has picked up the little one and is about to deposit him in the stock pot. But on the way there the little cook has grabbed a carving fork from a rack near the ceiling and stabs the big cook through the hand. Terrorized waitresses scream and somebody wants to call the police and an ambulance, neither of which is needed because, in the nick of time, a formidable waitress named Lola, a woman who could put a straitjacket on Joe Louis, enters the kitchen rolling back her sleeves. She separates the battling cooks. The iodine bottle and a roll of bandage do the rest and the crisis is over, except that in the dining

room some people complain that they have to wait for their dinner, since half a dozen lobsters, a steak and two orders of lamb chops have been carbonized during the fracas. The hostess explains to them that the food will be along in a little while—"a slight delay." Afterward the cooks make up over a drink.

When I took over the White Turkey I marveled at the meekness of the clientele. They would arrive like children going to school, sit where they were told, dutifully admire the flowers on the table, eat in orderly manner and leave quietly. On my first day at the Inn I stood in the lobby and observed the following scene with astonishment:

A man came in with his wife and two children. The man deposited his hat in the coat room, and while his wife took the children to the wash-room, he first cautiously surveyed and then admired the quaint interior. His family returned; they were ready to eat, and the man respectfully approached the hostess who was standing in the lobby. (She is called the Outer Hostess. Another, at the door of the dining room, is the Inner Hostess. A third, who functions inside the dining room, is the Executive Hostess.) The action begins:

MAN: A table for four, please.

OUTER HOSTESS (*sternly*): Have you a reservation?

MAN (*guiltily putting both hands on his chest*): No. Should I?

OUTER HOSTESS: Yes, you certainly should.

MAN (*apologetic*): Well, I didn't know about that. I didn't think about it. Do you think we can get something to eat?

OUTER HOSTESS: Well, I'll see. Wait here, please.

The Outer Hostess went to the door of the dining room and conferred with the Inner Hostess, who, in turn, entered the room and conferred with the Executive Hostess. The Inner Hostess returned to the door, nodded briefly to the O.H., who came back and told the man he was lucky—there was a free table. The four people were passed on to the Inner Hostess. As they approached the door, the Inner Hostess announced, "Four without," meaning, four without a reservation. The poor man, feeling as if he wasn't quite in order, was then taken in tow by the Executive Hostess and at last the family arrived at a table.

The "four without" routine immediately was abolished, as well as the hostesses' special titles, and the ladies were reminded that we were running an inn, not a battleship.

The plain American is so indoctrinated with respect for hostesses that he obeys their direction blindly and smiles gratefully while he is shunted about. He would never dream of arguing with a hostess. In a season of feeding thousands of people at the Inn, there has never been any revolt on the part of the customer. "Yes, ma'am" is what he always says.

In the department of human relations it cannot be expected that a restaurant hostess greet each guest as if he were a long-lost brother or father returning from the wars. A certain degree of civility, however, is possible, and the first step in reaching it is to get hostesses to forget that they are "ladies" and reduce them in rank to merely nice women, to flesh-and-blood women rather than the mechanized receptionists most of them are.

The main reasons why many a good man gets out of innkeeping are rising costs and labor troubles. The pendulum has swung the other way now—and occasionally there are abuses by the help instead of the employer. Here is an example.

In one of New York's top restaurants a man gave a dinner for two dozen people. When it was over, he paid his check and tipped those who had served him, including the wine waiter, to whom he handed a ten-dollar bill. The wine waiter put it in his pocket. The man asked, "Don't you say 'thank you' at least?"

"Why should I thank you? I serve you—you pay me. Besides, it's not more than what you ought to pay me anyway—fifteen per cent."

The man called the proprietor, who said that he was sorry, but there was nothing he could do—it happened again and again. "I have written to the union—they won't allow me to discharge him."

Aside from such incidents, much of the pleasure has gone out of innkeeping. The once comfortable business has been invaded by brash operators, free of all scruples, applying assembly-line methods to bed and table. They attempt to make amends by decoration, they paint false fronts on their places and pick names that promise repose or start the gastric juices flowing as you roll along the highway.

Unfortunately, the worst of them succeed. Having come from other businesses, they are unimpeded by tradition. They cut costs, use a substitute for butter or, perhaps, make hollandaise sauce that lasts for weeks and has the texture of custard. Their kitchen mechanics devise tricks, such as the one to make hamburgers juicy, which is simple and direct.

You soak the meat in ice water just before you throw it on the broiler or, rather, on that hot plate that serves in hurried cooking. It is remarkable that these mess halls have developed a clientele which recommends the places.

*J*ean *appeared and with him the chef I had engaged, Monsieur Tingaud.
"Don't let what this one has to say upset you," started Jean unhappily,
raising his hands. "Quelle catastrophe!" he wailed, looking with disgust
at the chef.*

*The chef broke in: "I hope monsieur will understand. First of all
I must say that I regret the matter—that is, I am in a way sorry. For I am
certain that I would have been happy here, and that we would have
understood each other. But I cannot come and cook here. Why not? Because, monsieur, I cannot afford it. Do you understand?"*

"Please come to the point, monsieur," said Jean.

"The world is vastly changing and everything with it," he went on.

*Jean became impatient. "We know, we know. Tell what has hap-
pened."*

*"One day I was walking down the Rue du Bac," started the chef, but
Jean let out a moan and ran his fingers through his hair and said, "He
has taken a job in a factory, can you understand that?"*

*The chef was now in a temper and, pushing Jean aside, said, "I have
been offered the position of executive director of the kitchens of the
Renault factory."*

*Jean put his fists on his hips and said, "He is in charge of a mess hall
for mechanics; he has folie de grandeur."*

*The chef answered, "Perhaps, perhaps, but neither of you could afford
to pay my salary—and the conditions, the conditions—you could not offer
me those in a thousand years." He held up one finger and pointed: "One
meal a day, one dish to cook. I come to work at nine, I go home at five.
Two weeks' holiday with pay. Pension, medical and dental and other
benefits. My kitchen of ten electric stoves looks very much like an
operating room."*

*Jean shook his head. "And you are proud of this? Tell me how many
of this one dish you serve a day?"*

"Seven thousand and some hundreds."

"*Well,* bon appétit, *Monsieur.*"

"*I am sorry, I did not mean to brag,*" said the chef.

"*Oh, don't be sorry,*" said Jean. "*There are still cooks in France with some pride!*"

Now they came close to each other and the chef yelled, "Pride for what? Pride to stand fourteen hours behind a stove, pride for being underpaid, and to cook a hundred things and listen to complaints and to have a miserable proprietor watch every gram of butter and cry in your ear? No, thank you." Without saying goodbye and in haste, Monsieur Tingaud stalked off in the direction of Notre Dame.

On the road to the Côte d'Azur there is the Hôtel de la Côte d'Or, relais gastronomique, *of which Monsieur Alexandre Dumaine calls himself, humbly, the* traiteur. *This is worthy of our stopping and remembering, for usually when a French restaurateur or hotelier, chef or proprietor gets the high accolade Mr. Dumaine has received, his head swells as big as the top of his chef's hat, he takes on airs and is difficult to be with. Monsieur Dumaine continues his fine traditions and is the same quiet, friendly person he was at the start. He sits in some part of his hotel reading the newspaper, and you can talk to him without being subjected to a lecture on* haute cuisine. *He merely wants you to enjoy the food.*

Bon jour monsieur Soulé I'm mrs Prendergast
my mother has reserved a Table — for us
this is my son John Armitage — II.

MONSIEUR SOULÉ

IN THE FASHIONABLE RESTAURANTS of large cities the guest is at times diffi-cult—he glares, shouts and complains. It takes a man of experience and tremendous stature to cope with a temperamental public.

The most strenuous customer-versus-proprietor battles occur in the smart restaurants of Paris and New York. This kind of restaurant, as a rule, is small. It is benefited by a certain type of guest and injured by another, and the latter must be discouraged from coming. In a man con-fronted daily with the task of separating the wanted from the un-wanted, a degree of arrogance is indispensable.

An ideal man in this respect is Monsieur Soulé, proprietor of the superb New York restaurant, Le Pavillon.

He is a museum piece, the composite of all the best proprietors and high priests of the table I have ever seen. On the right people Monsieur Soulé bestows a silent smile, reassuring and unchanging.

Soulé himself seems to be stuffed with the goodies of kitchen and cellar, and on a good day when all goes well, his face, round as the sun, shines as if the pastry cook had just passed his butter brush over it. He is perpetually examining every corner of his restaurant. He is a rotund but solid man, and he has a ballet dancer's agility; even when standing still he seems to spin, aware of everything that is happening on all sides. His sauces—and they are the first concern of the restaurateur—are perfection. It is a pleasure to watch Soulé stir the contents of his great pots, or to fish for lobster claws and mushrooms in wine sauces. But the rarest experience comes when, if you are lucky enough to be seated near the door, you can watch him throw somebody out of his distinguished establishment. I had that privilege recently.

A ponderous matron and steady restaurantgoer, whose big hats and Hattie Carnegie prints are part of the décor of many New York places, stood waiting at the door. She had the face of an angry mandrill and the complexion and voice of the late W. C. Fields. With her eyes snapping, she hissed at Monsieur Soulé, "Listen, I'm not in the habit—" That's as far as she got. Glaring back at her, Soulé said, "Madame, this street is crowded with restaurants, most of them empty and in need of clientele. Good day, madame." He waved her to the door, did one of his fast turns, and in that split second changed his expression and smiled his respects at an esteemed patron, M. Charles Boyer, who in turn complimented him with an actor's appreciation on the good performance he had given. Monsieur Soulé bowed gratefully and moved on to the carving table, where he devoted himself to slicing a rack of lamb.

II · *At Table*

And now L.B. sat, and others waited on him. But his training had been long and arduous, and he would never forget what he had learned. So while he sat, and thoroughly enjoyed sitting, part of him would always remain mentally standing —observing and studying those with whom he had changed places.

DOWN WHERE THE WÜRZBURGER FLOWS

I KNOW ABOUT BEER, because it flows in my veins; my great-grandfather was a brewer in the best hops country of southern Germany, and over the vast stone portal of the brewery was written:

Hopfen und Maltz
Gott erhalt's

The peculiarly built, long, heavy wagons which cradle the oaken barrels were pulled by stout Lippizaners, weighing tons apiece and the color of beer, with manes like foam. They moved with slow dignity and, when they came out of the brewery, pounding their heavy, shaggy hoofs on the creosote blocks of the pavement, sounded like thunder. This majestic tempo was kept up until the beer arrived in vast limestone caves, where it was rested, or *gelagered* (hence the word "lager" beer), for six months.

147

After that the barrels were carefully loaded again, and the beer was delivered to the various places which are called *Wirtschaften*, where it was poured and tasted with the ceremony and nervosity that is given in other regions of Europe to great wine.

As wine has bouquet, so has beer. It is said of good, dark beer that it tastes like licking a dusty windowpane. That may not be everyone's idea of pleasure, but an experienced beer drinker knows what I mean; it is a dusty, a fine antique, dusty, musty—a taste that is perfection.

As does wine, so does beer reflect its native landscape. If you have been out in the vineyards of France, the wine will bring them back to you. You can see the flowered fields of Alsace with the aid of a glass of Gewürtztraminer; you can conjure up the faces of the Bordelais when you drink their wine; and the Boxbeutel of Würzburg clearly reproduces for you the stony fields on which this superb wine grows.

Of beer, the same is true. The scene is more solid; it is a heavier canvas, determined in line and color. Not only does beer reflect; it is stronger, it also determines. It has created a certain kind of furniture, interiors, vehicles; influenced mores, dress and the shape of people. It has even changed language, medicine and the law.

In the south of Germany, whence the best brews come and where the cathedral of brewing, the Academy of Weihenstephan, is located, the number of breweries is easily determined in any given community simply by counting the church steeples. For every one there is a brewery.

Drinking here is a devotional rite, by people who have for generations given themselves to it. The South Germans are a kind of surviving Neanderthaler, with skulls of stone. In character they are comparable to the Irish, of the same manic-depressive character. Their soul is a ponderous mechanism, and when set in motion by sentimental impulse or agitated anger it moves the man slowly at first but with mountain-moving might.

The heavy beer is blamed for that.

The beer here has influenced the décor of the *Wirtschaft*, with heads of game on the wall and frescoes interwoven with poetry:

> *Leberwurscht für den Durscht*
> *Blunzeduft mit Kraut—*
> *Wenn der Bauer Hunger hat*
> *frisst ers z'amt der Haut.*

The author of this verse was my maternal grandfather, Ludwig Fischer.

Translate it I cannot, but it wants to say:

Liver sausage for the thirst
the aroma of blood sausage and cabbage
when the peasant is hungry
he devours it ("fressen" is not translatable)
"z'amt der Haut"—means with the skin.

The tables are solid and the influence of beer on the chairs is remarkable. They are heavy, made mostly of oak. The good ones have a face carved into the part against which you put your back. The seat is wooden also and so planed that it conforms to the anatomy of the local males; that is, you can place a large trunk on it and it will be safe and not wobble. Into the seat the four solid legs are placed, and here the Irish resemblance is again apparent. These legs are not glued or screwed into the seat, but merely inserted, so that with a good, strong twist of the wrist you can remove them and work with them as with a shillelagh.

Now as to the man who sits on the chair—he is self-contained and quiet (unless enraged), he is honest, loves his country, goes to church. Beer has also influenced him. First of all, he is there on its account and on no other. He enters the *Wirtschaft*, goes to his chair, and a grunt and a nod serve him for the first half hour. The waitress knows his wants and puts the first heavy stein in front of him.

During the first half hour, the true *Spezi*, as he is called—and which perhaps means "specialist"—folds his hands and contemplates his beer. He might lift his head and look beyond his part of the *Stammtisch* to see if any hostile element is present. (Anyone from another city is a foreigner.) If he sees a friend, there is another grunt. He does not call the waitress for another beer, because when he wants one he merely leaves the cover on his mug open in upstanding position; that is the signal to the waitress to hit him again.

He usually eats at home. If he eats at the *Wirtschaft*, he eats the same diet as his *Frau* prepares—radishes, pumpernickel, potato dumplings (which must be torn apart, not cut, or the cook's heart is broken), *Schweinebraten, Gänsbraten mit Rotkraut, Leberwurst und Blutwurst*.

All this gives him a liver like the geese of pâté de fois gras fame. He drinks himself to death at about the same age the American executive works himself to death.

149

GRANDFATHER AND THE *ZIPPERL*

REGENSBURG is a Bavarian city on the banks of the Danube, and it possesses one of the finest Gothic cathedrals. When I was little it had about sixty thousand inhabitants, first among whom was the Duke of Thurn und Taxis. He lived in a castle which it took fifteen minutes to pass; it stood in a park that encircled the city. The Duke retained the Spanish etiquette at his court; his servants wore livery and powdered wigs; he rode about in a gilded coach cradled in saffron leather and drawn by white horses. He supported several jewelers, the city's theater, a private orchestra and the race track.

Grandfather's brewery stood on a square facing the Duke's theater, in the oldest part of the town. His daughter, my mother, was born in Regensburg and was educated at the convent at Alt Oetting. Grandfather loved the city.

Attached to the brewery by mortgages were thirty-seven inns, all over the countryside, in which Grandfather's beer was sold. He had two kinds of beer: one a bittersweet, thick, black soupy brew; the other a blond beer, light-bodied, with much snowy foam, and bitter. Every spring Grandfather went on a round of visits to his inns, and my picture of happiness will always be one of him and his hunting wagon.

First the sound of the slim wheels on the gravel in the inner garden; then the deep liquid "clop, clop, clop" of the horse's hoofs as the wagon came out of the brewery through the tunnel, over creosote-soaked wooden blocks; and finally the clatter of the hoofs on the cobblestones in front of the house. Grandfather slowly climbing up in front, onto the reed basket seat of the delicate little wagon, almost turning it over on its red wheels, as he puts his great weight on its side.

He wore a loose green coat, with buttons cut from antler, a brush on his mountain hat, a whip for decoration in his big hands. He made a sound with his tongue, and the trotter lifted its knees up to its chest, and, weaving back and forth, its neck arched in a coy, young pose, it sailed out. From the back seat waved Grandfather's servant Alois, who always went with him. They stopped and drank and ate in all the inns, and bought calves for the butchery, which was part of the brewery. After years of experience Grandfather could drink thirty-six big stone mugs of beer in one evening. He ate heavy meals besides, hardly any vegetables, only dumplings and potatoes, potatoes and dumplings, and much meat.

In consequence of this diet, Grandfather had several times a year attacks of very painful gout, which in Bavaria is called *Zipperl.* Much of the time, one or the other of his legs was wrapped in cotton and elephantine bandages. If people came near it, even Mother, he chased them away with his stick, saying, "Ah, ah, ah" in an ecstasy of pain and widening his eyes as if he saw something very beautiful far away. Then he would rise up in his seat, while his voice changed to a whimpering "Jesus, Jesus, Jesus." He said he could feel the change in weather in his toes, through the thick bandages. But he did not stop eating or drinking.

He had a wheelchair at such times, and Alois had to push him on his visits to the other breweries or restaurants in Regensburg. A kind of track was built for this chair in the back yard of the house; it swung over the roof of the shack where the barrels were kept and came down to the ground in a wide serpentine. Then there were little wooden inclines, to make it possible to wheel Grandfather painlessly over the doorsteps, in front and in back of the house and out into the square.

On the ground floor of the house was a baker, and the stairway and all the rooms in the house smelled of freshly baked bread, nicest on cold winter days. The baker, white of face and clothes, could see Grandfather being wheeled out, and he would say, "The *Zipperl!* Aha! It's got you again, Herr Fischer!" and so said the policeman outside, while he made the streetcar wait, and so did all the other people. Everybody in the city knew Grandfather, and since life was without any other excitement, they had time to say, "Have you seen Herr Fischer? The *Zipperl* has him again!" And Grandfather said nothing but "Jesus, Jesus, God Almighty, ah ah ah, be careful, be careful, Alois! The *Zipperl!*"

*A*mong the birds that make good eating in the high Alps is the white grouse, locally called the snow chicken. It is also known as ptarmigan. It is the chameleon among birds, for its plumage adapts itself to the particular colors of the place in which it chooses to live. In the winter it is snow white. It lives at the edge of the timberline. Its flight is somewhat like that of the dove, and it nourishes itself carefully, so that there is barely need to season it when it is put in the oven. Its preferences are the young leaves and fruit of the juniper plant, the top branches of heather, the small buds of dwarf pine and alp roses, red bilberries, blueberries, cranberries, wild currants and sage. Its call is a throaty "kroegroegroe," difficult to imitate.

FILET DE SOLE COLBERT

SINCE GUSTL KNEW Brussels very well, I asked him to take me to its best restaurant, where I would be his host. He held down his lapels in the old gesture and said, "*Nonononon non, moi*, Monsieur Louis, *moi*." He would be the host, he insisted, or not even go in. The restaurant was the Filet de Sole, and it was a temple of good cooking. No bigger than an ordinary room, it was light and happy, white and gold, but on the ceiling were puffy cherubs in a bad rococo style, and from it hung an uncouth glass chandelier with arms, little arms on big arms, laded down with crystal, and with ruby and white frosted bulbs in its center.

There were as many maîtres d'hôtels and waiters and piccolos as there were guests, and the service was rapid and excellent. The best and worst thing about the restaurant was its proprietor, Paul Brouillard, an excellent chef. He looked like Toscanini, but younger, more like the man on the Eau de Quinine bottle, and he also assumed the gesture of that man when he spoke. He had taken over from the Tour d'Argent in Paris the very bad idea of tying on his fowls, before they came to the table, a tag with a number and the signature of the chef, as if it were a painting. So, attached to a roast capon that was magnificently cooked, well served and taken to pieces with a surgeon's clean cutting, there was unfortunately a tag, given to us as a souvenir, signed by Brouillard, and reading: *"Le Chapon Paul Brouillard, Numero 1978."*

On the cold buffet under the hideous chandelier was a wonderful display: white Brabant asparagus, jellied eels (for those who like them), Saint-Lambert strawberries, great dishes of puddings, galantines, cheeses. Indeed the entire menu read like music: *le lapin à la bière, les fricadelles sauce piquante, les choesels à la madère, la poularde rôtie, les carbonnades au lambic, les écrevisses, le rognon de veau, la tête de veau en tortue, le poulet sauté Sambre-et-Meuse, les tripes al djote, le cabillaud à la flamande, le maquereau aux groseilles, le pigeon à l'ardennaise, l'oie à l'instar de Vise, doreye de Verviers, les fromages de Huy, de Harzee, et de Herves.* One can hear the elegant hunger of Lamme Goedzack in De Coster's book.

All of it was good, but best of all was the melting filet de sole Colbert, the fish brought from Dover and not to be had better anywhere. If Monsieur Brouillard could have been made to stay in his kitchen, this would have been God's own restaurant. His prices were high, but one cannot cook with butter and use the best and not charge for it, and so that is as it should have been. But Monsieur Brouillard not only watched you eat, gluing himself to your table, wishing you good day and good-bye, he also pushed around his waiters, which should never happen, and at the end of the dinner came an unforgivable performance. He brought his three books, *"Mes trois livres de cuisine,"* and offered to sell them.

THE
S.S. *MESIAS*

En Route to Ecuador

"I am only stating that the food here was foul until they killed the cook," said a big man, a Hollander. He turned and, as if it were a rare animal that he wanted to catch without hurting it, he advanced to the rail of the ship with outstretched hands. He took hold of it, held it tightly to test whether it was solid, and then sank his huge body down on it. He was short-nosed, a man with shrimp-colored skin and a pink mustache, and he was drunk. A bottle of Mallorca stood on the table.

A dog came, a mongrel the color of a fox. He stopped, smelled the cuffs of the Hollander's trousers, and with stiff, dancing legs ran away, disappearing around a table.

The table might have stood in the family corner of a third-rate Italian restaurant. It was covered with cracked oilcloth on which stood greasy salt and pepper shakers; a river of red wine, half dried up, wound itself around a vase of breadsticks; and from the rim of a bowl of grated cheese blue flies and little bugs took off, circled under a lamp and landed again on the neck of the bottle of Mallorca.

Mallorca smells like absinthe. It gets milky when you pour it over ice and mix it with water. It's cheap enough for Indians to buy, and whole villages in Ecuador are in a stupor on Sundays and holidays, thanks to its powers.

The Hollander clasped and unclasped his hands and sank to his knees between the pink-and-white filigreed columns that held up the ship rail. He tried to reach one of the six chairs that stood around the table and fell headlong on a couch whose back rest leaned against a wooden wall of a most beautiful arsenic-green. A decayed awning patched with a raincoat shaded him.

A cow, hanging in a brace of canvas, came down past the awning, and for a while turned in silent circles, its eyes wide with hysteria. Then it dropped in a sudden lurch of a winch and turned again over an old Lincoln touring car. The Hollander snored and the little dog came back. He was surprised by the cow. He stopped and watched it for a second and then he ran on.

Nothing happened but the snore of the Hollander and the take-off of bees, mosquitoes and small bugs from the cheese bowl. It sounded like a military airdrome, very far away in memory and space.

Down my hand along the little finger walked a fly, a small, common fly with gray wings. She sailed from there for the rim of the cheese bowl and climbed up to its cover. Upside down, hanging from the metallic ceiling, she went along looking for food and stopping. She came to the edge of the lid and walked along it with six legs, I think, three of them on the inside and three on the outside of the lid. She hopped to the knob of the lid, stopped there to clean her wings with the last pair of legs, and then took off again.

With a humming drone she wrote some word in immense letters into the space between table top and awning. The last letter ended up near the raincoat. In the small circle of light over the lamp, like a performer in a circus, up under the roof of the tent, she stood still, and then with the sound of tearing cloth she dived down straight through the narrow space between the glass chimney and the shade, avoiding a bug that came from the opposite side, and soared up again into the warm air and the brilliant light under the lamp shade. She gained altitude once more and in two wide arcs shot down into an empty liqueur glass. I thought she would surely crash there, or get stuck in the slush at the bottom of the glass, but she had calculated in millimeters. She almost touched the glass, almost the walls, but in a maneuver too fast for observation she was out and had looped and set her course through the back rest of two bentwood chairs, over my nose, for the shining gold disk in the drunken Hollander's ear. There she stopped to clean her wings once more.

The raincoat patch on the awning moved, a small hairy hand came in, and then a golden eye looked down through a small opening. A monkey, with the motions of a woman taking off a tight dress, wiggled down through a hole no larger than a child's fist. With soft searches, carefully groping with his long legs and arms, and watching in back of him with the tip of his tail, he came down. Grimacing and pulling the skin above his metallic eyes into pleats and quickly straightening it out

again, sending furtive looks to left and right, he advanced over the table, stole a piece of sugar without stopping or looking at it, dropped it, and voyaged on to the shoulder of the sleeping Hollander. He reached into the man's pockets, found a coin, stuck it into his right cheek, then went to the man's face, looked into his ear and tried to pluck the small gold disk from it, pulled the lips apart and examined the teeth. The mongrel dog came on his third round, looked under the table, recognized the Hollander, looked into the kitchen and ran down the deck, which was split and uneven, like the floor of a neglected bowling alley.

The *Mesias* was occasionally chartered for trips to the Galápagos. She took mining machinery up the Magdalena River, underbid freight rates of the established steamship lines and was suspected of smuggling gold and helping people arrive and disappear. Most of the time, like a submerged old woman carrying above water only a garish hat decorated with banana leaves, she paraded up and down the coast from Chile to Colombia.

Her crew was half a dozen unshaven men who slept and drank and sang and whose brown limbs hung out of the carcass of the boat wherever the planking was gone. They lived on bananas, rice and the fish they caught. The captain was an amiable Italian with an upper and a lower stomach, divided by a belt. Since his cook had been killed he attended to the food himself, and first class were his spaghetti, risottos and soups. The captain's life was made cozy by an Indian girl, barefoot, with a pair of tinkling brass anklets on her right foot, and small hands with which she poured red wine into the captain's cloudy glasses and served Mallorca. She smelled of cheap soap, and her cotton house dress was too big for her: when she bent to serve someone across the table, her firm little body stood in it nude, with a small appendectomy scar and a medal of the Virgin hanging between her breasts.

I boarded the S.S. *Mesias* in Arica, a small, clean town beside a high cliff. The mile-wide cliffs change color from black to white as the birds fly away from them in an endless living cloud. They blot out the town, the liners, the horizon and the sun. Out over the green waters they drive, in close formation, their wings touching. It looks as if an immense carpet with an all-over design of birds were suddenly unrolled into the sea.

Hundreds of pelicans in reflective moods line the gunwales of the barges in the harbor. Here and there one sits alone in the water. Seals swim about and play, coming up out of deep water without warning and bumping the pelicans. The fat birds look annoyed, then ruffle themselves back into their dignity and unconcern.

On the day I was on board the *Mesias*, a Chilean boat had caught fire off the coast. The cattle had been thrown overboard and made to swim ashore. (From this disaster came the hysterical cow.) The steerage passengers had been taken off in lifeboats and the first-class passengers in a motor launch. There were only two of these, an American and his wife, and they chose to take the *Mesias* to Callao rather than stay a night at the town's hotel.

They had smart luggage. The man was over fifty, well groomed and elegant—not a businessman. The wife was athletic, gaunt, handsome and younger.

They seemed very fond of each other and had great consideration for each other's comfort. The captain came out of his kitchen and greeted them with his apron wound around the lower stomach. He offered them a drink; the Americans asked for a dry Martini, or some Scotch, but there was only red wine and Mallorca. They looked with suspicion at the glasses with the blue milk in them, tasted it, looked to left and right, and again at the glass, and drank it. "It's very cooling," they said.

The captain then showed them to their cabin. They came back immediately and wanted to get off the boat, but the two planks nailed together that reached over to the dock had been pulled in, and by bending low or sitting down you could look under the awning and see that the *Mesias* was moving out into the green water, toward the endless line of flying guano birds.

The Americans visited the cow on the lower deck. Later they stood arm in arm to watch the copper mountains, and he tried to take some moving pictures. He found the light too weak, but he took one of his wife anyway. The Indian girl set places at the captain's table and rang a dinner bell. The American asked the captain to let him sit at a separate table with his wife. The captain arranged this. They sat down; he pushed the chair for her and held her hand at the beginning of the meal.

The Hollander was awakened, and a Frenchman sat down at the table. He was in the diplomatic service and was visiting an oilfield at a place along the coast at which no large vessel stopped.

After the minestrone plates had been cleared away and the table was loaded with risotto, salad, bread and cheese, the captain and the Indian girl sat down and everyone ate in silence.

The mongrel dog came again; the wife of the American petted him and talked to him and offered him food. He ran away on his stiff drumstick legs and continued his parade around the boat. The woman asked to whom the dog belonged.

The captain wanted to give us some more of his risotto, and the Americans brought their glasses to the table, spilling much.

The Hollander was awake again, and he asked whether anyone wanted some rijstafel. "Have you ever eaten pio pio?" he asked next. "That's buffalo hide with shrimp. You take the buffalo hide and cut pieces the size of a poker chip out of it, but not quite so regular. You then drop them in hot oil. The basis of this dish is rice also. Have you ever eaten monkey liver?" He turned to the captain and said that he only wanted to point out that the basis of all these dishes was rice. He fell asleep again.

The Indian girl chased the flies away from him. The ocean was blood-red, the lamp lit. The captain said that the dog belonged to the cook who had been killed. He waited for a while and looked around for someone to ask him to tell the story of how the cook was killed, and when no one did he started by himself.

"We were loading cargo in Buenaventura. I was trying to sleep, when suddenly there was a loud scream outside my window, the sound of many feet running past and much cursing.

"There was a German ship docked not far from us and our cook had gone over to drink German beer. While he was gone we had a visit from a union delegate, a Communist elected by one of the ships in the harbor. We talked about this and that and he had a few drinks here and then he started back to shore.

"Just as my cook comes back and wants to come up the gangplank, the delegate gets hold of him and they get in an argument about the German beer the cook had been drinking.

"The union delegate shouted, 'Down with the Nazis! Down with the Fascists!' My cook said, 'What difference does it make—German beer, American beer, or Jewish beer—what difference does it make?' Diaz—that was the name of the union delegate—pushed him in the face, and as the cook raised his hands to protect himself, Diaz slipped a knife from his belt and ripped him open. We got the money together to fly him to Panama, and there he died. It was plain murder, and that dog that runs around here is his dog. He's looking for him."

The cook's dog had listened to the story and looked up at the captain, and then had gone on his rounds again, stopped at a dark spot in the planking and howled out to sea.

The heat of the engine made the place comfortable. Over the swells of water, wide as avenues, ran a luminous band of light to the moon. The sea was studded with the fins of sharks, each one a gleaming, golden plowshare stuck into a black field.

The little Indian girl wound up a portable victrola and Richard Tauber sang "*Dein ist mein ganzes Herz.*"

"I can't stand his singing," said the Frenchman to me. "He gives me the sensation of a waiter reaching up under my coat when I leave a restaurant."

The drunken Hollander pulled the captain's sleeve. "Last time I heard that song," he said, "was in Magdeburg—Malta—well, I am pointing out it was not exactly where the plan says it is. It was in Nell Sprout's, at the end of Kruger National Park. We were coming into the Equator with sixteen parrots and two monkeys; the ship's carpenter built the cages and the Governor of Venezuela came on board personally. I bought some cheese cookies. In the meantime the parrots were dying off. I was married at the time. We had them right there in back of the anchor winch. There were still fourteen parrots and two monkeys. One monkey was dead and the other was dying. They were given a proper burial at sea. The last parrot was buried off Southampton."

The Hollander made an involuntary underslung gesture with his hand to catch his chin and hold his head up. He missed and fell asleep. One after another everyone disappeared.

In the early-morning light a fishing boat crossed our course. The Hollander waved to it and climbed over a mountain of cargo to the rear deck, where the carpenter was busy building cages for his animals and birds. The dog followed him there, in advances and retreats, uncertain of his footing but determined to look there too for his master.

In a shelter that they had made of palm leaves, arm in arm, sat the Americans. The little Indian girl came out of the captain's cabin and stretched herself in the sun in the little piece of cloth that was her dress.

The Americans got off in Callao; the Hollander stayed on and left with the Frenchman at a small place just before the *Mesias* turned into the Guayas River.

The boat fought upstream half the time, and then ran quickly with the support of the tide. Small bouquets of water hyacinths floated past down to the sea. Dugouts with Indians and half-naked mulattoes and Negroes passed. Large rafts of balsa wood, complete households on them, with children, goats and dogs, and hammocks, swam along the river. Brown and black legs and banana leaves hung out of boats into the water, out of hammocks, down over bags of coffee; everywhere siesta. In the dugouts were oranges, pineapples, fighting cocks, pigs. Turkey buzzards sat in all the trees along the riverfront. Over the water, and so close that their bellies seemed to get wet, flew trains of pelicans, their wingbeat like a dancing lesson—one, two, three, four, glide. A cool wind came down the river; it began to smell of chocolate. The captain tinkled his engine bell, and the *Mesias* sighed in a slower tempo, turned, and, between launches that crowded together like young pigs feeding out of

161

the same trough, she squeezed to a wobbly dock and made fast in Guayaquil.

"Stay—today I'll make some lasagne à la bolognese," said the captain, who never seemed to wash himself.

To the pier came a group of youths and men with caps and rope. Two of them grabbed the lapels of my coat, others gave me a message; they seemed to have their hands in all my pockets. They all wanted to take my baggage to the Gran Hotel.

I am always unhappy when I leave a place—a hotel, a house, a boat— no matter how bad. For the first few hours on arriving in a new place an emotional sloppiness comes over me; I sat lost and homesick for the greasy *Mesias* in my room at the Gran Hotel. This house, half garage, half hospital, is excellently suited to make you unhappy. I went to the dining room, which is on the roof. I tasted the soup and got up and reached for my hat and walked back to the *Messias*.

The captain stood in the kitchen preparing his lasagne à la bolognese. In troubled moments there is nothing so reassuring, so kind to the soul, as to watch someone repair something or cook. The captain oiled the pan with his fingers, carefully placed strips of noodles along the bottom, and spread over them a paste which he had made out of ground beef and pork, some garlic, chopped onions, origanum, and a sauce prepared from Italian plum tomatoes. Over this he put another layer of noodles, and over the blanket of noodles he spread mozzarella cheese. Then came more paste, another sheet of noodles, and finally he carefully trimmed with scissors the noodles that hung down over the pan and put the whole thing in the oven. He cooked a lot, and he needed it.

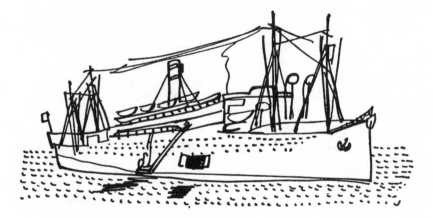

THE
DAY
WITH
HUNGER

THE TWO CABALLEROS were still snoring at the Swiss wallpaper—at a part where some poems by Hölderlin appeared in a Sunday supplement—and the door was blocked by the tilted chair. Through the cracks in the floor came smoke.

I went out to see if the hotel was on fire. The smoke rose in a twisted smeary column from under the building. The hotel stood on long poles, on which two monkeys on strings slid up and down, and the kitchen was under our room. A woman cook was below, barelegged in stockings of mud, a parrot on her shoulder and at her feet an assistant who fanned the flames.

As usual Aurelio had slept on the floor outside my room. He stood up in his poncho and disappeared to get our horses. An old proverb here says that half the journey is getting out of the inn.

The mayordomo was next to appear and ordered breakfast for us both.

A table was set on the veranda of the hotel. Out of a closet came a tablecloth reserved for distinguished guests; it was egg-stained and tomato-spotted. A handful of tinware, forks and spoons, was set down. The mayordomo put his revolver next to his plate and looked in the direction of the oven. The cook brought milk and coffee. Here in the land where some of the world's best coffee grows, if you love coffee you must bring your own and a percolator besides. In Ecuador and the rest of South America, in good and bad hotels alike, they cook the coffee long in advance, brewing a foul ink of it, which is cooled and kept in a bottle. Half a cupful of this dye is poured out, the sugar bowl emptied into it, and a little warm milk added on.

The mayordomo ate and drank and asked me why I did not eat. I had an omelet with tomato in front of me, and although I was very hungry and had not had a proper meal for days, I had no intention of eating it. I had wiped my fork and spoon and was starting on the cleaner end of the plate, when I looked across the square and saw a butcher stand. There under a big tree stood a wobbly box. It was covered with tin, an old oil can cut in pieces and nailed over it. An Indian woman with a baby tied to her back stood next to the box with a leg of mutton in her dirty fingers. Overhead was a cloud of flies, so thick that you could reach into it, squeeze a fistful together and throw them away. The woman had a machete and with this she carved the meat, the way you sharpen the end of a fence post. I sent Aurelio to buy two bananas for my breakfast.

For short intermissions we came out of the forest and then we rode into it again. The jungle has doors—like entrances to greenhouses. Outside there is a wall of earth, thickly covered with a rug of small leaves that resemble laurel. Sunk into these, solitary and apparently stemless, are little flowers, gentians. Then you come to an arrangement, bright as traffic lights, of pretty shrubs with tubiform flowers, copious reddish blossoms; and the chalk-colored blooms of geranium trees stand high in back. From a stagnant pond, crowded with weeds and small fat plants that resemble watercress, the black limbs of dead trees reach out, and on them sits an army of flies, bugs and beetles in the colors of sulphur, arsenic and copper.

There are rows of ferns on the green band of the wall, their compound fleshy fronds stuck into the turf; and then you are inside and a botanical monotony begins.

Against the flat green-gray curtain of the background soar the trees and the parasites that grow out of trees. In this steam bath are acacias, odoriferous flowers, yellow with binate spines three inches long, and fern trees with lacy leaves six feet in length. Bushes also grow on the trees, and everywhere are orchids.

From under our horses' hoofs came clouds of butterflies, some white and some with the pattern and color of mock turtle soup on their wings. After a while the very large orchids took on the shape of immense sauce boats standing and hanging on the branches. Under them were huge leaves that had decayed or been toasted crisp brown; they began to resemble filets of sole cooked in butter—the very brown ones like pompano cooked in a paper bag—and the orchids, which were a strong fine yellow, seemed like dishes of mayonnaise.

I smelled other cooking too. It seemed as if invisible cooks were hidden in the jungle, and with painful, accurate detail of shape, color and taste—and, above all, smell—held dish after dish under my nose only to take it away for a better one. I dreamed an immense bill of fare for the next few miles, a nightmare that began with assorted hors d'œuvre, céleri rémoulade, saucissons d'Arles, the hams of Poland, of Virginia, of York, of Westphalia, of the Ardennes and Bayonne, the choucroute garnie, the Tiroler Bauernschmaus. Then the soups, vichyssoise, germiny à l'oseille, onion soup au gratin, and marmite with marrow dumplings. The fish course followed: swordfish steaks, shad and roe, clam pan roast, cold barbue, and cold salmon. Confusion set in after this: hashed brown potatoes mixed with ham and eggs appeared. Pâté de foie gras, mackerel in tomato sauce, Bismarck herring and other agreeable pickles, bouillabaisse and pilaff with chicken livers, curry and chutney and Bombay duck, canard à la presse, and a tray of assorted cheeses—Camembert, Brie, Pont-l'Evêque, Roquefort.

After I had gone through all the bills of fare, I thought of restaurants and their proprietors, their décor, doormen, potted palms, white and gold interiors, cherubs, orchestras, coat racks, and of their service good and bad.

Of the vulgar tubs of butter at the Reine Pédauque, of the Restaurant Numa back of the Madeleine and its stacks of escargot plates. Of the big places in Copenhagen and Rotterdam with the red carpets, the immense waiters, and the terrines of soup in which, under a lake of melted butter, asparaguses thick as thumbs swam around. The carpets were dark as oxblood, and the people with stiff napkins tied around their necks sat eating for three hours. And Tyrol, and hunger from skiing, a different language spoken at every table in an inn as remote as the little Flexen in Zürrs; the Salontöchter in the Swiss hotels, the stew made with Steinpilze, the peasant women who brought the little strawberries down from the fields. The restaurant in the basement of the Grand Central Terminal in New York, the part with the counters on the right, where you are served by waiters who rank second in gruffness and bitter faces only to those of the Lafayette, but where you get the best ham and eggs in the world, and sea food and stews that are rare.

The Chinese restaurants; the Grotta Azzurra in downtown New York in a cellar with horrible murals, mostly frequented by political rabble, where they cook lobster with small Italian plum tomatoes and where a waiter who looks like d'Annunzio brings you half a dozen napkins with the lobster and three plates for the empty claws and shells; and then, a little farther uptown, Luchow's.

When I am in New York I usually cross Fourteenth Street and revolve the door of Luchow's on Sunday evenings. It is then that a small private miracle takes place. I sit down and watch for the arrival of occasional and peculiar guests. Where they come from I do not know. From a museum down the street, I think, where they are prepared for this visit with infinite care, where the men's noses are painted red, and the thin blue veins of too-good living are etched on their cheeks; where antique Prince Alberts are taken out of camphor and brushed.

Here I have seen a Schubert and two Brahmses, and on their arms lovely old Winterhalter ladies. One man who comes is a Lenbach portrait of Freiherr von Menzel the court painter, and another looks like my friend, the eighty-year-old K.K. Hofschauspieler of the Munich Theater, Konrad Dreher. For their entrances, the orchestra fiddles through forgotten Waldteufel music. It is sad and *hausgebacken;* it seems as if outside, instead of the bawdy street, there should be the stop for the green-and-white trolley car to Nymphenburg. The years of hopelessness and disgrace that have changed all this seem but a cloud of cigar smoke, rheumatism, beer and Kalbsbraten.

At about that part of the restaurant dream my horse stumbled; I woke up and began to smell cooking—real cooking. We came into a clearing again and I hoped that we might be near a small hacienda which perhaps belonged to someone who had a chicken on the fire, or that we were at least in the vicinity of the hut of a Salesian padre—these good men sometimes cook for themselves. Between two large walls of earth we saw a native hut from whose neat chimney smoke was rising; there was also some promise in washing that hung in the sun to dry, and in a well-fed dog.

I slid off my horse and found an oven at the back of the house, where an Indian woman was busy with food. She had a friendly face and she was reasonably clean. There was soup on the fire and she was busy cleaning out a monkey. She cut him up, going inside him with her knife, turning over the blade as if stirring stomach, liver, lungs, and then emptying him out. She singed off the hair and cooked him over an open fire. Another woman and a man came and sat down, and they ate the monkey, the man taking an arm and starting by eating the inside of the palm. He nibbled at the fingers and spat out the nails. The woman bit into the ears first. It was like eating a baby. My hunger was gone—I got on my horse and rode away.

Rafael de Gongotena came galloping back to me and wondered where I had been, and he said that we would be at the Hacienda El Triunfo in half an hour. He warned that ahead was a deep ravine bridged by two trees with earth stuffed in between, and said not to worry, the horse knew the bridge and would walk across and just to let him go.

The bridge came, and after it the hacienda. We were met by Don Antonio, the oldest son of the owner.

What music there can be in the sound of bath water running into a tub, in hearing a cocktail mixed; and what pleasure in a simple table laid, and a bottle of wine in a bucket. There was even a bath towel, a clean one, and a cake of soap.

*T*he man of the world was fond of apples. He ate them in place of dessert and they were selected with as much care and worry as were his vintage wines and the rare cigars he smoked. His favorite apple came from the Tyrol and was called the Calville apple. It grew on the sun-warmed foothills of the mountains around Meran and Bozen. In order to have its skin a uniform sulphur yellow without spots, reddish marks or roughness, the apple was grown inside a paper bag. The upper part of the apple had a bumpy surface, the meat was firm and snow white—it was handled as carefully as a sick bird. Taken from its paper bag, it went into a sheet of tissue paper, was wrapped in cotton, put into an individual stall in a large box, which in turn was heavily wrapped, cushioned in excelsior and shipped to France. The apple sold in the fruit shops of Paris for five francs.

VACATION

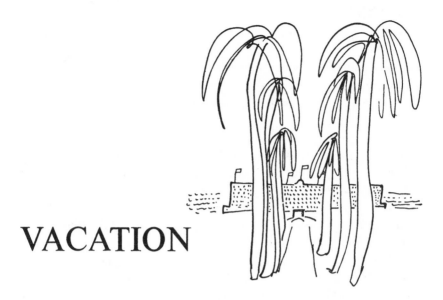

I ALWAYS TRIED to leave New York about four, in order to get out of the Holland Tunnel close to five. The ride over the Pulaski Skyway at that hour is one of the most exciting parts of a trip to the South. In the gaseous stretches of the Jersey landscape, half of it gone in shadows, stand drawbridges, factories, electric plants and immense tanks. They have the beauty of the devil, with green and yellow flames leaping from chimneys, with trains smearing black smoke over a gray horizon. The landscape is framed in a loop of light, an endless gleaming necklace, rolling over the hills and bridges, that is made up of headlights of on-coming cars. In snow or rain it is doubly enchanting. It is not all gas and oil and stink. We even saw a rabbit.

Barbara, who sat beside me, had her nose flattened against the window and saw the rabbit first. He scampered across the highway in the direction of Newark.

"Pappy!"

"Yes, darling."

"Tell me a story about a rabbit. A story about a rabbit, a rabbit, a rabbit."

Once upon a time a monkey and a rabbit met. The monkey said to the rabbit that it was a pity that he, the rabbit, could never sit still, but always had to look in back of him.

"Ha!" said the rabbit. "How about yourself? You can't sit still either. You always have to scratch yourself."

Both of them then agreed that for one whole day, from sunrise to sunset, they would sit side by side, and the rabbit would not look around and the monkey would not scratch himself.

The day on which they were going to do this arrived, and at the moment the sun rose the rabbit and the monkey met and sat down side by side.

Without batting a lid, the rabbit quietly looked down at the grass in front of him. The monkey sat still, his hands folded in his lap. They remained in this position for hours. The time passed very slowly, and it was midday when the monkey, who knew he could no longer sit still, said to the rabbit, "When I was a soldier, bullets hit me here, and here, and there, and there—" and wherever he pointed, at that spot on his body he quickly scratched himself.

The rabbit was no better off. He felt that he could not look another second at the grass in front of him, and he also began telling a story. "When I was a soldier," he said, "the enemy was hard after me. To escape him I had to jump like this, and like that, to the left and to the right." Like lightning, his eyes followed the motions of his limbs and every time he jumped he looked back.

Barbara, who was four years old, was asleep when I explained the moral of the story.

Before I fell asleep myself, we stopped at the Anglers' Rest in Seaford, Delaware. I tried to persuade the waitress who served us to bring Barbara some milk and vegetables, but Barbara didn't want any milk and vegetables.

"Well, honey, you can have spaghetti and meat balls," said the girl. "But why don't you order a submarine sandwich? My, that's good! Mmm."

"What is a submarine sandwich?"

"Well, a submarine sandwich comes two ways. The fifteen-cent one is seven inches long, and for a quarter you get one twelve inches long—"

"What's it made of?"

"It's made of Italian cheese, salami, Italian seasoning, hot peppers, lettuce and spiced ham; the cheese is put down first and then olive oil is put over it—it comes in a specially baked loaf of Italian bread."

Barbara ordered it and ate it, all of it, all of the fifteen-cent one, and drank some of my beer with it.

I wanted a cigar with my coffee. The girl brought me a cigar almost as long as the sandwich, mustard-colored, with large ribs running through the wrapper. It lit up like a torch, and when I asked her whether she had any other kind she said, "No, honey, just the five-cent one."

I asked for the bill. She wrote it on a piece of paper called "Guest check." She stuck a pencil in her hair and turned a knob on the radio.

A voice wailed, "Like a fool I didn't believe him and all the time I had a couple of detectives follow him. Why do I always have to hurt the people I love and why, why do the worst things always happen to the swellest people?"

"Good night, honey," said the waitress, and we left and drove to the Norfolk ferry.

Someone told me that you could go aboard the ferry boat at about eleven, get a room and bath and cross during the night, arriving in Norfolk at 7 A.M. The cabin looked like an illustration out of Dickens, the cast-iron bathtub was just large enough for Barbara, and the beds were two-story Army bunks. However, the ferry saves time.

The next day, I followed the Ocean Highway and turned inland as soon as it got warmer.

In New Orleans, Barbara was fascinated by another sandwich. This one was called "Martin's poorboy sandwich." She saw it in a little shop —outside of which hangs a sign showing a small boy who eats a sandwich larger than himself. A twenty-eight-inch loaf of bread is cut in half, loaded with sliced roast beef, lettuce and tomato, and the whole is soaked in gravy and costs ten cents. The sandwiches, which are sold in several establishments, were invented during the Depression and have made their inventor, a legless man, so rich that a colored chauffeur carries him from one "poorboy" place to the other. I refused, however, to go in there and buy two "poorboys," and so we arrived in tears at Antoine's restaurant.

This exquisite and sufficiently esteemed restaurant is all that one expects of it. It is blessed with a proprietor who honors his profession and worships his ancestors (I have counted 53 photographs of them on menus, on souvenirs, on postcards and in frames). He has a maître d'hôtel who is one of the few in that difficult calling who is free of all pomp. We ate in the 1820 Room, a private apartment in which hangs a large oil painting of Madame Antoine, a kind of Frau Sacher. Barbara was particularly elated because in a glass case along the wall of the room, among various personal belongings of Antoine Alciatore, the founder (1840–1885), there are a pair of baby shoes, the first pair he wore, kept right next to his shaving mug.

M. Isidor Cassou, the good headwaiter, an Adolphe Menjou type, supervised the dinner, and I had a terrible time because I had to eat the *spécialité de la maison, les huîtres Rockefeller.* I detest nothing so much as oysters when they are cooked, and these were covered with a green '
mud and done *au gratin.* During the ordeal, M. Roy L. Alciatore, the

grandson of Antoine, showed me a photograph in which he was shown eating the millionth order of this dish. I ate them quickly, almost swallowing the shell. M. Alciatore beamed and had a second order brought in.

The rest of the menu was superb cooking, particularly the pompano. It's an honest restaurant—the lights go out every time someone orders crêpes Suzette. The kitchen is badly lit; the chef stands in front of an old coal stove and cooks in heavy casseroles; everything is as it should be, and I hope it will forever stay that way, including the cedar sawdust that is sprinkled on the floor. It fills the rooms with an appetizing perfume. It smells like pencils being sharpened.

The road from New Orleans to Marco Island, where we went to go fishing, runs along the Gulf of Mexico and is in excellent condition. It will remain in Barbara's memory as a long line of dead black pigs. She counted fourteen of them. These pigs roam the country, half wild, and then, crossing the road, they are run over by the fast-moving cars. I had to tell several pig stories.

The captain of the fishing boat on Marco Island was very cooperative. He said, "I used to go barefoot, but now the place is getting fashionable, and out of consideration for the lady of the house, I wear shoes." We ran into a lot of fish, and I observed how much they resemble people.

Pulling them in became tiresome labor and at the end of it my arms hurt and the fishbox overflowed with them—all of them silently gulping. I wanted to let them go, but the captain said he could make something of them—fertilizer, I think.

Miami is Miami, and by no other name is there a city such as this. The hotel employees were as efficient and quick as dentists, and fingerprinted besides. Everything is to be had here from caviar to a Goodyear blimp. From a point of design and efficiency the new hotels in Miami Beach are models.

The main highway to Palm Beach was now an unending, open-all-night string of tourist cabins, orange- and papaya-juice pavilions, sea shells, carved coconuts and cypress-knee souvenir stands. There is another, quiet road along the ocean, one of the finest drives in the world.

An unforgettable picture presented itself to me at a turn in that road. It was past the S curve that leads to the Hutton castle in Palm Beach. This edifice always reminds me of an advertisement for breakfast food. I am certain that at night gnomes work there under the stairs of the baronial halls and in the vaulted cellars wrapping crunchy crackies, full of golden goodness, into bright packages and mailing them out in Josef Urban boxes.

The castle's garden faces the unceasing sound of the waves; the moon shone through the long, thin fins of palm leaves, and on a bulkhead near the sea sat a black gardener and a maid, engaged in ardent courtship. Beyond them, two tugs tried to get a steamer off a sandbank.

In Charleston, we stopped at a frequently and highly recommended restaurant. It is down near the slave market, and called Henry's. It is a restaurant of indifferent décor, which is often the sign of a very good place. On the tiled floor stood old Viennese bentwood chairs. The lighting fixtures are like those used in barber shops, and in the right rear corner of the restaurant's main dining room was a group of Negro waiters arranged according to size, the small ones in front, the tallest in back leaning against the sideboard. I thought they were about to sing some spirituals, but they were asleep with eyes wide open.

One of them exiled himself from the group and slouched over to our table. "There is two kinds of chowder on the menu," he said, "a black-fish chowder and a special one, a Charleston chowder." We ordered one of each, and when they were served they looked and tasted exactly alike, a white, sloppy paste, flavorless and lukewarm.

The next thing, some sea food which was recommended as a native dish, and *spécialité de la maison*, turned out to be another stew, a kind of rijstafel with small fish scales that got between your teeth, and other foreign substances thrown in.

On this trip we stayed at several hotels that belong to a chain which is owned by a man named Dinkler. They are a kind of traveling-salesman hotel, very clean and satisfactory. In each of them, in the center of immense lobbies, stands a statue of the founder—a grim-visaged executive. On everything is printed "This is a Dinkler Hotel," and the doorman sends you to the next Dinkler.

On the highway that leads to Newcastle and back to New York is a hill. When I was halfway down it a green traffic light shone ahead. A truck approached from the left over a crossroad and got stuck in the snow. Under the light, the hill was solid ice and it was too late to do anything. I pushed Barbara, who sat next to me, down on the floor, and then the crash came. The driver of the truck and his helper, two natives of Dover, were shaken up. The driver had a cut over his left eye, and we all had to go to a magistrate.

The driver and his helper were greeted by the magistrate as John and

Charlie, and everyone told the story of the accident. The magistrate listened carefully to all three versions and then he leaned back and asked a few questions. He seemed an honest man and he looked out of the window somewhat bewildered. It was a difficult case to decide. He asked a state trooper to drive him to the spot where the accident had taken place, and when he came back he lit a pipe and looked out of the window some more.

The driver sat on a bench in front of us, near an iron potbelly stove. He adjusted a small bandage over his eye. A little blood ran down over his face, and he wiped it away. The room was silent.

Barbara watched the man wipe the blood away. Then she said, "Pappy, why did you try to kill that poor man?"

The magistrate smiled gratefully. Nodding to me, he knocked on the table and said, "Guilty!"

YOU
SHALL
HAVE
MUSIC

THE BUTLER OPENED the door and ushered in a man who delivered a gift-wrapped case. Elsie indicated where she wanted it and told the butler to open the case.

The butler had undone the wrapping, and Elsie pointed to the wooden case and asked, "What's in it, Coombs?"

"Twelve quarts of Cointreau, milady."

"What will I do with twelve quarts of Cointreau?"

The butler pondered the problem and then his face became animated. "Give a party, milady," he said with a French jerk of his head.

"Of course," said Elsie. She turned and faced me and took a determined step forward, and her right hand reached for my left shoulder to steady herself and grabbed a handful of cloth. She held up a handkerchief with her free hand and waved it like a flag. She made *chk-chk* and said,

"Stevie"—I don't know why she called me Stevie, probably because a war was going on with Germany and she didn't like the Teutonic Ludwig—"Mother is going to do something for you. You know that enthusiasm in this world comes always fifty years too late to do the artist any good. Now, you don't care to be famous when you're dead and gone. You want what the world can offer you now." She stamped her foot. "And Mother is going to see that you get it. She will introduce you to the *beau monde*—you'll have a coming-out party. We'll get up a very careful list of people, and then we'll have a dinner for you, and by the time they serve coffee you can name your own price for your pictures, because you will be famous."

The butler came with a silver tray and presented a letter that had arrived with the liqueur. Mother glanced at it. "Now, isn't that thoughtful of dear Monsieur Cointreau. Here, read."

The note was in French, from M. Cointreau's New York agent, and said:

DEAR LADY MENDL,

Among the many things you have done in your long and shining career is one for which I am particularly grateful, and that is that you have made our liqueur, as an ingredient of the Lady Mendl Cocktail (⅓ gin, ⅓ grapefruit juice, 1 jigger of Cointreau), world famous. *Alors*, I am most happy to send you this case of Cointreau—with the assurance of etc. . . . etc. . . .

Elsie's face toughened and the voice went dry. She waved the letter as she handed it back to the butler, saying, "Charming letter, but if this is followed by a request for an endorsement and a picture of me without having to pay for it, we will say politely, '*Non, merci beaucoup.*' "

She grabbed my shoulder again, "Listen, Stevie, to what Mother says: Never let them run over you! Now we shall get busy with the menu, and after that with the list, and then send out the invitations. All we have to buy is a little champagne. The food Mother is going to pay for. Now, how do you like this for the menu? We'll keep it very simple.

"We'll start with soup—and Susan makes something very delicious, an oyster soup, and she has some kind of specialty that is served with it. The fish we dispense with, as oysters are both fish and soup and we want to keep it simple. The next thing is duck, which we can get without ration points, and with this we serve the small French peas with onions.

"For dessert we'll have chocolate soufflé. I myself never eat any dessert, but most people like it, and for ices it's too cold in California at dinner time. A few flowers aren't going to cost too much."

Sir Charles's record had finished playing. Mother was a woman for direct action. She immediately sent the butler to inform Sir Charles that there would be a party. Sir Charles arranged the seating of the guests and worried about all problems of protocol whenever a party was given. The secretary was informed and the cook. Elsie was smiling, for, as Charles had said, she loved nothing so much as a party.

A few days passed, and Mother added people to the list, and it was getting bigger and bigger. The weather was fine, and she decided that it could be held half inside, half outside the house. She said, "We'll place the rugged ones like Gary Cooper and Clark Gable outside," and then she added softly, "I think we ought to have a little music, Stevie."

I said, first of all, that Mother hated music; secondly, that all the brilliant and artistic people in town were on that list, who would make conversation; and, most important, that there was a war still going on and it wasn't the time for too much gaiety.

Mother looked at me a little hard at first, but then she kicked me in the ribs with her elbow and said, "You're right, Stevie. The brilliant people can make brilliant conversation, and this is no time for dancing and high jinks—why have music? Oh, you're so right, Stevie. What would Mother do without you to advise her? It's your party, dear, and everything must be exactly as you want it."

Charles had been listening, and when we were alone he said to me, "You know, dear boy, you're going to have music at your party. You know that, don't you? And what's more, you'll pay for it. One cannot win a war with the old girl. Watch out now, and remember what I said."

It was a week before the party, and I was up in my room. Some people had arrived for cocktails, and suddenly I heard music below. On the way to the living room I met Charles. I said, "I was shaving upstairs just now, and it seemed to me that I heard some music. Did you hear any?"

"Yes, of course. That's your music, dear boy, no doubt. Elsie is having a rehearsal of some kind. I told you you cannot win a war with the old girl."

The butler passed, and Charles said, "Who's making music, Coombs?"

"Milady is trying out an orchestra, Sir Charles," he said. "For the party."

"What did I tell you?" Charles walked to the bar, and when he came back he said, "She's an incredible woman. She has solved the problem so that we're having music and doing something for the boys at the same time. Come and see."

In a corner of the bar sat three sailors. One, a thin, long boy, was bent over a big guitar, which he called a "ghi-tar." The second had a small concertina and hummed through his nose. And the third played on a clarinet. They played cowboy songs, sad and muted.

The guitarist got up and said they would bring a little of that Texas sunshine into the house, and they sang "Pistol Packin' Mama" and then little-dogie songs, and while strumming the guitar the tallest did some Western yodeling.

"Now you can't possibly object to that," said Elsie. "And I hope it settles all your worries about the war, and all these dear boys ask for is a little drink and a ten-dollar bill each, that makes thirty dollars—now that's not too much for an evening's entertainment." Elsie looked like the bad queen again and left us.

Charles sat down and said to me, "Usually I'm the victim. This time she's done it to you. I offer ten quid if you can get out of paying for the music."

We were, that evening, only the family at dinner, and Elsie said, "Now, Stevie dear, you haven't told Mother how you liked the orchestra."

I hesitated.

"It's a gay note," said Elsie and continued, "Remember, Charles, those Neapolitan street singers we had in Venice, in their lovely costumes? Why, people went perfectly mad over them. They're fond of things like that. I'd say let's have them, now that I have found these boys who will come in their Navy suits. Well, Stevie?"

I said, "Look, Mother, I give up. I don't want any music, but you do—"

Mother looked a little hurt. She said, "Why don't we do this? We'll each pay for a musician. Stevie, you pay for one, Charles pays for one, and Mother pays for one. Now, that's very fair, don't you think?"

"I don't mind at all," said Charles and walked out of the room.

"I say," he said to me later in the corridor, "that's awfully cheeky of the old girl! And why do you let her do it? Why don't you put your foot down?"

"I'm sorry," I said. "It's not a complete defeat, but I lost the battle and I owe you—how much is ten quid?"

"Under these circumstances I wouldn't dream of holding you to it. She can make unholy complications. Anyway, we have a fine evening to look forward to—this dinner. Oh Lord, I've done the tables—you have all the crashing bores at yours with Elsie. I've had to sacrifice you to them. I've saved myself. I have Mary Pickford on my right and Olivia de Havilland on my left, Nadia Gardiner *en face*, Anita Colby and a new one"—he pulled out his notebook and put on the pince-nez and looked for the name—"Arlene Dahl. That makes a nice table."

The night before the party Mother's maid came to tell me that Lady Mendl wanted to speak to me.

Mother had a bed which was an antique and beautiful. She also had a great liking for lying on the floor, on a mattress covered with fur blankets. There she rested, supported by many pillows. On this mattress she exercised in yogi fashion, and occasionally stood on her head.

The room was softly lit. A fire burned in the chimney, and the one maid who refused to call Mother "milady" was arranging the pillows. Elsie punished her by calling her "Miss Bridget." The "Miss" was like a hiss.

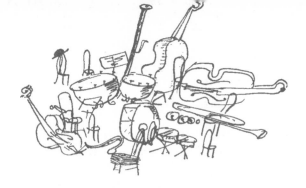

Mother was a wonderful portrait, like a very complicated rich little Christmas tree, beautifully ornamented, delicate, glittering here and there with jewels; she still had the white gloves on her hands and a turban about her head. She gave instructions to *Miss* Bridget to bring two rum punches. Then she said, "Are you satisfied, my dear, with the list of the guests? I don't think we have any deadwood. Only Charles has invited some awful people, that woman from Hungary—Hanky Panky or what's-her-name—and he wanted the monster, the Empty Stomach, who is fortunately unable to come—oh dear, Stevie. Anyway, we have a nice table. I've chosen the people myself."

Miss Bridget brought the drinks. Mother smiled. "Put the light on the Virgin, *Miss* Bridget."

The upper part of the room was in darkness. Miniature spotlights lit up small mirrors, flowers in vases, and now a sweet, very modern Madonna set in a mirrored frame.

"No, a little more to the right—good, now leave it that way, *Miss* Bridget. Thank you so much.

"Night is important, Stevie, because then you can light up things. Now, there is a wonderful man that Mother knows. Mother calls him "Nighty"—his real name is Mr. Nightingale, and so fitting—he functions at night. Because he belongs to the night he's the most perfect musician—what am I talking about? I have musicians on the brain—I mean, electrician. Mr. Nightingale is the most perfect electrician for the night, when you need them most—and, for that matter, also for the day. If ever you want to have anything done, call him.

"Now, dear Stevie, I have engaged Mr. Nightingale to light up the house and the garden tomorrow night. It will be a little like Versailles." She smiled sadly. "Dear Stevie, give Mother your hand. Would you terribly mind if Mother asked you for a great favor?"

"No, not at all."

"Stevie dear, do you mind if Mother gets a few people to make a little quiet night music?"

I said that I didn't mind and that we had all agreed on the sailors. Mother fell asleep, smiling.

Next day Mr. Nightingale was busy wiring trees, the house was torn apart, and all was upset. I went to Charles's room. He looked up as I entered and then tripped over boot trees and shoes. He scattered them with a kick of his foot. John had been sent to get extra chairs, and Charles was helpless. He was wearing gray felt bedroom slippers and magnificent British underwear, wool and white, and reaching from the ankles to his middle, and an upper piece with sleeves to his wrists. The number 38 was embroidered in red on it.

"What does the number on your underwear mean?"

"That's the year one bought it, dear boy, so one can keep track how long it lasts. I had this made in thirty-eight, and now we are forty-five—that's not bad. Of course, it's made in England, Hillditch and Keyes, Piccadilly." He pointed to a small tab and attached clasp beneath the knee. "This is to hold up the socks. It's attached to the underwear, so you don't have to wear those awkward garters. And this tab here below the stomach is another good thing. It keeps your shirt from riding up on you. And this band in the middle here—you lace it a bit, and it keeps you in shape. Now that's proper underwear for you.

"About tonight, you'll be lucky, dear boy, if you don't end up with Carmen Cavallero and his orchestra playing for dinner. Let me warn you, be prepared for surprises."

A few borrowed butlers and some men who worked for a caterer named Shields arrived, and it slowly got dark. Parties mean worry and are a great responsibility, especially when half of the guests are to be under the open, unpredictable California sky.

The hairdresser and his assistant arrived, and Elsie went upstairs to get dressed. Charles met me on the way to my room. He had a box of cigars and a bottle of whisky in his hands. He said, "I want to tell you that I am very fond of you," and he added, somewhat embarrassed, "I must ask you a favor, something personal. Would you mind coming to my room for a second where we can talk?"

In his room we sat down.

"The other day when we were at your little place on the beach with that ravishing creature, you made sport of me. I appreciate that you did it in front of me, but you told a story of how one day, coming early for dinner, you heard moaning inside the house and then found me listening to a recording of my own voice. I know you don't mean to hurt me, but women have no sense of humor—they believe stories like that.

"Now, dear boy, please don't tell that story again—you see, you must understand. It's the only thing I do really well, I assure you. Now I might be moved to sing a song or two tonight after dinner—you don't mind, do you? But you see, if while singing I looked at the audience and saw you leaning over to whoever is next to you, I'd know immediately that you were telling that fib again and my throat might go back on me. You know, I studied for years, with de Reszke, who said that I had an excellent voice. He even went so far as to say, 'Why don't you make a career of it, Charles?' "

He got up. We were both relieved that it was over. He handed me the box of cigars and the bottle of Scotch. "This is for your party, dear boy."

I went to dress, and when I came down the trees were lit up: the effect was as if green leopard skins were hung over the branches. The candles flickered, and the first guests arrived. They were a young and handsome couple in love, and to be married in a few days. She was pretty and a starlet, and the man was a very decent-looking and much decorated captain in the Air Force. They went to the bar and drank their cocktails.

Then down the stairs came Elsie, and she was magnificent—more royal than all the queens reigning at that time. She had over her shoulders a long pale-blue cape such as the officers of the French Foreign Legion wear. She was dressed in snow-white and wore all her medals, including the Croix de Guerre for her service in the field in the First World War. She wore a pair of long gloves, white, with jewels embroidered on them. The right glove had a diamond surrounded by blue stones; the left, a sapphire bracelet. In her hair she wore golden leaves, and she had on her big Indian necklace.

Two policemen came in and said that they were going to take care of traffic outside, and they each got a drink, and then there was commotion in the kitchen, and Mother said, "The only person that has a right to be temperamental in a house is the cook. Poor Susan has been working all day yesterday and today, and she prepared something special to go with the soup, and it's very delicate, and one of the men must have knocked it off the oven. And now she will be in a dreadful state. Go out and pacify her. Say a few nice things to her, Stevie."

When I got back the announcer had taken his place and the party was at its beginning. Suddenly Mother said, "Stevie, what about the music?"

The announcer pronounced, "Mr. Gilbert Miller, Mr. and Mrs. Rubinstein . . . Mr. Pinza . . . Miss Leonora Corbett, Mr. Charles Boyer . . . Mrs. Whitney . . ."

"Good evening . . . *bon soir* . . . *bon soir* . . . " Mother made brief conversation with the guests and introduced me. There was a pause, and then we heard music, a faint strumming barely audible over the hum of conversation. Mother said, "Go, Stevie, and tell them to play a little louder."

I went to where the music came from and saw that there was only one sailor, the one with the guitar, and I asked him where the others were. He said that they couldn't come because they had got drunk and were in the brig.

I went back to Mother.

"Miss Jeanette MacDonald . . . Sir Alexander Korda . . ."

"Good evening . . . good evening . . ."

In the next pause I told Mother about the missing sailors. I was sorry, I said, but only one musician had shown up. Charles came over. Elsie was, at the moment, introducing me to a newly arrived goddess. Charles waited, and then said, "Elsie, did you know that only one of the musicians has come? The others appear to be in lockup."

"I know, Charles dear," said Elsie, and to Marlene Dietrich she said, "I don't know what I'd do without dear Charles—he worries about every detail when we give a party." She looked at him and smiled her smile of dismissal, but Charles stayed; he wanted to ask something.

"Yes, Charles dear?"

"I say, whose musician is it, the one that's come?"

Mother pulled up her gloves. "Oh," she said with the bad-queen face, "not my musician, Charles, and certainly not Stevie's musician. It's your musician that came."

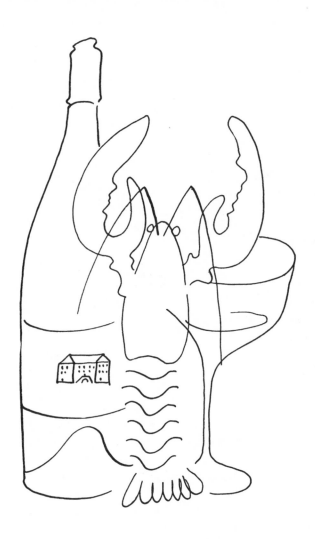

Headwaiter, tell me, this wine is all right, but what has happened to the famous vintages?"

"Monsieur, that is a sad story. It is sold for export to get the money to pay the loan to the Américains back. What folly! I cannot get a single bottle of good wine, of kirsch, or Cointreau, all on account of the Américains."

LES SAUCISSONS D'ARLES

"ONE REGRETS," said the waitress of the restaurant Au Bon Coin in Arles, "but one has no saucisson d'Arles. There is a kind of saucisson d'Arles that I can offer Monsieur, but it is not the *vrai* saucisson d'Arles, which, as Monsieur undoubtedly knows, is made from the meat of donkeys."

The waitress, who had the face of the true Arlésienne—a narrow oval commanded by an aquiline nose that has a smaller upper and a longer lower concave edge—looked at me with the brown eyes that go with this type of face and waited for my answer. Since few things in this world are *vrai* any more and made of the stuff they once were, I ordered the imitation saucisson d'Arles.

"After the saucisson may I suggest, Monsieur, la truite au bleu," continued the waitress, handing me a soiled piece of cardboard with a kindergarten kind of writing on it. Then, pointing with her pencil stub, she said, "After the truite, perhaps the côtelette de veau Provençale with a small salad. As to the order for the dessert, I will come back for it. To drink I can recommend to Monsieur *le petit vin du pays.* It has no name, but it is a good, light wine."

She wrote out the order in the same hand in which the menu was written, on a block of cheap paper. I kept nodding and she turned after every dish and sang out its name in the direction of the kitchen. The cook was listening through a windowlike opening through which he had stuck his head, nodding acknowledgment of the orders from the other end.

Halfway between the table and the kitchen, behind a bar, sat a woman with the calm face of the Mona Lisa, who listened, smiling with approval, and after the wine was ordered she turned majestically to take a small carafe from a zinc-covered bar and filled this with the *petit vin du pays*.

The *Guide Michelin* lists no famous restaurants in this region, and I had come to the restaurant Au Bon Coin upon the recommendation of a taxi driver I found standing in front of the Hôtel Jules César, which is the best in Arles, comfortable, but not of the luxury class. The restaurant Au Bon Coin is located in an old building, to which a cement box has been added by way of a terrace. The terrace has four windows at each side and a set of French doors that run the width of the structure. There are no fly screens, and, as in all such establishments, the selection of the color or material of curtains has not troubled anyone much. The tables in such places are sometimes alike, but the chairs certainly vary in design, or else the chairs are the same and then the tables belong to several styles.

Here there were four small tables seating two people each, two tables for four, and one large enough to seat ten to twelve people. The parquet hardwood floor ended where the French doors folded back, and at that part it was much scraped and cut from the gravel which extended from the doors to the sidewalk. On the day of my visit two of the small tables were outside on the gravel, and the one at which I sat down was shaded by a nearby tree.

The chef, who looked like a young mechanic rather than a cook, accompanied the waitress, who carried the saucisson d'Arles, and he excused himself for allowing it to come out of his kitchen. "It is regrettable," he said, "that people who have come from such faraway places as America to eat the real saucisson d'Arles in its place of origin have to content themselves with an imitation," which, he explained, was made of pork. The waitress staggered back through the gravel, then walked on the hard floor and took a tray from a stack; the woman at the bar handed her the small carafe of wine, which was placed on the tray—together with a glass—and brought to the table.

Into one corner of the terrace leaned a man dressed like a groom; he wore a tattered sporting jacket several sizes too big and an old cap. He came to life as another man, dressed in the same fashion but in clothes that fitted, came running through the restaurant. The well-dressed one was busy pulling on gloves, and as he came out on the gravel he was

met by a third man, who handed him a whip and led him to a waiting
horse and cart. After a clicking sound and cracking his whip smartly,
the man with the gloves sailed down the street behind his trotter. His
jacket was visible long after the shape and the color of horse and
wagon had become uncertain.

The sound of the hoofbeats fell away and the crunching of feet in
the sands, to which I turned, announced the waitress, who poured the
wine and asked for the bread ticket. I had just carefully detached the
badly perforated token when the clop, clop, clop of the trotter was
heard again, and as the horse came back up the boulevard, the entire
staff of the restaurant ran to the door, the guests arose from their tables,
and everybody shouted encouragement and praise. The cart went past,
the driver lowered his whip in salute and smiled with ownership's
pride. A puddle of water near the curb briefly mirrored his jacket.

"Monsieur is not eating his saucisson d'Arles?" said the waitress with
concern as she turned to the table, after having waved at the horseman.
She snapped her napkin at several dogs and eyed my table. "Go away,
Diane. Give me peace, Azore," she shouted. As the dogs moved under
the other tables and inside the restaurant the solicitous waitress said:
"But they are not as bad as all that, the saucissons, monsieur." She
pushed the plate toward me, put my fork on the plate atop the six
thin slices of saucisson d'Arles, which resembled disks of greasy red
marble, and then she went to another table, where she busied herself
ladling potage santé into the plate of a man who had the unmistakable

symptoms of a regular and satisfied patron of the establishment.

I poured myself another glass of wine from the cloudy glass jug, whose neck was full of fingerprints, and ate the sausages, which were good enough. Again the hoofbeats became audible, the staff once more rushed to the door, and this time the cart halted in front of the restaurant.

The magenta-colored nostrils of the horse distended and contracted; it was unhitched and taken to one of the trees, to which it was tied facing away from me, in a position that allowed it to swish the flies from its haunches as well as from my table.

The waitress came and wiped her face with the napkin and then threw it under her arm as she took away the plate on which the saucisson d'Arles had been. She said, "Don't derange yourself," forgetting the third-person address, "I shall be with you in a second and then I will not budge from this table again—the trout is on its way."

From then on, until the salad was cleared away, there was a crowd in front of and around my table, feeling the horse's legs and patting its rump. The chef found time to bring out carrot greens and feed them to the horse, and the owner stood with folded arms looking out into the street. Now and then he was almost pushed off the curb by the animal, which rubbed its head against the back of his multicolored tweed jacket.

He turned suddenly and put an end to the adoration of his horse by screaming for the waitress, whom he ordered to serve champagne to everyone. He took off the jacket and hung it over the vacant chair at my table and explained to me that he had acquired the horse that morning.

The Arlésienne let everything lie where it was and occupied herself with the order of the sportsman. She came back with champagne of an unknown brand, but, in the way of wine in France, nothing that comes out of a bottle is altogether bad, and this champagne, which had the color of thin light beer and its fragile white foam, was drinkable, and with the loud textiles it aided in establishing the free air of risk and reward that properly belongs around horses.

There was some singing later, and then after his coffee, whose piece of gray sugar he took from the saucer and sacrificed to his horse, the owner picked up his coat and, after brushing it with his hand, hung it over one shoulder. He untied the animal, looked at it once more, and led it away.

The waitress leaned against the tree and examined a bite on her arm inflicted by a horsefly.

"Who was that man?" I asked. She looked after him. He and the horse were stiffly walking down the exact center of the Boulevard des Lices.

"Oh, he," she said. "That is Monsieur the proprietor of this restaurant." She sucked the bite on her arm.

"And Madame," I asked, "is she the lady at the buffet?"

"*Non,*" answered the Arlésienne, "Madame and Monsieur have been divorced a long time. Madame lives in Paris."

I offer this overdetailed report on the character and personnel of this restaurant partly as a description of an average place in which I had a fair and reasonable meal, but chiefly to undo a cast-iron set of characters that live in the literature of travel. They are the half-witted, jovial owners of small restaurants and regional eating places who are usually called Papa or Mama, or *le bon Père So-and-so* or *la bonne Mère Catharine* or just *Monsieur le proprietaire* or *Madame la patronne*. They all suffer from the saccharine idiocy that infests Walt Disney's bunnies. Whether in Normandy, the Midi, or Provence, the cute inn-keeper of these reports always comes out of his kitchen rubbing his hands to explain the *spécialités de la maison*, and Madame then comes trotting from behind her buffet, from her arrangements of homemade, delicious pâtés, her special céleri ravigotte, from the secrets of her small andouilles, her priceless tartelettes and macédoines. She joins *le bon père* at the table of the tourist, and with many sad "Ohs" and shakings of the head they both bleat about the bad times one lives in and add to this a recital of their occupational ills. Later they speak of the past, nodding now with nostalgia but saying "Ah," instead of "Oh." The conversation of these figures is as static as their design, and you will hear them speak as they do now in articles written in 1898. Now as then in these stories they agree with every opinion—religious, political, economic, scientific or gastronomic—which the guest puts forward, and as that one tears himself away to say adieu—always after the most memorable meal of his life—they both come to the tavern gate and wave after him. I have met all kinds of *hôteliers*. In my travels I have looked in vain for Monsieur and Madame.

P.S. Arles is a good city to come back to. The Saucissons d'Arles are real again.

L.B., August 1948

*A*ll the marine charm of Les Sables-d'Olonne is packed into the old *port. There is a really good restaurant of no pretension called Chez Georges. Fish just pulled from the ocean can't be spoiled by the worst cook, but here is one who is worth shaking hands with. The chef's name is Courvoisier, and on his letterhead is written, "Only a hundred meters from the beach. Moderate prices. Kitchen entirely* au beurre!*"*

He has a sensible dish called Palourdes Farcies (the palourde *comes close to being a clam, and you can try this with a cherrystone-size clam as well as with a little-neck):*

RECIPE FOR BAKED CLAMS

First: Wash the clams in a little white wine; remove one shell.

Second: Make the dressing. Mix the ingredients according to your taste: parsley, shallot and garlic, finely chopped, lemon juice, salt and pepper, all mixed with butter.

Third: Put the above dressing over the clams and bake in a hot oven from seven to eight minutes. This dish of some twelve clams is a kind of maritime *Escargot.* It is served with a very light wine called Muscadet from grapes that grow in the valley of the Loire.

You eat here under a faded awning, and the wine costs fifty cents a full quart. Before you the masts of ships move slowly in and out of the harbor. Occasionally a small jovial man, with a belt let out to the last notch and with a face highly colored by both the weather and the bottle, will pass and look with sharp blue eyes into the restaurant and point to his ship, called Monique, *and to a sign that advertises* PROMENADE SUR MER. *Then, nursing a Pernod and eating* moules *or the above-described Palourdes Farcies, he will wait for an offer.*

THE
TREASURED CLIENT

THERE IS NO BILL of fare. The headwaiter recites the menu to you, first the various things to start with, like smoked salmon, caviar, goose-liver paste and things in oil and vinegar. Then he makes a pause and tells you about the soups, the fish and the lobsters and langoustes. Then he puts that down on his block and asks you about the next course, the meats, the game, the chicken, duck or goose, and when he has the order—and he will not be happy if you just take one dish—he calls the wine steward, who rattles off his beautiful litany of vintages with half-closed eyes. Then you sit back, and butter is brought, and bread, and a napkin unfolded in your lap, and you can look around.

There was that day a woman at the table opposite me, a treasured and spoiled client to whose table the headwaiter regularly returned like a mother bird to the nest of its young. You have seen her before. You have been pushed by her in an elevator at Saks Fifth Avenue. You've seen her in Buenos Aires or Palm Beach and listened to her complaints about the service in the best restaurants of New York or Beverly Hills.

She's ancient, formidable and grim, but she knows the good life and never stops chewing like a rabbit. You try to guess at her nationality but you can't decide. She's international and eternal. An assistant headwaiter was carving a chicken for her then, while she still munched whatever she had had before, and the wine waiter half filled her glass, watching her face, and then smiled as she nodded under the big hat, which wobbled in assent. She tapped the glass with a fingernail as a signal to pour more wine into it. She had eaten the breast of the bird after it had simmered over an alcohol lamp in a sauce for a while. She worked with a knife and fork, and then took the wing joints in her fingers and nibbled at them, and as a concession to elegance she stuck the two little fingers away from her hands as she chewed. She wiped the grease from her mouth after that and sat still again, and, after the headwaiter had bowed down to her and she had ordered the dessert, a box in which six peaches lay bedded in soft cotton was brought. While the assistant headwaiter, who had carved her chicken, was busy cutting up my duck, a younger man occupied himself with the peaches. The process was as adroit as the work of a precision machinist. He speared the fruit with a slim fork and with a sharp knife he made a small incision in the skin, then quickly he ran the knife around the peach and neatly placed the skin on a serving plate. She was the while picking her teeth and watching the two processes, alternating from the peach to the mirror of her compact, which she held up with her other hand to look at her teeth.

"Where have you been, Sebastian?" she inquired after looking up at the man.

He put the peach on her plate and, rubbing his hands, he said, "I was in Dortmund; I worked for the Boches in an armament factory." He spread out his fingers. "They are a little rough yet, Madame," he said, "but I take care of them and they are rapidly improving." He rubbed his hands nervously again.

She looked up at him the way a fish looks out of the window of an aquarium. For a moment she was afraid he would tell her more of his story. She asked next for a grape, and I said to myself, "What can you do with a grape?"

Sebastian brought a vaselike glass standing in a silver base. It was half filled with water. Then he brought the basket of fruit, and with special silver prongs he lifted a grape and dipped it into the water and slowly moved it up and down, and then placed it on her plate. She had coffee and brandy and eventually left with two purple patches on her cheeks, after the headwaiter had run outside to wake up her chauffeur.

TO BE A GOURMET

THERE IS A LOT of talk about the gourmet these days and about the rules and the art of eating—in fact, several magazines are devoted to this subject. Any restaurant that would try to satisfy the true gourmet would be bankrupt in a matter of weeks. The popular concept of the gourmet is that of a seallike, happy creature of Gargantuan appetite, who sticks a napkin inside his collar, dunks bread into the sauces and throws on the floor plates that are not properly heated. His nourishment is catalogued as caviar, pâté de foie gras, truffles, pheasant and crêpes Suzette. He drinks only the proper wine, but on closing his eyes and rinsing it in and out through his teeth he is able to tell you not only the age of the wine but also the number on the barrel in which it has been aged. He is thought of as a middle-aged man (never a woman), portly and jolly, given to reciting toasts that are spiked with French terms. His extravagant dinners take on the aspect of an eating contest rather than a good meal.

Actually, the true gourmet, like the true artist, is one of the unhappiest creatures existent. His trouble comes from so seldom finding what he constantly seeks: perfection.

To be a gourmet you must start early, as you must begin riding early to be a good horseman. You must live in France; your father must have been a gourmet. Nothing in life must interest you but your stomach. With hands trembling, you must approach the meal about which you have worried all day and risk dying of a stroke if it isn't perfect.

The last time I was at the Ritz in Paris I noticed a novice waiter, called a *piccolo,* standing in the dining room. He was about fourteen years old, with a student's pale face. Every so often he hid behind a marble column while he popped into his mouth, one by one, strawberries that he had swiped from the breakfast buffet. The captain on duty surprised him in the act and pulled him into the room, holding him gingerly by one ear. There in front of the buffet he delivered a long lecture, the gist of which was that the good things displayed there were only for the distinguished guests of the house. The captain, seeing that I had observed the scene, came to the table. "Very good boy, otherwise," he said. "He will be all right once he gets the hang of things." The boy, he explained, was the son of the owner of a tavern in Rouen; this man had a brother who was a maître d'hôtel at the Tour d'Argent, the famous Paris restaurant. When the boy was born, his father had written his brother to reserve for the boy a place as an apprentice, and because Monsieur the Maître d'Hôtel of the Tour d'Argent was a great friend of Monsieur the Maître d'Hôtel of the Ritz, the fortunate connection had been made, and the boy was thus in line for a fine career—after several years' apprenticeship. His counterpart below stairs, the one who becomes an apprentice in the kitchen, starts with peeling potatoes and scrubbing. In this climate the gourmet can survive. The climate of democracy is fatal to him.

At one time the gourmet had a chance in America. A horde of European chefs, maîtres d'hôtel, managers, waiters and cooks came to America.

Walking off the boats, they went straight to the newly erected large hotels, some of which, for several years, matched the standards of the European hotel de grand luxe.

One of the greatest hotels and restaurants of that time was the old Knickerbocker, owned and managed by a man named Regan, who walked through his hotel with two detectives because he was afraid that some foreign waiter might knife him. A complaint from a customer, in these days, was followed by immediate discharge.

When employees of the old Waldorf reported sick, they actually had to be in bed, for it was Mr. Boldt's habit to send detectives to their homes to check up.

As for hiring new help—that was no problem for management; outside the doors of every New York employment office were long lines of job seekers, each with a dossier of references from the best European houses.

As immigration became restricted, trained hotel personnel became fewer. Now virtually all of the old-timers have disappeared. Replacing them, particularly those employed in the kitchen, is one of the great problems of hotel keeping, for Americans don't like to be cooks.

Hotel managers tell you Americans make poor cooks. They say they lack the—"I don't know what." By the same rule it is said that no American makes a good musician or painter, but he does—once he is interested.

The fault is that no one has taken the trouble to make the profession of cooking attractive to young Americans—to inform them that being a good chef is one of the most satisfying, honored and remunerative callings. Another deterrent, perhaps, is the costume. The chef's traditional white hat, jacket and apron probably seem like sissy stuff to the prospective kitchen candidate.

America is a land of healthy appetites. It is not in the American character to live in order to eat. Rather, the reverse is true. Many try, but just as Americans don't make good gigolos, neither do they make good gourmets.

The desperate rituals of the various food fraternities and gourmet clubs are as authentic as the war dances Indians stage for tourists at Western railroad depots. The food served at the dinners of the societies is relatively good, as banquets go. The trouble with these affairs is not so much the cooking as the commercial note that is injected throughout the meal. You are accosted by salesmen for newly invented salad dressings, deep-frying fats or starchless spaghetti. These fellows are followed by liquor and champagne salesmen who creep around the table taking orders.

Such get-togethers fail to do anything for the cause, mainly because no good chef can prepare a truly superb meal for more than a dozen people.

Occasionally I am looked upon as a gourmet and when I go out with friends, they say, "Oh, let him order—he knows everything about food and wine."

Having been born in Europe and lived in hotels most of my life, I do know how to read a menu and can usually tell a poor restaurant by instinct. As for being a gourmet, I disqualify in every respect. I eat too much, drink too much and love company at the table. I use the menu without attention to rules. The geography of my stomach is antigourmet in the extreme. For example, I long for a small shack along

the Danube, at the side of the old stone bridge in Regensburg, Bavaria. There, over an open fire, in a kitchen two hundred years old and by a secret recipe kept in the family, sausages the size of a small finger are broiled.

They are served on a bed of sauerkraut, with the same brown beer my grandfather brewed. On a good day, I can eat a dozen of these for my second breakfast, around ten in the morning, and drink two quarts of that beer.

I remember with sadness an old fisherman in Miami on whose boat I worked long ago. There was a shack there, also on a pier, where we sold the fish. But we always kept one for ourselves, which we cooked in the shack. No fish has ever been better.

In the whole world there are no better lobsters than those that come from Maine. There are no better steaks anywhere than in America. I often go to the sea-food bar on the lower level of the Grand Central Station in New York to eat a clam pan roast. For Italian food I like Angelo's in Mulberry Street, or Tony's San Marino in East 53rd Street; for fish, Sweet's Restaurant near the fish market in downtown New York. The best German food is served by Luchow's, whose proprietor tries to keep the specialties of the house as authentically indigestible as they must be. The sauerbraten and potato pancakes there are superb, the red cabbage and lentil soup expertly cooked. Geese, venison and *Hasenpfeffer* are done as if Herr Walterspiel himself were at the oven, and you leave satisfied. If a prize were given for the treatment of beer, then it would go to this place. The pipes are kept clean, it's not too cold and there is enough of it drawn so that it is always fresh.

*P*rinces, generals, deep-sea captains are not allowed any humor. The captain of the United States always sends me a note, asking me to sit at the captain's table. My heart goes out to him. I would like to answer, "Dear Captain, let me invite you to my table. I sit upstairs in a small restaurant, alone, and would be very happy to have you join me."

THE SPAGHETTI TRAIN

I CAME INTO the dining car late. Patrizzi was finished with his breakfast
—that is, with the orange juice, toast, coffee and egg part of it. The
other passengers had left. The crew seated at the end of the car had
faces like wax figures in the bright sunlight.

Patrizzi lifted his nose and sniffed. "Spaghetti," he said. "Real
spaghetti?"

"Yes," said the steward, "we are eating now. Back there the cooks
are from Napoli."

"I'd very much like some of your spaghetti," said Patrizzi. "Enough
for me and my friend here."

The steward said the cooks would be delighted.

The spaghetti came, cooked with butter and garlic and with a handful
of chopped parsley strewn over it.

"Some people condemn the Italian kitchen," said Patrizzi, "and also
the French. They say they can't eat the food on account of the garlic.
Now there is no good cooking except with garlic—but in the hands of a
bad cook it is poisonous. It must be used with extreme care. The most
reckless are the English; once they take to cooking with garlic they

use it so freely it's impossible even for an Italian to eat it. For example, Somerset Maugham once served truffles wrapped in bacon, a very good dish. The truffles profit by the flavor of the bacon, the bacon is enhanced by the truffles, and I like it. But at that luncheon I bit into a truffle and inside was a whole clove of garlic. Both the truffle and bacon were ruined. And the garlic, which, incidentally, was also in the chicken we were served and on the toast that came with the cheese and in the salad —it was so predominant that the whole meal was ruined. Now take this spaghetti—simple, ultra-simple—but with a bouquet like the finest wine."

The train had stopped at a small station to wait for a clear track. Outside the window were the cars of a freight train. The boxcar doors were open, and inside were benches on which sat people most of whom had no shoes and all of whose eyes were fixed on the spaghetti and the bottle of wine on our table. I said that it seemed to me that in Italy there was a belief that God had made some people rich and others poor, and that the tragedy was that not only the rich but the poor also believed it, and consequently it would never change.

Patrizzi answered, "And don't you think this is as it should be and a very good arrangement? Have you ever seen an Italian peasant envious of those who have fine cars, or horses, or jewels? No, they admire those things, knowing they never can have them for themselves. They adopt a detachment, like people who go to the theater, or to an art gallery to admire priceless paintings. They are glad to know that these things exist, but they also know they never can own them. Just from looking at these things they derive a pleasure that possession never brings, because possession means worry." He snapped his finger. "More," he shouted back to the steward.

POULETS DE BRESSE

WHEN WE CAME the next day to Vienne, we wanted to stop at the famous Pyramide, once, and perhaps still, one of the great temples of gastronomy. On that day the chef-proprietor of the establishment was in an off mood or else the publicity he had received had caused him to suffer from *folie de grandeur:* he had several near nervous breakdowns in our presence, screamed in his kitchen and behaved in his dining room like a police official rather than a restaurateur. It is as damaging to a low bistro as to the best of restaurants when the proprietor discovers that he is a rare and remarkable man with his pots and bottles. Upon seeing his picture in various publications and reading a description of himself he becomes obese with acquired personality.

The specialties of the house here, besides a fine dish consisting of the tails of crayfish au gratin, is the chicken from Bresse. I have followed pigs on stilts looking for truffles and I know a little about the growing of grapes and the bottling of wine and the making of brandy, but the raising of chickens of Bresse is still a remote subject to me. It must, however, be a mammoth industry in France; for while you get hams from half a dozen places and even the sardine cans bear the names of various regions, the chicken served in a good restaurant in France is always from Bresse, and it is an excellent bird, as everyone will agree.

I was able to arrest the attention of the proprietor of the Pyramide long enough to ask him about the chicken. He told me: "Of chickens

I can tell you that they are never better than from September to February. Their meat then is well made and is not insipid. After February, the meat is not as tender nor as white. These we have now are young ones, four or five months old, and I am not too happy about them, for they have no character. We use them only for entrees. For the roasting chicken we must wait; it must be older. As for Bresse, I know as much about it as you do. I suppose Bresse is to chicken what Cologne is to water—some Eau de Cologne is made in Cologne, some in Paris. Some chickens come from Bresse; some people raise their own chickens of Bresse; some poulets de Bresse are raised right here in Vienne. At least those I serve are."

The chicken we were served was cooked in cream, flavored with estragon, and it was so-so. The wine, not being subject to the temper of cooks nor the season of chickens, was of the very best.

LADY MENDL'S DINING ROOM, VILLA TRIANON, VERSAILLES

THS WAS ONE of the happiest and most successful rooms conceived by Lady Mendl. It was a room resembling a tent built according to her design. It was of pale green and with a ceiling of green and white stripes. She had immense panes of glass placed so that there was the illusion of dining outdoors. On the side toward the house the room took on solidity, with statuary, a platform for the orchestra, and room for the reception of the guests and for coffee after dinner. It was like a most elegant private restaurant, well thought out, efficient and gay.

The dinners were exemplary and simple, and the rules laid down for the serving of meals were sensible. The basic laws were a cool room and hot plates, the floral decorations low, so that one could look across at the other people and talk to anyone without bending around a vase or candlesticks. Her love of things green and white went so far that the place cards were tropical leaves on which the names were written in white ink. The lighting was indirect and the service the ancient Russian, which is the most convenient for the guest at table as well as the help. It consists of a small rolling table, or, in the case of larger parties, of several of them. The food and the plates are placed thereon, and the servitors arrange the food on the plate and set it before the guest.

Since there was always a small green-and-white menu at the table the people knew what was coming, and they could choose more of the first course, if they liked that, or more of the second, if that course had more appeal to them.

The French service, the passing of the heavy silver platters, is awkward. Not infrequently the butler and footmen are hot and perspiring. They break up conversations as they lean down between people, passing the food. Frequently things are spilled. This style of service is not too easy on either guest or attendant.

I have never known any hostess, hotel manager, chef or maître d'hôtel who gave the attention to a party that Lady Mendl did. It started with an inspection of the room, with searching for dust with the white gloves. With acquainting herself anew with the chef and his problems. With seeing to the reception. That is, checking who received the guests and helped them from their cars, who opened the door for them, who took their coats, who showed them into the salon. She went over every detail of the service, and in the case of people whom she had not met she informed herself about them.

LUNCH WITH BOSY

THE RESTAURANT is called La Victoire, and the owner is also the head-waiter. There is also a chef, and a galley slave who can be seen from time to time as he comes from the vapors of the small kitchen and puts a stack of clean plates or silverware on a sideboard. This is a cheap-expensive restaurant—above those where you can eat reasonably well for a dollar and a half with a glass of wine.

This place has pretensions, but it serves the clientele of my novel and that is why I come here every day. The chef alone has integrity. He knocks about with his pots and pans in his small inferno, flashes of fire rising from his oven—and he has shown me a very primitive but sure way of telling when spaghetti is done. You throw one piece against the wall: if it sticks there, it's just right. If it falls off, let it cook a little longer.

One morning I took a long walk with my dog, Bosy, and stopped for lunch at La Victoire. Paris is nice to dogs. They are allowed to run free in most of the parks and on the streets and are admitted into all the restaurants that I know.

The proprietor came, rubbing his hands, and said to me, "Monsieur, I can recommend so and so and this and that"—and then he said, "And you son, what does he desire to eat?" ("Your son" is the form of address for a dog in Paris.) I said, "Oh, give him anything." The proprietor tilted his head and put his hands together and he said, "Perhaps a little meat, some vegetable in a little broth?" I said yes, that would be very nice.

The meal was served, for both the master and the dog. Bosy received great care—a napkin was placed on the floor and on it a silver bowl—and he ate with appetite. The headwaiter bent and talked to him, and the waiter picked up the empty dish and with the napkin wiped Bosy's mouth. I lit a cigar with the coffee and asked for the bill. I hate to look at restaurant bills and add them up, and a bill must really be outrageous before I make a fuss. But this one was. I called the waiter and said, "I'm afraid you gave me the wrong bill." "No, no, monsieur, that is your bill." I said, "But I only had the menu here—at one thousand two hundred francs—and who had the steak at five hundred, the string beans at one hundred and the consommé at eighty; and besides, you charge for two covers."

"Ah, monsieur, the second—that is for your son's lunch," he said. I had to pay.

LUCHOW'S

THE GERMAN DICTIONARY defines the word "*gemütlich*" as good-natured, jolly, agreeable, cheerful, hearty, simple and affectionate, full of feeling, comfortable, cozy, snug; and "*Gemütlichkeit*" as a state of mind, an easygoing disposition, good nature, geniality, pleasantness, a freedom from pecuniary or political cares, comfortableness.

Of the remaining few New York places that can call themselves restaurants, Luchow's triumphs in *Gemütlichkeit*. This quality, strong as the handshake of an old friend and a slap on the shoulder, is nowhere more honest. It enfolds you as you enter into the agreeable paneled halls.

A fragrance, delicate but not weak, and slightly male, rides the air. It composes itself of the aromas of solid cooking, of roast geese and ducks, of game and Huhn im Topf, of various things, sour and spicy, and tender cutlets simmering among *Steinpilze*.

Through it is wafted the bouquet of good wines, and above this hangs the blue cloud of the smoke of rare cigars. This obscures the stag and moose heads that are part of the décor, along with samples of the ironmonger's art.

The mood is supported by music equally enduring. The orchestra plays such aids to digestion as "Die Forelle" *von* Schubert, *The Tales of Hoffman, William Tell*, and "Sylvia," and such romantic fare as "The Evening Star." Occasionally a belly laugh echoes through the *Nibelungen*

Ring, for Luchow's clientele for the most part are an uninhibited and happy lot.

Every kind of restaurant finds its own public. Several of the best in New York have a patronage so select that they are checked into the premises with elaborate and embarrassing care and seated according to a rigid protocol.

Mr. Seute, now vice-president of Luchow's, but still functioning as the Herr Ober, is free of all the pretentiousness of his colleagues. He runs the restaurant, he directs traffic, and he places people with simple logic, where there is room. The doors are open and anyone is welcome. In the words of the venerable Mr. Seute: "You don't need a *gestarchte* shirt front to get in here. The only way you cannot come is *mitaus* a necktie."

It is as simple and as sound as this.

Along with the food, the authenticity of its atmosphere, it gives me restful ease and has ever since I have been in America. I find it one of those places in which the mind hums in harmony with its surroundings. I have spent many pleasant hours there, engaged in leaning back and looking at the assemblage of people. There are the large parties who call themselves "Our Bunch" and from whom most of the belly laughs issue.

At other tables sit priests, students, national figures (the late Jules Bache was a regular Sunday-night client), diplomats, politicians with Italian friends in race-track suits with pearl stickpins in their neckties, theatrical folk with broad-shouldered blondes who have brought along Mama and Papa. It is alive with children and with dogs. It is the most kaleidoscopic restaurant in New York. Its waiters are the last of their kind, upstanding citizens, without a trace of servility in their make-up.

They are very busy people and sometimes serve you *mitaus* a napkin. Also, they are apt to hand you the menu upside down and, a moment after handing it to you, take it back again, mumbling, "*Der Sauerbraten is aus*" and dramatically eliminate this delicacy from the menu with a bold stroke of a pencil stub, never longer than a smoked-out cigarette. They will then advise you about what's left in the kitchen, and also on anything else you want to know. It's a solid body of men, trustworthy and sound in the head. Their opinions are as definite as those of another race of philosophers, the New York taxi driver.

The only being, as yet, not in complete harmony with the establishment is Mr. Leonard Jan Mitchell, the new proprietor. He runs about the place with cautionary solicitude, worried lest he disturb anyone, much like a man whose wife has lost a glove in a movie theater and forgotten where she sat. It is most curious that a modern man who looks as if he were in training for the winter Olympics should find his happiness in being the curator of a Goulash and Wiener Schnitzel Emporium, worrying about the consistency of Nudel Soup.

It is to be hoped that this one flaw will be corrected, that a steady diet of Kartoffelknödel, of Wiener Schnitzel, and the greatest of the delights of Luchow's, the Pfannkuchen mit Preisselbeeren, together with the proper amounts of the various beers and good wines, will pad his cheeks, round out his stomach and put the roses on his nose.

We shall then no longer look at him with pity and suspicion and, as we did recently, ask Mr. Seute, a man of proper weight, "Who is that man there?"

And Mr. Seute will not have to answer ashamedly behind his menu, as he did, "Oh, that one, *mitaus* der stomach, *das ist der* Boss."

*L*ady Mendl liked dogs and people slim, and, while there was superb cooking and always enough at parties, when we were dining en famille there sometimes wasn't.

We sat at dinner in Versailles—Elsie, Charles, Hilda, Gayelord Hauser and I—and there were "bitkis" on the menu. This dish is a super chicken hamburger, the chicken being scraped and shredded before cooking, and served with a sauce in which sour cream plays a part. There were a great many of these bitkis, but they were the circumference of a quarter each. Soon we had eaten all but one, and eventually the one left in a small splotch of its fine sauce was passed again. The butler wandered around the table with it. I wanted it very badly; Hilda wanted it; Elsie was the only one with character enough to wave it away; Charles wanted it most of all. There was a great restraining all around, and finally, with anguish in his voice, Charles said, "Give it to the growing boy; he needs it most." With that he sadly pointed to the biggest man at the table—to Gayelord Hauser. For a moment there was hope, because Joseph held in his other hand a large silver dish filled with the most beautiful green spinach, cooked exactly to the doctor's liking and according to his recipe. We all were certain that the prophet of vegetable juice and roughage would ladle himself some of his own medicine. The good doctor was a disappointment; unashamed, he grabbed the last bitki, waving the look-younger-and-live-longer stuff away.

AMONG
THE ARABS

"You will enjoy the best we have to offer—a dish that is for sultans and kings," he said.

The result was, in truth, a memorable meal. Early that morning there arrived an old Arab with gray hair and beard. He poured water on the earth near a primitive, conical stove built of clay. Nearby a ram was tethered to a tree. The Arab slaughtered the animal by severing its head; he hung the body on the tree and let it bleed, while he removed the pelt and the intestines. He cut a strong forked limb from an olive tree, removed the bark, impaled the ram on it so that the crutch of the branch held it about a foot off the ground.

Inside the oven dry wood was burning. He frequently washed the ram's carcass and checked on the fire. All these preparations were done in silence.

When the oven was at last sufficiently hot, he took out the embers. Then he cleaned the ashes from the round opening on the top—the great waves of heat rising allowed him only to flick his hand over it, but the disturbed air blew the ashes away. He sprinkled water inside the oven; it hissed and turned to steam. Then he got a wire, secured the mutton to the branch and placed it inside the cone of the oven.

He mixed some mud and closed the opening on top, then took some of the dung of the animal and placed it in a cuplike depression which he made atop the oven. When this dung is dry, the meat is done. He made more mud, and wherever he saw steam escaping from the oven, he smeared mud and closed the cracks. He then washed his hands and wrapped up the head of the ram, the intestines, lung, heart, and so forth, all into the pelt, for that was his pay.

The cooking took two hours; at the end of that time an opening was made at the top of the oven. Protecting his hands with a towel, he lifted out the mutton and rushed it to a low table set up on the grass. The guests, seated on pillows, ate with their fingers. The outside of the ram had the texture of the crust of homemade bread. It was the most tasteful mutton I have ever experienced, truly fit for a pasha.

CAVIAR

IN PARIS THERE WAS a great gourmet who had Cartier construct a little gold ball which he wore on the other end of his watch chain. He would go to one of the good restaurants, have his plate heaped with caviar and then drop the golden sphere from a foot above the plate. If it passed through the caviar without effort, he pronounced it first rate. If the ball got stuck in its passage and did not reach the bottom of the plate, he sent the plate and the black stuff back to the kitchen.

I have never been quite this fussy when eating caviar, though I do not blame the gentleman for performing the ritual. Caviar has always been within my reach, since I was born into the hotel trade and raised therein. It was available in various grades in all the cold-food departments of the many establishments for which I worked.

The best caviar I ever found was in the old Ritz in New York, and to avail myself of some, I and several bus boys in the Banquet Department invented a system of thievery which worked very well for a while. The *garde-manger*, as the man in charge of caviar and other delicatessen is called, carefully weighed the cans of caviar, before and after each banquet. We overcame this problem by burying in the bottom of the can some object—usually a silver peppermill—which equaled in weight a large coffee cup of the stuff. The caviar was later enjoyed, in a corner of the magnificent Ritz ballroom, under a darkened crystal chandelier against priceless tapestry, and with some millionaire's leftover wine. Like all stolen things, it tasted wonderful. Those were the best caviar days I can remember.

Caviar is to dining what a sable coat is to a girl in evening dress. In those days of maîtres d'hôtel who were properly trained and knew their business, it was a compulsory item on the menu of any consequence. There was no escape. A birthday, a christening, New Year's, Christmas, a marriage, an engagement, state dinner—every occasion demanded it.

Even today it is not just snobbism that demands caviar, but, like the rites that go with High Mass, the solemn preparations of crêpes Suzette,

213

the flaming swords with lamb skewered on them, the serving of caviar makes for drama: the wheeling in of wagons, the blocks of ice in the shapes of swans, bears, turtles. (I have seen caviar served buried in the midriffs of reclining ice nudes bedded in ferns and roses.) All is silent except the gypsies' violins and the popping of champagne corks.

The people who sit at adjoining tables suddenly also must have caviar. The maître d'hôtel pushes back his cuffs and, with the smallest spoon in the establishment, carefully digs out a pigeon's-egg-sized portion and places it on your plate, at $7.50.

As a young man I had a cozy picture about caviar production. In my mind's eye I saw the broad mouth of a river, which I comfortably called the Malossol; in it a log of big Russkies, with beards like in *Boris Godunov*, were singing boat songs and wading and carefully lifting immense sturgeons out of the water while relieving them gently of their eggs with a soft, sluicy swish and then putting them back again, like milked cows let out to pasture. This tableau was in the style and colors of Chagall, and quite pleasant. I ate my caviar in relaxed, uncomplicated gourmand fashion.

I got straightened out after reading a journal devoted to the facts of life—a sturgeon's life, that is. After the sturgeon are caught, they are clubbed and their bellies slit open to remove the ovarian sac that contains the roe. The ovaries are then gently forced through a sieve of fine threads on a wooden frame to separate the eggs from the sac. The eggs are then processed with varying degrees of salt. The salting is done under directions of a *nastavnic*, a master taster. There aren't many of these masters around today, and caviar buyers swear that they can tell who prepared the roe just by rolling a sample of the eggs around on their tongues.

This rolling the eggs around the tongue is comparable to the wine-tasting legend, according to which a lover of a certain vintage can tell which barrel the wine comes from. I have at one time had the great pleasure of looking on as a blindfolded connoisseur was asked to decide whether the wine in a certain bottle was red or white—and he couldn't tell.

To make caviar, a lady sturgeon is needed, first of all. This fish, known to ichthyologists as *genus acipenser*, has twenty different species, varying widely in size and weight. The sterlet sturgeon never grows larger than three feet, while the giant beluga can get up to twenty-four feet in length, weigh in at one ton and live to be three hundred years old.

They mature in about fourteen years and, when caught, give up to three million-odd eggs.

Sturgeon live out most of their lives at the bottom of the sea, nosing around on the sofa-soft sea floor for the snails, tiny crabs and small fishes on which they must feed because of their toothlessness. In the spring, they go up large rivers to spawn and they sometimes do so later in the year as well for some mysterious reason. Today, almost all caviar comes from sturgeon that manage to survive in the Caspian Sea. The best for caviar are found in the southern, sweet water, the Iranian portion of the sea.

But the Caspian Sea wasn't always the only source of sturgeon. Before 1900 caviar was exported from the United States to Europe, competing favorably with the Russian product. The American caviar industry was centered in the East, but sturgeon were found as far west as the Sacramento River in California, and caviar for export was sold in San Francisco. Almost all of the United States caviar was sent to Europe, since Americans had so little taste for it at that time that caviar sandwiches were given away free in saloons with a glass of nickel beer, as they are given away today on planes, along with free cocktails.

But alas, caviar lovers, I must now sadden your hearts. Photographs taken from on high show that there is doom all around us. From the Caspian Sea to Astrakhan, the center of the Russian caviar industry, the water is evaporating, leaving only immense mud flats. The Volga is being diverted for other purposes; there are huge dams, and no one has bothered about installing fish ladders. In the other rivers of Russia, the royal fish is being killed off by industrial pollution. Like the American buffalo, the sturgeon seems to be headed for the museum and caviar for near extinction.

I don't know any of my young friends that would cross the street to get it anyway, and when they take a canape of it from a tray at a cocktail party they wear a disgusted look and ask whether there is a towel handy to wipe their hands on.

Although it is a "health food," maybe it is on the way out with the rococo way of life, with the old things, with kings and queens, monocles and sabres, Lubitsch films and Winterhalter ladies, agreeable afternoon seductions and the good wines of yesterday. So I shall examine it with *tristesse*—a last look before I step into the frozen-food locker and close the door after myself.

In France once, traveling off the high roads, I came to the city of Auch and met a man there who had the *Guide Michelin* in his hands, who told me that he followed this guide on his holidays. The way a man follows the races, he visited hotels and restaurants, to check on the quality and to complain if it was not as stated. His name was Michel Brodsky; he was a Russian of advanced years and not the most optimistic of people.

He showed me the book with the red cover, and he said, "You know the editors of this guide on eating, marching with the times, have become much less demanding than they were once; in fact, they now are disposed to great tolerance, so much so that the mere fact that a restaurant which offers its clientele a washroom that has a seat on its toilet is immediately awarded a star."

In the city of Auch, Monsieur Brodsky pointed out a small hotel especially recommended by the *Guide.* This place was the target of his critical interest: one of those ancient establishments of beaten exterior, in a side street, solid and somber, and of cozy warmth when you enter it. It had its good clientele, this old hotel. Soon, Monsieur Brodsky, with pad and pencil, was at the caviar, at the table next to me; he knocked on his glass with his caviar knife and the half-deaf maître d'hôtel came running and went through a Marcel Marceau act of agony in listening to the complaint and miming his apologies and concerns. Finally, he offered to take the blinis that had been served with the caviar back to the kitchen. Monsieur Brodsky, however, said that it was hopeless, for the cook who had turned out these would certainly not win a prize with his next attempt. Monsieur Brodsky said to me, "Look at it: it's a pancake, not a blini."

Blini is to caviar what ham is to ham and eggs. In Russia, caviar has always been an important part of life. Before the revolution caviar was eaten mostly during the two-week period before Lent, with blinis that were made of buckwheat mixed with white flour, sugar, salt and yeast to make a mixture that was left overnight to rise. The batter was then poured into hot cast-iron pans which had been lightly brushed with a feather dipped in grease. The pancakes—the size of a teacup saucer—were brought to the table where everyone's plate held some melted butter. With this, sour cream at room temperature and caviar—either fresh or pressed, sturgeon or salmon, depending on the financial status of the family—was served. In those days, too, the children took red caviar sandwiches to school with them, if they were lucky enough to have

parents who could afford to send them to school.

There are few people who know about caviar in America; oh, there is a Romanoff or an Obolensky who knows, but not many others. In America, caviar is served with an assortment of chopped-up onions, whites of eggs, yellows of eggs—and that is quite all right, if you want to kill the taste of it. I like it plain, with lemon only, and, of course, with those little thin blinis, which no one knows how to make any more. You have trouble getting them even in the best restaurants in Paris; and the Russians of the old school, who kept up tradition—alas, they are passing away, and with them the old-fashioned Russian restaurants. The young Russians don't care; they all become scientists.

There is one cardinal rule about eating caviar at a restaurant. Always go to places where a lot of it is consumed, for once a can is opened, it is the most perishable of articles and it quickly becomes not only unpalatable but turns dangerous. Caviar poisoning, while an elegant fashion of dying, is not pleasant.

The world of caviar eaters is small, and sooner or later you run into a fellow devotee. I met Monsieur Brodsky again in the bar of the good ship S.S. *United States*. The conversation was of caviar.

"You can eat the price of your passage in caviar on this ship alone. It is free; have some," said Monsieur Brodsky. "They buy eight thousand pounds a year for this ship. They run after you with it; it is the only place where you must say, 'Please, no more caviar.' You can have it at every meal and you get it until the farewell dinner whether you want it or not."

"Caviar?" said the steward in the bar.

"These, of course," said Monsieur Brodsky, "are not the eggs of the sterlet that were reserved for the Czar. These are a grade below, but very good stuff."

Caviar grading is an extremely specialized skill and requires many, many years of practice. The freshness of the fish, its size, the size and shape of the eggs and the fish's spawning time are all factors entering into the indefinable sense of taste that it takes an expert years to acquire.

After the caviar has been graded, it is stored in cans and kept under refrigeration until enough cans have accumulated to make up a shipment. The cans are sealed with a band of rubber which keeps air out and yet permits a little movement of the tops so that the caviar eggs don't get pressed too tightly against the can top and break, releasing the oil inside them.

For shipping purposes, three of the cans are sewn into a cloth sack. Eighteen of these sacks are then put into racks inside huge wooden kegs. The sacks and the kegs are always surrounded with ice, since caviar must be kept at a temperature of between 28° and 32° Fahrenheit.

During the war years, when refrigerated ships weren't available, no caviar came to the U.S. from Russia or Iran. Right after the war ended, an enterprising American importer filled the hold of a liberty ship with ice, loaded it up with caviar kegs packed right on the ice and brought it back to the caviar-starved gourmets of America.

The most common types of caviar are those from the beluga sturgeon, which have the largest eggs, and are preferred by Americans; the schipp and osetrina types, with medium-sized eggs from sturgeon that are usually less than half the size of the beluga; and the tiny eggs that come from the sevruga sturgeon, a comparatively small fish that grows to a length of only five feet. Europeans generally like the smaller sizes of caviar. The very special rare green-gold caviar that the Czar, Stalin and the Shah ate came from the bellies of the sterlet, and only a handful of other people have ever tasted it.

Within each type of caviar there are also a number of variations possible. The color of the caviar, for example, may range from light gray to coal black, depending upon how close to the spawning period the fish were caught. The closer to spawning, the more gray the caviar becomes.

I was becoming gray too, for we had had several vodkas and a great deal of the ship's supply of caviar. The steward came with a new tray.

"Would you care for a little more caviar, sir?" he asked.

"No, thank you."

To change the subject I started to talk about Tolstoi. "A great lover of caviar," said Monsieur Brodsky, so I got up and we walked to the little restaurant that is decorated with blue velvet and crystal chandeliers —and there on the table, in ice, was a can of caviar.

The rare black stuff that is so costly and so very delicious is brought to the United States in quantities of seventy tons a year. When you imagine all the people who can afford it—from the Oscar Award dinners in California, the state dinners for both our allies and enemies at the various embassies, the servings at countless de luxe restaurants all through America, the gourmet dinners offered in the sky by all the airlines and on board the ships that go to sea, and the millions of cocktail parties from La Jolla to Southampton—then seventy tons a year seems little. That it isn't more is due to the fact that most caviar is served with those abominable little teaspoons. Seventy tons a year *is* indeed but a small mound of black goodies for the richest nation on earth. I am speaking, of course, of the de luxe caviar, *malossol*, which means "slightly salted." There are lesser grades, which do not come within the calculation of the true caviar lover. They come in miserable little glass pots with metal cover. Year in, year out, in sun and snow, they frame salami and pastrami in the windows of delicatessen shops, together with pickle jars and smoked herrings. This kind is buckshot size, black glue that causes your teeth to stick together and locks your jaws, and is sold in great volume.

What many true caviar lovers call the very best, better even than malossol, is the slightly less expensive pressed caviar. Aristotle Onassis, a true caviar expert, eats this by preference. It is a staple in his diet and is kept at all restaurants and night clubs he frequents.

The Hotel de Paris in Monte Carlo, where Ari has his meals, is one of the last great restaurants. At a dinner given there by a Texan, the menu started with baked potatoes, hollowed out and filled with caviar, and very good.

Christian Dior used to put caviar on the bottom of small dishes and then have an egg cooked over them and serve the whole cold as an hors d'œuvre.

I have a preference for fresh caviar and will shamelessly attend a dinner party of awful people to partake of it, if I know the hostess has enough big serving spoons. Madame Vandable, the wife of the owner of Maxim's of Paris and an outspoken woman, once said, "*Mon Dieu,* Ludwig. You eat the stuff as if it were porridge." She is kind enough to send me a can of it packed in ice on my birthdays.

I met my caviar friend Brodsky again at the Pavillon Restaurant in New York, which, *Guide Michelin* or not, I consider the best French restaurant in the world, better than any on the Continent. Its maniacal proprietor, Monsieur Henri Soulé, has a passion for caviar, its service, its treatment, and he commands the best.

"Ah," says Monsieur Soulé, "no one knows what one suffers running a quality restaurant. You know the fish you see here swam yesterday in the Mediterranean. Today it is here. It has come from France to America, by jet through Customs, with a health certificate like you or I. *Un poisson français.* Alas, it was not always that way. At one time there was no caviar to be had—imagine!"

For years after the Russian revolution, the caviar industry remained at a complete halt. The operation of the grading and processing plants had been in the hands of a few non-Russian companies, the European caviar "houses" which, like the great merchant banking houses, had dynasties. But the revolution ended all that and the non-Russian interests were all expropriated. In 1924, the caviar industry slowly began to function again, under government ownership.

"Have you been in Russia lately?" asked Monsieur Brodsky of Monsieur Soulé. When you ask him something that has nothing to do with

food or the serving thereof, he turns deaf and runs away from your table, to cut up some meat on the heated silver service wagon. He was gone, sharpening two knives.

My friend Brodsky fell back into the subject of caviar again. "Today," he said, "the export of Soviet caviar is the responsibility of Prodintorg, the huge Soviet food trust." He then went on to explain the intricacies and operations of the caviar business.

The foreign caviar houses, which are the wholesalers of the trade, can only get their Russian caviar through Prodintorg. Until 1953, when the Iranians went into business for themselves, Persian caviar was also a Soviet monopoly, marketed only under a Russian label, and the Russians acted as does any capitalist monopoly—setting and maintaining prices at the highest level they felt the market could bear. Indeed, the way the Soviets ran the caviar trade bore a close resemblance to the kind of control the South African diamond monopoly still exerts over the world diamond trade. When the Soviet-Iran agreement was still in effect, the Russians even controlled the price and distribution of caviar in Iran itself, and no caviar was available there except that marketed under a Russian label, even thought it may have come from the shores of Iran itself.

The problem of price is just as pressing for a Russian or Iranian party-giver as for an American, since unpressed fresh sturgeon caviar is nearly as expensive in the two countries that produce it as in the countries that just eat it up, at $7.50 a spoonful, or at $36 a pound, which is what it sells for in a gourmet shop here. It is understandable why in the one and only fancy food store in Moscow, located in Ulitsa Gorkova, comparatively few people buy fresh sturgeon caviar, since it costs ninety rubles a pound, two hundred times the cost of bread. Red salmon caviar is far less expensive, of course, and comes packed in cellophane or plastic bags. In Iran, too, caviar is very expensive, selling for about $25 per pound in American money. But it isn't the cost alone that keeps Persian consumption of caviar down at a low level. *Khaviar* has never been as popular a dish there as in the Soviet Union, Europe or in present-day America.

On the other hand, caviar can be found on the menu of almost every Russian restaurant. It's rarely served very elegantly in the Soviet Union and is generally brought to the table in a small round glass dish, set in a silver-plated metal holder. The caviar itself varies greatly in quality, depending on the restaurant and the area of the country, but it is almost always of the sevruga variety, the cheapest type. Obviously, the Soviets reserve their more expensive, best-quality caviar either for export or for the use of high Soviet officials, although the Russian bureaucrats are showing a good deal more austerity about food and drink now than they did a few years ago, when an unlimited amount of caviar and vodka was s.o.p. at all official Soviet parties.

Now, however, the Russians face stiff competition from the Iranian product. The caviar houses in Paris, Hamburg, London and New York have begun to import more and more Persian caviar and less and less from Russia. The entire Iranian industry is nationalized, although there is some bootlegging of caviar in the large cities. The Iranians are exporting more than one hundred and fifty tons a year and rapidly learning the intricacies of the trade.

I said: "So the outlook is bright."

"The outlook!" Brodsky said. "What's an outlook today? On the one hand you have the lakes and rivers being polluted and the fish dying out; one the other hand you have an increase in caviar production. One goes crazy figuring out this world."

I called for a cigar. "We'll think about cigars," said Brodsky. "I suppose you smoke good Havana cigars—and there is another problem,

Fidel Castro. How long is that going to go on? Maybe suddenly there will be no more cigars, maybe suddenly there will be no more caviar. Now if one could talk to Khrushchev and say, 'Listen—what if you get to the moon, and meanwhile down here all the caviar is drying up and you lose the monopoly? Why don't you divert a few scientists to look after the problems of the sturgeon?' "

Another caviar friend passed our table, Mr. Gilbert Miller, connoisseur of food and wine, and a man who can afford both. He sat down at a table across from ours. He studied the card and asked for caviar.

He said: "This is the place for it in New York, you know."

I got up and started to leave as Brodsky said to Gilbert Miller, "You like caviar?"

"Very much," said Mr. Miller.

"Caviar is my specialty," said Monsieur Brodsky. "Incidentally, have you observed that the two most costly delicacies in the word are black caviar and truffles? My family was in the caviar business before the revolution; we supplied caviar to the Czar, to all the first families in Russia and to the great restaurants. Every Russian knew Michel Brodsky and Son, *Fournisseurs* to the Imperial Family. Our truck rolled in and out of the Kremlin and to the summer palace and the winter palace. Rasputin ate our caviar for breakfast, lunch and dinner—and so did Chaliapin. I will tell you all about caviar," said Michel Brodsky.

*W*e were seated in the Méditerranée, the restaurant that is home to me in Paris. St. Cucuface was eating moules, mussels cooked with garlic in a white wine sauce. He was eating them in the fashion of the French —that is, not with a fork but with the shell of one mussel, using its sharp edge to dislodge the flesh of the others and then scooping up the sauce.

Three tables away from us sat a monk in most serious habit, his pale face framed in a short black beard. He also ate mussels and had a quart bottle of Muscadet, a light wine from the valley of the Loire, in a cooler at his side.

"He comes here once a month," said St. Cucuface. "He is a padre in an abbey in Normandy and, surprisingly enough, was formerly the director of the Casino in Deauville. He comes here as the guest of Jean Subrenat, who is the owner of this place." Monsieur Subrenat, who is six feet tall, sat down at the padre's table, and, keeping an alert eye on the door for customers, said loudly enough for us to hear: *"Oh, how fast time passes! This is a sad, sad day for me. Today at exactly five in the evening the future father-in-law of my daughter will arrive here at the restaurant to ask me for her hand. Alas, all is arranged, and a good bottle awaits the agreement. An hour after that, at six, I lose my son also. He leaves for the Hotel Academy in Geneva, where he will, I hope, learn our trade properly. My son at least will come back; but my daughter has ideas of great grandeur in her head. She has chosen an architect. In these times! How she will miss her father's restaurant! She will think of it three times a day. She could have stayed here with me, and she would have had everything!"*

The padre nodded. The mussels were finished. He wiped his beard and, turning his kind and intelligent face upon Monsieur Subrenat, he salted his worldly advice with ecclesiastic consolation. Then, picking up bread crumbs from the tablecloth with a moistened finger, he calmly awaited the next course.

We went to rake for cockles, which are like our clams, except for
their almost globular structure, and they taste like Little Necks. I gave
the hostess a recipe, which I found in Grand Central Station's sea-food
bar, where a Greek chef who makes it wrote it down for me and showed
me how it's made. It is one of the best things to eat, simple to make—in
fact, nobody can go wrong. It's a meal in itself, and it costs very little.
You need paprika, chili sauce, sherry wine; also celery salt, Worcestershire sauce, butter according to your taste, and clams. I use cherrystones,
which are washed and brushed, and then placed in a deep pan with their
own liquid. For each portion of eight, add one pat of butter, a tablespoon
of chili sauce, ½ teaspoon of Worcestershire sauce, a few drops of
lemon juice and ½ cup of clam broth. Add a dash of celery salt and
paprika. Stir all this over a low fire for three minutes. Then add four
ounces of light cream or heavy cream, according to your taste, and one
ounce of sherry wine and keep stirring. When it comes to the boiling
point, pour it over dry toast in individual bowls. Add a pat of butter
and a dash of paprika and it is ready to serve. If you have made too
much of it, put the remainder into a container in your refrigerator. It will
be as good, warmed up, a week or a month later. It's called Clam Pan
Roast, if you ever want to order it in Grand Central Station's Oyster
Bar. I understand the recipe originally came from Maine.

226

TEXAS LEGEND

IF ANYWHERE IN TEXAS, one would expect to find a good restaurant in San Antonio. The local specialty, alas, is chili, this being the place where it is supposed to be exceptionally good. I don't think that there is such a thing as bad chili. Just chili is what I found it to be. Incidentally, chili is not a Mexican dish, as might be supposed, but a Texas invention. The flavor pervades the air of the eating places everywhere.

In one case, however, a tamale pie made with chili turned out to be a very delectable dish. The recipe is quite simple.

> 2 cups cornmeal mush
> 1 cup red kidney beans
> 1 onion, chopped
> 1 lb. chopped round steak
> 1 can tomatoes
> ¼ can tomato paste
> 1 teaspoon paprika
> 1 tablespoon chili powder (more or less, to taste)
> 1 bay leaf
> salt and pepper

Brown meat and onions, add tomatoes, tomato paste and seasonings and let simmer. Add cooked beans and mix well. Put mixture into casserole and cover with a layer of cornmeal mush. Bake at 350 degrees for 45 minutes.

Texas cattle are admittedly rangy because the climate is not favorable for fattening them. They are shipped to better pastures for that purpose, and then, after corn feeding, go to markets in the East. The local beef when it comes to the table has a curious pink pallor and a lack of flavor. It tastes as if it were a porous fiber from which, by chewing, you obtain a flavored liquid—not the taste of meat or soup. It has a warm, watery taste of no particular distinction.

Here and there an attempt has been made to create a restaurant in the Continental tradition. These are particularly unfortunate experiments. The French names on the menu do not suffice. The local liquor laws are not sympathetic to this kind of establishment, and the Texan, who will spend freely in New York or Paris, becomes Blue Plate-conscious at home. The dishes in these places are overflavored; everything is enhanced with the proprietor's private catechism of what cuisine consists of. He will spoil a perfectly good plain cucumber salad by placing a sweet pickle or a clove of garlic in it and flavor the dressing with the juice from the sweet-pickle jar. He will dust a good-enough strawberry soufflé with cinnamon and sugar, and cook a veal cutlet Milanaise until it is like tar paper.

The service everywhere is friendly, and you are treated as if you were a guest in a home, be it a drugstore, the lowest chili joint or the best club. Especially in Mexican restaurants, the servitor will attend you with solicitude. With a smile the aguacate is put down; with another, he brings the frijoles refritos, the enchiladas, the tortillas and the chicken mole, which is chicken cooked with chocolate, or the baked cabrito, which is young goat.

Thirty miles northeast of San Antonio is a village called New Braunfels. "You must go to New Braunfels. It's a little place—completely German. Everybody speaks German there, and you'll get some good beer and German food," said a Texas friend.

I drove to New Braunfels. In my mind's eye I saw a Black Forest village with cuckoo-clock houses and, in anticipation, I smelled sauerbraten, pigs' knuckles, roast goose. What a promise was the cool draught from a stein of lager in that arid landscape! What medicine for a throat seared by the pungency of chili and barbecue sauces! "Let's go!" I felt and looked better.

Yes, it was all described in our guidebook, and even a beer garden—the oasis in the desert. I stepped on the gas and we came to a village that was like any other: the repeated pattern of filling stations, motels, souvenir shops and road stands—not even the stack of a brewery.

We stopped at a gas station. A blond young man with blue eyes came toward us. Things looked promising. "Is there a German restaurant here?"

"Ja, ja, der iss vun right down the shdreed; it's called 'Ma and Pa's.'"

Ma and Pa's was devoid of all the visual attributes of a German restaurant—no antlers, steins, stained woodwork, comfortable wooden armchairs, not even checkered tablecloths, no evidence of beer being consumed. Our desolation was complete.

We ate a cheese sandwich and a turkey special, had two cups of coffee and paid. We went outside and found the proprietor sunning himself on the sidewalk.

"You don't have any German food here?"

He made a disgusted, all-dismissing downstroke with his right arm. "Naah, ve make it bevoor de war, denn ve stobbed it—becawz everybody vent kwazy here. You couldn't oben your drap. You say vun word of German, or but sauerkraut on de table, and they call you names, and they say 'To the benidentiary mit you.'"

I asked him in what part of Germany he had been born. He seemed surprised. He pointed down at the sidewalk. "I vas born ride here in New Braunfels. Of cuss, everything has changed. This was a nice place, like Germany, vunce. But now—bah!"

I am reasonably steady in moments of danger, but I am a coward when other people suffer or die. I got hungry from unhappiness again, and very thirsty, and tried to stretch out the return as much as I could. I came to a place with a restaurant that looked good; I ordered a big dinner, and it was very good. The plate was warm, and the wine was exceptional, a California dry white wine called Folle Blanche, a Schoonmaker wine, and it was clear, cold and served in a decent glass. I found an excuse for further delay: I said a few kind words to the proprietor and I asked him where the chef was.

"Second door to your right," he said.

It turned out to be the men's room; the proprietor had never heard the word "chef." I talked about cooks with him then, and he introduced me to the colored man who had prepared the meal; then we had brandy and I drove on.

THE BEST WAY TO SEE CUBA

THERE ARE SOME Cuban women who diet, who stay slim, who submit to the discipline of fashion, but they live abroad most of the year and come to Havana only for the season. They are a mere handful, and you find them on the pages of the high-fashion magazines. The Countess Comargo is one of these; she gave a dinner and dance at her palace, which is like a piece of Versailles transported to Havana. In Europe perhaps Don Carlos de Beistegui, Aristotle Socrates Onassis or Arturo Lopez may give a party like that; in America nobody can afford it any more.

Fifteen chefs are engaged to cook for two hundred. The garden is lit by thousands of candles; the service is of gold. The wines are the best, the food superb. It is the only really good meal I ever had in Cuba.

Here are the elite. The house has been searched for days by the police, for President Fulgencio Batista is coming. I am wearing an Italian midnight-blue dinner jacket; it is conservative, but I am outstandingly garish in this outfit, for every other man is in cloth of deepest black and the most serious cut. The ladies are in the latest Parisian creations. The jewels are fabulous; it's Cartier's windows emptied. In the shrubbery all around the building and behind the shutters of upstairs windows are sharpshooters with automatic weapons. Cubans will bet on anything; a man asks if I want to bet whether we have a quiet dinner or a bombing. Since bombs have been exploding almost nightly, this is a plausible wager.

"Don't worry," says another, "nothing will happen, while *he* is here—he's well guarded." Someone else says, "It is a safe bet he will not die in bed." And another says, "What are the odds on his getting through this dinner?" They speak of the difficulty of protecting anyone all the time.

Batista arrives late. He looks like a self-designed cross between Edward

G. Robinson and Charles Boyer. He is affable, stocky—the typical "strong man." He has à prodigious memory and is completely at ease. He has a good appetite at table and talks freely.

Toward the end of dinner the bands plays "Happy Birthday" in salute to the American ambassador. Batista speaks briefly and congratulates him, the ambassador says a few words of thanks, and then music is played for dancing.

When I got home from this party our maid, a sweet Negro girl named Juanita, was still up. A terrible thing had happened, she told us; a bomb had exploded nearby and knocked a picture off the wall in the dining room. Beneath the picture were some bottles on a sideboard—Scotch, which costs $4.35 a fifth here, and rum, which is very cheap. The picture had fallen on the Scotch, and Juanita showed me fragments of the bottle. I asked why it had not broken the rum, and she said, "Life is a gamble."

The bombings and bomb scares were part of the most casual revolution I ever saw. The guards around Batista's palace carried their rifles in a relaxed manner, smoked cigars and talked incessantly even on duty. It all seemed fuzzy. Most of my Cuban friends assured me that quite probably it would be over before my story appeared.

There are landscapes of great beauty in Cuba, of soft Pissarro and Cézanne color, and the tropical intensity of Gauguin. Most leaves on trees are round, the needles of the pines are soft, and some trees bear blossoms that look like the plumage of birds of paradise. The fields of sugar cane are of a green which is richer than any other. The earth is a moist burnt sienna.

There are mountains, hills and valleys; the vegetation varies in intensity from dense jungle to cultivated land—sugar here, tobacco there, oranges, bananas, pineapple.

The most radiantly beautiful object in nature here is the royal palm, which stands straight, perfectly balanced. Its silvered-gray trunk, which rises house-high, endows the land with splendor as do the columns of temples in Greece. Other palm trees, notably the coconut palm, lean this way and that, and have a generally unkempt appearance.

The royal palm stands anywhere, is sometimes found in rows a kilometer long, lining the lane to a farmhouse. It also stands as in a forest, and it may be found beside the house of the poorest farmer. "Farmer" is a word that does not apply here, really, for he is in most cases a worker in the cane fields and in the sugar mills, which employ him for three months of the year.

He lives in a house called a *bohio*, which is entirely constructed of the royal palm tree. The outside of this tree is hard and is used for the walls; the fronds are used for the thatched roof. Pigs and chickens share the house, and the pigs are fed the fruit of the royal palm, a kind of date unfit for people.

The food is beans, sugar cane, yams, potatoes, and here one sees that the potato is tropical and not Irish. These tuber plants grow virtually wild: "You stick them in the earth and they grow." The same with sugar cane—it grows with little attention; you cut it and it grows again.

Cubans like bananas when the skin is dark and spotted, and they eat them raw or fried or cooked in various exotic dishes. There are good pineapples, a red pulpy fruit called mammee, also cherimoyas, delicious heavy green, tree-borne fruit the size of a large apple, which taste like pineapple ice cream; oranges (which sell for a penny) and grapefruit of all the varieties we have in the States.

Greens such as spinach and string beans were formerly imported from the States. Now, Chinese, who have the patience for this kind of farming, raise them. The Cuban housewife of the upper classes does her shopping in American-style supermarkets and buys frozen vegetables at prices higher than those in the United States.

I found a tavern in Antibes that was simple and its food was good, but it is always hazardous to recommend anything to anyone in travel. One must say, "That day when I was there it was very good—for places change hands and mood. If René is still the proprietor of Chez René when you are in Antibes, then I can recommend it."

THE BEST
WAY TO SEE RIO

HIS EXCELLENCY, Assis Chateaubriand, whose full name is Dr. Francesco
de Assis Chateaubriand de Mello, Brazilian Ambassador to the Court of
St. James's, is a phenomenon, intricate and rare. A human jumping bean
with Napoleonic complexes, he nudges and budges, never sits still. He
wears a hat which resembles one used by Red Skelton in his most violent
comedy routines. It is gray felt and never the same shape and never does
it sit the same way on the ambassador's head; sometimes it faces back-
ward, sometimes left or right; sometimes it simply falls off.

On arriving at his post in London, the ambassador told the British that
he felt close to them, his maternal grandfather having roasted and eaten
an Anglican bishop.

It is because of Assis Chateaubriand that I am in Rio de Janeiro. I
sat near him during dinner at the house of Madame Schiaparelli in Paris
a year ago, and he hopped up and down on his seat there as he does here.
In a few minutes he had started as many arguments as there were candles
on the table. People were screaming to make themselves heard through
the cloud of words that swelled over the table. I had a pantomime going
with Chateaubriand. He is hard to understand, for he talks in three
clipped languages at double time. He talked about Rio, said I had to
come, and I got an idea of what it was like, although I did not understand a word he said. It is, however, exactly as he described it.

Now he was here in Rio, in the same formless gray hat, the dynamo running inside of him. He greeted me with friendly staccato talk and invited me to dinner. It is so hot that the tongues of cats are hanging out; anything you touch feels as if it came from an oven, but Assis Chateaubriand is wearing a wool suit, dark blue with stripes, and a woolen waistcoat, a shirt with stiff collar and a woolen tie. He said: "*J'adore la chaleur.*" He's lucky, for there is no air conditioning in the house where we are dining.

It is an elegant house and we are seated in a dining room without a draft of air, on upholstered chairs, and with a liveried servant who wears a starched collar and gloves on his hands, and with candles lit on the table. Assis Chateaubriand is hopping on his chair as he did in Paris, starting as many arguments as he had at Elsa Schiaparelli's. They serve shrimps with a red sauce that tastes of tomato and lobster and, with this, rice. Then turkey with peas and asparagus tips and fried potatoes. The conversation goes in eight directions, everybody screaming to someone else. The hostess on my left is screaming to the woman at the other end of the table. Between mouthfuls, Chatto, as he is known, throws additional fuel on the arguments. He shouts to ask if I found Rio the way he described it. I yelled back, "Yes, exactly so."

"Well," he says, "write some agreeable lies about us," and he lifts a glass of champagne. "Are you interested in agriculture?"

"Yes."

"We have a new coffee tree."

For the rest I have to rely on sign language and lip reading, but it seems they have a new coffee tree which is shorter, blossoms sooner and bears more beans.

The dessert is raspberry gelatine with ground coconut. Then comes coffee. Assis Chateaubriand goes to bed about four in the morning. He's up and gone at nine.

A Swiss-made cogwheel railroad runs to the top of the mountain on which stands the statue of Christ the Redeemer. You also can get there by car, over roads that ascend in serpentines and afford magnificent views of the city. There is a Chinese view framed in bamboo and purple blossoms; another is called the View of the Emperor's Table. You enter a jungle of immense trees, some with air roots and others covered with orchids. Ferns and magnificent palms line the road. Here are all the sounds peculiar to the deepest tropics, toads making many of them; and there is the constant screech and chatter of birds and monkeys. It is astonishing in its closeness, for you will see no wilder jungle even in the remote rain forest of the Amazon.

Some distance beneath the statue of the Saviour is the Hotel Corcovado, an inn run thirty years by Willy Timmermann and his wife. Typically German, Herr Timmermann—in the midst of this living tapestry literally choked with millions of exotic flowers of all colors—has set along the balustrade of the outdoor dining room twelve geraniums in cans. Each is watered every day and meticulously tended, as is everything else here. The chairs and tables are precisely arranged, and the waiters, trained by Willy himself, according to ancient usage, keep the right arm behind them as they lean forward and present things with the left. The only other place you could have observed such formal service was at the Hotel Kaiser Wilhelm in Berlin a century ago.

In the vast dining room is a large mahogany closet holding about three hundred glasses; each, although they are seldom used, is spotless. There is also a hundred-year-old clock that keeps time to the second. Frau Timmermann gets up at five A.M., Herr Timmermann at seven. Everything here shines.

The Brazilian beer Herr Timmermann serves is the best I have tasted outside Bavaria. The food is simple and good; the specialties are those of Luchow's Restaurant in New York. The cold consommé, cold roast beef and potato salad are superb. There are, incidentally, a thousand variations of potato salad; this is one of the best. As for wine, you may have German Riesling and Traminer, both of which keep well in the tropics. The great French whites, and even more the reds, suffer if kept long in this climate. Champagne keeps well but is very expensive. Chilean wines are drinkable. Native Brazilian wines are not very good. Herr Timmermann's prices, at present exchange rates, are very low.

"*Und*," says Herr Timmermann, "my place is respectable. *Ja, ja*, I could be a millionaire if I let the bars down. But no monkey business with me. Men with girls come here with Rolls-Royces or Mercedes-Benzes, but I have no room for anything that looks shady. I say, 'For one night I have no rooms, thank you and don't try again. This is a respectable place.'

A long time ago I wrote a story about the world's biggest hotel, so large that the chef used a motorboat to put the noodles in the soup. This hotel existed only in my imagination—until I came to Brazil. On one of the days when it was 102°, when the air was absolutely still, when the air conditioning had broken down, when putting on a necktie was like slipping into an overcoat, I decided to drive up to Petropolis, where the *cariocas* used to go over the weekend, to the Hotel Quitandinha, a super pleasure dome constructed during the Getulio Vargas regime.

It sits well in its scenery. It is as if you took the town of St. Moritz and all its hotels and kneaded them together to make one immense palatial hotel. If the exterior is large, the interior is bigger, like the home of a man who keeps elephants as house pets. It was decorated by Dorothy Draper with remarkable taste and courage. The chandeliers are like roller coasters suspended from the ceiling. There is a bird cage in one of the lobbies in which you could give riding lessons. A ballroom turns out to be a swimming pool. In the game rooms stand sixty roulette tables.

When I arrived, the room clerk, an affable, never-smiling little man, handed me the price list:

Double room, inside view	$ 4.00
Double room, outside view	6.00
Deluxe double room	7.00
Special-deluxe double room	9.00
Super-deluxe double room for four persons	22.00
Presidential apartment	35.00
Baby bed	1.00
Guest's servant's room	2.00

The presidential suite was rented and I contented myself with a special-deluxe room. The dining room functioned well under the new management. Everything was clean, pleasant, the air dry and cool, and the Hotel Quitandinha is to be recommended to anyone who has a long novel to write or for families with many children. They can get lost easily for the entire day. Since the passing of Getulio Vargas, it is a dead hotel. Gambling has stopped and there are merely the echoes of your footfalls as you walk the vast marble corridors. The person you see approaching from the other end of the lobby turns out to be your reflection in a huge mirror. But it was delightfully cool, inside and outside, with a beautiful view. I swam all alone in the pool, I had a drink all alone at the bar.

Before dinner I washed my hands in a marble retreat with enough fixtures for a regiment—and hung my cap in a coatroom on one of several thousand empty hooks—all chosen by Miss Draper—all polished brass.

In the vast dining room were eighteen guests, some with children who were very well behaved. The dinner was good. Melon and prosciutto, followed by a kind of shashlik with rice and beans; salad of hearts of palm; very good coffee; good native cigars. Three excellent Brahma brand beers and dinner, all of it $6.45—with music by the professor. At ten I was sleepy and wandered up the six kilometers or so to bed and to the first sound and dreamless sleep of my visit.

Morning at giant Hotel Quitandinha is glorious—Alpine light, a cool breeze, a magnificent panorama. And although this is only an hour from Rio, the climatic difference is as great as that between Palm Springs and the Adirondacks.

Solidly built, the hotel is almost completely soundproof. My room is beautifully furnished, the bed immense, the bathroom big with a king-size tub to match. Unusual in the tropics, there is abundant hot and cold water. The towels are too big to steal and there is a rug instead of a bath mat. Somebody must lose a lot of money on this place, for everything is kept in meticulous order. Who owns it? The room clerk says it belongs to the state, the headwaiter says an American corporation; nobody really seems to know.

SHIPOWNER

"MAY I SPEAK to you, sir, about provisions? There are a few things to consider. Wine and spaghetti we don't have to worry about, going to Italy. But I notice you drink bourbon whisky, and gin, and Guinness stout. Now, as for whisky—bourbon you cannot get at all in Italy, except at private houses, and perhaps in places like the Excelsior in Rome, or the Hassler. Ordinary whisky—all of it called "whisky"—is either made in Italy and put into real bottles, or else it is cut. Same with gin. So I suggest that we get a good supply of whisky and gin for the trip. Allow me to inform the signore that on shipboard, over salt water, one's thirst increases. Then I have noticed that the icebox is rather small, and we better take along some things that need not be put into the icebox. They make some very good conserves in France, and also there are imported things in cans. I have made a list. They can be stowed away in a cool place.

"Ship's cooking—mine, signore—is simple. The principle of the sea-going kitchen is that you can eat the food with one hand while the other holds the tiller—for we may have a rough sea and must allow for that. But that also means that you will eat well. For example, very good ravioli, which is pasta, meat and vegetable in one, and cheese over it, and you need only a fork and one hand. Also I must remind the signore that sometimes one arrives in a port where there is no restaurant, or let us say no good restaurant, or it is late, or the signore is too tired to go ashore and wants to eat on board where it is good and proper. For all this I have allowed, and made a list which I herewith submit to you."

All this made sense, and I gave my go-ahead to it without checking over the details. He thanked me for my confidence and backed away to go to the shops. Meanwhile the mate tanked up the fuel, scrubbed the deck, secured the spare anchor and ropes and washed the dinghy.

After a while a gay delivery truck painted marigold and cerulean blue rolled along the quay. The driver slowed down as he passed from yacht to yacht, almost stopped at the *Iphigenia*'s gangway, but then drove on until he came to the *Arche de Noé*, where he backed up to deliver the provisions.

Jambon de Paris, several varieties of herring in tins from Germany, the good mackerel of Captain Scott, hot chili sauce, beans from Heinz in America, corned beef, tins of soups, mayonnaise, saucissons de Lyon—he made trip after trip. Another truck followed with the beverages.

The captain came back and checked everything with me against the receipts from the shops. All these things seemed to cost their weight in precious metal, but then, as J. Pierpont Morgan said, if you have to think about the cost, you have no business owning a yacht.

As we cast off, the owner of the *Iphigenia*, his beautiful wife and the children waved from the high deck of their ship, and the Great Dane wagged its tail. We passed the *Christina* and, as the sun set, started on the voyage proper, going out into the calm Mediterranean between the two lighthouses of the port of Monaco, which is as neat and clean as a pastry shop.

The icebox door opened and closed quietly several times, and wonderful aromas filled the air. Then dinner was served. Light faded, the mate went below. Presently I heard his soft voice and the guitar. How often had I thought it folly—buying this boat. And now—how glad I was! Dear *Old Lady*, dear *Arche de Noé*.

A good wind pushed us along. Where the bow parted the waves, a million pearls of light danced on the water. The captain brought me a pillow, a cigar, a drink, tuned the radio to classical music and silently disappeared. We passed Menton. The mate came aft and hoisted a small Italian flag, for we were passing Ventimiglia. I had started on the long voyage.

Ile de
Parquerolles

THE ISLAND OF
PORQUEROLLES

IT LOOKED LIKE a Japanese print, an island covered with pine growth, but there seemed to be no place to land as we approached it from the sea. There was no use searching for its outline in the books and maps, for it might have been one of a hundred islands. As we came closer we saw that it was French by the flag that hung from the lighthouse tower. We saw another island to the right of it and passed in between them. Then there was a church steeple, some ship masts, a tower, and, turning to the left, there unfolded a pleasant harbor scene with a quay and some boats. We tied up and found ourselves on the island of Porquerolles, near Toulon.

We landed with the last drop of gas.

Porquerolles can be reached only by boat, and there are no cars on the island. It is a place of which I shall always think with pleasure.

There is a small hotel named, oddly enough, the same as my ship— L'Arche de Noé. It is one of the places most dear to me. Little, good, old houses that are hotels have always been my refuge and the only places in which I feel at home.

In the wobbly hours, when the motor almost got drowned and when the barometer was all the way down, I steered my turn and thought of what I would miss most in this world. Besides those I love, and my studio in New York, there appeared the memories of several taverns and the faces of people. One that came to mind was Alexandre Dumaine of the Hotel de la Côte d'Or in Saulieu. An unpretentious master of the great kitchen—and here, on Porquerolles, was another, the proprietor who is himself the chef, whose wife is at his side, in a house of a few tables and rooms, uncompromising, without airs. I never thought I would see a good kitchen like this again—large, light, spotless—and the chef, his every move for good purpose. To see butter being put on the inside of a casserole, vegetables cut up—that is all the therapy I need when I get disturbed.

*T*oni and Rocco always reminded me of the New York City Ballet. They were about the size and form of the dancers there and stood as if waiting to go on, Toni always grave, the other like a younger brother in rebellion and without responsibility.

On land they found small restaurants, taverns and marine eating places by asking the sailors of other ships or natives. To live cheaply and eat well, it is of advantage to dress up as a sailor. They both had immense appetites and demanded large portions of everything. The food was good, the prices unbelievably low. The mystery was what happened to the food. They swallowed, as pythons do goats, mountains of pasta, pastry and jugs of milk, but it never showed on them.

Between Toni and Rocco there were always small arguments, most of them having to do with their native town, Chiavari.

The boat had been pulled out of the water in the harbor of Antibes, and they were busy scraping marine growth and barnacles off the bottom. Rocco said, "You must say that the bread in Chiavari is better than here."

Toni, who was the more liberal-minded of the two, answered, "The bread is better here. I like it better. I don't like everything French, but French bread is better than the Italian in Chiavari. I saw the bakery here. They have a machine to mix the dough."

They scraped for a while; then Toni, who always spoke slowly and arranged his words carefully, said, "In Chiavari, I was eating bread once and bit on something, and I thought it was perhaps a grain of salt, but then I took it out of my mouth and saw that it was a tooth of a mouse. I took it to the baker—in Chiavari—the same where your mama gets the bread, and I saw him working, the baker in his undershirt, and the sweat from under his arms and his face dripped down into the dough. Since then I never ate bread with appetite in Chiavari."

There was a long pause, and then Rocco, who always answered back and had to have the last word, said from under the other side of the hull, "Perhaps that's what gives it its flavor."

244

THE SOUL OF AUSTRIA

ALL CLASSES of Austrians spend a good deal of their lives in restaurants, cafés, *Konditoreien* and small taverns which are called *Heurigen* and serve food with beer or wine. The beer is excellent, wine is the predominant beverage and it is good.

The most important dish is a schnitzel—which is a cutlet.

The schnitzel is what the Austrian would dream about when cast on a desert island. It comes dipped in bread crumbs and fried, with a slice of lemon and with lukewarm potato salad in which they sometimes put slivers of onion. It also comes *à la napolitaine*, with spaghetti. There are Holstein and paprika and many other kinds of schnitzel, and whether one is a minister, the president of Austria, an archduke or chimney sweep, at schnitzeltime the world can go hang.

The Hungarian, Polish and Czech kitchens have contributed to the Viennese menu. There are *Palatschinken* (pancakes in sour cream and cheese, with raisins). The famous *Kaiserschmarrn Pfannkuchen*, the apricot and plum dumplings, the *Apfelstrudels* with bread crumbs and other delights leave you gasping and with spots in front of your eyes. So most Austrians are well padded.

In outdoor seasons, the people like to wander up the hills around Vienna. In autumn, to drink the new wine, called the *Heurige,* they go out to places where there are simple taverns and gardens, shaded by vines on which the grapes still hang.

Here you find the true Viennese, the people. We are sitting in such a garden now, in early October. It is the garden of the house in which Beethoven composed the Sixth Symphony, the Pastorale. The place is without any great comfort, the tables and chairs are painted a pea-soup green, and ocher is on the walls of houses—yellow and a bitter mustard color are favorites in the pallete of Viennese house painters. There is a beloved shade called *"Schönbrunn Gelb"* and you come closest to it if you mix lemon yellow with Naples yellow and some deep ocher and apply it thickly. It is alight in the most verdant greenery, and in the Viennese landscape it reminds one of the colorations of Rome.

The seats are hard, pebbles cover the floor—there is murmured conversation. The wine and food are good and anyone can afford them. There is a quintet consisting of a double bass, a guitar, a concertina, a viola and a violin; they are first rate and one musician sings. The Viennese male voice is a little wheezy, like a peculiar instrument. In New York you can hear it in the Champagne Room of El Morocco, where the pianist renders Viennese folk songs in exactly that typical fashion. As all things Viennese, it is tinged with melancholia.

You don't get a table to yourself; the tables seat twelve, and you sit down where there is room. Karl Liebeszell and I sat down at the first available places, close to the orchestra, for they played rather quietly. We bowed to the table, saying, *"Guten Abend,"* and the others made room and bowed back—the only formality. They look at you with friendliness and offer you a true welcome. There is the inevitable little boy who, after having bored in his nose and contemplated you, climbs on your lap to examine you closer. He is restrained with kindness: *"Da komm her, Franzi,* the gentleman wants to be left alone." Little girls sit quietly at the side of their mamas; the men are holding a discussion and drinking the new wine, which flows like water but has hidden powers that make you wobble as you get up. Beware of young wine.

Having eaten and had the first bottle, one feels happy in this place. I cannot promise the traveler good weather, or a room at the Hotel Sacher, but I can guarantee that the mood here is genuine and as I have described it.

Austria is still an inexpensive country, and you get your money's worth. A good dinner in a tavern can be had for $1.50, a good room for $2. As far as Austrian hotels go, and also restaurants, I avoid the deluxe establishments and seek the taverns, places where the natives go.

There are some super-deluxe hotels that are first rate, but most of

that category suffer from the snobbism of their porters and maîtres d'hôtel (except the few hotels where the guest is known and treated like one of the family). They have grandiose names and smell of a peculiar kind of floor polish which is applied too frequently, by porters who skate over the parquet with brushes strapped to one foot. The rooms are crammed with furniture of a period no one can identify, the beds piled with cloud-shaped eiderdown quilts. Everywhere are heavy draperies, thick carpets, lace doilies and thousands of tassels. The opposite to this clutter is the modern hotel whose interior is naked living space, sterile as a hospital, sparsely furnished with tubular-legged chromium tables and chairs, the latter with sitting pads of leatherette. There are also some new motels in this super category, and I avoid them except the one or two where I am at home.

As I have said, I go to the inn, the *Gasthof*, which is inexpensive and friendly. The kitchen is spotless and you get good, plain Austrian food. In fancier establishments they try to imitate French cuisine and the results are neither one thing nor the other—they overseason, overdecorate and overserve the food.

Before driving back to Paris, I sat in the dining room of the Goldener Hirsch, a lovely cave in Salzburg, and with me was my friend the count, Karl Liebeszell. On this day he was unusually clear-minded and, as always, of uncompromising opinion and in good voice.

At the table next to us sat a group of Americans having a good time.

They were dressed as natives, the women in *dirndln* and the men in *Steirergwand*—gray suits which have a green edge stitched on lapels, pockets, the ends of the sleeves, and even down the side of the trousers. All wore mountain hats and were self-elected good-will ambassadors.

"Oh," said a very young and ardent woman in their group. "Oh, this lovely and beautiful land, this enchanting country of yours, and these warm-hearted and *gemütlich* Austrians—how I love them." She drank to us, and so did the others.

We raised our glasses. I drank. Count Liebeszell got up, but instead of drinking he paused.

Then he said: "Madame, I drink to the lovely country, but as far as the rest goes, my dear naïve and beautiful American lady, let me, an Austrian, make some things clear to you."

The room was silent—all knives, forks and glasses were put down. The service stopped and the waiters and boy apprentices stood with ears, eyes and mouths open.

Liebeszell said: "The Austrians who let Schubert starve to death, who dumped Mozart in a mass grave so that even today no one has any idea where he lies, who gave Hitler to the world, built the Mauthausen concentration camp, and of whom ninety per cent were good Nazis and most still are—they are not *gemütlich*, dear lady. Thank you."

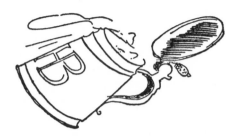

HOW I TOOK THE CURE

EVERY YEAR in the month of August, John Ringling North and I meet at the Hotel Vier Jahreszeiten, and from there we go forth to taste the brews of Munich.

These are the beers of the ancient breweries, which make Löwenbräu, Spatenbräu, Franziskaner, Paulaner and many others equally important. All are served in tall, heavy mugs at the right temperature and are so easily drinkable that you are surprised your vessel has to be refilled so soon. With these brews we eat the native food, which is enough to make any gourmet strangle on his napkin, throw his plate on the floor in disgust and cross our names off the sacred lists. The menus of the bourgeois places we visit are greasy and, in the twilight of the beer-hall interior, hard to read. Usually one asks the waitress—who is not addressed as *"Fräulein"* but respectfully as *"Frau,"* and by her proper name—what there is to eat.

The best cooking and service of this type are found at a place next to the Frauenkirche, called Das Nürnberger Bratwurstglöckl—the Nuremberg Sausage Bell. This place seats about a hundred people, is filled from 11 A.M. to late at night, and everything is served in a hushed atmosphere (no one speaks loudly here unless he's a foreigner or a Prussian, which in Bavaria is considered worse), and the beer is treated with loving care.

In a kitchen that looks like a cuckoo clock—old Munich's wood-paneled interior—the cooking is done over a large, open charcoal roaster. They have wonderful bread, a kind of sourdough, and peasant loaves and *Laugen Pretzel*, a salty twist which is delicious.

On the menu appears a surrealist poem that makes no sense at all but somehow belongs here. It's written in archaic German:

> *Steckk an die Schweinen braten*
> *Dazu die Hüner jung!*
> *Darauf mag uns geraten*
> *Ein frischer, freier trunk.*

I will not attempt to translate—it's impossible. It's like one of those subliminal images flashed on movie screens—you don't see it, but it makes you suddenly go to a fountain and deposit a dime for a drink. This verse, somehow, enlivens your appetite.

I am very happy here. I was taken to this place years ago when I was a small boy. I sat on the same hard chairs, and at the table are the same people of my childhood; they say, "*Guten Appetit.*" They are Munich citizens of the old school.

You sit down wherever you can find an empty chair. There is a *Stammtisch* for the regulars, but to be entitled to a seat there you must come year in and year out. Johnny and I sit with Frau Schlemmer, who says, "*Ja san Sie wieder da—ja Grüss eahne Gott,*" which is Bavarian for hello. There is *Ochsenfleisch mit Gemüse*—boiled beef with kohlrabi —excellent; it costs sixty cents, U.S. There is *Schweinsbraten* (not *Schweinebraten*) with *Knödl*, also sixty cents—a superb roast pig with very tender dumplings, and many other dishes. But we eat the bratwurst with sauerkraut at thirty cents for four. The bratwurst which comes on a pewter plate has a bit of kraut under it such as you get nowhere else in the world. The sausages are the size of a lady's little finger, and for them I will gladly trade at any time the very best caviar and the most costly pâté de foie gras. This is a sausage from heaven. It never lets you down, summer or winter, year after year—it is always a delight. In vain I have tried for two decades to get the recipes for this sausage-and-sauerkraut, but they are better kept than our atomic secrets.

When staying in Munich, you take on Munich character; that is, you talk only about important things, like beer, or food. And this is how Johnny and I sat, eating and drinking beer. Munich was celebrating its eight-hundredth year of existence. The city was filled with flags, brass bands played everywhere, and a special anniversary brew was made. We had had our third plate of sausages and the fourth beer when someone sat down at the table—"*Grüss Gott*"—and unfolded a paper.

We saw a headline which said that Voroshilov had declared that he expected to live two hundred years. Johnny stopped picking his teeth as he read this.

"I've just been thinking," he said, pointing at the headline with his toothpick, "that when Munich celebrates its one-thousandth anniversary, this place will still be here—these sausages and this beer *but* neither you nor I nor our children will be here. It makes me very sad."

I said: "Well, maybe the Russians will invent something so that we'll still be here. Life is too short—we're almost gone and we haven't started . . . really."

A Munich citizen overheard me. "Yes," he said. "Take me, I am a doctor. You're almost forty before you become a doctor—and then it's nearly over. Do you mind my asking how old you are?"

"I'm sixty."

"Oh, you're just a kid—I'm seventy-five," said the doctor. "But every year it goes quicker—well, *Grüss Gott.*"

"I have a chance," said Johnny, "to get old. Maybe a hundred or so, because I at least take care of myself. But *you—*"

"But I what?"

"Well, I've known you for—how many years? Ten at least. Did you ever do anything?"

"Anything for what?"

"Well, to get in condition—to keep fit?"

I liked that. I have never seen Johnny except in restaurants surrounded with bottles and platters and bowls. He has to put down a fork or spoon or glass to shake hands with you, and his conversation is always about his last seven-course meal.

"And you," I finally said, "what do you do except eat and drink?"

He looked up in surprise and said, putting down his fork, "Don't you know? Haven't I told you about Doctor Buchinger's Clinic in Überlingen on the Bodensee? I go there every year for a month, and come out like a newborn baby. I lost eighteen pounds last time—didn't I ever tell you about this?" He turned and asked Frau Schlemmer to bring us each another mug of beer. "I'm going there in ten days. Why don't you come with me? Now listen to me: Consider your car—you have the oil changed, don't you? You have the engine overhauled once in a while, don't you? You look after it—well, your body is the same." I never heard Johnny talk so much about anything—including his circus. "Our lions, tigers, monkeys, elephants," he went on, "they have one fasting day a week—and they're on a diet the rest of the time. They stay fit.

"Logic, logic, logic—it makes sense. Don't put it off. Doctor Buchinger's is famous—it's full all the time, but I'll get you in. Wait a minute." He got up and telephoned to Überlingen on the Bodensee. The call was delayed. People in this beer hall seldom ever telephone, especially long distance. Nobody is ever paged at his table. The place was upset and people were looking at us with displeasure; we were disturbing the *Gemütlichkeit* of the Bratwurstglöckl. Finally the call came through: The Clinic am Bodensee said that they would be happy to have me, but I had to come right away.

"*Jah*—are you sick?" asked Frau Schlemmer.

"*Nein*," I said.

Johnny explained, "He's going for an *Entschlackungskur*." *Entschlackung* is, as are most German words, very apt. It means cleaning out a stopped-up grease trap.

"*Ach*—you poor man," said Frau Schlemmer. "You better eat another plate of sausages."

"Yes," said Johnny, "you better. Because you won't get anything like them at Doctor Buchinger's."

"What do you get?"

"Nothing—you fast, like a hermit. A little fruit the first day, then a cup of tea a day—not real tea, herb tea. Doctor Buchinger plants it himself."

The waitress said, "But why? You are not fat, either of you."

"Well, we're not fat in Munich, but in America we are. Besides, it's

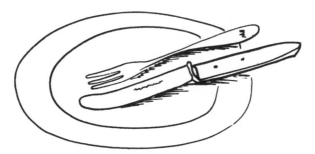

the *Entschlackung*. Bring me also a plate of sausages, Frau Schlemmer," said Johnny, and as we stowed our portions away he added, "You know that's the beauty of this—now we can eat as much as we want. It all comes off, you'll not know yourself, you feel like jumping over horses when you leave Doctor Buchinger's. You'll be a young mountain goat, born anew. Frau Schlemmer, the bill, please."

I said, "No, you have done so much for me; let me have this one." In these places you tell the waitress what you had and she makes out the bill. She has about twenty guests to serve and she can't remember everything, yet nobody ever cheats. Frau Schlemmer took a pencil stub from the bun of hair at the back of her head and a small pad from her bag. These bags are peculiar to Munich waitresses. They are stout leather *portemonnaies* suspended from the waist by a chain. Moistening the end of her pencil, Frau Schlemmer said, "Now, then, what did we have?"

I said, "Five plates of Würstl for me and five for him."

"Ten times one mark, fifty pfennige makes fifteen marks. How many bread?"

"Three for me and two for Johnny."

"How many beers?"

"Four seidels each."

"Makes eight times seventy-five pfennigs—*Fünf mal acht ist vierzig,* carry four—" Seven times eight was always a very difficult problem for me in school in Bavaria but Frau Schlemmer had a calculating machine for a head and instantly pronounced: "*sechs mark achtzig*—is altogether—twenty-two marks, ten per cent service, makes twenty-four marks and two pfennige. *Danke vielmals, danke sehr. Auf Wiedersehen.* Come soon again—*Grüss Gott!*"

"I told them," said Johnny, "you would be in Überlingen tomorrow evening. No use rushing there, which gives us a chance for a last memorial meal tomorrow before you drive off. Now we can go to the

Platzl and have a little Spaten Brew Special. It doesn't matter now; it all comes off in Überlingen."

We drank to the health of Herr Doktor Buchinger, tried a few liters of the most marvelous of this year's Stark beer and went back to the Hotel Vier Jahreszeiten.

The next day I packed. But before I drove off to the Bodensee, which is part Swiss, Austrian and German, and known also as Lake Constance, we went to another famous place with the same quality of food, atmosphere and prices, where they put on your table a small barrel of beer, which you can tap yourself. There we each ate a *Kalbshaxe*—leg of veal —with pan-browned potatoes. For dessert, radishes and cheese. Here, too, the beer was magnificent. At last we clinked glasses *auf Wiedersehen*. Johnny paid, shook my hand, and I drove off alone, in the mood in which one goes to perform a serious duty such as assisting at the funeral of a dear friend.

The road from Munich to Überlingen is four hours' easy driving through pleasant landscape, with mountains to the left and rolling cattle land to the right. This is the direct way and as I intended to go. But as the reality of things became clear to me—the absolute regimen (Johnny had told me no cigars, no drinking—on your honor)—I thought it would be good if I arrived late and had a last meal somewhere en route.

The pine scent of the Alps and the mountain breezes that fan the waters of the Bodensee are always good for an appetite. There is an inn above the village of Sipplingen—a *Gasthof* called Haldenhof—with a wide view over the lake. Its specialty, as in Munich, is the simplest and best—homemade black bread, peasant bacon and those things are called *Bauernspeck und selbstgebackenes Brot*. It's eaten out on the terrace high above the lake, under spreading linden trees overlooking the ancient ruin of Hohenfels, where seven hundred years ago a local troubadour (*Minnesinger*) praised the local wine. Chickens run about, sit on the chairs and on unoccupied tables. The wine is not a Montrachet to be sure; but it is good—and even better when wine is about to be taken away from you. Altogether the clouds, which are like immense white bolsters, drift in the direction of Überlingen. Yes, there is a telephone, and I put in a call to Doctor Buchinger's sanatorium. The operator who tries to get me the number contemplates my face with sadness as she waits for the call to go through.

"*Ja, bitte, das Sanatorium am Bodensee, Doktor Buchinger, bitte. . . .*

Ja, der Herr Doktor is unable to speak to you." A ray of hope. Maybe the Herr Doktor has a contagious *Krankheit* and the sanatorium is quarantined, but this hope fades away when the sanatorium reports that Doctor Buchinger is on vacation in Italy.

"But the sanatorium—"

"Oh, *ja, ja;* the sanatorium is open. Who is talking?" The Fräulein of the Haldenhof hands me the phone.

"Oh," said a female voice that rang pure and clear like an early church bell. She seemed to know where I was and what I was doing. "You can come as late as eleven P.M., Herr Bemelmans." There was some reproach in her tone. "Everything is ready, we are waiting for you." I paid the bill. Everybody in this region knows about Dr. B.

The Fräulein and the innkeeper shook hands with me, as if it were an interment. "*Grüss Gott,*" they said, and "Come and see us after." They waved goodbye as I drove down the lake road that leads inevitably to Überlingen.

There was time for a last stop. There on the main street of Überlingen is an inn called the Pike—Hotel Hecht. It deserves an award for gastronomy. Although Irish stew is on the menu, as well as roast beef, the thing to order here is the Bodensee Felchen (lake salmon) and also, occasionally, salmon trout. Luckily they had a trout, and it came in an oblong silver casserole, plain boiled, with young potatoes and melted butter. This is a royal repast, and the *Überlinger Spitalwein* goes along perfectly with it. The plates were cold, the service so-so, but on a last meal like this one doesn't quibble. Besides, the fish and potatoes were steaming. The wine was a little below room temperature, which is tepid, but it is claimed that this brings out the full flavor.

Here they are prejudiced against bringing wine to the table in a bucket of ice. Even at such a restaurant as Walterspiel's in Munich, you must argue to have a Moselle, a Traminer, a Rhine wine or a French white wine put in ice. In any case, it isn't done without the sommelier raising eyebrows and mumbling to the waiter, "*Nah ya—Amerikaner,* what can you expect?" I always cut them right short at the beginning, saying: "We are American savages—put it in ice and put ice in the glasses—do you mind?" That shuts them up. Anyway, here I had arrived at the last station. I drank my coffee, paid my bill and marched to my fate—out of the Hotel Hecht.

It was raining heavily. The porter opened a huge umbrella and went for my car. It was early evening in the rest of the world, but in Überlingen it was deadest night. Not even the street lights were on. A solitary lamp lit the hotel entrance and shed its light on a poster on which appeared in large Gothic printing: *"Kurort Überlingen."*

Überlingen calls itself a *Kurort* on account of its balmy air, curative waters, woodsy promenades and absolute quiet. The poster announced the current week's goings on, printed under the heading: ENTERTAIN-MENT

It read as follows:

MONTAG
Rest day for the *Kurorchester.*
DIENSTAG 3 P.M.
Kurkonzert in the *Kurpark.*
MITTWOCH 3 P.M.
Kurkonzert in the *Kurpark.*
DONNERSTAG 3 P.M.
Kurkonzert in the *Kurpark.*
FREITAG 3 P.M.
Kurkonzert in the *Kurpark.*
SAMSTAG 3 P.M.
Kurkonzert in the *Kurpark.*
SONNTAG 3 P.M.
Grosses Kurkonzert in the Grosse Kursaal

At last my wet car appeared in the silent street. I took the wheel. The porter put out the light. The Hotel Hecht was dark.

The rain continued; the last stop I made before committing myself was at a gas station, the only place in Überlingen where, at three minutes to eleven, there was light. The attendant filled the tank, checked the tires, water and oil, and then pointed to the first of a series of small, neatly lettered white-and-green signs that led up a hill. Each one of them read: *"To Dr. Buchinger's Clinic am Bodensee."*

I advise prospective builders of clinics to visit Überlingen. It is the gayest, most refreshing and intelligent institutional building I have ever seen. Like a modern hotel or the promenade deck on shipboard, it lacks all that makes sanatoria unpleasant to enter. It stands in a park over-looking the lake, with magnificent trees growing almost through the building; brilliant colors and vast expanses of glass make it bright inside and out. On entering, there is a blackboard on which a tailor announces that his shop specializes in "taking in" skirts and trousers. The gaiety is

underlined by a sign taken from a railroad coach which says: *Nonsmoker.*

As inviting as the place is its personnel. Instead of a sleepy, rheumy night porter, a radiant, young, efficient girl, with the bluest eyes I have ever seen, received me at eleven P.M. She directed her frank gaze to my face and asked in that bell-clear voice, *"Haben Sie heute schon etwas gegessen?"*

"Ja, ja," I said.

Her eyes veiled a little and she said in a serious voice, looking the way one's mother does when trying to detect a lie, "You are coming here to fast. You understand that, yes?"

I said, *"Ja, Fräulein,* of course."

Again she corrected me, saying, *"Schwester* Marie Louise."

I said, "Yes, indeed, I intend to, *Schwester."*

"Also," she said, "tomorrow we start in earnest."

I was shown to a nice room with a balcony, and *Schwester* Marie Louise gave me a small bottle. "Tomorrow," she said, "before you eat anything; for the laboratory." The word for an empty stomach in German is *nüchtern,* another apt expression meaning you are *clear.* I was very *nüchtern* now and experienced a terrible thirst and hunger. I went to sleep and had a dream that was more like Buchenwald than Buchinger. I woke up to sunshine and blue sky.

The furniture on the balcony outside my plate-glass window was gay and dewy, the first rays of the morning sun shone into my bed and I picked up the telephone and said, "I would like to order breakfast— please."

The *Mädchen*-in-uniform who answered asked, "What?" She did not seem to understand me. I repeated my request, saying I would like to have some ham and eggs, coffee, rolls and butter and first a melon, ripe—very ripe.

The *Schwester* said, "Do you know where you are, Herr Bemelmans?"

I said, "Yes. At Doctor Buchinger's Sanatorium am Bodensee."

"Well, there is no breakfast, Herr Bemelmans. You are fasting, remember?"

"Not even a cup of coffee?"

"Not even a cup of coffee."

I said I thought it started after breakfast. After all, one gets breakfast anywhere in the world—in jail, in the Army, anywhere. The day starts with breakfast.

"Now then, Herr Bemelmans, you are not cooperating—there is no breakfast here. I am sorry. You may have a cup of herb tea—after being weighed."

"Would you kindly connect me with Herr Doktor Buchinger?" I asked in desperation.

"Doktor Buchinger is vacationing in Italy. Now, please . . ."

Probably stuffing himself with osso buco, spaghetti and cannelloni, I thought. I slowly put down the receiver in hopelessness.

A Fata Morgana aroma of coffee invaded my nose and I took a bath and dressed. There was a knock on the door.

"Oh," said another clear-eyed *Schwester*, "you are already dressed, Herr Bemelmans!"

"But why not, *Fräulein?*"

Once more I was corrected.

"*Schwester* Annerose, please—and please undress again," she said sternly. "I will wait outside." She took the little bottle.

I said, "Undress—why?"

She said, "Please put on your pajamas and robe and slippers, and then we go to weigh ourselves."

"But, *Schwester,* can't I go as I am?"

"No."

"Why not, *Schwester?*"

"Because we must weigh every morning."

"Well, dear *Schwester,* if I go every morning dressed as I am, it will be the same."

"It's one of the rules. Why do you object?"

"I dislike walking around like a patient in a hospital. I hate to wear slippers and a robe except in my bedroom. Besides—I never wear pajamas."

The *Schwester* was very sweet, but her face hardened. She said, putting her hands over her heart in a religious motion, "Please do it for *me.*" She added: "The robe will do."

This helplessness in the hands of a woman in absolute authority brought back long-forgotten days of childhood. Suddenly, as I undressed, I found I was being taken advantage of in a nursery way. It is the habit of European nurses, when a child hates a certain dish (in my case a dreadful soup called *Sago Suppe* that had fishlike eyes floating in it),

259

to blow on a hot spoonful and say, "Now, one spoon for Mammie, one for Pappie, one for Opapa, one for Omama, one for Uncle Henri. And the last one, now—it's almost over—for *me*." So I removed my trousers, shoes, stockings and shirt, hung up my coat and, putting on the bathrobe and slippers, followed the *Schwester* with the bottle to a room marked "Weighing Room."

"So now, one hundred eighty-six pounds. *Danke schön,* Herr Bemelmans." They all pronounced my awkward name in clear, precise tones—*Bémélmàns*—also as in school.

When I came back to my room I found a basket, the size that the figure of Little Red Riding Hood might carry in a marionette show, and in it were exactly twelve fresh raspberries. I smelled toast and ham and eggs and coffee again.

Schwester Annerose said, "Today you're on fruit. Tomorrow we start in earnest. You are free now to do anything you want." I wanted to drive down to the nearest tavern.

I was given a pamphlet entitled *The Theory of Fasting:*

We all have complete sympathy for you if, before you begin fasting, you have fear. It is natural when you take the cure for the first time. But you will soon see that it isn't bad. You will feel no pangs of

hunger, you will be surprised how light you feel. It needs, however, a bit of confidence and optimism on your part. Over and over again we make the observation that those patients who wholeheartedly say *yes*— and let things go their way—are most benefited.

Think of it—forty thousand people have fasted here and every year there are more who want to.

There followed some clinical explanation of what happens to your interior in this process of *Entschlackung*.

You will, as in all major changes in life, have difficulty acclimating yourself the first few days. Not enough to eat, no alcohol or tobacco— all these denials the patient must overcome, and no small matter. So hand yourself over completely and with confidence to the doctors, the *Schwestern* and all workers in this house, for all are concerned with your well-being. We start with one or two days of fruit, after which you receive a draught of *Glaubersalz*—warm—which, while mild, will effect a thorough and intense purge. This is followed by a rush of water into the intestine, which will cause a great thirst and this will be quenched with a cup of tea at noon. In the days following, you will receive, four times a day, warm drinks. Tea in the morning, at noon a mug of vegetable brew—and then you go to bed, where *Schwester* will give you a liverpack, a hot-water bottle.

To suggest to you a better way of living, the evening hours are devoted to music, and lectures by the doctors. A few hints to especially take to heart:

Talk about Lucullan adventures only makes it more difficult. Radios and typewriters are not desired, as absolute quiet is important to the cure.

After the cure it is necessary to adjust the body for seven days back to regular living and a gradual increase in food accomplishes this. Do not clandestinely go to restaurants. Avoid the excitement of cinemas, or coffee. Become, instead, conscious of nature and the calm that surrounds you.

Please understand us: we are not an institute of morality in which your behavior is censured; we appeal to your good will and cooperation, and now we hope with all our heart that the cure will bring you health and freshness and, beyond that, have an inner meaning for you.

The *Schwester* in charge of me announced that we had progressed now to the point where one of the *Kurdoktors* would give me a thorough examination.

I had an hour before the doctor wanted to see me. I walked about the institute and its grounds. In one of the bright dining rooms, those who had done their stint were munching their proper foods, all looking smug and healthy. In the rest of the building the *Schwestern* were busy preparing the hot-water bottles, and through an open door I saw in orderly rows cups ready for the herb tea. I encountered fellow patients in the various corridors and on the walks of the parks—Valkyries, Farouks, Butterballs bouncing along—meatballs sitting on benches, popovers and soufflés in human form—none of them depressing. There were merely what one sees in a German landscape, or beer garden, brewery or office. A wave of terrible hunger came over me and it all seemed like a comical nightmare. I thought it would make a very fine musical and I sat on a bench and made the first stanza of a song. It started:

> *"I will always be singing—*
> *In praise of Überlingen . . ."*

I become irritated at feeding time when there is nothing to eat. Also, I get annoyed when asked to answer personal questions on a paper. A doctor without an ounce of humor sat behind his desk and asked when and where I was born, what my profession was, and why I had decided to take the cure.

When and where I was born he could read in my passport; also my profession, on the register of the sanatorium; and evidently I had not come to gain weight in Überlingen. He asked me to undress and began a very thorough examination. He tapped me with a hammer and said, using my name in its most accusative form: "Herr Bemelmans—you have a swollen liver."

"Yes," I said, "why not?" Ass of a doctor—neither he nor I would be here without defects.

"How much do you drink, Herr Bemelmans?"

I told him, and he looked personally offended and made tests with my eyes following his finger down to my nose and away again. He measured me and said, "You have fallen arches, Herr Bemelmans"—a condition I was unaware of until now. He said it with moral indignation.

He took my blood pressure and looked in my mouth. "How much do you smoke a day, Herr Bemelmans?"

"Oh, sixteen to twenty cigars."

"*Hm, hm,*" he mumbled, and observed that I had some very intricate bridgework. "*Er hat ja Brücken, und Brücken,*" he said, addressing me in the third person. "We shall have to take an electrograph of the heart," he said, and marked on a printed form the various massages, intestinal baths and other beneficial treatments I should get. He said he would visit me in my room at eight-thirty in the morning the day after tomorrow.

I am sorry. I cannot tell you about the cure and its benefits. I fell into black despair, which I suppose came from my empty stomach.

I went to my room and picked up the telephone. The little church-bell voice answered, and I said, "Will you be so kind as to make out my bill? I am leaving."

"*Nein,*" said the *Schwester* there.

I said, "Yes, *liebe Schwester,* please. I am sorry. You are all so nice and sweet—but this is not for me. I prefer to drop dead tomorrow at the Bratwurstglöckl."

The good woman who made up my room came in and said, "*Aber,* Herr Bemelmans, you can go in the woods there and smoke a cigar—nobody sees you. They all sneak out for a snack—nobody minds."

I said, "Thank you and bless you, but it's more than that." The *Hausmeister,* as the porter in such places is called, brought my car, and my baggage was put in it. In the dining room the cured fatties about to be sprung looked at me with contempt. Once again it was like being thrown out of boarding school, with all the good children eying you. Only the dear *Schwester* Annerose said goodbye with sympathy.

I always have a sensation of great joy when saying farewell to places of strictness and denial. I drove out whistling in high good humor like a bird on the wing.

Johnny stuck it out, a man of will power and moral fiber. I tried to corrupt him. I had a sort of CARE package made up containing a dozen *Bratwürste,* headcheese, smoked *Kassler Rippchen* and a barrel of *Spatenbräu,* and sent it to him at the sanatorium am Bodensee; also menus from Maxim's, the Méditerranée, the Escargot de Montorgueil and Joseph's in Paris. But he stayed a whole month and lost thirty-one pounds. On account of Doctor Buchinger's Clinic am Bodensee I gained eight. But I can recommend the place highly to people of character.

June 14, 1962

MY DEAR FRIEND:

I had dinner last night in your restaurant with a titled friend who is not very affluent and who wanted a duck.

I know that you don't specialize in ducks, but the duck was on the menu and I ordered it, rôti, *with petits pois à la Française.*

The waiter must have had a crise de nerfs *or some domestic upset, for he was in a terrible mood. I ordered as usual a double Jus de Pamplemousse,* nature, *which was served. Then when I told the maître d'hôtel later to bring a second double* jus, *the waiter snapped at him, "But he's already had one." I know that waiter is one of your trusted aides, but it is bad enough to have to drink Jus de Pamplemousse with your duck, and it started out badly.*

Then came the duck. I said to him, as I saw him start with the legs, that we did not want the legs. So he took the legs and desosséed *them with his back turned to me. Then he sliced the left side of the breast of the duck, very thin, and spirited the carcass into a receptacle that already contained another piece*

264

of leftover food. He did all this covering the maneuver with his derrière
*and his coat, and put the duck into the lower, closed part of the side-board. I observed all this. There was served a greasy piece of skin (I like
the duck very browned, to a crisp). Then the leg,* tranché *to look like
the breast. Then he put over this* une soupe de petits pois et de sauce et
du bacon et c'était épouvantable—à vomir. *I called the* maître d'hôtel,
*who explained that in this restaurant usually one served a half a duck
for two people. Well, not to me. So I will not write about this, except I
will place it into an imaginary restaurant called* Le Morpion *in Nanterres
or somewhere else, where I need to complain. You owe me a duck—a
small one, properly* rôti, *and I am sorry to have to write this letter, but
there is no excuse to do a foul trick like that to a bon client, so knock
their heads together.*

Toujours,
LUDWIG

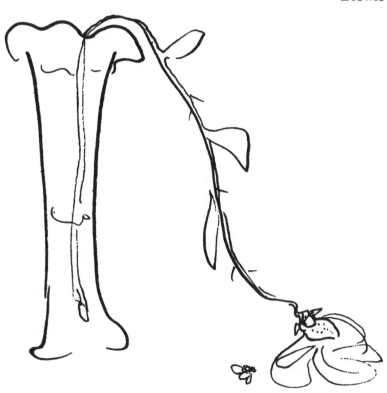

In the spring and summer of 1962, on his last trip to Europe, L. B. kept a journal. In it were notes to himself of things to write about later. The pieces following in this section—unpolished and heretofore unpublished—are from this journal.

THE FRENCH TRAIN

THIS IS THE END of trains. The Orient Express is already finished and not running any more. This one, the train excessively advertised in glowing phrases and with much praise, is, like all European trains *de grand luxe*, a memory.

This one is an assassin. It takes you by the head and shoulders and shakes you as if it were after your life. It assaults you with a concert of clanking, shrieking, knocking noises, such as you must go into a factory to hear; it sways and rattles along, so that you feel at times you will fly off the rails with it. If you fall asleep you will have terrible nightmares and wake up to gruesome reality, see the desolate night scenes when the train comes to abrupt halts and starts to wobble and to jerk, to dance, and the people come dancing along. That was some meal; it is in your memory now—the most awful of meals at table.

It is hard to get on this train—for what reason? Are so many people afraid to fly? Are so many flying that there is not room in the sky? And today, being the beginning of Whitsunday, and I am going in the opposite direction of the crowd, why did I have trouble getting a ticket and a cabin, a single old, dirty cabin on this miserable train? I tried to get one at the station—impossible. I tried to get one at a travelers bureau —sold out. Finally I went to the concierge, who said, "Perhaps I can get you a seat—and a place at the first sitting, a reserved seat at table. You better reserve it—the train will be jammed. But why don't you fly?" No, now I wanted to see what it was like. The flight in the Caravelle is wonderful, and planes all day long. Finally he got a place. I got on the train; it was car fourteen, which is really thirteen—all the way back of the station, the last car. Outside the station really. Then came the first jerk, and the train moved on. In the dining room, by the time I got there, everyone was seated and eating. I asked the headwaiter, or conductor, for my seat. He was busy putting out wine and beer bottles, and said, "Sorry, but the place has been taken." One had to be there, in place, at the beginning of the meal or else wait for the second service, which was at 10 P.M. Would I mind waiting in the bar?

The bar was jammed also, but a stool was found. Now the crowding was explained: They were all members of a traveling club, English, and knew one another, and they were very jolly, and the men all smoked pipes. They were nice people, estate agents, owners of garages and shops, and they exchanged very sober talk. The barman was unhappy, there being small tips. Every little while the train let out a sound like the scream of a woman seeing a mouse and being frightened by it. These women here, all of them were very good, and not very happy with this voyage, and not comfortable, being shaken continually like a lot of puddings on small plates, and not fitting into the narrow berths, and apparently exhausted by a two weeks' holiday and rushed from the Eiffel Tower to the Vatican—*Did you see the Pope? Did you? We did, and we're not Catholics, we saw him, we're not either*—with 28,000 people. It was spectacular. The smoke thickens; it's not the best tobacco; the eyes burn.

Well, they are having their chicken in there, reports one; that means another half hour. Now will you have another lager? I don't like this beer. (The only beers they have on board are Kronenbourg Alsace and Fuerstenberg—and it's ice cold, and not to the liking of these people, although they are all very nice about it.)

The meal is awful: a soup like in prison, made of carrots shredded and some kind of gruel, watery, in silver battered pots; then a sole, which is not bad, *meunière;* a red wine—a Bordeaux, iced, or at least the bottle is ice cold—perhaps people ask for that; and then a Buck, or Guinea Hen —it seems precooked with black olives and is in a gooey stew, and the black little sheafs of where the feathers have been are still in the skin of the animal—a decomposed kind of meat from overcooking; with it, very good *petits pois,* as they should be, and potatoes and, after, cheeses. There is a new cheese here, le Bleu de Bresse, which I discovered when I ate with the help in a private villa. (The help know what is good; they ignored the wine cellar and drank a bottle distinguished by the fact that it did not have a label on it—this was made at the villa by old Robert. Then a very good bread, round peasant loaf, and this wonderful cheese.)

"What is the matter now?" The train rolls into a station, change of engines, with a lot of fuss. Banging, whistling, finally the dessert, a soupy ice, fruit, in a basket, good. Coffee—Nescafé. The bill is low—for all, including wine and coffee, tip and taxes, about $4. But a good deal for France. You see that in everything an American price level is aimed at. The British find it higher than in England. The crew is overworked; there is no time for elegance. (Their white coats are spattered and seem to have been used for days.) There is no longer any time for talking or slow, careful service; it is a rush, the rush they complain about as being "American."

Had lunch at the Hotel de Paris in Monte Carlo. A young piccolo served the bread with two forks, and he dropped it on the carpet. He turned around and looked carefully to see if anyone had observed him, picked up the roll with his hand and then saw that I had watched him. He turned red and said, " 'Scusa." I asked him to bring me a spoon and a fork. He had held the two forks in this position—((—so I showed him how to do it like this—()—with a spoon on the left under side and a fork on the right, both in the right hand. He was baffled. I told him that I had learned how to do it at his age.

The cooking of the Hotel de Paris is superb. I ordered spaghetti Bolognese and it was as light as a soufflé. Very nice maître d'hôtel gave me table number five. "Because," he said, "five is a number that always comes out at the center roulette table at the casino." I gave the number to someone yesterday and it came out twice in a row.

L'OUSTAU DE

BAUMANIÈRE

TRIP TO LES BAUX: L'Oustau de Baumanière, restaurant and hotel marked with highest notes in *Guide Michelin* and virtually a Lourdes of the Gourmets. CHEF: Proprietor M. Raymond Thuilier.

Arrival at Baumanière, haunted place of rocks, suicidal landscape, a small domain embedded in walls of rock. By small I mean Central Park in New York, surrounded by Hotel Plaza-size boulders. A sign that points to Baumanière also says "Valley of Hell"; above that, Baumanière, small village. Then on left are some stables, buildings that house guests—drive on and up and there is a swimming pool and the restaurant. This has the character of a vaulted monastery or castle. The chairs and tables super solid. The wine waiter looks like a blacksmith and wears such an apron. There are a lot of real women around, and waiters—all very nice people and at ease. The food comes on little wagons which are rolled from a pantry outside the kitchen—that is, between kitchen and dining room. Inside is a loudspeaker in the kitchen, and the kitchen is relatively small. The oven here is very hot. On the left side is the altar part of the oven where M. Thuilier functions; he has a great many small casseroles, in which with a "Besen" he makes his sauces. In back, facing the oven, is a large wooden table and here a man makes the *croutes*, the dough into which a good many things are packed to be baked.

The menu is compact and consists of various recommendations, four in each section, to start with, to fish with, to meat with, to dessert with —finish. The wine card is large, but it's best to trust that powerful sommelier, who, *tutoyezing* the proprietor, is therefore either very close to him or is his brother.

There is a young non-maître-d'hôtel type of maître d'hôtel who must also be a relative, smells of garlic and is very friendly besides. He has the menus in his hands, and as you enter you are not taken to your table, but, holding the menu like the toreador does the muleta, to make the bull go —forward and to the right—he smiles and conducts to a small vaulted fireplace and refectory chair place. Again castle, church, convent air must be marvelous and cool in summer but is now, with a mistral blowing the trees to shreds and no fire going, rather cold. But you go in there, like it or not, to "compose your menu."

One thing M. Thuilier systematically runs his place, and you better submit to routine and the suggestions, for here there is only one rule.

Now the menu is made, and there is the wine waiter, *bon*. You wait, others are waiting, and then you get your table assigned. The soup is wonderful, the baked-in lamb and its kidney is heavenly, the dessert is a dream. The wine is fine, the coffee good; seven times or ten a little wagon has been rolled to your table. The bisque of homard was so good I asked for a second helping, and for that the wagon was rolled out and in again—so that it is hot, hot plate, hot ladle, hot customer in praise. Steam runs down your face. It is the best; it cannot be made better.

Otherwise is the hotel, a grim Spanish-style room, and I have never cut myself with a bedsheet. That one had a fold in the center and as I slid into bed I got cut. I suppose people wearing silk pajamas can sleep with comfort there, but I had not put them on.

The towels also are hard. The water is hot, the willingness great. There is one attendant there, and in this land of Tarascon and other comedians, this one is worth a study. He has a thin, long nose and gives very "fool" answers that are wise.

Monsieur Thuilier shows me his house—rows upon rows of books, an entire library, and here is *ma salle d'eau*—local expression for washroom. He is about in apron and jacket but never in chef's hat. Only chef I know who is not.

In the morning his cooks also are without it. I ask them, they say, "Oh, we put it on at eleven." In wine cellar which is naturally cool—that is, not air-conditioned—is a great deal of wine and all good. The master's hearing is not too good—he leans sideways to hear. Great friend of animals, and many people with dogs come here, dogs admitted to place and dining room. The house cat wears a bell to warn mice and birds. Cat not allowed in kitchen. Waits at door. M. Thuilier like all great chefs a little off center. In wine cellar keeps extra pair of shoes cool, for hot feet at oven.

He does not believe much in vegetables. I ask for vegetables. "Sorry— have you asparagus?" (In season now and plenty.)

"No."

"String beans?"

"N-o-o."

"Carrots?"

"N-n-o-o."

"Perhaps some petits pois?"

"Yes."

Brings petits pois, came from a can, were small and sort of dented in four places like a sucked-in tennis ball and no good at all. When one eats here, you best have no liver trouble and follow the master. What does the master eat? Very strict regime, for seventeen years—no sauces, no wine, no smoking—but he makes the very best sauces and orders his altar boys with the various casseroles, "Take this one off, put this one on the fire." Nothing must come to a very sudden heat, to boil. The butter used in cooking is thrown away and new butter is used to put on the dish when it is served.

Where did he serve his apprenticeship?

"*Alors*, that is a long story."

There is the only riding academy at which I have seen happy horses and there are signs—"Be careful of your horse," "Be nice to him, he is a good friend." All is very neat, well fed, and a drillmaster who trains the riders in the best Russian manner (he is French). All this belongs to M. Thuilier—vineyards, houses, terrain, the hotel, the trees, the plants.

Take road to Arles, twenty-five kilometers away. Black mood in nature, the depressing, nerve-eating wind of the region, the many cypresses in rows to break up the flow of air, the mood of Arles, the Van Gogh depression. They have removed the bridge he had painted; they are not proud of him here. But now everything becomes clear: law practice, Thuilier, and another.

Monsieur Thuilier was a lawyer in Paris, and he fell in love, married, and he wanted to get away from the parquets of the Seine. Looked around, found wild lands, bought the property in Les Baux, long ago, developed them into his various interests. Made the restaurant, and started his various hobbies, among them cooking. He also paints, patient pictures of flowers, on an easel. He puts them before himself, a pot, a bouquet, and then a canvas, and those are his afternoons—landscapes of Les Baux, a picture of his old dog, of his pots. None of women, and horses are rather complicated also, although he loves them.

When I asked him how the reception on television up here was, said, "Nothing now."

I said: "Wh-hy?"

He said that he had turned his set off a while ago. (He did not mean to be funny.)

Return to Nice, one tank full of gas. Eighteen liters.

273

I bought the first good cherries I saw in Monte Carlo—Italian cherries—and when I got back to the villa I said to Madame Sabatini, "Here, help yourself." So she took one, saying, "Now I must make a wish, with the first cerise of the year." She closed her eyes.

She is a remarkable woman, well into her sixties, who takes care of the whole house and the kitchen while her husband, a decade older, cares for the grounds.

I asked, "Will you tell me what you wished?"

She said, "I wished that I may have many more years of work and usefulness—I and my husband. I do not at all envy the rich, who are all of them unhappy. Work is what I like."

Menus

L.B. was never of the classic mold of Menu Collectors. Actually, menus, after being studied and ordered from, were for him fortuitously available sketching pads. As such they were kept by him, and it is from among them that the following selection has been made. The sketches from the backs of the menus have been appropriately distributed throughout this book.

Le Pavillon

MENU

Caviar Malossol 8.00   Saumon Gumé 3.00   Anguille Gumée 2.75
Gambon de Bayonne 2.50   Goie Gras Truffé 6.00   Grapefruit 1.00
Little Necks 1.50   Cherrystones 1.50   Melon 1.50
Cocktails: Lobster 5.00   Shrimps 3.00   Crab Meat 4.00

Oeufs

Brouillé au Parmesan 3.00   Omelette Pavillon 5.00   Cocotte Périgourdine 3.00
Poché Bénédictine 3.50   Groids à la Gelée 1.75   Plat aux Rognons 3.25
Mollet aux Epinards 3.25   Omelette Gorestière 3.50   Grit Andalouse 3.00   Gimbale des Gourmets 3.25

Poissons

Délices de Sole Polignac 4.50   Gimbale de Crab Meat Newburg 5.50   Homard Xavier 7.50
Moules au Chablis 4.25   Suprême de Striped Bass Dugléré 4.50   Grenouilles Provençale 4.75
Goujonnette de Sole, Sauce Moutarde 4.50   Gruite de Rivière, Beurre Noisette 4.75
Spécialités: Homard 7.50   Sole Anglaise   Moules 3.50

Plats du Jour

CONTRE FILET PAVILLON 6.50   LA POULARDE BASQUAISE (Pour 2) 12.00
Suprême de Pintadon Carmen 5.50   Coeur de Gilet Biarrotte 8.50   Pigeonneau aux Olives 6.00
Caneton aux Cerises (Pour 2) 15.00   Médaillon de Veau Smitane 5.00   Ris de Veau Meunière 5.25
Côte de Volaille Pojarsky 5.25   Rognon de Veau Ardennaise 5.00   Goie de Veau à l'Anglaise 4.75

Spécialités: Châteaubriand (Pour 2) 18.00   Volaille (selon grosseur)   Ris de Veau 6.00

Grillades

Poularde   Reine   Grain   Poussin   Canard   Pigeon
Selle d'Agneau   Carré d'Agneau

Plats Froids

Poularde à la Gelée à l'Estragon 5.50   Langue Givrée 3.25   Gambon d'York 3.50
Gerrine de Canard 4.50   Boeuf Mode à la Gelée 5.00   Gerrine de Volaille 4.50

Légumes

Coeur de Céleri à la Moëlle 2.50   Epinards au Velouté 1.50   Petits Pois aux Laitues 1.75
Courgette Gines Herbes 2.00   Haricots Verts au Beurre 1.75   Choux-Gleurs au Gratin 2.50
Laitue Braisé au Gus 2.00   Champignons Grillés sur Toast 2.75   Artichaut à l'Huile 2.00

Entremets

Patisserie Pavillon 2.00   Soufflés Tous Parfums 3.25   Crêpes Pavillon 3.25
Désir de Roi 2.50   Cerises Gubilée 3.50   Poire Hélène 3.00
Pêche Melba 2.50   Macédoine de Gruits aux Liqueurs 2.50   Coupe aux Marrons 2.50
Glaces: Vanille 1.00   Chocolat (Menier) 1.00   Gramboise 1.00   Moka 1.00   Citron 1.00   Graise 1.00
Café .70   Demi Tasse .60   Bread and Butter .75

LES HORS D'ŒUVRE CHAUDS
DE

MAXIM'S

Pissaladière - Petite bouchée d'ici
Crêpes Maxim's - Moules Frites - Ramequin
Quiche lorraine - Parmesane de Collioure
Petites "Spéciales" grillées américaine
Toasts à la moelle - Chipolatas sur Toasts
Toasts chauds au foie gras
Tarte aux poireaux - Choux farcis
Rissoles de foie gras
Rissoles de volaille - Rissoles du Père Antoine

Parmi

LES GRANDES SPÉCIALITÉS

MAXIM'S

qui vous seront présentées au cours de la Saison :

LE CONSOMMÉ AU FOIE GRAS ★ LA CRÈME DE MARENNES

LES ŒUFS POCHÉS SANS-GÊNE (RECETTE P. SALLES & MONTAGNÉ) ★ L'OMELETTE RICHEMOND

LA COQUILLE SAINT-JACQUES PRÉSIDENT CHAIX ★ LA SOLE ALBERT
LES DÉLICES DE SOLE ALEX HUMBERT
LA DEMOISELLE DE CHERBOURG "RUE ROYALE"

LES NOISETTES D'AGNEAU EDOUARD VII ★ LE RIS DE VEAU ENTIER EN COCOTTE
LE GIGOT BRAISÉ A L'INDIENNE ★ LE CARRÉ D'AGNEAU AUX PETITS LÉGUMES
LA POULARDE EN COCOTTE MAXIM'S ★ LE CANARD NANTAIS A L'ANANAS
LE PIGEON EN COMPOTE NIÇOISE ★ LE CIVET DE LIÈVRE D'ÉDOUARD NIGNON
LES GRIVES A LA FRANÇAISE (E. NIGNON) ★ LES ALOUETTES BONNE FEMME (ESCOFFIER)
LE RABLE DE LIÈVRE GRAND VENEUR
LA LONGE DE VEAU PRINCE ORLOFF
LA DINDE DES ARTISTES (RECETTE D'ALEXANDRE DUMAS)
L'ESCALOPE DE FOIE GRAS ET SES TRUFFES FRAICHES (CRÉATION)

LA CROÛTE AUX FRUITS D'ALFRED GOISET
LES CRÊPES FOURRÉES VEUVE JOYEUSE

nous vous proposons
AUJOURD'HUI :

La Bisque de Homard. 550.

La Demoiselle de Cherbourg "Rue Royale" 1600.

Les Grives doubles à la Française

MENU

CLASSIQUE DU GRAND VÉFOUR

	Couvert-Beurre 180	Céleris en branche	2
Pamplemousse	300	Caviar frais	
Mœlle sur toast	450	Terrines	6
Jambon d'York	750	Bayonne	8
Foie gras des Landes	950	Quimperlaise	7
Lobster Cocktail	950	L'Assortiment Landais	8

LES POTAGES

Bisque de Homard	500	Consommé double en tasse (chaud ou en gelée) 2	
Tortue claire en tasse	350	Crème Vichyssoise	4
Germiny	450		

LES POISSONS

Le toast de Crevettes Rothschild	500	Sole au plat " Vefour"	9

LES ŒUFS

Œufs plat Louis Oliver	850	Œufs cocotte Opéra	4
Œufs Véfour	750	Œufs André Leconte	5
	Œufs en gelée	250	

LES ENTRÉES

Les Rognons flambés à l'Armagnac	950	Tournedos sauté Belle Hélène	8
Ballotines de volaille Duc de Chartres	950	Steack au poivre	7
Pigeon " Prince Rainier III"	1100	Noix de Ris de Veau au Xerès	8

LES GRILLADES

Chateaubriand grillé Béarnaise (2 pers.)	1.900	Steack minute Paillard	7
Mixed Grill	850	Côte d'Agneau haricots verts	8
Demi-Poulet grillé Américaine (2 pers.)	1.700	Rognons grillés au Bacon	9

Entrecôte grillée comme à Porteneuve (2 personnes) 1.800

CARTE DU JOUR

POISSONS

```
Brochettes de Scampis Meunière 650
Filets de Soles Marguerie      750
Sole de Roche Belle Meunière   750
Coquilles St.Jacques au Safran 750
I/2 Homard  Chantecler       I.200
```

ENTREES

```
Côtes de veau Biarrotte        750
Carrè d'Agneau Sarladaise      950
Entrecôte Marcahnd de vin(2)I.800
```

LES DESSERTS

Crêpes Belle Otero	4
Pâtisserie Maison	3
Meringues glacées	3
Glaces au choix	3
Les Soufflés au choix	4
Fruits rafraîchis	3
Coupe Jack	3
Oranges Orientales	3
Poires " Vefour"	4

NOTA : Ce menu est composé de la façon suivant

    1 menu classique comportant nos spéciali
en rouge.
1 Menu du jour.

Chacun de ces Menus possède la gamme habitue
des Mets

	NF
COUVERT 300	3,00

		NF
BELONS 000, les six.................	1.080	10,80
LE SAUMON FUMÉ	1.000	10,00
JAMBON DE PARME	850	8,50
FOIE GRAS GELÉE DE RUBIS	1.100	11,00
LES RILLETTES À L'OIE	300	3,00

		NF
PETITE MARMITE	400	4,00
SAINT-GERMAIN AUX CROUTONS. ..	400	4,00
CONSOMMÉ DOUBLÉ EN TASSE	300	3,00

ŒUFS GRATINÉS LAPÉROUSE	400	4,00
ŒUFS BROUILLÉS BERGÈRE	400	4,00
LES ŒUFS À LA GELÉE	400	4,00

		NF			NF
SALADE DE LANGOUSTE JÉRÔME ..	1.700	17,00	DÉLICES DE SOLE SONIA	900	9,00
SUPRÊME DE TURBOT ST-GERMAIN.	850	8,50	MERLAN RICHELIEU	500	5,00
LA TIMBALE DES AUGUSTINS	1.000	10,00	LA TRUITE AU VIN BLANC..........	750	7,50
MATELOTE D'ANGUILLE bourguignonne.	850	8,50	GRATIN DE Langoustine LAPÉROUSE..	1.000	10,00
LANGOUSTE BABINSKI	1.900	19,00	MOUSSELINES DE BROCHET St-Michel	800	8,00
LA TRUITE À LA GELÉE	750	7,50	LES COQUILLES ST-JACQUES Pépère..	750	7,50

	2	3	4			NF
				ROGNONS DE VEAU JAMAIS MIEUX.	1.100	11,00
			NF	JAMBON BRAISÉ gratins Augustins.....	700	7,00
	30	36	44	FOIE DE VEAU À L'ANGLAISE......	850	8,50
LE CANETON DE COLETTE 3.000	3.600	4.400		ÉTUVE DE BŒUF MACONNAISE	700	7,00
RIS DE VEAU AUX PETITS POIS....	1.050	10,50		LE DESIR DES GOURMETS	800	8,00
CÔTE DE VEAU ORLOFF	850	8,50		STEACK SAUTÉ LAPÉROUSE........	900	9,00
CURRY DE VOLAILLE À L'INDIENNE.	900	9,00		SELLE ET CARRÉ D'AGNEAU (selon gros.)		
LE PIGEON ROTI	1.200	12,00		LE MARCASSIN SAUTÉ ST-HUBERT..	11.00	11,00
POULARDE POÊLÉE Docteur (le quart).	750	7,50				
LA BÉCASSE NAVIGATEUR	2.800	28,00				

		NF			NF
FONDS D'ARTICHAUT FLORENTINE..	350	3,50	HARICOTS VERTS AU BEURRE......	350	3,50
LES CHAMPIGNONS LAPÉROUSE.....	350	3,50	CŒUR DE LAITUE BRAISÉ	250	2,50
GRATIN DU QUAI	300	3,00	GRATIN SYDNEY	400	4,00
POMMES	250	2,50	PETITS POIS À LA FRANÇAISE......	350	3,50
ENDIVES MEUNIÈRES	300	3,00	POINTES D'ASPERGES Petit-Duc......	750	7,50

LA POIRE LAPÉROUSE.............	450	4,50
TOUS LES FROMAGES	250	2,50
SOUFFLÉ AU GRAND MARNIER.....	500	5,00
LES CRÊPRES MONA..............	450	4,50
BANANES FLAMBÉES	400	4,00
CRÈME FRAICHE	250	2,50
FRUITS MELBA	450	4,50
GLACE VANILLE	250	2,50
FRUITS AUX LIQUEURS	500	5,00

CAFÉ	130	1,30

51, Quai des Grands-Augustins, PARIS (6ᵉ. — Tél. : DANton 68-64

Menu

DINER

Ccuvert 200
Caviar 1600 - Saumon Fu[...]
Grape Fruit 250
Fines Belons 1/2 Dz. ·500
Marennes extra 1/2 Dz. 800
Escargots de Bourgogne 1/2 Dz. 280
Tous les Hors-d'Oeuvre 450 - Saucisson Chaud 450
Parfait de Foie Gras dans sa Gelée au Porto 1.200
Jambonneau de Paris 350 - Jambon de Bayonne-d'York 550
Terrine de Volaille-de de Bécasse 750 - Terrine Maison 350

LES POTAGES

Petite Marmite Henri IV	300	Bisque de Homard 800
Consommé au Tapioca	200	Cressonniere 200	Lamballe 200

LES POISSONS

Delices de Sole Lucas 700
Filets de Merlan Richelieu 450

Quenelles de Brochet Armoricaine	750	Rougets au Gratin	600
Turbot Poché Sce Mousseline	650	Raie au Beurre Noir	450
Supreme de Barbue Dugléré	600	Moules Mariniere	450
Morue Pochée au Beurre Fondu	550	Coquille St-Jacques Provencale	600

Homard ou Langouste S.G.

LES ENTREES

Volaille de Bresse en Cocotte Mascotte 750
Medaillon de Veau Malesherbes 650

Noisette d'Agneau aux Laitues	750	Rognon Flambé Lucas	750
Ris de Veau Braisé aux Olives	650	Tournedos Massena	700
Cervelle Florentine	600	Jambon a la Mode de Chablis	600
Bécasse Flambée à notre Manière	2500	Noisette de Marcassin St Hubert	1200

Quartier de Pauillac Sarladaise S.G

LES ROTS

Poularde - Reine - Grain   S.G.   Carré ou Selle d'Agneau   S.G.

LE BUFFET FROID

Jambon d'York 550 Langue Ecarlate 550   1/4 de Volaille de Bresse   650
Parfait de Foie Gras dans sa Gelée au Porto 1.200 - Terrine de Volaille-de Lièvre 650 - de Perdreau 750

LES LEGUMES

Haricots Verts Frais 400 Aubergines 250 Courgettes 250   Petits Pois a la Française 300
Artichaut 250   Fonds d'Artichauts 300 - Sauce Hollandaise 400 Tomates 250 Endives 250
Champignons sur Toast 250   Chou-Fleur 200 Epinards 200 Pâtes 200

LES ENTREMETS - LES FRUITS

Crêpes Flambées au Grand Marnier 350 Soufflé Lucas 400 Bananes Flambées 300 Croute aux Fruits 350
Pomme Lucas 300   Poire Belle Hélène 350   Pot de Crème Vanille ou Chocolat 200
Ananas au Kirsch 400   Salade d'Oranges 350   - Fruits Rafraichis 350 - Pèche Melba 350
Meringue Glacée 300 Glace Vanille 250   Coupe Jack 300   Tartelette aux Fruits 250
Rais in 350 - Poire - Pomme 250   Mandarine = Noix
Tous Les Fromages 200   Café 120   Sanka 150

SERVICE NON COMPRIS

Service et -VENTE DE VINS EN VILLE 'Prix Special'

Aligoté 1954 la Bout 550 1/2 Bout 280

Nos spécialités : Le Gratin de Champignons Lucas - La Sole de ma Tante Marie - La Timbale Mauresque
Le Canard Rouennais à la Presse - La Poularde étuvée au Porto avec la mousse des prairies - Le Rognon flambé Lucas

RESTAURANT LUCAS CARTON, 9 Place de la Madeleine   Téléph. Anjou 22-90
~ Grands et Petits Salons ~   22-91

CRÉATIONS ET SPÉCIALITÉS

LARUE

Déjeuner

Hors-d'œuvre chauds : Les Rognons de Veau à la Valançay.
Les Feuilletés Richemonde. - Le Saucisson de Lyon chaud.

LUNDI. .. .. Filet de Turbotin au Corton.
Cassoulet d'Oie à la Castelnaudary.

MARDI .. .. Petit Bar grillé Sauce Moutarde.
Civet de Garenne à la Française.

MERCREDI. Matelote d'Anguille au Champagne.
Gigot d'Agneau Rôti au Plat Larue.

JEUDI. .. .. Filets de Sole Nantaise.
Pièce de Bœuf braisée de 7 heures à
la Noailles.

VENDREDI. Pâté chaud de Saumon à la Antonin
Carême.

SAMEDI. .. .. Quenelles de Brochet à la Nantua.
Jambonneau braisé aux Haricots rouges
au Chambertin.

Dîner

POTAGES :
Consommé Rubis - Consommé de Volaille Larue
Consommé Bortchok - Crème Germiny aux Profiteroles
Coulis d'Écrevisses à la Brillat Savarin
Petite marmite à la moelle - Ox-tail soup
Bortsch de petite Russie

POISSONS :
Filets de Sole Nantaise - Filets de Sole Chimay
Filets de Sole Royale - Sole Strogonoff
Sole farcie Thérèse - Sole Camille Cerf
Petite Barbue étuvée au Corton
Petite Barbue Palestrina - Truite Saumonée Belgrand
Turbotin étuvé au Champagne
Laitance de Carpe à l'Alsacienne
Gratin d'Écrevisses à la Nantua
Homard à l'Armoricaine - Homard à la Cussy
Langouste à la Doria

ENTRÉES :
Foies de Canard à la Polignac
Côtelette de Volaille Maréchal
Poularde de Bresse grillée à la Grimaldi
Poularde de Bresse des Gastronomes
Poularde de Bresse au Champagne
Poularde de Bresse étuvée au Chambertin
Le Chapon en pâte à la Barbey d'Aurévilly
Caneton Nantais aux Figues
Caneton froid à la Derby
La Dodine de Caneton aux Perles Noires
Caille à la Souwaroff
Bécasse au Fumet Flambée Fine Champagne
Caille à la Païva
Bécasse Rôtie sur Canapé Larue
Les Truffes en Feuilletés à la Talleyrand
Le Parfait de Foie gras Larue à la gelée de Porto

ENTREMETS :
Soufflé aux Framboises - Soufflé Larue - Soufflé Praliné
Poire Schouwaloff - Poire à la Rosemonde - Poire Hélène
Ananas à la Royal - Pomme Karolinska
Pudding léger Montmorency - Pêche Cardinal
Crêpes Suzette au Grand Marnier - Crêpes Marquise
Crêpes Larue - Le Soufflé glacé Lamberty

Restaurant LARUE

C. DUPLAT, Succr d'Ed. NIGNON
27, Rue Royale - 3, Place de la Madeleine
Tél. : Anjou 10-10 et 10-11

MENU GASTRONOMIQUE A 1500 FRANCS
VIN COMPRIS
4 plats au choix
et 1/2 bouteille de Bordeaux Supérieur blanc ou rouge

ŒUF EN GELÉE · JAMBON DE BAYONNE
PORTUGAISES DE CLAIRES · HORS-D'ŒUVRE
ŒUFS PLAT AU BACON · OMELETTE BASQUAISE

✳

FILETS DE SOLE CHAPON FIN
TURBOT SAUCE HOLLANDAISE
ALOSE GRILLÉE SAUCE GRIBICHE
LAMPROIE BORDELAISE

✳

AGNEAU DE PAUILLAC POMMES NOUVELLES
ENTRECOTE BORDELAISE POMMES SOUFFLÉES
BROCHETTE DE FILET DE BŒUF BÉARNAISE
POULET EN COCOTTE FORESTIÈRE

✳

POIRE CHAPON FIN
FRUITS RAFRAICHIS AU CHAMPAGNE
PÊCHE FLAMBÉE AU KIRSCH
CRÈMES FRITES BORDELAISE

✳

ROUSSEAU FRÈRES IMP

OREILLER DE LA BELLE AURORE

PATE CHAUD ROUENNAISE

BRIOCHE DE FOIE GRAS

TERRINE DE GRIVES AU GENIEVRE

BARQUETTE PYRAMIDE

TRUITE FARCIE BRAISEE AU PORTO

GRATIN DE QUEUES D'ECREVISSES

TURBOT AU CHAMPAGNE

VOLAILLE DE BRESSE A LA CREME

RIZ PILAFF

CANARD GRILLE SAUCE BEARNAISE

GRATIN DAUPHINOIS

FROMAGE SAINT-MARCELLIN

GLACE DU JOUR

GATEAUX SUCCES

ENTREMETS VARIES

CORBEILLES DE FRUITS

Restaurant Point, La Pyramide   Vienne (Isère)
Téléphone : o-96

Foie gras frais	12.75
Bisque de homards	4.75
Mousse de grives	7.25
Galantine de faisan au foie gras	7.75
Feuilleté de ris de veau	6.50
Ballottine de saumon	9.75

Pâté de Saumon chaud	12.75
Rougets en papillotes	8.50
Homards à la crème	13.75
Ecrevisses à la crème	13.50
Ombles chevalier au beurre blanc	9.75
Truites au bleu	8.50
Filets de soles au Vermouth	9.95

Couvert

Gigot d'agneau en croûte	13.25
Poularde à l'estragon	12.50
Cailles au foie gras	9.75
Entrecôte « Baumanière »	12.75
Rognons au Madère	9.75
Pintadeau aux morilles	12.75

Soufflé à l'orange	5.75
Crêpes « Baumanière »	5.75
Vacherin aux marrons	5.50
Crème glacée	3.50
Toutes les pâtisseries	6.00

ce en plus

Münchner Schmankerl

Milzwurst abgebräunt mit Salat	1.50	Schweinsherz vom Rost mit gemischtem Salat	2.30
Kälberfüße abgebräunt, gem. Salat	1.50	Schweinsniere gebraten mit gemischtem Salat	2.20
Kalbszüngerl gebacken, Sce. Remoulade und Kartoffelsalat	2.20	Ochsenlende gesotten auf Holzteller mit Meerrettich	2.80
Schweinszüngerl auf Kraut, Salzkartoffeln	2.10	Kalbs- oder Schweinshaxen gebraten mit Salatplatte von 3.60 bis 8.—	
Backkopf mit gemischtem Salat	2.—	½ Kalbshaxe abgebr. mit gem. Salat ab 3.—	
Kalbskopf „Schildkröten Art" mit Salzkartoffeln	2.—		

Suppen

Kraftbrühe mit Hausmacher-Omelette	—.50
Gulaschsuppe	—.60
Tiroler Speckknödelsuppe	—.70
Bouillon mit Ei	—.80
Tasso Schildkrötensuppe	—.90

Fische

Goldbarschfilet gebacken, Sr. remoulade und Kartoffelsalat	2.—
Karpfen blau mit frischer Butter und Salzkartoffeln	2.70
Karpfen gebacken mit Mayonnaisensalat	2.90
Donauschill vom Rost mit Kräuterbutter und Salzkartoffeln	2.50

Geflügel

½ Wiener Backhendl m. gem. Salat 4.50 5.—	5.50
½ Brathendl mit gemischtem Salat 4.50 5.—	5.50

Fleischgerichte

Hammelragout mit Spaghetti	2.20
Kalbsbräten mit gemischtem Salat	2.10
Kalbsschulter mit Rosenkohl, Bratkartoffeln	2.20
Rosenspitz „englisch", grüne Bohnen und Bratkartoffeln	2.20
Fränkischer Schweinsschlegel mit Reis, Salat	2.10
Schweinsbraten mit Semmelknödel u. Salat	2.10

Pfannengerichte (10—15 Min.)

Schweinskotelette „Doria", Bratkartoffeln und Salat	2.30
Wiener Schnitzel mit gemischtem Salat	2.60
Rumpsteak mit Zwiebel, Butterbohnen und pommes frites	2.90
Filetschnitte mit Spiegelei, Selleriesalat und Bratkartoffeln	3.30
(ohne Ei)	2.90
Hammelchops am Spieß, Kräuterbutter Bohnen und pommes frites	2.90
Rumpsteak „Weinhändler Art" mit Butterbohnen und pommes frites (mit Zwiebelmus bestrichen, in Rotwein gedämpft, mit Parmesan überbacken)	3.90
Hofbräu-Spezial-Topf	3.60
Château-Briand (doppeltes Filetstück) (für 2 Personen) Prinzeßbohnen, Pariser Karotten, pommes frites, Kräuterbutter	6.50

Würste

1 Paar Weißwürste	1.10
1 Paar Regensburger mit Kraut	1.—
2 Paar Schweinswürstl mit Kraut	1.20
2 Paar Wiener Würstel mit Kraut	1.20
1 Paar Pfälzer mit Kraut	1.10
1 Paar Pfälzer mit Linsen	1.20

Semmel oder Brezen —.08   Schwarzbrot —.07

Vorzügliche Zigarren, Virginier und Zigaretten aller bekannten Marken · Zur Erinnerung si

Speisen·Karte

Spezialitäten von Heute

Donnerstag, den 29. Januar 1953

Münchner Schlachtschüssel	2.—
Kalbszüngerl mit Steinpilzen, Kartoffelbrei und Salat	2.20
Kalbsleber mit Speck, Bratkartoffeln und Bohnensalat	2.80
Garniertes Sauerkraut	2.80
Rehrücken mit Kartoffelcroquettes und Preißelbeeren	3.20

Eier-u. Mehlspeisen

2 Stück Spiegel- oder Rühreier mit Schinken und Salat oder Speck	2.50
Omelette confiture	2.50
Spaghetti mit Schinken und Salat	1.90

Kalte Speisen

1 Portion roher Schinken mit Butter und Schwarzbrot	2.60
Ansbacher Pressack	1.—
Hausgemachter Fränk. Geleger	1.—
Fein gemischter Aufschnitt	2.—
Kaltes Ripperl mit Kartoffelsalat	1.90
Sulzkotelette mit Bratkartoffeln	2.—
Schwedenplatte	2.25
Geräucherte Pökelzunge mit Aspik	2.25
Tatar-Beefsteak mit Ei	2.40
Port. gekochter Schinken m. Butter u. Brot	2.25
Münchner Brotzeit	2.25
Roastbeef kalt, Sc. remoulade und Bratkart.	2.60
Hofbräuplatte für 2 Personen	5.40
Gänseleberpastete in der Terrine mit Butter und Toast	8.—
Kalter Schweinsbraten mit Butter	2.—

Pikante Kleinigkeiten

Schweinsknöcherlsulz	1.10
Warme Käseschnitte	1.60
Bismarck- oder Brathering	—.50
Ochsenmaulsalat	1.—
Matjesfilet auf Eis mit Salzkartoffeln	1.20
Italienischer Salat	1.20
Wurstsalat	1.20
Remouladeneier	1.20
Russische Eier	2.—

Käse

Gervais garniert	1.50
Emmentaler mit Butter	1.—
Edamer mit Butter	1.—
Camembert mit Butter	1.—
Roquefort m. Pumpernickel	1.20

Kompott

Apfelmus	—.—
Pflaumen	—.60
Gemischtes Kompott	—.80

Kuchen

Buttercremetorte	—.80
Englischer Kuchen	—.50

Salate u. Beilagen

Selleriesalat	—.50
Chicoréesalat	—.60
Endiviensalat	—.40
Krautsalat	—.40
Kartoffelsalat	—.35
Salatplatte	1.—
Bohnensalat	—.50
Semmelknödel	—.35
Spaghetti	—.40
Rosenkohl	—.60
Meerrettichgemüse	—.60

Unseren lieben Gästen

recht guatn Appetit

und ein baldiges Wiederschaun!

Die Hofbräuwirtsleute
Franz u. Thea Trimborn

Original-Hofbräuhaus-Krüge und Speisenkarten an den bezeichneten Ständen zu haben

Anheuser-Busch, Michelob....Glass 15   Seidel or Shell 30
Ballentine's Ale .... " 15   "   25
Prior Special Brew............ " 20   "   35

FINE SELECTION
of WINES

PRIVATE DINING ROOMS FOR SPECIAL DINNERS OR BEEF STEAK PARTIES

APPETIZERS

Fresh Caviar	2 75
Canape of Caviar	1 00
Canape Lucullus	1 35
Eggs a la Russe	90
Tidbits Mixed	
Oxmouth Salad	85
Herring Salad	60
Fried Herring, Pickled	45
Herring Filet, Wine Sauce	50
Herring Filet with Mustard Sauce	50
Filet of Maatjes Herring, Plain	45
Filet of Marinierte Herring	45
Pickled or Roll Herring	45
French Boneless Sardines	60
Norwegian Brisling Sardines, per Box	45
Iceland Gabelsbissen	35
Anchovies in Oil, per Portion	50
Shrimp Cocktail	65
Crabflakes Ravigote	1 00
Crabflake or Lobster Cocktail	95
Vegetable Juice	25
Tomato or Sour Kraut Juice	20
Orange, Pineapple or Grapefruit Juice	25
Goose Fat, per portion	25

OYSTERS & CLAMS

Diamond Point Oysters	45	75
Blue Point Oysters	35	60
Cherrystone Clams	40	75
Little Neck Clams	35	60
Clam Juice Cocktail		50
Oyster or Clams Casino 1 00	Clam Omelette	85
Oyster or Clam Fry		80
Oyster or Clam Stew 55 with Cream		65

(Cocktail Sauce, 5c. extra)

COLD DISHES

*SMOKED NOVA SCOTIA SALMON	1 35
*SMOKED LAKE STURGEON	1 35
LACHS SCHINKEN	1 15
Luchow's Special Cold Cuts	1 75
Swedish Platter, (per cover)	1 75
Sliced Breast of Chicken	1 50
Sliced Turkey, (white meat only)	1 25
*Eels in Jelly 75 *Smoked Eel	85
*Cold Cuts (for 1) 1 25 Own Selection	85
Mixed Sausage	75
*Blood Sausage	75
*Pork Chop in Jelly	75
Ham or Beer Sausage	85
*Pig's Knuckle in Jelly	85
Oxmouth Salad	85
*Home Made Head Cheese, Vinaigrette	85
*Boiled Ham	85
Westphaelian Style Ham	1 35
Julienne Westphaelian Style Ham, Asparagus	1 65
*Roast Beef	1 00
*Beef Tongue, Smoked	95
Beef Steak a la Tartara	1 00
Knacksausage	50
Smoked Brunswick Style Liver Sausage	85
Smoked Thuringian Style Blood Sausage	85
Mett Sausage	85
*Country Made Cervelat Sausage	95
*Home Made Liver Sausage	85
Salami	95
Crabflakes a la Ravigote	1 00
Tomatoes Stuffed with Crabflakes	85
Half Lobster, Mayonnaise	1 25
Whole Lobster, Mayonnaise	2 00 & up

Dishes Marked (*), Are Served with Potato Salad

Special Dinner – $1.75

Served from 5 to 9 P. M.

Shrimp or Fruit Cocktail
Marinated Herring or Pickled Herring
Oysters or Clams on Half Shell
Smoked Eel   Herring Salad   Suize Vinaigrette
Vegetable Juice   Oxmouth Salad
Pineapple or Tomato Juice

• • •

Green Pea Soup, Country Style
Consomme, Egg Barley
Home Made Noodle Soup

• • •

Radishes   Olives

• • •

Filet of Boston Scrod au Four
Parsley Potato   Escarolle Salad

Creamed Chicken a la Frascatti with Fresh
Mushrooms en Bordure
Roast Young Lamb, Mint Sauce
Smoked Brisket of Beef
Chopped Veal Steak Saute
Gypsy Goulash with Spaetzle
Sour Pot Roast, Potato Pancake

Roast Prime Ribs of Beef 2 00
Half Spring Chicken, Paprika Sauce 2 00
Grilled Sirloin Steak 2 75

Brussel Sprouts or Baked Beans, Bretonne

• • •

Bavarian Vanilla Cream, Fruit Sauce

Mocha Cream Tart	Lemon Meringue Pie
Apple Crumb Cake	Butter Cake
Fruit Compote	Home Made Stolle
Apple Strudel	Cheese Cake
Ice Cream	Water Ices
Pies	

Any Kind of Cheese with Pumpernickle

• • •

Coffee   Tea   or   Milk

FISH & SEAFOOD
TO ORDER

PLANKED BONELESS SAVANAH SHAD	1 75
SHAD ROE, Bacon, Idaho Baked Potato	1 65
Fried L. I. Scallops, Tartar Sauce, Salad	1 50
Jumbo Frogs Legs Saute Meuniere, Salad	1 35
Cucumber Smelts en Casserole, Potato Salad	1 25
Steamed Finnan Haddy, Spinach, Potato	1 35
Broiled Bluefish, Baked Potato	1 35
Broiled Codfish, Creamed Potatoes	95
Boiled Haddock, Mustard Butter, Potatoes	95
Sea Bass, Split and Broiled, Potatoes in Cream	95
Sea Trout Saute, Mixed Salad	95
Crabmeat au Gratin	1 50
Fried Filet of Sole, Tartar Sauce, Potato Salad	95
BROILED STATE of MAINE LOBSTER, from	2 00
Lobster a la Newburgh in Chafing Dish, (for 1)	2 00

STEAKS & CHOPS

Chopped Sirloin Steak, French Fried Potatoes	90
Sirloin Steak 2 25 en Casserole	2 75
Sirloin Steak a la Jardiniera, (Fresh)	3 00
Sirloin Steak a la Mayer	2 25
Double Sirloin Steak 4 00 en Casserole	4 50
Tenderloin Steak 2 50 Double	4 00
Planked Steak, Fresh Vegetables, per Person	3 00
Porterhouse Steak 3 75 Double	6 50
Steak Minute, Potatoes 1 75 a Jardiniere	2 50
Filet Mignon (1) 1 85 a la Jardiniere	2 50
Family Porterhouse 7 50 Club Steak	6 50
Lamb Chops 1 25 Breaded, Tomato Sauce	1 35
Grilled Calf's Liver Steak, Bacon, Potatoes	1 35
Broiled Ham Steak 1 25 Pork Chops	1 00
Calf's Liver Saute, Bacon, Potatoes	1 25
Veal Chop, Plain	1 35

With Onions, Sauce Bordelaise or Bearnaise, 25c. extra
With Stewed Mushrooms, 35c. extra Per Person

SPECIAL

New Dill Pickle 20
Ripe Olives 30
Imported Pickled Onions
Celery 40

Green Pea Soup, Country
Green Pea Soup Marmite
Home Made Noodle Soup
Cup Consomme Marrow
Potage St. Hubertus 30

SPE
Fresh California
Medallion of Fat
Guinea Hen on
Royal Jumbo Sq
Baby Partridge
FRESH KILLED SPRING
SWEETBREADS, SOUS C
ENGLISH MUTTON CHO
HAMBURGER STEAK A
IRISH BACON, BROILED
HOTHOUSE BABY LAMB
HOTHOUSE BABY LAMB
FRENCH RACK TENDER

HOME MADE BOCKWU
*CREAMED CHICKEN A
*SMOKED BRISKET OF B
*ROAST YOUNG LAMB,
*Gypsy Goulash, Sour Kra
Chopped Veal Steak Saut
Two Poached Eggs on Ri
*Capon Cutlets, New Carr
Pancake with Plum Sau
Potato Pancakes with Ap
JULIENNE of WESTPHA
Lachs Schinken,
Jardiniere of Fresh Vegeta
French Pig's Feet, Grilled
Chicken Fricassee, Home
Boiled Fowl Marmite, Bo
Grilled Home Made Sausa
Hamburger Steak, Fried O
*Sour Pot Roast with Potat
Pig's Knuckle, Sour Kraut
*Boiled Short Ribs, Horse-
Roast Prime Ribs of Beef,

Creamed Fresh Spinach 3
New Green Peas 40
Red Cabbage 35   Ne
New String Beans 40
Giant Asparagus 65
Stewed Tomatoes 25

Saute 25   New Bermu
Idaho Baked 25   Julienne
Boiled 20   Mash
Au Gratin 35   Potato

Riverb DISHES

FINE SELECTION of WINES

Schaefer's
Ruppert's   Trommer's
R & H Premium   Rheingold, Extra Dry
Eichler's   Loewer's

Glass 15   Seidel or Shell 25

Luchow's HOUSE SPECIALTIES

Veal Chop Breaded, Spinach, Potatoes	1 35
Calf's Head en Vinaigrette, Potato	1 00
Broiled Fresh Mushrooms on Toast	1 00
Short Ribs en Casserole, Sour Kraut	1 35
Short Ribs en Casserole, Bourgeoise	1 35
Boiled Short Ribs with Noodles, Marmite	1 35
Domestic Frankfurters, Sour Kraut, Potatoes	65
Imported Frankfurters, Sour Kraut, Potatoes	85
Filet of Veal Goulash with Rice	1 00
Ragout of Tenderloin, Kidneys, Mushrooms	1 35
Hamburger Steak Luchow, Fried Potatoes	1 15
Sirloin Steak Saute, Viennoise	2 50
Veal Cutlet, Paprika Sauce, Noodles	1 35
Luchow's Veal Cutlet with Asparagus	1 85
Veal Cutlet Natural, Holstein 1 65 Breaded	1 50
Chicken Luchow en Casserole	2 75
Broiled Spring Chicken, Half 1 25 Whole	2 25
Paprika Chicken, Home Made Noodles	1 50
Chicken a la King in Chafing Dish	1 75
Tyrolienne Alps Ragout	1 50
Filet of Veal (2), Mushrooms, Vegetables	2 50
Potato Pancakes 50 with Apple Sauce	65

SALADS

Chicory, Escarolle or Romaine	30	55
Knob Celery	35	65
Combination	40	75
Hearts of Lettuce	25	45
Lettuce and Tomatoes	30	55
Sliced Tomatoes	25	40
Cole Slaw	20	35
Asparagus Tips		50
Potato	15	25
Fruit or Grapefruit	40	75
Fresh Vegetable	45	85
Watercress 40	Cucumber	50
Crabflakes 1 60	Shrimp	1 00
Chicken 1 15	Lobster	1 75
Sweet Pickles 25	Pickled Beets	30
Sliced Bermuda Onions 25	Herring	60
Cucumber with Cream Dressing 65		

DRESSINGS

Roquefort 25   Ravigote 15   Lemon 15
Mayonnaise 15   Russian 15   Tartar Sauce 15

CHEESE, Etc.

Canadian Oka	45
Del Bel Paese	45
Camembert	40
Fromage De Brie	40
Gorgonzola	50
Imported Switzerland	40—75
Pot Cheese	35—50
Liederkranz	35
Limburger	40
Imported Blue Cheese, (Roquefort Type)	40
Imported Gruyera	35
Liptauer	45
Edam	40
Golden Rich	40
Liptauer Garni	65
Cuban Guava Jelly	25
Cream Cheese	25
American	20
Saltines, Whole Wheat or Graham Crackers	15
Toast	15

RAREBITS

Welsh Rarebit	55
Long Island Rarebit	65
Golden Buck	70
Yorkshire Rarebit	80

HOME MADE PASTRY Etc.

Mocha Cream Tart 35 Apple Crumb Cake	30
Lemon Meringue Pie 30 Butter Cake	20
Bavarian Vanilla Cream, Fruit Sauce	25
STRAWBERRY SHORTCAKE	65
STRAWBERRY TARTLET 50 with ICE CREAM	60
HOME MADE STOLLE	25
Home Made Apple Strudel	30
Cheese Cake	25
Vienna Coffee Ring or Snail	20
Charlotte Russe	25
Fruit Tartlet	35
Cup Custard	25
Cold Rice Pudding, Fruit Sauce	30
Cold Rice Pudding, Ice Cream	40
Apple Pie 30 a la Mode	40
Apple Pie, Whipped Cream	40
Plain Pancake	70
Pancake with Apple	85
French Pancakes	90
Omelette Confiture au Rum	1 25
Macaroons 30 Lady Fingers	20
Assorted Cakes 30 Meringue Panache	50

FRUITS & COMPOTES

FRESH STRAWBERRIES AND CREAM	50
BAKED APPLE 25 with Cream	30
FRESH HOTHOUSE RHUBARB	40
Fresh Strawberry Compote	40
Fresh Sliced Pineapple	40
Preserved Peaches	40
Mixed Compote	40
Grapefruit, Half 30 Orange	20
Preserved Cherries	40
Imported Kransberries	35
Preserved Pineapple or Pears	35
Fruit Cocktail	40
Preserved Figs	40
Red Currant Jelly 25 Stewed Prunes	25
Bar-le-Duc	35
Natural Honey	25
Apple Sauce 25 Raspberry Jam	25
Cuban Guava Jelly	25

ICE CREAM or ICES

Strawberry Cup	55
Nesselrode Ice Cream	45
Rum and Raisin Ice Cream	45
Ice Cream Fruit Cup	55
French Walnut Ice Cream	45
French Strawberry Ice Cream	45
French Pistachio Ice Cream	45
French Vanilla or Coffee	45
Ice Cream Fruit Cup, Angostura	55
French Ice Cream Parfait	50
Chocolate or Vanilla	30
Biscuit Tortoni	30
Pineapple, Raspberry, Orange or Lemon Ice	30
Baked Alaska 1 25 (for 2)	2 00

COFFEE, TEA, Etc.

Coffee with Cream, (pot for 1)	20
Demi (for 1) 15 with Cream	20
Tea (pot for 1)	20
Chocolate or Cocoa	30
Coffee Glace	35
Milk or Buttermilk, glass	15
Coffee in Percolater, Demi 25 Large	35
Kaffee Hag, Postum or Sanka 20 Percolater	25-35
Iced Tea or Iced Coffee 20 Pot	25

EGGS, Etc.

Two Eggs, Boiled, Fried or Poached	45
Three Eggs, Scrambled	60
Spanish Omelette	80
Two Fried Eggs with Spinach, Potatoes	80
Ham or Bacon and Eggs	80
Ham Omelette	80
Home Made Noodle Omelette	50
Plain Omelette	55
Omelette with Westphaelian Ham	90

Marinierte Herring, (to take home in jars) 80c. & $1.50

Our Celebrated Coffee: 1 lb. 50c.   3 lbs. 90c.   5 lbs. $1.25

Our Celebrated Home Made Stollen, small $2 00   large $3 00

E SERVED
AY

Monday, March 23rd, 1942

Chow Chow 25	
Stuffed Olives 35	
Radishes 25	
Olives 20	

Consomme, Egg Barley 25

Marmite 75   Kraftsuppe 35
Soup, Small 35   Regular 50
Clear Turtle Soup 50

RDER
Hollandaise 1 50
chow 2 50
asserole 3 50
esh Vegetables 1 50
1 65
LUCHOW 2 75
1 50
POTATO 1 50
1 35
POTATO 1 25
NG BEANS, POTATO 1 35
EAK, BOUQUETIERE 1 65
1 25

POTATOES 85
HROOMS, BORDURE 1 00
E, FRIED POTATOES 1 00
ED POTATOES 1 00
85
85
85
65
90
65
us Vinaigrette 1 65
2 50
95
75
Breast, Casserole 1 65
1 35
oes 90
85
1 00
role Panashee 1 25
1 00
tra Cut 2 35

Brussel Sprouts 40
Egg Plant 30
raut 25   Wine Kraut 45
Carrots 50   Carrots 35
Cauliflower Hollandaise 50
Stewed Mushrooms 65

wn 30   French Fried 25
Balls 30   Fried Sweets 35
Hashed in Cream 30
40   Cottage Fried 40
TO SERVE

III · Fancies

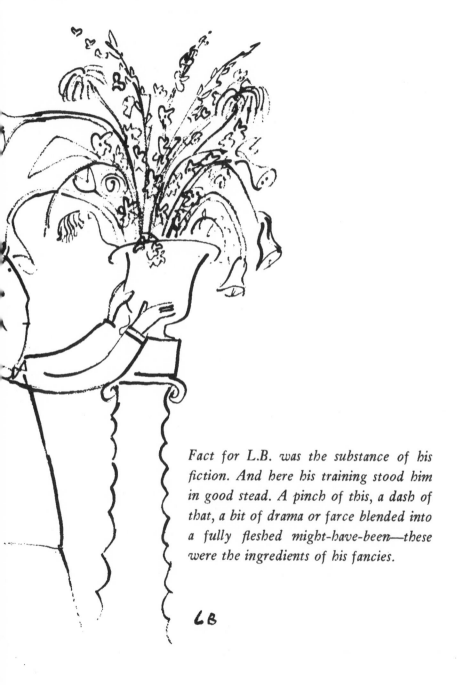

Fact for L.B. was the substance of his fiction. And here his training stood him in good stead. A pinch of this, a dash of that, a bit of drama or farce blended into a fully fleshed might-have-been—these were the ingredients of his fancies.

LB

THE ELEPHANT CUTLET

ONCE UPON A TIME there were two men in Vienna who wanted to open a restaurant. One was a dentist who was tired of fixing teeth and always wanted to own a restaurant, and the other a famous cook by the name of Souphans.

The dentist was, however, a little afraid. "There are," he said, "already too many restaurants in Vienna, restaurants of every kind, Viennese, French, Italian, Chinese, American, American-Chinese, Portuguese, Armenian, Dietary, Vegetarian, Jewish, Wine and Beer restaurants—in short, all sorts of restaurants."

But the chef had an Idea. "There is one kind of restaurant that Vienna has not," he said.

"What kind?" said the dentist.

"A restaurant such as has never existed before, a restaurant for cutlets from every animal in the world."

The dentist was afraid, but finally he agreed, and the famous chef went out to buy a house, tables and chairs, and engaged help, pots and pans and had a sign painted with big red letters ten feet high saying: "CUTLETS FROM EVERY ANIMAL IN THE WORLD"

The first customer that entered the door was a distinguished lady, a countess. She sat down and asked for an elephant cutlet.

"How would Madame like this elephant cutlet cooked?" said the waiter.

"Oh, Milanaise, sauté in butter, with a little spaghetti over it, on that a filet of anchovy, and an olive on top," she said.

"That is very nice," said the waiter and went out to order it.

"Jessas Maria und Joseph!" said the dentist when he heard the order, and he turned to the chef and cried, "What did I tell you? Now what are we going to do?"

The chef said nothing; he put on a clean apron and walked into the dining room to the table of the lady. There he bowed, bent down to her and said, "Madame has ordered an elephant cutlet?"

"Yes," said the countess.

"With spaghetti and a filet of anchovy and an olive?"

"Yes."

"Madame is all alone?"

"Yes, yes."

"Madame expects no one else?"

"No."

"And Madame wants only one cutlet?"

"Yes," said the lady, "but why all these questions?"

"Because," said the chef, "because, Madame, I am very sorry, but for one cutlet we cannot cut up our elephant."

Christmas in Tyrol

IN THE HIGH WORLD of the mountain tops, at the edge of glaciers, up where the eagles soar over the fields of rock, mosses and dwarf pines, lived Tobias Amrainer, a hunter, his wife and five children. The youngest of these was Christopher, four and a half; after him came Agnes and Crescentia, who were six and seven. Then the oldest girl in the family, Mary, ten years old, and a boy whose name was Franzi. Franzi was twelve.

Wedged between immense boulders and weather-beaten to the color of the surrounding stone stood the hut of the hunter. The house was built of heavy timber, calked with moss, and it looked like the cabins of the settlers in the American West. It had a stout roof that was weighed down with big stones. Inside was one long room and along the side of it in two partitions were built-in bunks on which parents and children bedded themselves on straw sacks. There was a stove made of stone, the windows were small, and when one opened the door, it was like opening that of an airplane high in the sky, for outside there were clouds, the stars, and the crags of mountains on which chamois and mountain goats danced. Here, the fearless hunter still finds game plentiful.

The children of the Amrainers looked like the same child at various ages. They were all cut from the same wood. They had yellow hair, almost bleached to whiteness. The eyes of the father gave the girls a direct courageous look, and the boys the gaze of the hunter who forever searches among rocks and in the greenery, steadily and without missing anything that stood, lay, flew or moved.

There were no arguments, for mountain people talk little; and there was nothing for the children to fight over, for the fields and mountains were filled with the things that were their toys. Work and play exhausted them so that they were off in dreams the moment they fell into bed. In summer they were barefoot, in winter they wore heavy shoes, and slowly they grew through each other's clothes. The greatest longevity was in the leather shorts of the boys. These last a lifetime, and the older they are, and the more one slides over rocks with them, the softer they get, and the more proud one is of them.

Most of the time their humble meal was a kind of porridge steaming in a large, black cast-iron pan. On Sundays a pat of butter was put in the center of it. The children who sat around the table with the parents, all eating out of the same pan, were busy with their spoons, making depressions or tracing small channels in the mush, so as to lead some of the molten butter to their side. The advantage of this kind of cooking was that there weren't any dishes to wash and dry and put away. Everybody licked his spoon clean and stuck it into a wooden rack on the wall, and the pan in winter was cleaned with snow, and in summer with the sand of the brook that passed close to the house.

In a drawer of the table there were knives and forks, and a carving set, and even coffee spoons, but when these were placed on the table it was a high holiday, or else a feast day. This last occurred when the father had shot a piece of game, and there was meat for dinner. Occasionally he would shoot a chamois or a deer, and then he would cut it up with his hunting knife. From the skin of these animals came the long-lasting leather pants.

They got up at daylight and went to bed soon after dusk. There was no radio—only the song of birds, the calls of the animals in the forest, the howling of foxes, and the steady song of the wind. The most fearful sounds in this concert were the thunder in summer and the rumble of avalanches in winter. These children had a frugal life and many chores to do. However, they also had great pleasures. They knew secret patches in the forest below, where small delicious strawberries grew wild. They found aged trees whose trunks were filled with black honey. They learned how to tell weather; they ran and sang, jumped and slept, and listened to the echoes of their voices; and they were tough and hard of muscle.

Summer was easier on the family than winter, as it is most everywhere. But here the summer was short. And the best thing about winter was waiting for Christmas. If they were lucky, on the day before Christmas they were all bundled up, and they put on the heavy hobnail boots and the parents walked ahead down through the snow, making a path which the children followed. It took sometimes six hours to get to the town of

Lech, but it was worth it. They went to the inn, called the Old Post.

The innkeeper there, Ambrose Maybock, was married to the sister of the children's mother. The aunt had no children of her own, so she invited the family down every year to celebrate Christmas at the inn. During the holidays there were no guests and the Old Post was empty.

At last it was Christmas time again!

On the night before the Amrainers went down the mountain, it was hard for the children to go to sleep because of the expectations that lay in the wonderful world below. The great pleasure of eating at someone else's table, the joy of sleeping in a real soft bed! They would jump on the mattresses and dive head down into the pillows, and cover and uncover themselves with the down-filled comforter. Even more exciting was to find that the bed was like a picture book covered with paintings all over. They would wash themselves without urging, for there the water which they poured from a pitcher into a porcelain basin was warm. Up in the high world, they had to break the ice first. And finally there would be the arrival of Santa Claus, and everybody would receive a gift. It was a wonder that they went to sleep at all, the night before the Christmas trip to Lech.

It was snowing as they came down. They had started before noon, and now the sun was low. Finally they came to the door of the inn and each in turn knocked the snow from his boots.

As you walk in the door of the inn, you enter a vaulted hall. To the right, a stone step down, you walk over worn brick slabs to the kitchen. Through this you come to another hall, which smells of hay and of animals. In this hall, unless you are familiar with it, you will trip over the threshold that leads to a paneled and vaulted room, the woodwork of which is so aged and beautiful that the museums of Innsbruck and Salzburg have wanted to tear it out and take it away. Another object they wished to buy is the ancient Tyrolean tile stove. The windows of this room are small and leaded. A guitar hangs on the wall. From the ceiling a wood-carved figure of a postilion blowing his horn is suspended, and in a niche stands an old wooden statue of Saint Christopher, the most revered saint of the mountains.

This room, forty feet long and twenty-eight feet wide, is the living and dining room for the guests as well as the innkeeper. The most comfortable table in winter is the one close to the stove. At this table congregate most evenings the priest, the burgomaster of the village, a few peasants, and the guardian of the peace, who is called a gendarme in Austria, a word borrowed from the French, meaning the "armed gent."

Ambrose Maybock, the innkeeper, is usually down in his cellar, which is dank with the seepage of rain and melting snow. The barrels of wine therefore are resting on wooden beams; the hams and sausages hang from the ceiling.

The wine is a clear, red, light native wine with which the regular guests are as satisfied as they are with the fare Frau Maybock prepares on her old-fashioned stove. Once this stove is fired with pine wood and hot, it takes two and a half hours to roast a good-sized goose in its big oven. In Tyrol this is the bird to celebrate with. It is stuffed with apples, and every fifteen minutes it is pulled out, the sizzling fat drained off and the gravy poured over the goose until it is a rich golden brown all over.

And now as the children and the parents walked in, the setting sun looked through the kitchen window. It played its rays upon the vapors that rose from the oven, tinting them pink; it placed the shadow of Frau Maybock among the copper pots that hung against the snow-white wall and these now flashed in its last rays.

"Anni," said Frau Maybock to the girl who was waitress, chambermaid and assistant cook, "go to the window, Anni, and see if they're coming—the bird is almost ready."

As Anni was about to go to the window, the Amrainers all came into the kitchen, and they were greeted and each in turn embraced.

Frau Maybock went for the last time to the oven and pulled out the goose and she poured the fat over it, and then she said, "Anni, go and tell them that it's ready."

Anni shouted down the cellar, to call Ambrose Maybock; she ran into the stable to call old Florian, the stablehand; then she went outside to find the five children who had run out and were riding down a hill on an old sleigh.

"Just once more," cried the children, and pulled the sleigh uphill.

The Christmas trees stood all about in fields and forest, in all sizes, and were there for the taking. Winter had festooned them with snow and ice. The cold winds had given them shape: some seemed like bent old men with long beards, snow white and sparkling, that flowed down into the white fields; others looked like children kneeling, and the oldest and tallest looked like the most beautiful Christmas trees, sparkling as if millions of diamonds had been showered on them.

The windows of the village glowed now as the copper pots had a

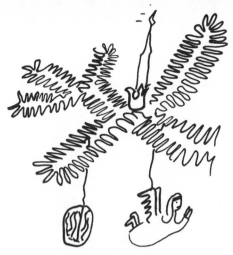

minute ago, and the little old bent snowmen that were the outdoor Christmas trees had the color of the vapors in the kitchen. Snow fell with a muted sound. High up, the icy peaks were aflame in the last sunlight, and blue shadows ran down the hills. Here and there a star flickered and then shone on steadily.

The children's mother had to come and get them into the house. They were unwrapped and then they stood looking at the Christmas tree. It filled the room with its pine, pitch and Christmas smell. Wax candles lit it up. Walnuts which had been rolled in silver paper and hung on the branches glittered. There were cookies baked in the shapes of stars and angels, and the rest of the tree's decoration were hard, small, red-cheeked apples. Over all shone a golden paper star pressed flat against the ceiling, for the tree was a good-sized one.

"Tell them it's ready and on the table," said Frau Maybock once more, and Anni went and called down the cellar for the innkeeper to come up. He usually came the third time he was called. He was busy below, looking after his costume in which he would later appear as Santa Claus. The boots were in order, the beard made of flax, the sack in which he would bring the gifts was filled.

"Tobias, art thou coming?" shouted Frau Maybock, and in the paneled room the mother of the children said, "Papa has always got to be the last one."

"Here I am," said Amrainer. He bent low to enter the room. He pulled his hat from his thick black hair and hung it next to his coat and then he smiled at his family, rubbing his hands that were big and strong. He picked up his youngest and gave him a ride on his knee.

Tobias Amrainer, even when he smiled, resembled a bird of prey. His hair stood about his head like the feathers of a ruffled buzzard. In his light gray eyes, the pupils were two sharp black dots and what they looked at they fixed on, as if he were looking over his gunsight at a difficult target.

"Put Christopher down," said Frau Amrainer to her husband. The good smell of roast goose floated through the whole inn. The children were seated, and the arrival of the holiday bird was expected any minute now. The innkeeper brought milk for the children and a jug of wine for the grown people. He sat down in his place at the head of the table and folded his hands. After a while he looked impatiently at the door that led to the entrance hall. The rest of the assembly also looked toward the door, for they heard steps in the hall. Then the door opened, and tripping over the threshold there entered a stranger, who, in a foreign dialect, by way of greeting, said, or rather issued, an order, which was: "Good evening."

The words came out of him sharply, right after he had regained his balance.

The first impression was that a very important person had lost his way in the mountains.

The new arrival wore a high fur hat, a long fur coat with attached fur collar. On his feet were galoshes probably lined with fur. His hands were in thick gloves. The only part of him that seemed to be cold was the bulbous red nose that supported his spectacles.

It was icy cold outside now, and warm inside the room, and perhaps the stranger's glasses had clouded, or else his vision was poor in spite of them, for he gave no sign of noticing anyone in the room. He turned and found an empty table, close to where he stood, and after hanging his coat on a hook on the wall and his fur hat over the arm of a chair near the stove, he sat down.

If a pack of dogs had been at his heels, they would not have been quicker or more thorough at getting a clear whiff of the man than the silent observers in the corner of the room. Besides their good instincts, they possessed thorough knowledge of the pelts of animals and they had identified the fur hat as native muskrat, the collar of the coat as badger and its lining rabbit. Therefore they decided that this was not the very important person of first appearance, but simply an individual dressed for warmth, perhaps a small-game hunter, stalking about in his trophies.

He was puffing as he tried to pull off his galoshes—he issued a whistling sound as he pulled—and they eventually came off. They were not fur lined, but their thickness was explained by two pairs of heavy, long woolen socks, which he rolled down. They were of gray wool, with red heels and toes, and when he had peeled them off there was a third pair, short, thin black socks, such as people wear in the city, and these he kept on.

From a battered briefcase he took a pair of mouse-colored felt slippers. He put his feet into these and while he was still bent to the floor his voice of command was heard again. He addressed himself to no one in particular. Sounding like a bullfrog in agony, he croaked—without saying anything at all. It wasn't a word; it was a large croaking sound of impatience that he made, and at the same time he held up his hand. When the people looked his way and he thought that he had their attention, he spoke.

"Where does one wash one's hands?" he growled. Whatever had melted from the glory of his first appearance he replaced with the forcefulness of his unwrapped person.

He was now a thin man, standing, without the benefit of his three pairs of stockings and the heavy galoshes, five foot five. He seemed without a neck but had ears like large red-dyed potato chips attached to the side of his face. He addressed himself to the stove.

"I asked, where does one wash one's hands?" he boomed once more, with the overshoes in his hands.

While he shouted, Anni, the servant girl, came from the kitchen. She was carrying the roasted goose. She stopped at the table of the rugged stranger and, tilting her head in the direction he was to go, she said, "Out in the hall, second door to the right."

At the table everyone turned to the golden-brown bird. Ambrose Maybock sharpened his knife and expertly took it apart.

As they began to eat, the stranger came back into the room, tripping once more over the threshold. He slammed the door, sat down and slapped his briefcase on the table. He searched in several pockets for a pencil and looked at some papers, while an assortment of unpleasant expressions passed over his face. "So," he said eventually, and then he demanded, "Bill of fare."

Ambrose Maybock put down his knife and fork and, walking over to the stranger, addressed him in the native, familiar "thou" rather than the more formal "you," saying to him, "There's enough food if thou art hungry. Wouldst sit with us?"

"Who are you?" exploded the visitor.

"I'm the innkeeper," said Maybock.

"Oh," said the other, pulling out his wallet and taking from it a large white visiting card which he handed to the owner of the Old Post. On the card there were two lines, for the man's title was of such importance that it ran from one end to the other, and beneath that was his name. The title was too much for the innkeeper. He had never come into contact with anyone that mighty. The name was simpler—he could make that out. It was Dr. Julius Stickle. The important man became impatient and he said, "If you can't read, let me tell you who I am. I am the Ober-ministerialrat Doctor Julius Stickle."

The innkeeper said, "Oh."

The high official before him paused and then he said, "What I would like to know is by what right you call this—huh—a hotel. I have been out in the snow, then outside in the hall—no one asked me where I came from or what I wanted." He took in some air and with mounting tension he continued: "My luggage is still out in the hall. I have a room reserved here and I want to eat. I want to eat alone. I want to eat off a clean tablecloth. I want first of all a bill of fare—and a wine card. I want some attention!"

The innkeeper walked back to his own table undisturbed and sat down, and the small white card went from hand to hand.

The official's important title seemed to be written all over his face. The way his breath came out of his nostrils, the way the eyeglasses quivered when he moved his head, all the small jerks and stiff postures were indicative of a man who knew his own weight and worth.

The innkeeper's wife still studied the card slowly, lip-reading the magnificent name and title. The highest man in the land that had ever come to Lech was old Francis Joseph, who looked more like Santa Claus than an emperor—and he had made no demands. He had been friendly and humble. The local doctor was the most important person next to the priest, and both these were old friends and looked after you, body and soul. The important official there on the bench looked as if he brought trouble, and his title removed him from ordinary humanity altogether, for *ober* means upper, over or above the rest, and *ministerialrat* means ministerial. It was a cold and uncomfortable label, and Frau Maybock wondered what such a rare individual could possibly want under the roof of the Old Post.

Frau Maybock said that she could make some soup for the stranger, or a veal cutlet with potato salad, or perhaps an omelet. She said this across the room from where she sat and was about to get up when the

official screamed, "Is there another inn in this—huh—place?"

"Yes," said Maybock. "Two and a half hours over the mountain."

The official retired into silence and the innkeeper put some of the goose on a plate, added stuffing and vegetables, poured a ladle of sauce over it, and, filling a glass with wine, handed the plate and the glass to Anni. She put it in front of the guest, and as she brought him bread, knife and fork and a napkin she wished him a good appetite, as is the custom of the country.

The official was hungry and thirsty. He lifted the wineglass, his nostrils dilated, and he looked to the ceiling in despair as he found the wine unworthy, but he emptied the glass. He swallowed his food without any pleasure, looking sideways out of his face, as a dog does when it fears that another will take its bone away. When he had finished, he pushed the plate away, glad that it was over. When he was asked if he wanted more or any dessert, he lifted his hand and yelled, "No."

At last he turned, so that he did not have to face the family in the corner. While he was searching in his bag, the door opened and the village gendarme came in. He sat down with the stranger, who had taken a Viennese newspaper from his bag.

The gendarme leaned over and jovially said, "May I ask what brings thee to our village?"

The official opened his large newspaper and, shielding himself with it from the gendarme, he snapped, "I haven't the least intention of entering into a conversation with you."

The gendarme, with his feelings badly hurt, moved to another table, and the innkeeper gave him the visiting card to read.

Standing on one of the lowest rungs of the ladder of officialdom, the gendarme had proper understanding of the importance of the other. In fact he was obliged to salute him any time he met him on the street.

Frau Maybock was about to leave the room, carrying a large platter heaped with the carcass of the goose. She stopped in front of the new guest and, turning her head, said to Anni, "When he wants to go to bed, take him up to number five."

Anni, who was still eating, said, "Ahum."

On other such evenings there was singing and dancing, and the gendarme would open the collar of his tight uniform, light his pipe and take down the guitar.

Tonight the room was quiet. The innkeeper wanted to wait until the official had gone to bed before donning his Santa Claus costume and handing out the presents.

The children were impatient. Christopher had sat near the end of the bench, making up-and-down movements with his arms and slowly working his way toward the edge.

"Christopher, be quiet," his mother had said several times and he had answered, "I don't want to." She had to pull him back and then he started to kick the bottom of the bench with the heel of his only pair of shoes. It sounded like woodchopping, for Christopher, as a result of daily fights with his brothers and encounters with nature, was as strong as a small ox.

"Christopher, be quiet," said the mother again.

While the others sat close together and talked, he finally got away by making squirming movements with arms and shoulders along the stove. Eventually he was free and he directed his steps toward the object of his attention. He picked the official's fur hat off the arm of the chair and, unobserved, he played with it for a while, putting it on and making faces, taking it off, trying to make something else like a rabbit out of it and turning it inside out. At one time the official put down his paper and looked at him, but said nothing, for he did not see his hat. Christopher at that moment was sitting on it.

From where Christopher sat, he could see that near the stove, on a hooked rug, there was a cat with her kittens. He now proceeded toward that spot, using the fur hat as a pillow to slide on. He was very earnest and determined, and the kittens, one by one, were put into the fur hat.

"Mama, look," said Christopher when he had accomplished this. His mother didn't look; she just said, "Christopher, be quiet."

But the official looked. He screamed, "My hat!" and he jumped up. He took hold of the fur hat, but Christopher would not let go—he twisted the hat and the cats fell out. The official also held on. Christopher was experienced in close fighting. Suddenly the Herr Oberministerialrat felt a stinging pain in his lower left leg, resulting from a sudden hard kick

with a hobnail boot. The principle of self-defense is an eye for an eye and a tooth for a tooth. The injured Oberministerialrat could not kick Christopher's shins, because he would have lost his balance. He swung and delivered a smack to his right cheek. The slapped Christopher screamed but kept holding onto the fur hat.

If in the mountains an injured member of a family is unable to defend himself, the others do it for him. While the mother picked Christopher off the floor, the brother and sisters fell on the Herr Oberministerialrat, and it took the gendarme to restore order.

The official groaned as he came out of the fight assisted by the gendarme—his face was red, his nose blue. He fought for breath at first and sat down on the bench. He raised both his arms to breathe, wiped his face, and then his fist came down on the table so hard the glasses jumped.

"In all my days I have never—never—had an experience like this. One must come to the backwoods for something like this to happen to one."

Anni brought the fur hat to the official's table. It looked like a half-plucked animal. The official held it up, showing it to the gendarme.

"You, there, saw what passed here."

The gendarme got up and, standing at attention, with his hands on the seams of his trousers and his heels together, said loudly, "Yes, Herr Oberministerialrat."

"I ask you," the official screamed, "I ask you, is that a way to bring up children?"

There was no answer.

"Go finish thy milk," said Frau Amrainer to Christopher.

The father of the children stuffed his pipe.

"Unbelievable," screamed the official. He got up and put on his pince-nez, and, looking them over, he said rather quietly, "How quaint." And then he yelled, "Why don't you give the blasted brat some candy as a reward for kicking an official of the Austrian government!" Reminded of the pain by his own words, he suddenly sat down. He turned his attention to his leg. The pain he felt there was reflected in his face. Breathing heavily, he pulled up his trouser leg and carefully rolled down the stocking. There was the mark of the hobnails, a blue half circle. "Like the bite of a wild animal," he said bitterly.

"This is not the last you'll hear of this," said the official, holding his leg in the direction of the adversaries.

The innkeeper approached. He took his pipe out of his mouth and looked at the leg. After a while he said to the official, "Smear a little pitch on it."

"Pitch?"

"Yes. Pitch, the kind the shoemaker uses. Smear it on. In a day it'll be gone!"

The official leaned back, exhausted. With half-closed eyes he waved the innkeeper away, and then he said, "I have been looking forward to this—as a sort of vacation. I have been told so much of the quaintness of the mountaineers—the rugged, the golden-hearted, simple people of the Alps. Simple they are—to the point of idiocy; and rugged—as a band of assassins."

Anni approached him.

"Here is some pitch," she said, holding a pot toward him. In the pot was a stick such as one uses to grease wagon wheels with.

"Go away," groaned the official. "I suppose you have never heard of a doctor hereabouts. You cure yourselves with herbs and pitch and magic. Go send for a doctor."

"Thou needst a doctor for this?" asked the innkeeper, unbelieving.

"A doctor right away," cried the official, looking at his wound.

The gendarme, seeing a chance to escape, came to attention. He saluted and announced that he would run to the village to get the doctor. Maybock said that it would be best to celebrate Christmas in the children's room.

The parents got the children to leave, and they all said good night to the official. He let them pass in silence and when they were out of the room he said to Anni, "What is going to happen to a country, when people like that are allowed to put children into the world." He changed his tone from one of sad comment, and in the voice of command he snapped, "How long does it take the doctor to come here?"

"Three hours, maybe four," said Anni, and then there was silence.

The innkeeper, who was Santa Claus that night, came very late and he avoided the dining room, where he had always made his appearance before. He climbed by way of the hayloft and the stable up to the room where the children waited, and here the presents were given.

For old Florian, the stablehand, there was a pipe; for Anni, some wool; for the children, skates, a wind-up train, a whistle to call birds, a pocketknife, a pair of gloves; for the children's mother, a silken shawl; and for the father, Tobias Amrainer, a box with six clips of ammunition: .65-caliber steel-jacket bullets.

This last gift was always the most gratefully accepted. Tobias Amrainer would open it and look into the box as if it contained rare jewels. The eyes of his wife would be on him during the whole ceremony of receiving the gift. She would sigh; every Christmas it was the one unhappy moment for her.

The hunter had brought a present for Santa Claus. It was a beautiful chamois brush. It is worn on the hats of mountain people and is made of the long, fine hairs that grow along the spine of the chamois, from the shoulders down to the hindquarters. They are dark and tipped white at the end, and a good brush of them is a rare thing and much valued.

Tobias Amrainer took the ammunition and put it into his jacket. He was the best hunter in the region and he believed that the high world belonged to those that live up there and brave its dangers and that it was right and proper to hunt in order to eat and to dress yourself.

The government took a different view of him. In the eyes of the law, Tobias Amrainer was a poacher.

The official was alone in the dining room. He had been pacing up and down with a limp. Anni, whose many duties included that of turning out the last light and locking up, sat in a corner knitting.

The official looked at his watch. "Where is that blasted doctor?"

"Over the mountain," said Anni.

"Will he come?"

"Maybe."

"What do you mean, 'maybe'?"

"Oh, for a scratch like that he isn't going to saddle his horse and ride through the snow on Christmas Eve," said Anni.

"Do I have to break my neck before I can get a doctor in this place?"
Anni didn't answer because she was yawning.

"The gendarme will tell him who I am, I hope."

"Oh, thou canst be certain of that."

The official wiped vapor from the window and gazed out into the
night. Anni yawned again.

She yawned several times and leaned back, closing her eyes, and then
she put the knitting away and asked, "When dost thou want to go to
bed?"

"Let us have it understood," said the official, "that I am not used to
being addressed like a peasant. When you speak to me, you address me
by my title; when you ask me something, you ask, 'What does the Herr
Official desire?' You may also tell that to these—" he pointed with his
thumb in the direction of the door—"yokels."

"I'm going to bed," said Anni resolutely. "Please say good night to
the Herr Official for me." She was about to go.

"Good night, Anni," he said, somewhat pacified.

"Is he leaving tomorrow?" she asked with the door handle pressed
down.

"No," said the important man. "He is going to stay a long time, perhaps a year, perhaps even two."

"That's a fine Christmas present for the Old Post," groaned Frau
Maybock when Anni told her.

The wife of the mountaineer was upset. "Tobias," she said, "I see
black. Thou knowest that on every day of the year, but today I fear for
thee. The priest threatens thee with hell-fire and purgatory, the burgomaster wants thee to leave the mountains. I feel like throwing the ammunition into the river. Oh, Lord, what is going to become of us."

That night, the children slept, but the parents were awake in the next
room. Early the next day the Amrainers left to return to their hut up in
the high world.

Far to the left over a hill the golden minute hand on the church steeple
of the village of Lech was almost up to the full hour, and the small hand
was at nine. From where the Amrainers stood they could see the doctor's
horse, walking along the road below, across a field and a hill. The horse
was almost at the inn.

"Tobias," said the mother, "as long as the official is down there, we'd
better stay on our mountain."

*O*n Christmas Eve, Frau Maybock was
draining fat from more geese than she had
ever cooked before at one time, while her
husband made trip after trip to the cellar to
make the Tyrolean Christmas beverage
called "glow wine," of which, on that day,
every child receives a small glass. It is made
as follows for a gathering like the one at the
inn: Take four quarts of good dry red wine;
add a pound and a half of sugar and an
ounce of cinnamon, if possible using cinnamon sticks and breaking them into small
pieces. Throw a few cloves into the pot
(earthenware if available) and heat to the
boiling point. Serve it hot.

It's a good drink to thaw out frozen and
lonesome souls, it's a good stopper for colds,
it's a quick warmer of the inner man when
he comes down from the mountain, and
it's the best recipe for the fatigue that follows skiing.

ABOUT CLOUDS AND LEBKUCHEN

On the top of a mountain Hansi was in the land of clouds. He had come as high up as the clouds sailed when he looked at them from the streets of Innsbruck.

The clouds rolled along the streets here, making dense fog—silver white at times, gray and black at others. They rolled toward whatever they wanted and took it away so no one could see it. Houses, people, horses and wagons, even churches—steeples and all—disappeared one second and just as suddenly came back the next.

People got lost. On such days, they walked into wrong houses and bumped their heads. It was told of Seppl that on such a foggy day he put his horses in the kitchen and went to bed in the stable, and Uncle Herman remembers when it was so foggy that somebody whom he could not see looked at Uncle Herman's watch.

If such things happened to strong men who lived here all the time, it was best for a little boy to stay indoors when clouds were low, storms threatened and an icy wind blew from the glaciers.

On one such a day Hansi spent much time in the kitchen. He sat on a little box and whittled kindling from pieces of pine wood. There was much need for this. Three big stoves heated the large house and ate up a lot of wood.

The kitchen was a very busy place.

Aunt Amalie sat at the wide kitchen table with Lieserl at her side. She unpacked a little chest which stood on six glass legs that were round and of deep blue.

This interesting box was covered with what had at one time been purple velvet, and was very artfully decorated all over with little ornaments in silver and rows of very small sea shells which ran along the edges and of which many had fallen off.

A golden thimble with some writing on it came out first, then a small prayerbook with ivory corners and a golden lock—and a big package of letters tied with a blue ribbon that held a little bunch of dried flowers.

"Hansi, come here and look!" Lieserl had seen some old pictures that were in the box. She knew them. "It's your Uncle Herman when he was young—ha, ha!" Little Uncle Herman swam on a big pillow with lace around it. He looked scared and was a baby with no hair.

"I don't believe it," said Hansi, who thought that Uncle Herman had always had a long beard and smoked a pipe, even when he was a baby. No, Uncle Herman never was a baby.

"Here is what I'm looking for," said Aunt Amalie, and she took out a worn notebook. Its leaves had come loose from the binding. The paper, which was yellow with age, was carefully lined and filled with the first recipes Aunt Amalie had collected.

Aunt Amalie looked for the page on which was written how to make Lebkuchen—the wonderful brown Christmas cakes—and there it was.

"Lieserl, first of all we need that big wooden bowl over there and a tablespoon. Hansi, please get the scales in the larder—and whistle while you are in there. You have already eaten too many dried apples—look at your stomach!"

A big pan was buttered and the dough was stretched with a rolling pin until it was as thin as Hansi's little finger.

The real fun started when the dough was cut into shapes of trees, people, rabbits, and many, many kinds of things—whatever came into one's mind. The pieces were then put on the pan and pushed into the oven to bake for half an hour.

Soon the house smelled from cellar to roof like a big Lebkuchen. Lieserl's cheeks were red from the heat of the oven. Her nose got into the powdered sugar and was white, and she held her arms far away from herself because they were covered with dough.

Waldl as usual slept on the bench next to the oven and opened one eye from time to time to see if anything worth eating was brought out. He did not care for Lebkuchen—no real dog does.

That evening when the cakes had cooled off and Uncle Herman was home, they all sat around the table. On the table were little pots in which was a paste that is made by putting a little water in a cupful of powdered sugar and adding some color to it. One pot is red, another blue—any color one likes. The paste is put in a little cone of paper which is easy to make by just rolling a white sheet and leaving a little opening on the end the size of a pinhead. By squeezing the color out of this tube one can make pictures.

Hansi made a cake with Uncle Herman on it, and Lieserl made an angel.

WEDDING IN TYROL

"THE HONORABLE BRIDE and the honorable groom invite you!"

With these words, after knocking on the ground three times with a flower-decorated pole, the man who is called the "inviter" goes from house to house and announces the wedding. It is not enough for him to visit the immediate family; he must go up to the last peasant houses, wherever friends live.

A wedding in Tyrol is a celebration attended by a few hundred people. They come from the Mountain and they come up from the Land.

One must have endurance and good lungs just to recite the announcement of the meal:

> *Twelve cooks have baked with fat and flour*
> *and prepared the table for this happy hour.*
> *They stirred and steamed and weighed things right.*
> *Come all of you, bring appetite;*
> *you have never eaten such fare—*
> *there's enough for a hundred pair.*
> *Start with the soup, eat dumplings and fish,*
> *calf's-head and kidneys, as much as you wish,*
> *roast geese and pigeons, mutton and deer,*
> *and wash it down with wine and beer.*
> *Let's make the bride's father run to the cave:*
> *this is no day on which to save.*
> *And let all sorrow be forsaken—*
> *drink when the bridal wreath is taken,*
> *pour it down and again make room*
> *in your cups to toast the groom.*
> *Start the shooting and the band*
> *for we will proclaim in all the land*
> *that the customs of the good old days*
> *and that our forefathers' ways*
> *honored are and well observed.*
> *After that there will be served*
> *Gugelhupf with coffee and cream.*
> *Come on foot, come with your team;*
> *from valleys deep, from mountains tall,*
> *hurry and assemble all.*

The bride and groom come on horseback to the church. She carries a spinning wheel to the altar and he his hunting gun. They drink the wine, and blessed bread is cut. The ring is clumsily put on the bride's finger, and once there it will go to the grave on her hand.

The young men dance before the door of the church, and the bridesmaids, wearing small, crownlike, golden wreaths in their hair, stand about like candles on a cake.

There is an old custom in this region called the wedding race. It is run from the church to the inn, and whether in the great heat of summer or bitterest winter cold, the racers wear only a shirt and long white trousers; on their heads are stocking caps with long red and white ribbons attached to their tassels. After they have all drunk a toast from one glass, the last drinker throws the glass high in the air, and that is the signal for the start. At the actual wedding the runners are young. At a golden wedding the old men run, and there was one time when the dozen runners carried on their shoulders the weight of a thousand years—the youngest was seventy-four.

After the runners, the groom lifts his bride on his horse and rides her down to the inn, followed by the music. Once all the guests are in the room, the inviter pounds his stick against the floor boards and waits for silence. He leaves his place next to the bride and ceremoniously takes up a position facing the groom. Then both of them turn to face the assembled guests, and the inviter gravely speaks:

"Now, honorable groom, I have turned this way and that and observed all the good people here, and among them I see your dear father and mother, and that is of great good fortune. Thank God that those most dear to your heart are here on this day. Now walk toward your father—now then, go—and look into his eyes and take both of his hands in yours, and say to him, 'God bless you, God thank you, and God keep you!' And, holding him by the hands, think of everything he has given you—your life, your mountains, and the house that has sheltered you."

The inviter waits and then knocks on the floor again. "As you have gone to your father, so now look toward your mother. Go now and turn to your beloved mother and say again, 'God bless you, God thank you, and God keep you!' And, holding her hands, think back over all she has done for you. Think of how she carried you under her heart for nine months and brought you into the world with pain. Think back over the years when she fed you patiently, and promise her that you shall never abandon her in this life, and that as long as you have a crust of bread you will share it with her."

Into this tearful moment, after his third pounding of the stick, the music crashes, the doors open, and the vapors of the kitchen roll into the room. The first of the two feasts begins. There is hard drinking and eating, and dancing until past sunset. The second feast, at ten, is as elaborate as the first. The inviter, who is the master of ceremonies and of great importance, remains beside the bride from morning till night.

S chweinerei," *screamed Herr Stolz, a Gauleiter of Regensburg. He made himself well heard above the music of the three-piece orchestra which played behind him. He pointed at the small, grayish pork cutlet with his knife and fork. He pushed the plate, in one shove, toward his wife so that the small piece of meat almost hopped out of the dish. But before the poor woman, who saw meat rarely, who ate at home before they went out and contented herself with a sip from his beer and an ersatz-buttered roll, could reach for a fork, he had retrieved the plate. He hammered at the edge of it with the knife and looked around.*

"Frau Saltner," he shouted as the waitress came to the table. "Frau Saltner, it is a disgrace and a Schweinerei *to put a plate like this in front of me, to call this a portion of* Schweinefleisch *and to charge one mark and fifty pfennigs for it."*

"Please, Papa," said Frau Stolz, patting the left sleeve of the Gauleiter.

"Shut your mouth," he said to her. "This doesn't concern you. You have nothing at all to do with it."

The hands of his poor wife sank back into her lap, and with worried, devoted eyes she looked at the Gauleiter's face.

"But, Herr Gau—" the scared waitress began to answer.

He shut her up with the knife held high. "Don't tell me again, Frau Saltner. Don't tell me again there's a war going on."

On such occasions, the music stopped. The Herr Gauleiter addressed

*himself to the beer garden, which was filled with those citizens of Regens-
burg who did not find themselves at the front or in concentration camps,
who had enough substance, leisure and license to contemplate the beau-
ties of the bridge and its reflection, to count the smokestacks of the
breweries and to order a meal. Their digestion was helped along by the
patriotic airs and the waltzes of the band and fortified by the broadcasts
of the Ministry of Information.*

*The Gauleiter stopped to look at the food which Frau Saltner had
placed before him. He took knife and fork, and for several minutes he
labored efficiently in the oval-shaped, heavy porcelain dish, stabbing, cutting, swishing sauce up the sides, and soaking it up with pieces of dumpling. While his mouth was still full, so that he could hardly say Pfaff,
and only a dry piece of dumpling was left in a corner, he pushed the
dish away and mumbled, "That goddamned Pfaff. I can't eat any more.
Take it away, Frau Saltner. My appetite is gone." His chair grated in the
sand as he turned to call after Frau Saltner, who had taken his rejected
dish away—he wanted to order an additional beer.*

TALES OF THE SOUTH AMERICAN GENERAL

IN THE DAYS when the King of Spain's only concern was that no one should clip a second off his record run from San Sebastian to Biarritz . . .

Amidst the boom-tara of unending fiestas, of gala dinners in blossom-lined ballrooms in which a thousand songbirds were released, half of them to be swept out the next day . . .

In the good old days when the amateur mechanic, the Marqués Ricardo Soreano, amused himself by pushing a button under his table that ingeniously released a menagerie of tigers, lions and crocodiles, which suddenly stared into the dining room through the large plate-glass windows and frightened his guests to death . . .

When the young and radiant Natasha Brailovski shot herself through the heart over her father's grave with a ridiculously small jeweled revolver that was practically made by Cartier . . .

. . . and the handsome, immaculately groomed Antonio de Portago, dream man of the American debutantes, married, had all his debts paid, and later died for Franco . . .

When, at the height of its fashion, this affluent municipality was graced with the presence of both the Grand Dukes, Dmitri and Boris; and the unbelievably beautiful Bebecita de Gainza—who set the fashion in Biarritz with her chic mother, Selmira de Gainza—married Nicki de Sangro . . . When Elsa Maxwell promoted the dressmaker Patou and introduced the O'Briens to society . . .

At that time there lived in his villa in Biarritz, in seclusion and in comparative simplicity, the South American general, Leonidas Erosa.

The Villa Amelita stood in vast grounds along the road that leads from Biarritz to Saint Jean de Luz. The varied landscape composed itself of opposites, and achieved harmony out of princely households set against the bonhomie of sardine fishermen's houses and their craft, of the fragrance that the sun drew from the fallen needles of pine trees, and the mimosa that was tended with extreme care in the gardens of the Villa Amelita.

No one was anonymous here, or footsore. Nothing merited the attention of the tourist in this good corner of France. It was blessed by an absence of museums, venerable cathedrals, ancient monasteries, historic curios, or scenic wonders. It was doubly protected by the total absence of cheap lodgings.

Like most wealthy South Americans, Leonidas Erosa preferred to live in France rather than in his native land. He had been home to Ecuador on two occasions, but he had quarreled with his relatives and left after a few days. He had never been to the Argentine to visit the properties that were the source of his enormous wealth. Out of respect for the famous Erosa herds, the Argentine republic had made him an honorary general, and he used the title on every possible occasion.

On a day when von Uff, onetime president of the Dresdner Bank, an expert in disaster, who had amassed a fortune during the German inflation, told the American expatriates that it was high time to close the shutters of their villas, pack up and go home, Señor Alfonso Lopez appeared at the ornamental bronze gate of the Villa Amelita.

He found Leonidas Erosa at a large table in the tower of the villa looking out at the sea. In front of him was an assortment of silver dishes. A butler poured wine for him, Roederer 1928 brut, which the General drank like lemonade. He had finished a kidney stew and asked for more wine when the sand crunched under the small feet of his visitor.

Don Alfonso was excited and warm; he stuttered and fanned himself with his bowler. The purpose of his visit, he said, was to give the General a warning. He knew someone, he said, who had the confidence of Gamelin. He advised the general's immediate departure.

He said, "I believe that this time they will steal everything, the Mona Lisa, the wine, the silver."

The General asked where he should go.

"New York, of course," said Don Alfonso; "there is no other place left fit to live in. Good hotels, opera, night clubs, people, all the pleasures . . ."

"I am not an opera man," said the General. "I don't like to go out to eat. I would hate to leave all this now and then have the French cover themselves with glory and hang up victory emblems while I am in America. I love this place, I am happy here—I will stay here. And now I wish to pray."

Leonidas Erosa stopped at each of the fourteen stations of the cross which stood along a path that led from the tower to the villa. Don Alfonso, who was an opera man, walked about and hummed an aria, and when both were done, they went into the villa.

The General and Don Alfonso lunched together in the baroque dining room. After coffee and cigars, Don Leonidas advised his visitor to remain calm, and he said goodbye to him in front of a forty-thousand-dollar bouquet of roses painted by Renoir.

The interior of the Villa Amelita was an auctioneer's paradise of flowered carpets, tassels and draperies, Biedermeier, and Louis Seize. Of the many rooms, General Erosa's bedroom was the most museumlike. It was a shrine dedicated to the memory of his dead wife. Three full-faced and two profile paintings of Donna Amelita hung here, and with them a portrait of the General's daughter, Beatriz Mercedes, who was now married to an Englishman and living in London. Donna Beatriz resembled her Peruvian mother closely.

The furniture in this room, as in all the others, was ornate. On a rosewood table whose marble top was supported by the golden legs of two cranes reposed the Erosa family album, bound in velvet, embossed, and the size of a lexicon. In a large glass case next to the rosewood table were preserved a number of relics of the General's marriage: his wife's wedding dress, the small doll-like madonna to which she had prayed, a sword and silver spurs, two dried bouquets of flowers, and a row of the scented candles which had burned at her bier. Four people could have slept in the General's bed, which was heavily inlaid with mother-of-

pearl. Over it, on a branch, sat a stuffed condor which the General had shot in South America. At the door of the bedroom, on a golden bracket, swung a polished turtle shell containing holy water.

The General was awakened by the sun each morning when his valet drew back the tasseled curtains. Although he was seventy, he was still a man of tremendous strength. He had the torso of a bull, and almost no neck whatever. People who saw him sitting in bed thought a very tall man would get up, but his powerful legs were extremely short. His arms and legs were covered with black hair, and his chest looked like a sofa ripped open.

The General's day was as evenly divided as the face of a watch. From the moment he woke he was passed from one pair of hands to another, like someone in a flying trapeze act. The valet dressed him, walked him to the private chapel of the villa and pushed him through a carved oaken door. On the other side the curé would take him over, whisper a few devout sentiments in his ear, guide him to a pew, and begin to say the Mass. With the General knelt his entire household, except Miss Graves, whom the lonesome General kept on as a companion and who belonged to the Church of England. Anselmo served as altar boy. He repeated the Latin service day after day without knowing the meaning of the words and went through the ritual with automatic precision. He had learned it thoroughly as a child.

The curé stayed for breakfast, blessed the bread and brought the gossip of Biarritz into the glass-enclosed veranda where he and the General ate. After breakfast the chef would appear, bringing with him Escoffier's *Guide Culinaire* and a heavy scrapbook filled with recipes and menus. He and the General nearly always had a difficult time rowing through a sea of soups, sauces, ragouts and all the ingredients that go into them. They disagreed about what birds to cook, what to garnish and stuff them with, and how to balance it all with the proper savory, the right wine and the General's mood. This was the hour in which the General was most alert. He aroused the temper of his French chef, the table was struck and voices were raised. It was fortunate that the curé was present to bring master and servant back into proper accord. As the chef left, Miss Graves entered.

The curé waited for that moment as a dog waits for a bone, because it was then that the General called for a silver casket in which he kept his cigars, and from it presented the man of God with a soft, round, perfectly balanced brunette cigar—a British cabinet selection. The two men always lit their cigars with separate matches.

After the curé left, Miss Graves read the mail, which consisted of daily appeals for help from charitable organizations, and occasionally a letter from the General's daughter. On those rare occasions when the General decided to answer a letter, he would inform Miss Graves of his sentiments and she would translate them into a polite and brief answer.

At ten the General proceeded to the lookout tower, followed by a butler who carried an elaborate assemblage of copper marmites. This equipment had been designed for an outing in the Pyrenees, but was used to transport the General's second breakfast, which consisted of meat puddings, small curries, sweetbreads, kidney stews and coquilles of sea food.

At eleven Professor Hubert Roselius, a German refugee portraitist, waited for the General in a small garden house, where he was at work on one of a series of portraits of the General in a soldierly coat, holding a sword and looking into the distance. Herr Professor Roselius was only a mediocre painter and had no talent for business, but even to his dull senses it was clear that a man who had three pictures and a statue of Napoleon in his library, who walked with his right hand stuck into

his coat and insisted on being addressed as "General," might secretly fancy himself to resemble the Emperor. Herr Professor Roselius had remarked on this curious accident, after having several swallows of Napoleon brandy served in an inhaler with a large golden N engraved on its belly, and the result was his present commission and what seemed to be a life work ahead. The finished pictures, all of them more like Bonaparte than like Erosa, were stored one after another in an attic, like the scenery of plays that had ended their run, and immediately a new one was begun.

The General's lunch was served at one, in the lookout tower whenever the weather permitted. He usually ate in the company of his doctor or Miss Graves. After luncheon he went to sleep for an hour and was awakened by the masseur, who appeared at three. At four, having passed through swells of soapsuds, sponging, slapping and rubbing, kneading, and the heat of the electric cabinet, he was taken to his swimming pool. He swam up and down three times, like a large turtle, and crawled out, to be dried and placed in the sun.

The Paris papers arrived then, and tea was served on the terrace of the pool. Miss Graves read to him the items that interested her, which were mostly about the Court and the Royal Family; she avoided the more disturbing news. She had to stop reading sometimes when military planes flew overhead, but the General did not regard them either with interest or with anxiety.

After tea, with Anselmo beside him, he made the stations of the cross once more. Then the valet took over and helped him dress for dinner.

There were always guests. While the food was on the table, the General's appetite confined his thoughts and hands to his knife, fork and spoon. He smoked one of his fine cigars after dinner, and for dessert slowly peeled himself a Calville apple. After he had finished, he always looked from face to face around the table, as if he were sorry for them all, got up abruptly and went to his bedroom. The valet undressed him, drew the curtains and left. For a moment the trapeze act seemed suspended. In sudden fright, because there were no outstretched hands to catch him, he yelled for the Indian. Anselmo came in then and stayed with the General until he fell asleep.

Shortly after the visit of Señor Lopez, the peace of the Villa Amelita was disturbed by two visits from the authorities. The first time it was the agents of the Deuxième Bureau. They hustled Herr Professor Roselius off but allowed the General's laundresses—two German women whom he called the Andirons because they looked exactly alike—to remain at the villa. They were even permitted to keep the little radio with which they listened, as they bent over their washtubs, to the broadcasts from Cologne.

A few weeks later the villa was visited by a French army surgeon who wanted to be shown over the grounds with a view to converting the villa into a hospital for convalescent officers. It was admirably suited for that purpose, he told the General as he left.

The General was disturbed at the thought of having to give up his villa, and the loss of his portrait painter also bothered him. He could find no satisfactory way of filling in the time between eleven and twelve every morning. One day while he was in the lookout tower he received a visit from the chef. Truffles and Malossol caviar and Miss Graves's Earl Grey Blend tea and the kind of pâté de foie gras that the General was so fond of were difficult to obtain. There was, of course, the pâté which came from Strasbourg and which most people considered good enough, but the General would not eat it. The pâté de foie gras he liked was flown in from Czechoslovakia by plane and processed by the chef at the Ritz in Paris. Monsieur Auzello, the director of the Ritz, had written to explain that on account of conditions in Czechoslovakia no more was being received and there were only six jars left, which he

was forwarding. After that, the chef said glumly, it was the Strasbourg pâté or none.

Two days later General Erosa received a telegram from Alfonso Lopez in Paris informing him that all arrangements for his departure had been completed. The General left his villa and walked down to the lookout tower. He saw Anselmo stretched out on the rocks below and called to him. When Anselmo had mounted the stairs, General Erosa flung one arm around his shoulder affectionately and with his silver-headed cane he pointed out to sea. Soon, he said, a ship would be anchored there, ready to take them away. Anselmo nodded. Like waiting children, he and the General looked out over the blue water.

Señor Lopez in striped trousers and high collar, accompanied by a beautiful and compact young secretary, came to the Palace Hotel and rendered a financial report. The General received him in the salon of his suite. He signed several documents and listened to him, playing with the tassels of his dressing gown and admiring the long slim legs of the secretary.

At the end of the meeting, before he could say, "I salute you," and bid Lopez adieu, Señor Lopez, who had planted himself out of reach of the General's handshake in the center of the salon, addressed him, turning the large diamond on the ring finger of his left hand with the delicate thumb and index finger of the right.

"I came chiefly in the matter of the chef," he said. "I came to recommend his instant dismissal."

He looked at Leonidas Erosa, who had suddenly come to attention.

"My dear Leonidas, allow me to say beforehand that no one has greater admiration for the talents, the imagination, the originality of Monsieur Vitasse. It has always been an inestimable privilege to eat at your table, dear friend. In his capacity as a cook, I am the first to salute him; for the rest, he is a crook and belongs in jail."

"What has he done?" said the General impatiently.

"He has missed his profession," said Lopez. "He should have been the chief of a band of brigands, instead of just a chef," said Lopez. He reached into his portfolio for the fat dossier on the affairs of Jacques Vitasse.

"Every time you light a cigar, every time you drink a glass of Vichy, my friend, every time you engage an automobile, this robber baron holds out his red hands and takes his tribute. He collects commissions from the vegetables, the meat, the flowers, the hotel. He did it for years in Biarritz, too. He has cost you a fortune."

"You are not telling me anything new," said the General wearily. "These commissions are time-honored prerogatives of chefs and butlers, and who am I to challenge that? That is as it should be. That is no reason to call the man a crook," said the General with every sign of annoyance.

"I have said before," said Lopez, "that I understand your attachment to Monsieur Vitasse. I grant you, also, that he is not a pioneer in this form of exploitation. But there is more, my friend."

"He has been with me for thirty years," said the General.

Señor Lopez searched for some invoices. "Here," he said, "look at these figures."

"You know I don't like to look at figures. Tell me about it," said the General, handing the papers back to him. "Or, still better, don't tell me about it. I detest this kind of shabby affair."

"I will be as brief as possible," said Señor Lopez. "Before we go any further, did you give Monsieur Vitasse authority to buy provisions for

the Hacienda Miraflores which are to accompany you on your voyage aboard the ship?"

"Yes, yes, yes," said the General.

"Allow me one more question, Leonidas. Did you evoke in him any idea about what you wanted, and to what limits he could go?"

"No," said the General, loud as an irritated child. "I always leave that to him. And stop playing inquisitor, Alfonso!"

"Well, he has prospered vastly on this business, my dear friend. Just for example, do you know that he has bought one thousand wax candles, and sixty cases of turtle soup? Look here! Ancora Brand, Genuine Clear Green Turtle Soup with Sherry Wine."

"That is extremely wise of him. I am very fond of turtle soup. And as for the candles, you know that the electricity at the hacienda fails regularly. What is wrong about that? That is foresighted."

"Just one more thing," Señor Lopez said, "and then I will go. Surely there is dog food at the hacienda, with several thousand head of cattle. But let that go—it's not important. What I wish to bring to your attention is the matter of the wine."

He took a bill from the dossier. "Here is an item for twenty-four cases of sherry, Sandeman Three Star, bought at a private sale—so private that only Monsieur Vitasse knew about it. This same sherry is to be had at a dozen wineshops for almost half the price he charges here. The second item is for two hundred and sixty-eight cases of Dom Perignon—I grant you it is rare, but here, please look at this, so I will not be accused later of having invented these charges. Here is a quotation from the owner of a night club—if you please—who has some of it left, and offers it at eight dollars a case less than the chef was able to get it for—and what do you say to that?"

"I will speak to him," said the General. He called for Plaschke. "Albert, get hold of the old maniac. Tell him to come here immediately."

"I'll leave these papers and bills. Just show them to him," said Alfonso Lopez, and left abruptly with the pretty secretary.

"A glass of sherry, Monsieur Vitasse?" said the General as the chef came in.

"You are very kind. Yes, thank you, I will have a glass of sherry," said the chef. He reached back to pull up the chair to which Leonidas Erosa had motioned.

Plaschke brought two glasses of sherry and left.

The General folded his hands and looked at the chef, who brushed the ends of his mustache, parted his beard and held up the glass. He looked through the pale golden liquid, waved the glass back and forth under his nose and finally took a sip.

"It's the Sandeman Three Star," said the chef. "It's excellent. We have twenty-four cases of it. I was very fortunate in obtaining it. You can't get it in the open market any more. I bought it at a private sale. A friend was so good as to inform me—Monsieur André Buffoni, the sommelier of the Kiss Royale."

The General looked quietly at the chef. He agreed that the sherry was excellent. He swung the cord and tassel of his dressing gown in a circle and said, "I have just had a long conversation with Señor Lopez." The chef moved to the edge of his seat and opened his mouth, but the General stopped him from speaking by holding up his hand. He took the dossier and handed it to the chef. "The notes attached to this," he observed, "are not my own; they come from the hand of Señor Lopez."

The chef looked at the bills and moved forward again, but the General still stopped him from speaking.

The chef, whose purple veins had disappeared in the high coloration of his face, walked knock-kneed over to the window. He held the papers to the light, examined them with small, stupid eyes, and then stared down into the park.

Slowly trimming the end of a cigar, turning it between his lips and carefully lighting it, the General got up and walked to the tabouret on which the giant inhaler stood, and placed both his hands at the sides of the cool glass. Looking down at the salamander, he said, "The manifestations of Señor Lopez have nothing to do with the sympathy and esteem which unite us. Be assured, my dear Monsieur Vitasse, that I detest situations like this one. Allow me to make another observation: I count on your services, I count on having them for many years. The methods you choose to employ, Monsieur Vitasse, are your own."

The General blew smoke rings, and the chef stared at the top of a streetcar below without seeing it.

"We are sailing for Ecuador in a few days," said the General, pleased with his speeches, and grateful that the chef had listened in absolute silence. "Our Villa Amelita there is as modern as this hotel and almost as large. It stands, however, in a terrain that is foreign to you. The distances are immense, and the language difficult for you. You will find dealing with tradesmen irksome. It is not like here where you can pick up a telephone, or Paris where you could run across the street for a banquet. I am thinking only of your well-being when I suggest that . . ."

He began again as the chef's ears colored anew. "When I suggest that some of the vast responsibilities that go with running a household as large as this be put on other shoulders, so that you can devote all your time to the work that is the most important—to the kitchen. Let an intermediary worry about the provisions. Let us say Monsieur Lopez— someone who speaks Spanish—could come and . . ."

The chef turned around. He looked murderously at the General.

"I propose the following arrangement," said the General, who was angry himself. "I hate to worry every time I sit at the table and eat, or open a bottle of wine, whether you have received your proper share. You confine yourself to cooking from now on. And you stop taking money from grocers, butchers and wine merchants! I in turn will make up the difference and add it to your salary. Let me know how much it is."

"You couldn't afford it," sneered the chef. He threw the papers on the floor and walked out of the apartment, slamming the door.

The *Céfalo* progressed slowly against an incoming tide. The General and Miss Graves stood on deck and watched the magnificent panorama of New York pass them. They walked to starboard to see the Statue of Liberty, and they waited until the pilot was taken off. Two destroyers passed them and sailors waved, and the little girl in the yellow coat ran into the General and almost knocked him down. The rhythm of the machinery accelerated, the ship began to vibrate and pound, and the water changed to a deeper color.

On a chair like the one Plaschke had provided for the *Xenaide Ybirricos,* but of sturdier construction, sat the General, and Miss Graves was at his right.

The *Céfalo* slowly began to rock. The silhouette of the Atlantic Highlands rose and sank over the handrail, although there was neither wind nor sea. As the ship's bell rang, two stewards rolled a wagon out on deck. They were engaged in animated conversation. On the top shelf of the wagon, without a napkin under them, stood rows of thick-lipped cups, a pile of saucers heavy as stones, a large can containing saltine biscuits, and a steaming zinc pitcher. One of the stewards poured hot consommé into the cups, the way one waters flowerpots standing in a row, without stopping between cups. The second reached into the can and placed two saltine crackers on each saucer. They kept

on talking while one pushed the wagon and the other placed the cups on saucers and handed them out to the passengers. Everybody else was served before they came to Miss Graves and the General. They had two cups left. One of the stewards filled a cup and then turned the battered pitcher upside down. Only a few drops fell out of it. He smiled at the General and shouted to his comrade: "Julius, run down and get some more *Kraftbrühe—mach' schnell!*"

Miss Graves reached for the cup. At the bottom of it floated the debris that is found in the last helpings of clam broth—a gray, sandy residue. She held the cup up and smelled it. "Bouillon," she said, and gave it back to the steward.

"Never mind more soup, Julius!" yelled the steward down the stairs, and gave Miss Graves's cup to the General.

"Not for me," said the General, "thank you."

"It's good for you," said the steward.

"Thank you," said the General.

"Wait till the sea air gets you, you'll have an appetite all right," said the steward. He mopped the spilled soup from the top of the wagon with a towel, which he wrung out over the side of the ship and resumed the conversation with his colleague.

"Who recommended this boat to me?" muttered the General. "It's worse than the *Xenaide Ybirricos*."

An officer appeared on deck. He came closer, walking loosely with his head rocking back and forth. His hair was cut very short and parted with a wet comb, and he was dressed in a white uniform decorated with the stripes of an admiral. He was a man of unusual format: head, eyes, feet and hands, nose, ears, nostrils, teeth—everything was extra large and very simple in construction. His face was blank and pink, and he had pale-blue, water-clear eyes. He advanced toward people searching their countenances as if he had lost something and they knew where it was; then he waited for a signal of friendship and, at the least encouragement, pointed his lips and then parted them, smiling like the full moon. He took the person's hand and wrapped it in his own as in warm dough. With his head wobbling, he asked questions in a resonant, warm voice, and answered with patience, after a long look out to sea, the nautical conundrums which are addressed to all ships' captains.

When he greeted the General, he assured him that everything would be done to make the voyage agreeable. He informed him that he and Miss Graves were to sit at his table; then he bowed, shook hands and left. "Gulbransson," he had said, introducing himself. "Captain Kasper Gulbransson."

The dining room of the *Céfalo* was amidships, two decks down, the low ceiling held up by iron columns that were painted brown and gold. Old mahogany and brown leather swivel chairs were fastened to the brown floor, and this tedious and practical color scheme was relieved by olive-green linoleum, emerald chintz curtains and two Kelly-green doors that led into the kitchen.

The captain got up as they came in, and bowed. The General sat to his left and Miss Graves to his right.

In the center of the room, on the first day of sailing, was a cold buffet, and everybody helped themselves. Plaschke came just in time. "No dead fish for me, Albert, please," pleaded the General. "Just get me some cold chicken, a slice of Virginia ham, a little green salad." He had a demitasse afterward up on deck.

In the afternoon, just as the General got up from his sleep, the wagon with the cups came again—the same cups in which the consommé had been served. Now tea was offered in them. The General and Miss Graves were sleeping, and it passed them by.

"Oh, God," groaned Leonidas Erosa that evening, when Miss Graves read him the dinner menu: Herring Salad; Scotch Broth; Grilled Fresh Pork Tenderloin or Cold Roast Goose with Celery Knob Salad; Cold Rice Pudding with Fruit Sauce.

"That Scotch broth is the bouillon from this morning with barley thrown in. Is there anything more revolting than a salad made of herring? I am going to starve to death on this ship," said the General. "I hated rice pudding even as a child. Oh, where is Vitasse?"

"The chef is eating in the second class. He has a cabin in the second class," said Plaschke.

"Go and tell him," said the General, "that I want a bottle of champagne in my cabin, and—you know, Albert—something simple: a little turtle soup out of the can, just warmed up. That is all I would like to have."

Plaschke came back with a bottle of Dom Perignon and a message from the chef, which said that the provisions were in the hold of the ship and the hold was locked and would not be opened until next morning.

Monsieur Vitasse was in the galley, sitting in a cozy corner which was the combination office and dining room of the cook. He waited for the chief cook to finish dishing out the food for the passengers who ate at the second sitting.

Adolfo Guzman, the chef of the *Céfalo*, was a specialist with leftovers, an economical garrison cook. He was a sergeant in that army in which Jacques Vitasse was a marshal with every campaign ribbon and the Legion of Honor pinned on his chest. The chef had made that clear immediately in the way he had walked through the kitchen, the fashion in which he had listened to the apologies of Herr Guzman and looked into his inadequate iceboxes. Iceboxes were the love of Monsieur Vitasse. One of his pronouncements was "The icebox is more important than the oven."

Adolfo Guzman had opened the greasy doors, one after the other, of his refrigerator and had recited the contents: "Beef, for boiling. We have boiled beef on the menu every Tuesday. And pork," he said, "they

335

love pork roasted. Veal for steamed kalbsbrust on Wednesday. Goose
and chicken for the captain's dinner. Duck I don't have. Here is lamb,
for stew, and the vegetables. And here—" he pointed at a tub in which
beef was marinated—"this is for sauerbraten on Thursday, with potato
pancakes."

"Ah, yes," said Vitasse, "a kind of boeuf à la mode."

"Sausages they also like." He showed garlands of sausages up on
hooks. "Hams and bacon an Monday. Before we get in, we have a
Beer Evening—you know, music and beer and sauerkraut—mit ham and
sausages."

"Ah, oui," said the chef with understanding. "Choucroute à l'Alsacienne. Very nice, very nice." He wiped his hands on Mr. Guzman's
apron. He was getting hungry.

"You know, of course," said Vitasse, "in cooking, it is not the material but what is done with it. A bad cook can ruin the best food—a
good cook perform miracles with practically nothing."

"Ah, yes," agreed the chef of the *Céfalo*.

"May I have a casserole, Monsieur Guzman—may I make a little
dish, for you and me?"

"But certainly," said Guzman.

"And for my friend, Herr Plaschke?"

"I am honored, monsieur," said Adolfo Guzman.

"Good." The chef put his hand on the shoulder of his colleague.
"Now, while I go to get some wine from my cabin, I want you to
prepare the following: One pound of mushrooms, some sweet butter,
one shallot chopped, one cup of brown sauce. I see you have that there
on your oven. One half teaspoon of chopped parsley. You have all that
down, Monsieur Guzman? *Eh bien.* As for the meat, I will cut it myself
when I return."

The chef went to his cabin and returned with a bottle of the Sandeman sherry and a bottle of champagne. A table was set in the corner of
the kitchen, the oven was cleared, and two casseroles waited there for
Monsieur Vitasse, who removed his coat, rolled up his sleeves and tied
a borrowed apron around his middle. He expertly cut a beef tenderloin
in large dice, put it into a casserole of hot fat for two minutes, drained
off the fat and removed the meat from the pan, while he simmered the
clean and dry mushrooms in melted butter in the second casserole. He
added salt and pepper with an elegant swish, poured the right quantity
of dry sherry out of the bottle, without bothering to measure it in a

cup, and sprayed parsley over the dish.

"Tarragon," he said to Adolfo Guzman, "and chervil." He shook the casserole back and forth, violently, mixing all the ingredients with quick jerks.

Mr. Plaschke appeared, sat down quietly and unfolded his napkin.

"Dinner is served," said the chef.

Adolfo Guzman ate as if he were in church. They mopped up the sauce on their plates with pieces of bread. After the bottle of champagne, Mr. Guzman offered brandy. It was sticky and sweet. Monsieur Vitasse drank it like medicine, holding his breath. He directed the conversation to his illustrious past, going back to his apprenticeship in the kitchen of the great Escoffier. He talked of ovens, and particularly of iceboxes, and of the people he had cooked for. Adolfo Guzman, who was the natural son of the proprietor of a German rathskeller in Buenos Aires, nodded continually in agreement and took all the lessons to heart.

Captain Gulbransson pointed his lips as if he were about to kiss the General. Tapping with his spoon at the edge of his soup plate as a signal that he was through, and looking into the faces of his guests, he began to sing the praises of the S.S. *Céfalo's* cuisine.

The captain had started off with one of his cook's specialties—a thick purée of lentils in which slices of sausage floated half submerged.

"Since I stopped smoking and drinking, I eat much better," said the captain. "Everything tastes so much better. My advice to young men is never start smoking and drinking. You don't enjoy your food if you do. I lost weight when I went ashore, eating in restaurants, throwing my money away. I said to myself, why spend your good money when you can live so much better on board?"

The steward bent over the table with a thick porcelain platter of meat covered by another brown sauce.

"Taste this sauerbraten," said the captain. "Only my mother, who was German, made it better. You won't get a sauerbraten like this anywhere in the world. And the potato pancakes—taste them—like snow! They melt in your mouth."

The potato pancakes were soggy, large, gray-blue and crisply fried at the edges. The General fiddled around with his knife and fork. "It's always that way the first day out. Wait till tomorrow," said the captain, consoling the General.

He picked up the menu and read: "Quesos Surtidos, Galletas de Sodas Tostadas, Frutas Frescas en Temporada."

The General wanted nothing. He held up his hands and ran out of the room.

"Give me the cheese," said Captain Gulbransson. "A nice ripe Liederkranz and the soda crackers."

"Anibal—I am an extremely moral man, Anibal. All my appetites and all my play, dear Anibal, were only to decorate the lonesome house in which I lived. And now it is all over. Still I pray to her soft eyes, to her young mouth, to the pulses in her wrists. Anibal, you never pray, and here my voice is praying again over the water. Again I die for her in loneliness—again she comes to me in the water. Oh, I am thirsty like an ox, Plaschke. Life is not vertical at all—it's horizontal; life is nothing you can collect or stack up. This is one day like any other day—like the day on which I was nineteen or thirty-five. It's Thursday, Plaschke, and as long as any other. The rest of life is filled with such small moments that I can tell you all of them in three seconds. When you have lost your first love, you have lost all the women in the world, Anibal. Why is it that the more women you have, the more lonesome you are? And why is it, Anibal, that coffee is never better than in the kitchen of a whorehouse—and that nothing is as awful as the need for it?"

These were the last spoken words of Leonidas Erosa.

Oh, but that boy was really mean!
He built himself a guillotine!
He was unmoved by the last look
The frightened chickens gave the cook.
He ate them roasted, grilled and frito!
Oh, what a horror was Pepito!

339

GERMINY À L'OSEILLE

"I met a most extraordinary man today," said Sir Charles to Lady Mendl, who was arranging the elephants in her jade menagerie. "Gallant Frenchman, colonel in the last war—like us, too old to fight in this one —lives in Benedict Canyon—a bona fide resident of Hollywood. Built himself a house and a pool—has some land there, and a cow. Good fellow."

"Ha!" said Elsie. "A cow." She had politeness in her inattention. She picked up a word now and then and repeated it, and then went her own way again.

"His own milk," said Sir Charles, "cream and butter. He has started a small farm, with boxes of cement, and there he raises his own snails, and, in the brook on his property, small fresh-water lobsters—which are called crayfish here. Excellent cook besides. Name is Count Bobino. He's coming here for cocktails. Elsie, he's bringing a friend, a very important man, and a great gourmet. They live for each other. The count cooks and the other eats, and they talk about the great meals they have had the way other men brag about their amours. Munchin is the name of the other one—French also—but he owns twelve hotels, international industrialist, steamship lines, he builds whole cities—and his appetite is tremendous."

Elsie was with her seashells. "How remarkable," she said, for Charles had paused, and "How remarkable" fitted almost any pause.

"Elsie dear, Mr. Munchin once ordered dinner for six people. Hors d'oeuvres, soup, fish, meat, salad, dessert and coffee. He said to the waiter, 'Bring the hors d'oeuvres'—and he ate all six of them. And the waiter said, 'Should I bring more?' "

"More what?" said Elsie, arranging the shells.

" 'More hors d'oeuvres,' the waiter said. 'No, bring the soup for everybody,' said Munchin, and he ate all the soup, the fish, the six meats, the sweets, cheeses, salads—and the waiter asked, 'What about the other people?' And Munchin said, 'Oh, they'll be along later. Give me the bill for this and let them pay for their own dinner.' "

The footman announced Count Bobino, who had come without his friend. Mr. Munchin, he explained, had got hungry again. There was a fabulous new *charcuterie*, a German delicatessen, near the Farmers' Market, where every kind of sausage could be had, and this had been discovered by Mr. Munchin. He had stopped and ordered a liverwurst sandwich, liverwurst being the specialty of the house. The proprietor had sliced a French type of bread, for Mr. Munchin had shown him how large he wanted the sandwich, and then had put a large sausage into the meat-slicing machine with the circular, rotating knife. But he could not make the sandwich, for as the slices came off, Mr. Munchin picked them up with his fingers and ate them. He ate almost the entire liverwurst, and the count could not get Munchin out of the delicatessen store. He wrote down the address and said that there was the best assortment of spices, of things in sour sauces, of hams, a mountain of the most delicious rosy smoked cuts of loins of pork, and every sausage imaginable.

The count then explained that he had made a great culinary discovery. "I have found a hill where sour grass grows," he announced poetically with a great sweep of his right arm. He turned to Elsie. "The queen of all the soups in the world, as you know, dear lady, is Germiny à l'Oseille. I have succeeded in raising almost everything I need for it. Also my farm produces the eggs and butter. You take the yolks of six eggs, which you dilute with a quarter pint of cream; put on the fire and stir until the preparation gives signs of boiling. The sour grass—which is really a kind of sour leafy plant called sorrel—you take three ounces and shred them and cook them in butter ahead of time, and add to the one and one half pints of white consommé, and then the yolks of the six eggs with the cream, and stir all this until it reaches the boiling point. But do not let it boil."

Elsie listened politely but heard nothing of what was said. Normally she was interested in cooking and especially in soups, but now she was thinking of other things, most probably her dog. The count paused.

She was polite again. "But these things run into money," she said. "The cow and all that."

"Ah, but, dear lady," said the count, arranging his monocle, "the cow is always there. You have it for years."

"Of course," said Elsie.

The count got up. "Dear lady," he said, bending over Elsie's hand, "milk and cream and butter are rare now. You will allow me to send them to you. And as for the consommé, I have made a great discovery. As you know, Lady Mendl, the basis of consommé is the chicken. The old way, you had to buy two soup chickens. You had the trouble of cooking them. It takes hours, it's tiresome. You know what I do now? I buy canned noodle soup. I throw the noodles away—I don't want them —and begin with what is left. The can of noodle soup is only twenty or thirty cents."

Elsie got up. She thought he was leaving and she staggered toward the door and she smiled, but the count was an intense man. He talked about his cow; the barnyard odor moved back into the house. Elsie was smiling bitterly, and there was no way of rescuing her; he had a firm grip on her arm. He walked her around the room.

Finally she took a stance and stopped him by saying firmly, "You must take me to see your lovely farm someday."

He kissed her hand once more and backed out of the room, promising to send eggs, snails, crayfish, butter and sour grass. After he was gone Elsie said, "What a charming, generous man, but the next time I wish he'd have cocktails with the cook. And how fortunate that what's-his-name, his friend, the Empty Stomach, didn't come along."

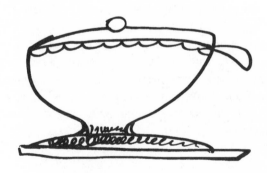

ROMANOFF'S
FOR LUNCH

THE RIGHT HAND of Ludlow Mumm, the one he wrote with, was in bandages as the result of a railroad accident some fifty miles out of Los Angeles. The writer leaned forward with a painful move and picked up the phone with his left hand.

"Good morning," said a cheery voice. "This is the Wildgans Chase Agency. You're having lunch with Mr. Wildgans at Romanoff's. Mr. Wildgans wants to discuss the contract with you. We're sending a car

for you. It will be there in fifteen minutes. You will find it under the porte-cochere of your hotel."

Ludlow Mumm stepped out on the balcony of his suite and looked down the front of the Beverly Hills Hotel.

"I would have called it a marquee," he said, and went back into the room.

He took a dictionary out of his bag, and, holding it between his legs and opening it with his good hand, he searched under the letter P.

" 'Porte-cochere,' " he read, " 'a large gateway through which a carriage may drive into a court; an extension of a porch; a roof over a driveway.' "

He turned the pages and looked under M.

" 'Marquee,' " he read, " 'a tent; a window awning; an awning raised as a temporary shelter from the curb to the door of a dwelling or a public building.'

"She's absolutely right," said the writer, and put the book away.

He walked back out on the balcony, lifted himself on the toes of his small feet, leaned over the banister, enjoying the scene, and scratched his soft brown beard. He had grown it to cover up at least part of a round face that was kind to the point of idiocy.

Ludlow Mumm would have been happiest as a lay brother of a religious order, one not too penitent. He would have fitted ideally into the cloth of that happy group of monks who brew sweet liqueurs to the glory of God in France.

He looked down again, smiling. On a balcony beneath him, stretched on a chaise longue which was covered with an immense bath towel, was all that is real and good in a sometimes lazily shifting female form, unclothed, inhaling and exhaling deeply, and occasionally running her fingers through her platinum-blond hair.

Women, in the life of Ludlow Mumm, took the roles of mothers, sweethearts, good wives, sisters and little girls. Those that disturbed other men were regarded by him as remarkable adornments in that ever-beautiful green valley through whose dewy grass the padre in his sandals wandered with uplifted heart.

"Porte-cochere," repeated the conscientious scribe, looking once more down at the front of the hotel.

Then he went back into his suite again, picked up his hat with the unbandaged left hand and walked to the elevator.

The happy first impression of the correctness and efficiency of the Wildgans Chase Agency was underlined when, exactly fifteen minutes after the telephone call, a black, polished Buick limousine purred up along the avenue of palm trees and stopped smoothly under the porte-cochere.

The alert, uniformed driver, who had never seen Mumm before this moment, touched his cap and smiled. The doorman opened the door, and as Ludlow sat down the driver said, "Good morning, Mr. Mumm. Welcome to California."

As the car swung down and halted for the stop sign at the crossing of Sunset and Rodeo, the driver jumped from his seat and made Ludlow Mumm comfortable, suggesting that he move into the left corner of the car. He pulled down the arm rest for the injured member.

"Toni is my name," he said, and was back up front.

"You're in good hands, sir," he said, "when you're with Wildgans Chase. You'll get plenty for that accident. We had you insured from the moment you left New York."

The writer leaned back and smiled. The palm trees swam by and Toni identified the lovely homes of the stars along the route.

"I can get you anything you want in this town," said Toni.

By the time they arrived at Romanoff's, he had arranged for a car and chauffeur; for some color film for the writer's magazine Kodak; and he had promised to smooth out any difficulties and overcome all shortages and needs that would arise during the writer's stay.

Toni stopped the car and ran into the restaurant, announcing Ludlow Mumm to the headwaiter, who at once took him to one of the good tables.

"Mr. Wildgans," said Joe, the maître d'hôtel, "is up there now at the first table. He's expecting you. He'll be here in a little while."

Arty Wildgans, a portly, ruddy man, slowly came down the line: like a bucket in the hands of a fire brigade, he was handed on from one person to the next.

"The first thing I always say is 'Hello,' " he said cheerily as he finally arrived and sat down.

Looking over Mumm's head, he waved and smiled at several people in the rear of the room.

"And how are the folks back East?" he asked, picking up the menu.

Without waiting for the answer, he looked up at the waiter and said, "How's the Vichyssoise today?"

"Well," said the waiter with indignation in his voice, "Joe Schenck just had some!"

"All right, all right," countered Wildgans, equally agitated. "Let's have that to start with—and what else did Joe Schenck have?"

"The boeuf à la mode with gnocchi," said the waiter bitterly.

"All right, we'll take the beef à la mode with the genukki, too," said Wildgans. "Or do you want something different? . . . Hello, Al," he said with a wave of the hand to a man who approached the table. He made the introductions: "Al Leinwand—Ludlow Mumm, the great writer. You heard of him."

"Sure," said Al Leinwand.

Al Leinwand, a fierce man and rival agent, a birdlike creature with the head of a hawk on a sparrow's body, glared into the room over Ludlow Mumm's head, in that peculiar Hollywood restaurant manner in which one is never with the eyes where the ears are.

"Go on," said Wildgans, "about the accident."

Mumm recited the story of the derailment in which he had injured his hand, and Leinwand, who, like everyone here, was able to top any story, listened with an unhappy expression of impatience. Suddenly he cut the report short. Following the swaying rump of a girl in a Vertés print with his eyes, the small man said, "I read all about your accident, Mumm. I could have been in that wreck too." He looked briefly at Wildgans as if excusing himself for an omission and added: "In fact, I almost was."

He nodded at a producer three tables away. "I had reservations on that same train. Only, at the last minute, I was held over in New York. Well, so long."

Wildgans salted his Vichyssoise.

"You made him very unhappy," he said to Mumm. "He's heartbroken he wasn't in that wreck. He's got to be in everything. Well," he said, stirring the cold soup, "how do you like it out here?"

The writer smiled and was about to say something when Arty Wildgans turned from his plate, looked up and said an indifferent "Hello" to a beautiful and exotic creature, a woman in her best years, who stretched out to him her carmine-gloved arms, pointed her lips and made the sound of kissing several times as she sat down.

"Arty, mind if I sit down here for a minute?" she asked reproachfully, with a heavy foreign accent.

"Ludlow Mumm, the writer," said Wildgans and introduced the actress.

347

She talked into the small mirror of her compact, saying "Hello" with a quick glance at Mumm.

"Darling," she said, still reproachfully, "you promised as a favor to get me a test with Vashvily."

"I will," said Wildgans. "I'm crazy about that bit you did in *Jetsam.* I saw it yesterday. It was marvelous. Just a little more of that the next time and then Vanya Vashvily can't throw it in my face that you are nothing but a character woman and I can defeat him."

She purred and put her arm through his. A fourth person joined the group, a sagging individual in a pale-blue sports coat, a musician, also with a heavy accent, who took a match from the table and relit his soggy cigar.

"You know Vogelsang," said Wildgans and explained that the man was a famous composer of background music.

"You are Austrian?" asked the character woman, while Wildgans, whose client Vogelsang was, said to Mumm, "Great talent. He did the score for *Magdalene.*"

"Ja, Ja," said Vogelsang, or rather, "Yoh, Yoh."

"Ah, Austrians," she said with throaty laughter, "such *gemütliche* people, Austrians. Well, maybe not—nobody is *gemütlich* any more, except Arty here.

"You know Russians, kind, sing, dance, help everybody, suddenly turn into wild animals, beat innocents. Ach, prrrppzzt—man is terrible. Well, nice to have seen you."

Mr. Vogelsang, with the back of his trousers hanging sadly, stuck his wet cigar deep into his mouth, made a Continental bow to the character woman, and left.

"I don't agree with what you said about the Russians at all," said Ludlow Mumm to the character woman. "I can't agree with you at all on that. I think they're a great people."

"I hope you are right," said the actress. "I am one of them."

She turned to Wildgans.

"Would you like to have a cheap thrill, Arty? I am going to have a massage and you can come and talk to me."

She was up and without waiting for the answer she sailed off, throwing kisses.

"I always inherit these dogs," said Wildgans, starting to cut the boeuf à la mode.

"Nobody else wants to have anything to do with them . . . just because I have a soft heart and can't say no. Of course, that dame will never be anything but a character woman, but I haven't the heart to tell her that. I could have told her five years ago when she came out here."

They both ate—Wildgans in haste, and Mumm with enjoyment of the sauce, which he mopped up with pieces of bread after he had eaten all the gnocchi.

"We have to get something blight-resisting for this table," remarked Wildgans as a tall, ascetic-looking man came up to the table with his hands in his coat pockets.

The unhappy-looking, pale individual stared at Wildgans, and without any change of expression in his face and tired voice he said, "I'm still dazed. I fell off my filing cabinet last night when I got your note."

"What did you expect?" said Wildgans.

"I expected a check—money—for the difference between what they said they'd agree to and what I'm getting."

He stared at Wildgans and Wildgans said, "You know Ludlow Mumm, the writer."

Without taking his eyes off Wildgans, the tall, thin man said, "Hello, Mumm," and continued: "Listen, Wildgans, I'm just a thin, tired Jew. I don't want anything for nothing. I only ask to be paid for my work, and when I'm not, I get unhappy and the fountain doesn't spurt."

"I'll see Moses Fable tomorrow," said Wildgans.

"Why not today?" said the man.

"Tomorrow is a better day. I'm a little dull today," said Wildgans.

"Did you hear that, Mumm?" asked the thin man. "He said, 'I'm a little dull today!' Why make an exception? Why not just say, 'I'm Arty'?"

Wildgans laughed and handed him a cigar. Jerome Hack rolled it in his long fingers, smelled it and examined it with his unhappy black eyes.

"What are you staring at the cigar for? It's good. I gave it to you."

"Get busy, Wildgans, and do something," Jerome Hack said as he left.

"Great talent," said Wildgans after the departing writer. "On the same

lot as you are—a mechanic, great on construction—turns out rough-and-tumble musicals—cops-and-robbers—anything you want. Very dependable—great sense of humor—a very legitimate guy."

The waiter put the check down and Wildgans signed it.

He drove back to the hotel with Mumm.

"Well," he said, "I think we had a very fruitful talk. Goodbye, Lud. I'll call you."

"How about the story? When do I start to work?" asked Mumm, leaning forward, ready to get out of the car.

"Oh, about the picture," said Wildgans. "Listen, Mumm, take it easy. Get settled first and don't worry about the picture. These days you can hang a sign outside a theater saying 'No Picture Today' and close up and they'll break down the doors. You don't have to show no picture —just turn out the lights and get a couple of guys to drag wet overcoats throug the aisles and step on the feet of the audience."

*A*h," said Maurice, "*I know of a little restaurant at the end of the pier in Santa Monica. I dislike ostentation. I am fed up with places like Romanoff's and Larue's. Always the same menu, always the same faces—horrible people—the same awful faces. I am very fond of this little place. The* spécialité de la maison *is abalone steak.*"

"*I'm feeling much better. Yesterday I had lunch out somewhere, in a restaurant near the Paramount Studio, very nice. I prefer Romanoff's, however. At Romanoff's one meets the awful people one knows. At that other place there are the awful people one doesn't know.*"

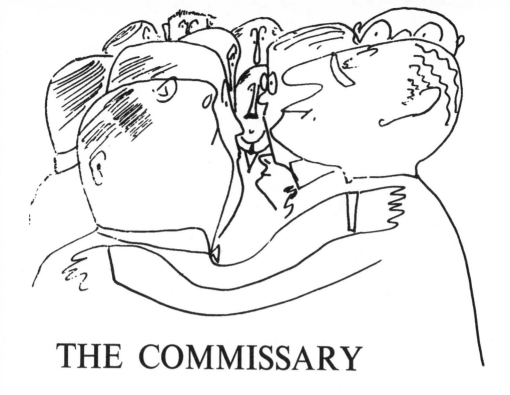

THE COMMISSARY

AT NOON, the electricians on the various stages of the vast lot of Olympia Pictures threw their switches and the large family that worked on the Olympia lot began their leisurely trek toward the cafeterias and the commissary.

At one, the bells of the carillon with which Moses Fable had endowed a Methodist church that stood on a lot adjoining the studio began to ring their changes and the high executives in the administration building started to salivate.

A motherly woman known as Ma Gundel, in white with broad white shoes on her aching feet, would come out of the kitchen then, carrying a large wicker basket which contained various kinds of bread. In the basket were sour-dough bread, sweet rye, Russian rye, matzoth, French bread, pumpernickel, Swedish crisp, potato bread and Viennese rolls. She covered this with a napkin and put it in the center of the round table at which Moses Fable lunched and walked back through the commissary to get large kosher pickles, almost electric with their sharp, salty tang. She also brought red and green tomatoes, pickled; a dish with chopped chicken liver, Bismarck herring, sliced smoked salmon, sour cream, chives, scallions, immense sticks of Utah celery, radishes, and more

353

pickles; and other good and salty delicatessen according to the day of the week.

Her last trip was for Dr. Brown's Celery Tonic, Pepsi-Cola, Coca-Cola, and bottles of milk and buttermilk.

All this done, she sat on a chair outside the executive dining room and looked into the large commissary at the assembled stars, bit actors and extras, who, in the various costumes of the parts they played, sat there and ate and talked.

Nuns from religious spectacles sat next to gangsters; Gestapo captains ate in peace with the French Underground; and maharajahs were seated below untouchables at another table.

Ma Gundel could have retired years ago under the pension plan which enveloped all regular employees of Olympia. But she loved pictures and could not tear herself away from the forever-exciting scene of their making. She followed every production with interest. Moses Fable valued her criticism and had been known to consult with her seriously when casting important features. She was a person of consequence and everybody put his arms around her.

Ma Gundel rested her feet and awaited the arrival of Moses Fable and his guests.

Moses Fable and Olympia were made for each other. No player in Hollywood could have come near the perfect portrayal that he gave as president of the corporation. If he had limited his work to impersonating himself, his huge salary would have been earned.

There was a solid air about him as he walked through the pandemonium of the plant in his conservative gray suits. The thin veins on his massive cheeks were like the engraving on gilt-edged securities.

He moved with weight and deliberation, and when he wanted to look around he turned with the whole elliptical body, slowly and steadily, as a statue is moved.

"Here at Olympia," he was fond of saying, "we have both time and money in unlimited quantities!"

In his solid fashion, he was outstandingly different from his competitors, who always ran and always seemed to suspect that someone was listening behind them.

A beneficiary of mankind in the mass, as he liked to think of himself, Moses Fable also richly rewarded those around him he thought worthy. He was interested in the last individual of his large family.

"Anyone can come and see me at any hour of the day and also the night, if it's important enough" was another of his favorite sayings.

But, if he was kind and human, he was not gullible, and while he spoke ordinarily with the rich organ of a psalm-singer holding himself in, once he was confronted with roguery, when he found lurking skimmers trying to dip their ladles in the rich Olympia broth, when his treasures were threatened, or he caught the competition trying to wander off with one of his stars, he became dangerously agile and emitted the sounds of a knife-grinder.

The procession of his virtues is not complete without citing his courage. He was envied and admired for the fortitude with which he regularly threw good money after bad and thereby regularly attained large grosses and fabulous successes with even his worst pictures.

With the same rare mixture of a peasant's cunning and an impresario's play of hunches, he chose people. If he saw talent and good will he was generous with time and money, he forgave the beginner his mistakes and allowed for occasional failure in old hands.

He read people through his sharp rimless glasses and he filed away what he found. The intricate cabinet in his head never mislaid information. It was a piece of occult furniture that belonged among the paraphernalia of stargazers and spiritualists; it was of paramount importance in his complicated industry, but would have wrecked any other kind of business had it made use of it.

He was given to speeches. His winged words, uncensored, flew out over banquet tables and into the nation's press. He was upswept by his own words and believed everything he said.

The carillon in the church across the street was still ringing when Ludlow Mumm followed another girl guide into the inner office of Moses Fable. She left the shy writer standing in the doorway.

The executives who stood in a group in the center of the room slowly moved toward him. They all talked: some to one another in the center of the circle; others shouted over the heads of people who stood between them; and some carried on conversations on the outside.

Vanya Vashvily was talking to a director.

"What did the picture show?" he asked.

"The picture finally revealed," said the director, "that toward the end of the colon there is a small pocket, and in this, food gets stuck and infects the whole system. They'll operate tomorrow and then she'll have to stay on a corrective diet for a while."

Moses Fable slowly moved his massive form and said to the director

who was with Vashvily, "Who are you talking about, Sandor?"

"That Mexican, Dolores Tarant."

"But I thought she was a nice girl," said Fable.

"Certainly, she *is* a nice girl. She's more beautiful than ever, great talent," said the director, reassuring his employer.

"That's the one we had the teeth straightened, isn't it?" asked Moses Fable.

"Straightened and capped," replied Vashvily.

"Well," said the fatherly Fable with concern, "you had better take care and tell the hospital people to cover them with Vaseline if they're going to give her a total anesthetic, because the ether dissolves those plastic teeth."

"Right, Mr. Fable," said the director, and made a note.

"What is this, the emergency ward?" asked Moses Fable, looking past Vashvily at the door and pointing with slow, deliberate gesture at Ludlow Mumm, who stood there with his bandaged hand.

Vashvily turned around.

"Oh, hello," he said. "That's one of my boys, Mr. Fable. Ludlow Mumm, the great writer."

"I beg your pardon," said Fable, slowly approaching the writer. "It's a great pleasure to have you with us, Mr. Mumm. I want you to meet some of the people here. Wolfgang Liebestod, head of our musical department; Raoul de Bourggraff, head of the art department; John St. Clair; Sandor Thrilling, the director you've heard about."

Mumm shook hands without surprise. In a town that contains firms like Utter McKinley, the undertakers; a real estate firm of Read and Wright; two Prinzmetals; a LeRoy Prinz; a Jack Skirball; a Jerry Rothschild; a law firm by the name of Dull and Twist; and musicians called Amphitheatrof and Bakaleinakoff, he had become accustomed to unusual and distinctive names.

"Bob Evervess of the story department and Mr. Envelove of the legal end. Come on boys, let's go," said Moses Fable, and, taking hold of the writer, he advanced with him through the door as the pealing of the carillon faded away.

"Mr. Mumm," said Fable, "you sit over there."

He indicated the chair opposite his own, but before he released him from the strong grip with which he had transported him from the executive suite, over the lawn and through the commissary into the private dining room, he said, "I hope you're feeling at home here. I hope you'll be with us a long time, Mr. Mumm, and I hope they're treating you right. If they don't, you come and see me. It's not like over at those windbags'—" he nodded in the direction of another studio—"where you have to wade through fourteen secretaries before you can see anybody. Remember, here, you can see me any hour of the day, and if it's important, any hour of the night."

He gave Mumm a smile and started to tear open a telegram which his secretary had brought to him.

He sat down and the executives followed. Fable looked madder and madder as he read.

"So, what you tukking?" said Mrs. Gundel, and began to recite the day's menu.

Fable looked at her and said, "Just a minute," and then turned to the table and he held up the telegram.

"Gentlemen," he said, "I have to go to Washington next Friday to explain some elemental things down there."

He hit the table and the pince-nez trembled.

"Judas Priest," he cried, "they talk about inflation, and of course I'm right up there next to Louis B. Mayer and maybe this year I'll be ahead of him, right on top of the list. People like me are always the target because we earn the biggest salary in the United States."

"Mebbe, da spacial billa fare you vant?" said Mrs. Gundel with a trace of impatience.

"Oh, bring me anything," said Fable.

"Da borscht." She looked around and everybody nodded. To the newcomer, Mumm, Ma Gundel said in her best dialect and as if she were in a radio serial, "Vait till you taste the borscht! You'll going to lick by you de fingehs."

Repeating the order to herself, she walked out of the room.

Moses Fable took a pickle in his hand and continued: "All right, so what—I pay ninety-two per cent in taxes! My cars are up on blocks. I eat here the sixty-cent lunch in the commissary. What else do they want me to do? They can back up a truck to my home and take my forty pairs of old shoes away and the rags I have hanging in my closet, they can have those too. It doesn't mean a thing to me."

The pickle crackled as he bit into it.

"But if those idiots in Washington would sit down for a moment and think, they would see that I and the handful of men that earn the kind of money I make don't mean a thing. It's the morons, the millions that never had a goddamn thing. The father used to make thirty bucks, now he works in a defense plant. He brings home $110 a week, with time, overtime and double pay on Sunday. The mother makes $80. That makes $190, and little Rosie, the riveter, brings in another $60. That makes it $250 a week.

"They never knew that kind of money before, and somehow they manage to buy the last icebox and the last radio. Every dream has come true—the house is painted and they go to the pictures every night, which is all very well and as it should be. But they forget who they owe it to. They owe it to the sixty economic royalists that made it all possible. To the damned and discredited people who built up the industries of this country. The steel men, the oil men, the motor makers, the bankers, and people like you and I who worked overtime and Sundays all our lives, and who carry the responsibility.

"What did they ever do? Those bastards have never given anything to anybody or worked beyond what they had to to keep from starving! They are lazy, mean and grabbing.

"Now comes that withholding tax and they're asked to give up a measly twenty per cent. That's what hurts—and in Washington, they scream and blame it on us. 'Look at Fable and his fabulous salary!' they say.

"But that's too easy, gentlemen. They're just trying to get out of that mess in Washington and so that's why they blame people like me. But I'm tired of keeping quiet. I've just rehearsed, gentlemen, what I'm going to tell them in Washington Friday."

The executives nodded and murmured their approval.

Moses Fable felt for his spoon.

"What a picture! What a documentary I could make about those bums in Washington!" he said bitterly.

"But again, I impress upon you, gentlemen, that we are not in the business of propaganda but in the business of entertainment, and I refuse to use the gigantic resources of this organization to further my personal aims or to influence public opinion. If such pictures are to be made—" he nodded in the direction of the other studio—"let them stick their necks out. I am not pro this or pro that. I just want to be fair and I'll tell them what's on my mind. But those flag-waving phonies, they have to beat the drum. They think they can save the world. I don't want to save the world. I just want to entertain the masses of the people."

Moses Fable had kept his eyes fixed in a hypnotic stare at Mumm during the entire speech. Now he was ready to eat. He stood up and bent forward, reaching into the glass jar for a new pickle. In a slow and deliberate manner he waved the pickle and then pointed with it at each individual at the table.

"I hope I haven't hurt anybody's feelings," he said and sat down and, with a cracking sound, bit into the sour delicacy.

"Nu, so drink your cawfee," said Ma Gundel.

"I don't want any coffee, Ma," said Fable.

"No Linzertorte?"

"No Linzertorte."

At the end of the meal he walked over to Mumm and took a grip on his arm again.

"I'll be back in a few days," he said, "and remember, you can come and see me any time. And good luck to you."

He walked, with his hand on Ludlow Mumm's shoulder, through the commissary, and stood outside with him in the sun. Then, as Mumm walked away, he lifted his right arm in farewell greeting and Mumm waved his bandaged arm in return. Moses Fable stepped into the car, the one which was not on blocks, and drove away.

SERVANT TROUBLE

Mumm was on time. It was exactly seven. As he approached the heavy iron-bound door it automatically opened. An old-fashioned German of some sixty years with close-cropped hair stood in the hall. Vashvily, who was in a blue velvet house jacket, adjusted his hearing aid and, after greeting Ludlow Mumm, mixed a Martini.

"You better take your drink to the table," he said, "and have it there."

The butler, who stood waiting in the dining room, pushed a heavy Venetian baroque chair under Mumm.

The face of a woman who looked like Hindenburg, only with two buns of yellow hair at the sides of her face, appeared in the door. She was the butler's wife. She handed two plates of home-made noodle soup to her husband.

"Beer or wine?" asked the man.

Mumm asked for beer.

As the butler left the room, Vashvily said in a tone of confidence, "I had a very nice colored man before they came—was with me for years. I hope to get him back."

The butler came and took the plates away. He put a bottle of beer next to Mumm's plate and also an opener. Mrs. Hindenburg came and handed bread around.

There was absolute silence until they had gone. Then Vashvily whispered, "You know, I take sun baths; I have a small terrace upstairs where I take sun baths."

The man came in again and put two very large and very hot plates on the table and there was silence again until he went out through the door, back into the kitchen.

"I told you about the terrace where I take my sun baths," said the producer. "Well, next to this terrace are two trees. I'd have them cut down, but the place doesn't belong to me. They're eucalyptus trees and they are very disorderly, always dropping things. Leaves fall out of them and pods, and even pieces of the bark."

Mrs. Hindenburg and her husband marched in, he with sauerbraten and potato pancakes, and she with a jardiniere of fresh vegetables, topped by two fried eggs. After they had marched out again, the producer lowered his voice and looked at the door.

"So, my terrace is full of leaves that fall out of those trees, so I tell this son-of-a-bitch to clean it up. They've got nothing to do but to take care of me, no laundry, no cleaning windows, nothing. Well, after a week, I'm up to my ankles in dead leaves up there. So, two more days pass. You know, I'm just out of the hospital and I'm not supposed to exert myself, so I say to him—"

There was absolute silence again as the man came back into the room. He looked sternly at the plates and the producer started eating with fine remarks about the cooking and compliments for Mrs. Hindenburg.

Later, Mumm turned around and looked at the Braque, admiring it, and also at an anonymous still life which Vashvily had picked up in a junk shop downtown and put into a good frame.

(In a telephone conversation, the day after the liberation-of-Paris celebration, when Cassard had excused himself for his behavior, he had also said about Vashvily, "A man of taste, not the run of insensible producers. You can talk about anything with him. He is well informed. He has traveled. He knows food and wine and plays the piano beautifully. He has read everything. Only, when he starts talking about pictures he turns into an absolute idiot.")

Mr. and Mrs. Hindenburg passed the platters once more. The sour pot roast was good, the potato pancakes light and small, and both men took more.

"So I say to the son-of-a-bitch," continued Vashvily, as the door swung closed again, "just to shame him into it, I said, 'All right, if you're so busy, I'll clean them up myself—the leaves.'"

Mumm shook his head.

There was another period of silence during the clearing of the plates, after which Mrs. Hindenburg put a large cut-glass bowl of stewed apricots in the center of the table and the butler brushed the crumbs off the tablecloth and put down the dessert plates and the silver.

"Coffee," he asked without the inflection of a question.

"Yes, in the other room," answered Vashvily, equally flat.

They were gone again.

"I said, 'All right, I'll clean up myself if you're so busy,'" repeated the producer. "So what do you think he does? He comes up to my terrace and hands me a broom and a dustpan!"

"I don't believe it," said Mumm in astonishment.

"That's nothing," said the producer. "Wait till you hear the rest. So I clean up the leaves myself, and when I'm halfway through, he comes again—I'm just resting. . . . Well, he stands there and he takes the broom out of my hand and I say to myself, 'At last.' But he just takes the broom and turns it around and he says, 'I guess I'd better get you a new broom. This one is just about worn out.'"

The conversation was cut again. The man came in, folded his arms and, standing by the leaded window, stared at the table.

Mrs. Hindenburg carried the tray with the coffee into the living room, past him. Vashvily made haste with his apricots and they both got up.

The candles were snuffed out and the dining-room doors shut behind the wife after she had said a grim "Good night."

Vashvily said, "The first thing they asked when they came was 'How often do you entertain?' He said, 'What time do you eat?' and in the same breath she said, 'Not later than seven-thirty.' And when it's seven and the guests have not arrived, he stands at the window there and glowers through the Venetian blinds. Well," whispered Vashvily, "he won't glower much longer."

"It's very hard these days," said Mumm.

"Hell, they have a sitting room and a bedroom and two bathrooms with dressing room. I pay them four hundred dollars a month. Guests only once or twice a week. Use of a car. What more do they want?"

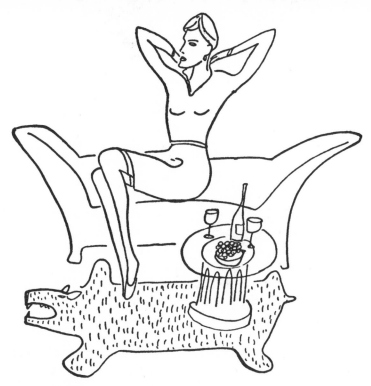

SNOWY NIGHT
IN MALIBU

Betsy Allbright, the silent-picture star, arranged the seating for her dinner party. Lieutenant Casey McMahon, her fourth husband, was busy playing along the beach, throwing pieces of driftwood for his giant black schnauzer to retrieve from the Malibu waves. The lieutenant was out of the Army only a week, and Betsy Allbright stopped occasionally and lifted her eyes from the table and looked out through the plate-glass window, watching his youthful leaps and runs, and the dives he did into the ocean.

"Tell him to come in and get dressed," she said to Auguste. "And here—" she handed the butler a large vase that was in the center of the table—"take these artificial flowers out of here. They make such awful noises."

The modern house was insulated against the sounds of the sea, and the soundproofing extended to the telephone, which did not ring but an-

nounced calls with a soft green light. Tom, the chauffeur, came down the stairs and told Betsy Allbright that Maurice Cassard was on the wire.

"Betsy darling," said Cassard, "I depend on you. I am bringing her down tonight—put in a good word for me. She is infatuated with that crêpe Suzette, Buddy van der Lynn; she has mentioned his name three times today already. Tell her about actors. . . ."

"Let me have a look at her first," said Betsy, "and then I'll do what's good for you."

Miss Allbright's secretary used a special typewriter with letters large enough so that the old actress could read menus, messages and place cards without using glasses.

She put Cassard on her left and Belinda next to her husband. Ludlow Mumm was on Belinda's left. An old admirer, Sir Gerald Graveline, the distinguished actor, was seated on Betsy's right.

"Now, go ahead and tell him to put away that goddamn dog and get dressed. They'll all be on time tonight," she said. "What time is it, Auguste?"

"I should say we're nearing seven, Madame," replied the butler.

She came down at eight-thirty, in gold lamé this time, her hair wound like fresh bread in a yellow twist on top of her head. She wore a broad emerald necklace, and from her wrist to the floor hung a chiffon handkerchief to match her necklace. Around her waist was a girdle of leopard skin and gold leaf.

The sun-tanned lieutenant had exchanged the uniform for a dinner jacket. He was romantic and lithe. He moved about as if he were on a set, playing the parts of several young men at the same time, all of them keen and debonair, standing in the four corners of the room.

"I've got to go to a funeral Thursday," said Betsy Allbright. "I just found out that I've got nothing but beach wear and evening dresses, so tomorrow remind me to get some things sent out from Adrian's. . . . I told him to go to the Mayos, or to the Walter Reed, but he had his own ideas. All the good people are dying now," she said, looking over the table.

The young man walked back and forth and occasionally mumbled by way of answering.

"We were just talking about poor Sam," said Betsy Allbright to Cassard as he came into the room.

"Ah, yes," said Cassard. "Poor Sam. What a pity!"

"Six months ago, when he first told me what was wrong with him, I said to him, go to the Mayo Clinic. There is a doctor. He did this throat for me. You know, the Mayos, what they said to me ten years ago? They said, you better have that goiter out or your life won't be worth a nickel. So they sent me to this man that I wanted to send Sam to, and he took it out—you can hardly see the scar. And the Mayos, they operated on my leg." She shook with laughter. "When you see me here, Maurice, you see only half of me. I left most of it in clinics all over the world—and what isn't cut out is sewn up. . . .

"Give him a cocktail," she said to the lieutenant, who was chewing his lip. He came forward and bowed to Belinda, pressing his neat mustache on her hand.

Sir Gerald arrived. He greeted the hostess and the lieutenant and then the other guests in proper sequence.

"The funniest thing is," said the hostess to Cassard, "that the poor bastard gave a couple of million dollars to build a wing on this god-damned hospital, just to die in it. That's gratitude!"

Cassard said hello to the host. The lieutenant, who had kept a British accent intact through two and a half years of service with the Canadians, slapped Cassard's back.

"You are glad to be back?" asked Cassard.

"Awfully," said the host. "Been playing on the sand with the dahg all afternoon."

"Are you in pictures?"

"I've been approached by several agents, and there is talk of giving me a part at Olympia."

"And what are you going to play?"

"Oh, something in Galilean homespun. But there," said the lieutenant, with raised voice, and holding his glass in the direction of Sir Gerald, "is the man who should play the lead, not—what's his name?"

"Thank you. Thank you very much, dear boy," said Sir Gerald, "but there are three roles in this world that I do not care to play. They are, in fact, not playable. They are: Christ, Shakespeare and Jeeves. You start with six strikes against you when you try to portray any of them."

"Well, I dare say you'd be good—better than anyone else, anyway," Lady Graveline said. "He's so tired, the poor darling. All his activities—the radio, the screen, and all the things he does besides. I'm glad they didn't ask him. I'd hate to have him step out of *Monte Cristo* to do *The Mount*."

"Well, that wouldn't be a serial," said Betsy Allbright.

Sir Gerald turned to get a drink.

"I don't know anything about pictures any more. I've got money in them—that's all," said Betsy Allbright. "I finance one or two a year and I look at one or two a year and I take a lot of trouble selecting them—more than the Academy Award people take."

Sir Gerald said to Mumm: "It's fatal for actors to come out here. Oh, how fatal this place is for talent!

"We have lived in Paris, in London, in Stockholm and it's been wonderful, but you come out here and something happens to you. I wish I had the courage to leave and go back to the stage. Well, for me it's too late, but I pity the young ones. I don't have to tell you. You can see for yourself what happens to actors out here. God—I believe in a hard life for actors—to try and try again—to meet with misfortune—to walk into managers' offices and sit there and wait for a part and to have that a matter of life and death. Out of that, sir, came actors."

The lieutenant nodded gravely.

"The same holds true of your work, doesn't it, Mr. Mumm? A garret —turn-down—and misery—and try and try again?"

"That is true of all that is art," said Ludlow Mumm, stroking his beard.

"As far as actresses go—"

Sir Gerald held up both his hands. "Take that girl, that awfully silly girl. She's a new discovery and now she's a star. What's her name? Whether it rains or shines, whether the piece is happy or sad, she's always the same."

"Ah, but she has something," said the host.

"Well, all right. You mean she has breasts. Well, dear boy, acting is not done with the breasts, if you allow me."

When they had sat down to dinner, Mumm asked: "Did you all see that awful picture of Mussolini in today's paper?"

"I say, such a thing could never happen in England," said Lady

Graveline. "I mean the girl hanging next to him, upside down."

"I wonder how they kept her skirts from falling down over her head," said Cassard.

"Rather good legs," said the lieutenant.

Sir Gerald occasionally absented himself in mind from the table; he frequently closed his eyes and dozed off. When he awoke he sat up and pulled open his eyelids, which were like a large bird's. He awoke now and leaned toward the hostess with blank eyes.

"We were just talking about Mussolini," she said loudly, as if she could thereby recall the entire conversation to him.

"Oh yes, good fellow—made the trains run on time."

There was loud laughter at the other end of the table. "Who's the silly ass?" Sir Gerald asked his hostess.

She kicked him in the side with her elbow.

"My new husband," she said.

"Oh, dear," said the great actor.

The ruddy lieutenant reached for the card that leaned against the candlestick and read the menu.

"Excellent dinner, darling," he said in a pause across the table. "May I congratulate you, particularly on the selection of the wine. Claret goes well with filet mignon, particularly a full-bodied claret like this—"

"You'll have to thank Dennis for that," said Betsy Allbright. "That's all I ever got out of my first marriage. He made me wine-conscious, and he taught me how to pronounce 'Auguste' in French—and a few other things."

Betsy Allbright moved the open-toed sandal on her right foot over to the buzzer and pressed down on it. "More wine, Auguste."

The butler carefully poured the claret from a crystal decanter. The host lifted his glass, held it against the light of the candle and slowly turned the stem between thumb and index finger, studying the color carefully. Overseas he had been stationed at a replacement center close to the Château Lafite, and he had made the study of French wines, and particularly of the local vintages, his concern.

"What year, Auguste?" he asked eventually, after sipping some of the wine and letting it roll over his tongue.

The butler, who had taken the menu card and was using it to scrape bread crumbs off the table, straightened up. He said, "No year, monsieur. Just Sonny Boy California Claret."

"Oh," said the lieutenant and put the glass down. He turned to Belinda.

"A kind of *vin ordinaire*," he said.

"Precisely, monsieur," said the butler over his shoulder, continuing with the crumbs.

"For that—not bad at all," said the lieutenant.

At that moment Betsy Allbright suffered an almost uncontrollable impulse to throw her glass of Sonny Boy California Claret into her husband's face, but she turned her head and looked out through the wide, plate-glass window at the sea.

"The war does funny things, even to wines," said the lieutenant. "No one would ever have thought of serving this before."

"I must say I've grown to like these wines," said Cassard. "I have this claret regularly with my meals, and I think it is getting better and better every year. I say to myself—perhaps the Américains are learning to make good wine after all."

"Na-a-ah," said the lieutenant, forgetting his accent. "You're wrong there, Maurice. It's because you've been away from home so long—you forget about good wine. Think back. Take a St. Emilion or a Pouilly—a Montrachet—or, better still, a Bâtard Montrachet. That's what I mean when I speak of good wine."

The butler placed one of his blue hands over the other and pressed both to his chest. He sighed.

"Ah, monsieur, *vous avez bien raison.*"

"Cut out that foreign talk and get the coffee," said Betsy to the butler. "And the brandy," she shouted after him. "That special Santa Monica Brandy—from Thrifty's!"

The lieutenant returned to Belinda.

Sir Gerald was engaged in solving the color problem.

"I've given it a lot of thought, Mr. Mumm," he said, "and I have a theory of my own about it. I say the color question doesn't exist at all in America—not the way you people think it does—I mean, it isn't hopeless at all. We have some friends in Santa Barbara, the Barbarians, I call them—hahaha—and I go there frequently. I will tell you what I have observed there. These friends of ours run a large establishment and they employ Negro help. Now, these Negroes are married and they have children and the children are allowed about the grounds, and I have observed that the children are several degrees lighter than their parents —and that solves the problem. A few more generations, and these people will have bleached themselves completely and the question will no longer exist."

The hostess got up. There was conversation in the living room, and drinks, and most of the guests went into the card room. Betsy Allbright was alone with Belinda. "Why don't you marry him?" she asked.

"Maurice?"

"Hasn't he asked you?"

"He asks me every day."

"Well, you're crazy if you don't. You couldn't do better in this town," said Betsy Allbright. "At least he's got a mind. He's devoted to you— my God, he worships the ground you walk on—and for a Frenchman that's something. How long has it been going on? Four months, isn't it? Well, that's a long time. You don't find anybody like that again out here. You better grab him."

"I don't know," said Belinda.

"Anybody else?"

"Well," said Belinda, "sometimes I think I like Buddy van der Lynn— he's sweet."

"He's an actor. Listen to me, Belinda. Don't ever marry an actor."

"What's wrong with actors?"

"Everything. To begin with, I can't think of them as men. They're not men—they're boys—and then, suddenly, they get old."

Betsy Allbright half filled the inhaler with brandy. She warmed the body of the glass in the palm of her hand, rotating it with slow, expert motion.

"I'll tell you about actors, Belinda," she said and turned to look for the butler. She scratched her abdomen and her scalp. She looked into the dining room.

"Hey, Auguste, leave the table alone and bring us a bucket of champagne—bring us the Krug *sans année*—the private *cuvée* that I keep for special occasions," she said to the butler, who was blowing out candles.

"I'd like you to look at some pictures of happy married life out here." Betsy Allbright was offering the family album, enhanced in Hollywood fashion.

"Auguste," she screamed, "tell Tom to run off the picture."

"The old silent?" asked Auguste, who knew the moods of bitter nostalgia that overcame his mistress on such evenings.

"Yes, the old silent," she said. *"Snowy Night."*

COME RAIN,
COME SHINE

MUMM AND CASSARD were going in to lunch.

"When something like this happens," said Cassard, "they spray embalming fluid all over the place. When something goes wrong, the people in this village can hear you think. They come and stand next to you, and they know. It's like dogs that can smell whether you're afraid of them or not, and they bite you if you are afraid. They can smell whether your option has been taken up, or whether a big deal has fallen through. They know by looking at you that your picture is a failure, and they cool off instantly. You will notice that they don't shake hands with you. They take your hand to push you away."

The cool reception of the man who opened the door at Romanoff's bore out this truth. He used to trumpet a nasal greeting, saying, "And how are you today, Mr. Cassard? And how do you do, Mr. Mumm?" Today he just said "Hello." And inside the reception was very formal and they were demoted and taken through the length of the restaurant to where the discarded wives of producers sit and where the minute steak takes an hour. The good waiter from the front, Mr. Reinhardt, came back and looked at them with some sympathy, but he said he was sorry he could not wait on them. He seemed to look at them out of a shattered mirror, so broken with worry was his face.

"You're only as good as your last picture, here," said Cassard.

The ever-placid Mumm looked around and saw people he had never seen before. It was as if he were in another restaurant. And Cassard looked up as a girl smiled at him. She had a man with her.

"May I present my husband?" she said. "Mr. Copfee."

They got up and shook hands.

"Who is that?" asked Mumm.

"That," said Cassard, "was a call girl a month ago. She came once to visit me. Her price was thirty dollars and worth it. She came to my beach house. *Alors*, she is now a respectably married woman!"

Mrs. Copfee went about from table to table, introducing the new husband, and everybody smiled.

"She seems to have had a large clientele," said Cassard. "And very solid!"

"You must admit," said Mumm, "that they are tolerant here. Now, in no other city could a woman like that who decides to get married—I mean, in a small town like this—suddenly change her life and face the community and be accepted. I think it's very nice and very tolerant."

"*Alors*," said Cassard. "If they weren't tolerant out here, where would they be? They'd have no one to talk to."

"We were talking about tolerance," said Cassard as Vashvily and Belinda came in.

"God!" said Belinda. "You have to be tolerant in this world, but out here you have to be especially tolerant or you choke with hate. Gee, it's easy to hate these guys, if you let yourself. They're so awful. Every one a heel, every one a procurer, every one a talker! Look at them. I told a story to Moses Fable—we stopped at his table to say hello. You know, the silly jerk didn't listen to me at all. For the first part, he was watching the door, and when I came to the second, he turned that fish-face of his and listened to a conversation on our right. At the end he laughed, but he was looking past me—trying to read the lips of some guy who had just come in and was talking to Vanya . . ."

"Somebody just offered me a job," said Vashvily, "thinking this would be a good time." He patted her hand. "Well, don't let it get you," he said. "If he doesn't take up your option, somebody else will."

They ordered.

"Mr. Mumm is leaving. He is going to New York to do a profile on Moses Fable," said Cassard to an assistant director of Olympia who stopped. "And then he is going to write a novel."

"Well, that's nice," said the assistant director. "Good luck, Mr. Mumm, and a nice trip east."

They had to pass Moses Fable's table as they left, but there were no greetings. Fable was suddenly interested in a large slab of mocha cake, and the others looked straight ahead.

Mumm drove back to the hotel. He dragged his traveling bag out of the closet. The valet had become lax.

"Your tickets are here," said Miss Princip, dabbing at her eyes. She was typing out several unbelievable checks to the Collector of Internal Revenue; and when they were added up, together with the hotel bill, the last tips, and the check he had told her to make out for herself, they left Ludlow Mumm a shocking balance in only three figures.

Mumm signed the checks and spent the rest of the day winding up his business.

The next day, when he was ready to leave for the train, Mumm walked to the cigar counter in the lobby to buy supplies for his trip. His finger moved slowly from the Cuban corner back to the Robert Burns Panatelas. The surprised girl had the box in her hand and was ready to bring it up out of the glass case when Ludlow Mumm felt himself tapped on the shoulder by a bellboy.

"Call for you, Mr. Mumm," he said. And Mumm thought he heard the old respectful ring in the boy's voice. "Will you take it in the booth?" he asked. Now with an unmistakable upswing in his voice: "It's the Wildgans Chase Agency," he said, folding back the door of the telephone booth and handing the instrument to the writer.

"Mr. Mumm," said the cheerful girl with ecstasy, "let me be the first to congratulate you—"

"On what?" asked Mumm.

"It will be in tomorrow's *Reporter*. Haven't you heard? They had a sneak preview of *Will You Marry Me?* Just a moment, Mr. Wildgans wants to tell you himself."

"Well, it's in the bag, Mumm," said Arty Wildgans. "Listen! The audience was in stitches. They rolled in the aisles. They stamped and whistled. It's great, and everybody is talking about it. I just had Moses Fable on the phone. He's crying. He wants to offer you a straight contract for seven years—anything you want—and double what you're getting now. But we'll make it tough for him—real tough!"

The girl took over again. "Mr. Mumm," she said, "you're having lunch with Mr. Wildgans at Romanoff's. The car will be under the porte-cochere of your hotel in fifteen minutes!"

MOCAMBO

THREE PEOPLE CAME into the night club.

"In this village of glass houses," said Cassard to himself, "you can't get away from anybody."

He told Belinda about Jerome Hack, the writer at Olympia, who had ordered the cheap corsage of one orchid that morning at the flower shop.

Hack stood at the door and spoke to the headwaiter, who snapped his fingers and then indicated a table in front of the one at which Cassard and Belinda were sitting.

With Hack were an old man and an old woman. The woman had refused to leave her fur coat in the checkroom. The old man looked back with bewilderment at the sofa in the lobby, which was upholstered in artificial grass.

"*Bon soir*, Monsieur Hack," said the captain, and steered the group to their table.

Cassard saw that the cheap corsage was pinned to the woman's fur coat. The table was decorated with a small vase of flowers, and a bottle of champagne stood in a cooler at the side.

One of the waiters handed a menu to the woman, but the headwaiter took it away from her again and said, "Everything is already ordered."

"You didn't have to go to all that trouble, Jerry," said the old man, unfolding his napkin.

"Oh, it's all right, Pop," said Hack. "Look at the birds. Ever seen anything like that?"

The woman had just finished surveying the room with a mixture of curiosity and disdain. She now turned and looked at the birds.

"What is the name of this place?" she asked in a flat, hard voice.

"Mocambo," said Hack. "It's the leading night club here."

She turned and stared through her pince-nez at Belinda and Cassard, and then, with suspicion, at the column painted like a candy stick that stands in the center of the room.

The orchestra tuned up.

"My God," said the woman. "I left the room key in the door." She clasped and unclasped her hands again, and looked in her bag and then at the old man.

"That's all right, Ma," he said.

She turned to look once more at Belinda and Cassard. The lighting fixtures were reflected again in her rimless pince-nez. The soft putty chin and cheeks, the crepy throat, all shone rosy in the dim light.

The waiter put a large silver dish down before her.

She asked shrilly, and again with suspicion, "What's that?"

"Cracked crab," answered the young man. "Try it. You'll like it."

She looked at the food for a while and picked up the very small fork.

"There's Gary Cooper and his wife," said Hack as the music began. "Hello, Coop," he said as the star passed.

The woman turned her head too late. The soft bulges all swayed. She used her arm as a wedge against the table to turn her body and stopped eating to wait until Cooper came by again. Then she bestowed a smile on him.

The old man at the table smiled too. He had a kind face, honest and good, deeply lined, loose skin draped over a strong, good frame, and large ears. He smiled shyly. He looked for the kind of fork that his wife was using, and then he looked at Hack and smiled again gratefully, and ate. He looked up whenever the writer pointed out celebrities.

The waiter opened Cassard's wine and poured it. The orchestra played and the birds had come to life. The smaller fluttered in group flights from one end of the room to the other; the larger stretched their wings and hopped about, or hung upside down from limbs, looking into the room and screeching; and some beat out the rhythm of the music with extended, furiously colored wings.

"Look at Emil Coleman," said Cassard to Belinda. "You know what he reminds me of? When I was a child my father brought me home a toy from a Paris exhibition—a Russian Easter egg, made of wood, and on the outside of it a man was painted, and when you twisted it, it came apart; but inside it was another egg, just like the one on the outside— and then another and another. That's what Coleman reminds me of— the man painted on the outside and the inside of that wooden Russian Easter egg. I can listen to his music forever."

"I like it, too. I just love to sit here quietly."

"We like everybody tonight," said Cassard.

Belinda lifted her glass.

"To friendship!" he said.

"To our friendship," she said. "Let me buy the next bottle."

The waiter filled the glasses again and Belinda asked him for paper and pencil. She sent the name of Vanya Vashvily's song to Coleman, who nodded and started it as soon as he was through with the conga he had been playing.

Cassard looked again at the three people in front of him.

The headwaiter came and bent down. "How was the chicken, madame?" he asked the old woman.

She was taken by surprise. Her mouth hardened into a small, bitter line, and she placed her round arms away from herself, with all fingers separated, as if she had eaten with her hands and the fingers were covered with fat, and she looked at him and said something, and then looked away, embarrassed, out over the dance floor. After the headwaiter was gone, she looked after him and then folded her hands.

Hack sat at the side of the table, his chair turned toward the floor and his legs crossed, and he drummed with his fork on the table. The old man looked at the people that passed by and smiled at everybody.

After the Danny Spellbinder melody, the dancing stopped and a waiter wound his way past the tables, holding a platter high above his head. As he brought it down, a small birthday cake appeared on it, and as he came to Hack's table the orchestra played "Happy Birthday to You."

The maître d'hôtel handed a knife to the woman. "Will Madame cut the cake?" he said.

Everyone in the room looked at her. She raised the knife and cut the cake. People smiled and applauded, and now the old man was embarrassed, but he looked up and when he saw the people smile, he smiled and bowed, and somebody handed him a cigar.

The old man had not touched the champagne; the woman had slowly sipped it all evening long. He bent over to Hack, who called the waiter and ordered a rye and ginger ale for him.

The music started again and the birds flew. Cassard watched the table and Belinda was far away.

So it went on until the crowd thinned and the music stopped. Hack had ordered more drinks for the old man and now he sat close to him. He held the man's hand in his and he looked at him.

"Do you love me?" he asked. "Have you loved me as much as if I'd been your own son?"

"Sure, Jerry," said the old man.

"You know I loved you, Pop, a hundred times more than if you'd been my own father."

"We loved you as much as if you'd been our own," said the woman.

Then none of them said anything. The young man looked at the man he called Pop and the old man looked sadly at the birds.

"Well," said Hack, "I just wanted to ask you—you know, like man to man, across the table. You loved me? That's the truth, isn't it?"

"Sure, it's the truth," said the old man.

The woman pulled the new gray fur coat up over her shoulders and she looked at her wrist watch.

"Hey—pssst, *garçon, l'addition*," said Hack.

The bill came. Hack turned it upside down without looking at it. On the back, the total for food and drink was added with a red pencil. Hack took a golden pencil and signed the bill and reached into his coat for his wallet.

The woman watched all this sharply and with petulance, and her hand moved, opening and closing into a fist and tapping on the table.

Hack put a five-dollar bill on the plate for the waiter. He took another five-dollar bill from a packet of money and then picked out a twenty-dollar bill and folded it small.

The captain bowed and called the headwaiter. The waiter said, "*Merci*, Monsieur Hack," and the headwaiter said, "*Merci*, Monsieur Hack."

The woman's mouth was compressed and her eyes hard with enmity.

"Remember, Pop," said Hack, "when we had the stationery and candy up in Fordham? Remember how glad we were when somebody came in and bought a stick of chewing gum?"

The old man looked down sadly and nodded.

"Try and get some now," said the woman.

"I'll get you all you want. I can get anything," said Hack sharply, for the first time looking at her and turning his chair to face her. "What was it you used to say to me?"

"I used to say you were a show-off," said the woman.

"And what else did you used to say to me?" He leaned toward her. She had a new wrist watch that was on a black elastic cord. He pulled it away from her arm, half an inch or so, and let it snap back into her soft flesh.

"Jerry," said the old man, and he lifted the empty split bottle of ginger ale, holding it upside down and waving it like a miniature club, threateningly and with a sad smile.

"Jerry, don't talk to your Mom that way."

They got up.

"You shouldn't spend so much money on us," said the old man. "The hotel room, and the flowers, and the coat for Mom, and this dinner—"

"Forget it," said Hack as he straightened out the smart double-breasted jacket of his gray suit. "Forget it, Pop. I'll charge it up to entertaining."

They filed out.

"This is the saddest, most heartbreaking and lonesomest place in the whole wide world," said Cassard.

"I know," said Belinda, who had been silently crying.

*T*he Herr Professor ate a small goulash with great appetite and wiped the plate with the last piece of bread. The beer we were served was the first he had had since the end of the war. He told me, with the coffee, that he was always hungry. He said, "You know, I dream often, very often, about my stamp collection. I owned a very good one. At the beginning of this dream I always carry my album to the large walnut desk that stood in my private office at the clinic, and I sit down and open it, and, stuck on the transparent paper of the album, which is like waxed paper, I find the most beautiful slices of sausage—instead of my rare stamps. There is salami, mortadella, liverwurst and cervelat, and as I turn the pages I come to slices of smoked tongue, and then to hams—every kind of ham I have eaten on my travels, Westphalian, Prague, and prosciutto. The collection ends with an assortment of cold meats in which chicken predominates. The last time I had this dream I succeeded in carefully removing a large snow-white slice of breast of capon from the sandwich paper. I gently put this into my shoe and carefully put the shoe on, so that no one would discover it. I wanted to take the slice of capon home to my wife. I got out of the clinic, but from there on frightful things happened, always with the shoe. I had to walk through a street newly tarred, still smoking and hot; I came to another that was strewn with broken glass. My foot began to ache terribly, and I took the shoe off to see if the slice of capon was still there. An ambulance came along and picked me up and took me back to the clinic. One of the doctors there, none of whom I knew, said, 'Herr Professor, we shall have to amputate the leg.' I protested, and that was when my wife woke me."

GUTEN APPETIT

HE GAVE THE SIGNAL of the gourmets, the index finger and thumb arranged into a ring and the eyebrows lifted, and he said that the kitchen here was fantastic—"Wait until you taste it." The kitchen was under the direction of Frau Lampe, famous for her cooking. A woman worth her weight in gold, specializing in solid, plain food, simply cooked.

She was the high priestess of cooking, and the General said: "As far as I am concerned—much more important than the *beaux arts*, or sports, or politics, for the welfare of a nation is *die Kochkunst*. Look at France, another country where it is esteemed." They clinked glasses again, and for once Papa said, *"D'accord."*

"Now then, I must warn you, Your Excellency Herr General, she has a temper."

Papa smiled indulgently; he understood.

"Any good cook worth her salt has," he said. It was late now. Papa would pay a visit to the kitchen the next day.

Papa was a military gourmet; he liked good food and would drive far to get to a restaurant where they made a dish to his liking. But always mindful of his figure, he ate very carefully, very little, and preferred plain things to rich ones. He especially liked vegetables, salads and fresh fruit. He wanted to combine the visit to the kitchen with brief instructions to the cook. I was taken along because I had turned the pages of a German dictionary and knew a few phrases of the language, and this was a sort of *visite de famille*, rather than a military one. Mama, of course, in the Spanish tradition, had never been in any kitchen any-where and would not come now.

Hohenlinden was a romantic castle such as one imagines along the Rhine and the Moselle, with battlements and towers that once had been of use in war. It had a façade toward the Moselle that made it look like an ivy-colored ruin when seen from below, but when one came up the winding road it had another face. From that side, it was still castle, but very modern. In front of it was a parking place big enough to use as a parade ground. It had an immense garage, a park with a swimming pool, and inside everything except the furniture was modern.

There were immense halls, a Rittersaal—as the large salon was called—carved ceilings the outstanding characteristic of the place was an abundance of lavatories everywhere. Almost every door we opened contained one with immense porcelain fittings, most of them for the use of men. Wide stairways, again carved, overlarge rooms with dressing rooms and elaborate baths.

The kitchen was in the basement. Frau Lampe was in front of her oven and in back of her was her staff. It was as if they were a battery of heavy artillery drawn up for battle. Frau Lampe was immaculate, as was her kitchen, and a very unusual woman: a figure made of sacks of flour, and a pink, egg-shaped balloon of a head on top of which golden noodles seemed to be stacked. She looked like something a mad baker might have created, an immense, swollen loaf of flesh, moving on wheels, on rounded calves which spilled over her shoes. She moved with deliberate and majestic ease, rowing the air with her solid round arms—she was like the Grand Romulus getting under way. She turned and waved at her staff and called out their names: Frau Scheitholz, Frau Kueppersbusch, Frau Unterer. These were the senior assistants, and then came Anneliese, Gertrude, Hildegard and half a dozen others, and from the pantry appeared two stout scullery maids, and out of the "walk-in" icebox a butcher, Herman Nickel, who came to sharp attention with a loud "phlump" of his rubber boots.

Frau Lampe put them at ease by saying, "*Tya—macht nur weiter Kinners.*"

She used *Tya* instead of the German *Ja*, and she said *Kinners* instead of *Kinder*, which is dialect. Even with her as a yardstick, the *Kinners* were a solid group, not outrightly unfriendly at this presentation, but not happy either, and looking with quick glances at Papa when he did not look at them.

The kitchen was spotless, and in the old tradition with an immense oven in the center of the white-tiled room. Frau Lampe said, "*Tya*, here we cook with coal—not gas or electricity."

She had one complaint: the water in the neighborhood contained a great deal of chalk. Water was very important, and the water in that basin was for cooking only—she never used tap water. The water of the region was hard, and even this water, which came from the Black Forest springs of Freudenstadt, had a content that formed *Kesselstein*, and therefore the *Wasserschiff*, as the container for this water was called, was always kept meticulously clean inside and out. Frau Lampe did not like anything newfangled, and when Papa told her that I spoke some German, she gave me a brief nod and went into giving a lecture on the oven: *Tya*, she had it installed herself, she was here for twenty-three years now, and as one could see everything had been thought of—the oven was accessible from four sides, old-fashioned, heated with coal, and in her opinion only *Steinkohle* was acceptable as a fuel for a *Küchenkohlenherd*.

Papa looked at the largest copper casserole that stood on the oven, and Frau Lampe explained that this was the stockpot, and that just as the oven was the altar of the kitchen, the stockpot was the heart; and half the battle in good cooking was won when the stock was good, and only the best materials went into that; and there were no recipes, no theories, no things that one could read in books—it came only by long and bitter experience, the art of making stock—and there could be no good stock, she said meaningfully, without the best materials—and then the good things would come. *Tya*—that is all about this pot of stock. She went back to her lecture on the oven.

There are few people even in Germany who understand the proper care of a *Küchenkohlenherd*. The *Ofenkehrer* has to come at least twice a year and clear the ducts. The surface of the oven is cleaned with a moist rag and sand every day, then washed, then rubbed in with a little oil, and polished—*Tya, tya*—but then what comes out of such an oven, Fräulein? Well, you will see what comes out of it!

"*Tya, und* here—come here for a second, Herr General. Here is the bake oven and Frau Holle, the pastry cook, and her assistant Gretchen. *Tya*, the big *Backofen*, and the table for making apple strudel, and tarts and cakes and cookies, and above that the things like kettledrums in which to whip up creams, and the stuff for soufflés—*tya*, we have everything. . . ."

Papa was very pleased with the inspection and was ready to go. He bowed toward Frau Lampe and he told me to convey his pleasure to her and how very glad he was that she was at the castle.

The brigade of assistants around her all stopped what they were doing, the way a mechanical toy with many figures stops working. One held the rag he was cleaning with to the spot he was cleaning; another, who had bent over a pot stirring, remained bent but stopped stirring and looked up; a third, who was carrying something, carried but stood still; and only Herman Nickel clapped himself to attention again, also mechanically twisting his head to look at the General, and although he was now a civilian, he held a stiff salute. Papa answered his salute and the hand slapped itself down to the side of his trousers.

"*Tya*," said Frau Lampe. She was honored that His Excellency the Herr General had come down into her kitchen, and she was sure that Hohenlinden would please him. She was able to feed up to two hundred people at a time here—and this hospitable house had had under its roof some very important people. The Fuehrer himself had slept here— Marshal Goering, also Herr von Ribbentrop.

Papa suddenly became himself, his bonhomie left him, and he took his stance, pulled at his gloves and said, "I hope that you have changed the linen since."

"*Tya, natürlich*," said Frau Lampe.

For an instant the whites of the eyes of Frau Lampe had enlarged and there seemed another face on her body. The egg-shaped curves became disturbed and shifted, and the mouth was pressed into a straight line. Then she turned to the "*Kinners*" and in a sergeant's voice ordered them to get on with their work, and the mechanical toy started again, pounding, turning, stirring and polishing.

One would never think that one could reduce in Germany—but we all lost weight, on account of too much food.

Our first meal at Hohenlinden was the start of many sessions that raised your pulse, gave you expansions in the stomach, a feeling of strangulation, and when you looked at the cook you got vertigo in addition. The first meal was a salad of head of veal, then a soup with little eyes of fat floating on it and with parsley chopped into it; submerged in each plate lay a gray submarine-shaped liver dumpling. Then came a roast stuffed goose, with red cabbage, and applesauce and salad served at the same time, and potatoes. Always *Kartoffel*. The dessert was a gruesome cold paste, dye-colored red and called *Rote Grütze*. The coffee was served at the same time as the dessert in large cups and with milk. We exchanged hopeless looks while all this was brought in. I thought of the *pensionnat* and how I would like to throw my plate on the floor. We barely touched the food.

At the end Frau Lampe came in, propelled herself to where Papa sat, and, leaning forward from her buttocks, ignoring us and looking at Papa, she said, "*Hats nicht wohl bekommen*, Herr General?" which means, "Has it not become you well." Frau Lampe was used to having her food appreciated, and she liked to see the plates clear and empty with nothing but bones on them—also, what was *los?* She gave the explanation herself: the change of air and the excitement—that was it.

"You have to get used to my cooking, and when you are used to it, you will like it," she said. Everybody did and we were no exception. "*Tya*—better *appetit* the next time."

We had observed her entrance with great amusement, for we had expected an explosion. We had hoped to see Papa in action, reducing Frau Lampe to a trembling carcass and kicking her downstairs forever.

However, nothing happened; he looked at her with the kindest face he could manage, and, wiping his mouth with his napkin—and adjusting his mustache—he said, "Excellent, Frau Lampe."

Papa always made a point of remembering the name of the people under him.

He didn't even ask that black coffee, in small cups, be brought into the salon or on the terrace.

Mama, who had eaten black bread and salad and had not touched anything else, looked ill. We had eaten some goose. The wine was good, if a little sweet. We all got up silently and went out. To avoid any discussion, Papa quickly drove off with Auguste. He explained later to Mama that he could not fire the cook or the rest of the help the first week we were there—it would look very bad. He would adjust things and soon the menus would be in order. He commanded us to have patience. After all it was a foreign country, and they did their best.

The problem was dealt with in various ways. Papa, who inclined to vegetables, asked for spinach, carrots, celery and asparagus, but when they came to the table they were not to his liking. Frau Lampe managed to make vegetables unpalatable by cutting them in a fashion to which we were not accustomed, or presenting them so they were floating in butter or covered with bread crumbs or awful to taste—or even to look

at—and impossible to eat. Also they said they could not get this or that at the market or at the commissary, although we saw that it was to be had in stores and got it at other houses. It was no use complaining. Anyone talking to Frau Lampe now got a hysterical look and was menaced by the arms held out like a fat crab about to pinch you. She had changed completely.

Mama lived off some things her maid prepared. Finally Papa had the courage to tell General von der Linde that he did not have the palate to appreciate Frau Lampe's cooking—and neither did any of the rest of the family.

The General was very surprised and a little hurt. He brought a French cookbook that had been translated into German: it was taken to Frau Lampe. She looked at it, held it in her hands, leafed through it for several minutes, got redder and redder, and finally threw it on the kitchen table and walked off and up to her room. She came back in time to cook a supper of what she took to be light cooking in the French manner. It too was inedible.

We hardly ate anything of what came to the table. That is, we took a little part of this or of that. We were hungry, and some of it, once you stopped hating it, wasn't too bad to eat. There is no worse punishment for a cook than having things sent back to the kitchen untouched—or plates half full of food not eaten. Frau Lampe became furious and shot her eyes into the dishes as they came back. Finally, by a process of elimination, she had reduced the menu to simple things like plain consommé or soups without "*Einlagen*," as the dumplings, marrow bones, *Schinkenflecken* or other additions were called. Schnitzels, plain or à la Viennoise we liked (à la Holstein, with a fried egg, we sent back and it never came again). A kind of German *fricassée de volaille*, also a *Gulasch* with sour cream and sauerkraut, were good; so was *Rostbraten* with onions, and plain salads. With the exception of compotes we refused all desserts and *Torten*. *Torten* were the specialty of the house, and in the beginning they came in unbelievable sizes and in colors, like nail enamel and plastic toys, or covered with all kinds of *glacé* fruit and frosting.

If Papa had had the courage to talk to Frau Lampe in the kitchen, it would have perhaps been possible to eat. But now she felt unappreciated and neglected, and she had become hostile.

It is in the nature of the military man, and especially one who gets as far as general, to see things through—and so Papa decided that somehow he would bring Frau Lampe into line—as he tried with us—correct the demoralization that had taken the place of discipline in her kitchen, and make it work properly.

The occasion of this new attack on the kitchen was a luncheon he had to give, to celebrate the anniversary of the regiment. At first it was to be a dinner and dance, but in view of the difficulties of such an undertaking, Papa changed it to a luncheon for a hundred and twenty officers and their wives.

That he thought Frau Lampe, or rather he, could handle.

He made up the menu beforehand. Her beloved *Ochsenmaulsalat* had been modified into an aspic. Then there would be something she was sure to be able to make: *quenelles de brochet*. There weren't any remarkable fish in the Moselle except the pike. Pike, on account of its dry, flaky flesh, is made into dumplings and served with a sauce. It is one of the most liked dishes in the French kitchen. After that there would be roast chicken, salad and ice cream. There was no danger in any of these dishes. He asked for Frau Lampe. She came in, she was hot, her face looked like a lacquered duck—the plum and egg curves had gone out of it. Papa attempted to charm her and offered her a seat with his most elegant gesture. He asked me to read the menu to her, and she said, *Tya*, she could do all that but what was the fish dish like? That was· what he wanted to talk to her about. The pike was the most common fish caught in the waters of the Moselle. It was also a common fish in France, but it was not the most delicate of fishes. There was, however, a time-honored, simple recipe in the French kitchen, and he thought that it might be added to the cookbook of Frau Lampe and enrich her cuisine.

"*Tya*—fish cakes and fish balls I know how to make," said Frau Lampe with lightning flashes around the eyes.

"*Oui, oui, madame, d'accord,*" said Papa. "Fish cakes and fish balls are very good and they are appreciated in France. However, these are a sort of glorified fish ball—very good—extremely delicate in taste and easy to make. I have had it written down for you, Madame Lampe, in German." Papa picked up the recipe and gave it to Frau Lampe, who read it with great suspicion, as if someone had handed her an outrageous bill for something she had never bought.

"In a mortar pound the flesh of the pike, adding one half pound of frangipane."

"What is frangipane?"

I translated: "It's made of flour, yolks of eggs, salt, pepper, nutmeg and melted butter and diluted over boiled milk. You stir and boil, and then let it cool, and add it to the fish meat; now you work the mortar thoroughly to make the fish combine with beef marrow, then you put it into the refrigerator. When you cook the *quenelles*, you make elongated balls of the stuff you have in the mortar, with your hands covered with flour and on a flour-covered board—"

Now Frau Lampe exploded: "*Tya, tya,* all that is very *schön und gut,* and you don't have to explain to me—or show me how I should make it—I know how to make it, I am a cook—it's like marrow dumplings, except with pike—but for these fish balls we need pike, and there is no pike."

I translated this to my father.

He asked: "But all these fishermen, and the fishboxes in the Moselle —what are they doing?"

"There is no pike, Your Excellency Herr General," said Frau Lampe, "and you want to know why? Because your soldiers steal them all— they break open the fishboxes at night, and what they don't steal swims away. On the black market perhaps you can get all the pike you want —I think your soldiers can tell you where. But a decent German *Hausfrau* cannot buy any pike anywhere, so if you get the pike for me, I will make you those dumplings, and now may I go?"

Frau Lampe went back down into her kitchen and knocked about with her pots and pans and screamed at her help.

In an old house in Paris
that was covered with vines
lived twelve little girls
in two straight lines.
In two straight lines they broke their bread
and brushed their teeth and went to bed.

MADAME
L'AMBASSADRICE

A GRAY ROLLS-ROYCE convertible of postwar design stood below and a chauffeur in uniform and cap to match beside it. On the way to the restaurant, breaking a silence which had lasted from the Arc de Triomphe to the Alexander Bridge, Madame l'Ambassadrice remarked: "*J'ai un grand appetit.*"

St. Cucuface leaned toward me and said, "Isn't it remarkable that a woman like Madame l'Ambassadrice, who has both great charm and great intelligence, should also speak the most beautiful French." She smiled a smile that lasted until we arrived at the restaurant.

In this exclusive and most carefully run restaurant, a reception committee consisting of doorman, door opener, coat hander, coat taker, inside-door opener, up-the-stairs pointer, director, headwaiter, assistant headwaiter and, farther on, captain, waiter and bus boy, bowed and whispered: "*Mon Prince*, Madame l'Ambassadrice, Monsieur le Comte."

The director himself attached himself to the table to arrange the menu.

"Caviar—and the thinnest of blinis," he recommended.

"*Oui*," said Madame l'Ambassadrice with perfect pronunciation.

"A cup of *Germiny*—sorrel soup—with eggs beaten in it."

"*Oui*," said Madame and nodded assent.

"After, a little sole, with lobster claws."

"*Ah, oui.* I would like that very much," she said.

"Then a specialty of the house: a tender chicken of Bresse perhaps, in our fashion: sautéed, with *morilles*, which grow only in the month of May."

"*Parfait*—exactly what I want."

"A soufflé Armagnac—"

"*Merveilleux, merveilleux*," she sang.

"And to drink." The director closed his eyes; he sniffed at his finger tips, which he held cupped together close to his nose, as though he were smelling a rose in bud. Then he whispered, "I have something to offer you: a Rhine wine, 1920, made when they pressed the grapes with the skin. There's only one bottle of it left in the world. I have kept it for my best clients—*oui, alors*—after that, Bollinger '34, Extra Dry." He stabbed the block on which he had written the order with his pencil, signed his elaborate initials and thrust the paper at the second in command, who did an about-face and ran. The priceless bottle came and was opened with every possible precaution; the inside of the neck was carefully wiped, and then the director himself poured the first half glass. He rinsed it through his teeth, washed it against the insides of his cheeks, and finally, tilting his head back, he swallowed it, gurgling with delight. He seemed unable to express his ecstasy in words and resorted to pantomine. Then, rolling his eyes upward, he poured the wine and stood by to watch the effect.

Madame l'Ambassadrice said, "Chin-chin," and swallowed. She looked at the director as he had looked at her, and, repeating his pantomime and rolling her eyes, she said, "*Merveilleux.*"

The director stiffened, bowed deeply and said slowly, "Always at your service, Madame l'Ambassadrice." He then backed away bowing, and it was as if Erich von Stroheim had received the grand cross of the Legion of Honor.

St. Cucuface gave me a significant look. He had tasted the wine and so had I. It was as dark as syrup and quite undrinkable, something indeed rare and very difficult to obtain in even a mediocre restaurant in France.

St. Cucuface tasted the wine once more, leaned toward me, and shamelessly and while looking straight at her and holding her hand tenderly above the table, he said: "Isn't it remarkable that a woman who is beautiful as well as intelligent not only knows how to order a magnificent dinner but on top of that is a connoisseur of wines."

Madame l'Ambassadrice looked at him meltingly. Then she picked up the caviar fork and scratched her head.

The dinner was very good and only spoiled by too much food and an overattentive staff. After the coffee and brandy, the waiter brought a small package tied with a ribbon. "For your dog, Monsieur le Comte, with our compliments," he said.

"They are so thoughtful," said Madame l'Ambassadrice.

We floated for a while in the bilious tedium of after-dinner conversation. Madame l'Ambassadrice said that she planned to fly to Cannes to meet the Ambassador and that she intended to send the car separately with a chauffeur, as she hated long drives. St. Cucuface looked very thoughtful and lit one of Madame l'Ambassadrice's cigars. He snapped his fingers and six waiters came running. Their faces dropped when Cucuface asked for the bill.

While the bill was being computed I wondered what would happen, for I knew that St. Cucuface had only two hundred francs in his pocket. They picked the one waiter who had an honest face to bring the bill to the table. It was upside down, lying on a gold plate large enough to hold a church collection. Then the company of bandits began to assemble. In a half circle about six feet away they moved restlessly about like sea gulls sailing hopefully over a ship about to dump its garbage. The lesser ones dusted tables with their napkins. All of them kept casting quick glances at the plate and all of them seemed near a state of inner collapse, like gamblers seeing their last hope fade. They twisted their napkins in their hands, pushed chairs about, pulled at the lapels of their jackets, tailcoats and on the ends of their noses.

None of them seemed able to leave the scene of impending disaster. There was the compulsion that brings a murderer to the grave of his victim. St. Cucuface studied the bill carefully and now they began to look at him with the utmost contempt. Some of them even gave vent to their feelings by slapping the napkins down on the cleared-off tables, pretending they were brushing away old toothpicks, bread crumbs and other dinner debris.

St. Cucuface then did an incredible thing: he asked for a pencil and began to add up the bill. Naturally he found several mistakes, none of them in favor of the guests.

Madame l'Ambassadrice was beginning to be annoyed. She began powdering her face and looking at her teeth in the mirror of her compact.

"*Alors?*" she said, and managed to get an authentic French shading of annoyance into the word.

At this point there began a well-rehearsed pantomime of consternation, surprise and injury, played by the bandits. They stood in a row in back of the headwaiter, who impersonated an innocent citizen wrongly accused. He studied the bill carefully, and suddenly seemed to discover something. "*Ah, oui,*" he said, "we have forgotten something. We have forgotten to charge for the second helping of caviar that everyone had. As for the total, Monsieur le Comte, I am not Einstein, but I can add correctly. Where is the error? Show me." He set the gold plate down with a bang.

St. Cucuface took the bill. "Look," he said, and pointed to the error.

"Oh, that," said the headwaiter airily, "that is in the wrong column. *Alors*, that can happen now and then; it is merely an oversight of the cashier—"

"Let's get out of here," said Madame l'Ambassadrice loudly.

"Oversight! Why is it you never make an oversight in favor of the guest?" asked St. Cucuface.

The chorus now mumbled and made various gestures of hopelessness and disgust, such as holding both arms away from the body and shrugging the shoulders. They looked bitterly at St. Cucuface.

The restaurant was crowded, and Madame l'Ambassadrice had recognized several friends and had flashed friendly signals with her dinner rings at them.

"You are a band of thieves," said Cucuface loudly, waving his arms.

The headwaiter, on behalf of his staff, said: "*M-o-n-s-i-e-u-r.*" He said it very well and he stuck a finger in his high collar and pulled it forward for purposes of ventilation.

St. Cucuface and the headwaiter were now ready to begin the main assault. This fascinating contest is a necessary part of the repertory of every French establishment and reaches its finest form in a restaurant of the category called *"Exceptionelle."* No one enjoys it more than the participants. The *aficionados* of this form of entertainment at nearby tables all turned their good ears our way. It promised to be a good fight.

Madame l'Ambassadrice spoiled it. She struck the table with her jewel-weighted hand.

"Shut up, all of you," she screamed.

The gallery nodded appreciatively. "Shut up," "Nuts" and "O.K." and also "K.O." had been taken over into the French language. They approved highly of the "shut up" as being direct and expressive.

Unfortunately at this moment the director came to the table. He wore the widest of smiles and completely spoiled the mood. He had in his hand a bottle of cognac so old that the label had been almost worn off by time alone. Fresh balloon glasses had been brought in, three men became very busy warming them in the palms of their moist and nervous hands, and then the golden brandy was poured with generosity and the compliments of the house.

Madame l'Ambassadrice said, "Chin-chin," and we clinked glasses.

"That is all very well and good," St. Cucuface started to say, but Madame l'Ambassadrice had had enough.

"You have nothing to say. This is my dinner," she announced imperiously, and produced a golden pencil set with rubies.

As if suddenly fresh candles had been placed on the tables, the faces of all the bandits lit up. The headwaiter paled several degrees from his former cockscomb red.

St. Cucuface tried again to engage him—but the mood was gone, the game was won.

The atmosphere of conflict had softened and the anger collapsed as softly as a child's balloon sinks to earth. Madame called the director and from behind her heavy iridium-and-sapphire make-up box, which she held to her face, she gestured with the emeralds on her right hand, waving green lights—a signal which everyone immediately understood to mean that she wanted the check.

St. Cucuface was not quite quick enough to take it, as it appeared like magic. She initialed it and instructed the director to take ample care of the help in the matter of *pourboires*.

"I simply cannot understand you," said St. Cucuface. "Imagine—

these robbers charging you four thousand francs for that Rhine wine, and then on top of it, making a mistake in adding up the bill. If you *will* put up with things like that—"

"I am sorry, Cucu," said Madame l'Ambassadrice. "I am very fond of you, but I will not have you making scenes in restaurants on account of your—whatever it is—outraged sense of proportion, or values, or something."

She put on lipstick and poked at her hair. She took the pencil and scratched her head with it. "It's the same thing every time we go out, Cucu, you and I, and I will not have it!" And then, remembering her perfect French, she added with finality, "*Je n'aime pas ça* at all! I forbid you to pay another bill."

"Well, if you want to be a fool," said St. Cucuface, "and if it makes you feel better, it's O.K. with me."

Madame passed the bowing heads and was handed down the stairs. The inner doorman opened the door of the restaurant and the outer doorman opened the door of the Rolls-Royce.

In the street, Madame l'Ambassadrice, whom we had permitted to drink the entire bottle of the rare Rhine wine, suddenly spoke English. The car was there, but not the chauffeur. She swayed a little and then she said, "Where is that old bastard?"

She informed us that her chauffeur made a habit of going into one of the bistros in the side streets while he was waiting and that sometimes he stayed too long and drank too much. We walked around awhile, peering into various cafés, and the Restaurant Lucullus even sent out a posse of waiters to search in others, but nowhere was he to be found.

"The Prince is an excellent driver," said St. Cucuface. I took the wheel, and a few minutes later my incognito almost exploded: I drove the wrong way down a one-way street. A gendarme with the face of the true French *flic* blew his whistle violently. He crossed the street and approached the car with his notebook in hand. When he was close enough to see the license plate, he seemed to slowly arrive at the realization that this was an American car. He also began to remember the instructions of the Commissariat du Tourisme: to be polite to foreigners from hard-money countries. He gradually achieved a smile and touched his cap with a fat hand as he asked me for my license. I told him I didn't have it. "Your passport?" "I'm sorry, it's in my hotel."

He was joined by a colleague, to whom he gave the details. They held a long consultation in back of the car. Finally they came back and

the first gendarme asked, "You are a visitor here, monsieur?"

"Yes," I said.

"Tell him you are an American," said Madame l'Ambassadrice, "and they'll let you go."

"You are American, monsieur?"

"Yes."

"You have a very beautiful car," he said, smiling now like the full moon. "And if I may make an observation, you do not have the face of a 'gangster.'" They both laughed and swayed like musical-comedy cops. "And you say that your papers are at the hotel?"

"Yes."

"Well, we choose to believe you, monsieur. Proceed. And, monsieur, if you insist on driving into one-way streets, sooner or later we shall have an accident!" He playfully wagged his finger and again saluted. We drove Madame l'Ambassadrice home without further incident.

Cucuface took the package for his dog out of the car and we waited until Madame l'Ambassadrice had gone upstairs, and then started home.

"In June it sometimes becomes very hot in Paris," he said as we walked back down the Avenue de Bois. "Also the tourists begin to appear in great hordes and take over the city. Then it is time to leave." I had to walk fast to keep in step with him.

"Do you object to long drives?" he asked. When I told him that I liked nothing better he said, "We shall do Madame l'Ambassadrice a great favor. We shall offer to drive her car to Cannes. The chauffeur she has is quite unreliable, as we know; let her send him on a train. Of course she must pay for the gas."

After half an hour's walk, which ended along the Quai des Grands-Augustins on the left bank of the Seine not far from the restaurant where we had dined, we came to the house in which St. Cucuface lived.

The building trembled every time the subway passed, and since it was at the bottom of the incline toward the Place St. Michel, all the trucks and buses changed to second gear, and plaster rained softly down at night from the ceilings of houses along the Quai. We went up six flights of stairs, which sagged like those at the Hotel St. Julien le Pauvre, and became narrower as we came up to the *mansarde* of the building, in which the Count's apartment was situated.

I expected to hear the bark or the whine of a dog, but the place was silent as we entered, and a silvery light came through the large windows.

The view was sufficient compensation for the climb. Through a window, past a small terrace, one could see the Eiffel Tower to the left, and past Notre Dame to the right, up to Montmartre in the distance. And within this triangle was all that is most beautiful in Paris.

The moon was full, and the clouds were edged with the mauve and violet hues that Dufy smears into his pictures of the Paris sky. The beam of the searchlight atop the Eiffel Tower swept ceaselessly over the city, and overhead could be heard the soft murmur of the throttled-down motors of a transatlantic plane, its signal lights blinking on and off as it headed for Orly Field. Notre Dame was illuminated, and the light reflected from its white stones edged the towers and spires and the metalwork on the nearby roofs with a soft golden halo.

St. Cucuface opened the French window onto the terrace and came back with folding chairs. He pointed out various landmarks. "There is my Guardian Angel," he said, pointing to a golden figure on a roof across the river. He described the buildings and named the spires, and while he talked he slowly untied the package from the Restaurant Lucullus. He took from it a leg of chicken. He brought a folding card table, salt and pepper, a bottle of wine and a stick of bread which was neither long nor short, but of the in-between size which is called *un bâtard* in French bakeries.

Pointing at the lighted cathedral, I asked if this was due to the observance of some special holy day.

"No, that we owe to the alert proprietor of the famous restaurant, the Tour d'Argent," explained St. Cucuface.

"A rich South American gave a dinner there for some friends on the eve of the Fourteenth of July—Bastille Day, our Independence Day—and on that occasion the cathedral was lighted, and from the windows of the restaurant which is on the roof the view of the cathedral is superb. One of the men who attended the party gave a dinner several days later, when there was no holiday. He was very disappointed that the cathedral was not lighted, and complained to the proprietor. To please his guests the proprietor then called the Secretary of the Diocese, and arrangements were made to light the cathedral. The price agreed on was then added to the bill at the restaurant, and now when you order dinner at the Tour d'Argent, the maître d'hôtel asks you what you want in the way of food and wine, and also whether or not you want the cathedral lighted. The money goes to the poor and everyone is happy. In such matters we French are exceedingly rational."

St. Cucuface poured wine and then went back through the window again. He reappeared with more dog-bone packages. "Let's see what we have," he said, and began to separate the various kinds of meat. Putting a bone to one side, he remarked, "Some of this actually goes to a dog."

He put the food away in the kitchenette of his apartment, which was tucked away under the various levels of the roof of the old house like a swallow's nest.

He then wrapped a bone in a piece of paper and tied it with the string. The Place Vendôme is an hour away. He offered to walk part of the way home with me.

Along the Quai des Grands-Augustins is a stone wall crowded with the famous wooden stalls from which secondhand books and old prints are sold. These were closed and secured with iron bands from which hung ancient and complicated padlocks. Along the stone wall is a break and a cobblestone roadway leads down to the paved banks of the Seine. On this part of the river, long black barges are moored. They bear Dutch and Belgian names and are meticulously clean. Beyond a bridge, toward the Place de la Concorde, three gray fireboats are tied up. Under the bridge a man and a woman slept back-to-back on a mattress, covered with a blanket and a tarpaulin bearing a stenciled *U.S.A.* Beside the mattress stood a baby carriage covered with a sack.

St. Cucuface made a chirping sound. The sack began to stir and out of the baby carriage jumped a small dog. As if he had never doubted his coming, or even known hunger, he stretched himself, yawned and waited politely until St. Cucuface had unwrapped the bone. He took it in his teeth with the utmost delicacy and made his way with great dignity to some stones that lay in a patch of light that came from a window of one of the barges. In the light he showed himself to be a white, long-tailed fox terrier with a black mask. A few yards above, from beyond the bookstalls, the windows of the Restaurant Lucullus shone down. Occasionally there was the whistle of the doorman, the rattle of an answering taxi and then a sound of the doors being slammed.

The honking of the horns of the buses mingled with the rumble of heavy trucks laboring upward to the corner brightened by the glass-enclosed sidewalk terrace of the Brasserie la Perigourdine.

"Will you ever go back?" I asked.

"To the Restaurant Lucullus?"

"Yes."

"But certainly."

"Won't they resent it?"

"Not in the least. That was a comedy; I knew it and they knew it. I am one of the most scrupulous of people. There are those who would go back there and collect their percentage on the dinner, and they would get it without any argument whatsoever, and whenever they wished they could have a free meal."

In the pauses between street noises, the fox terrier could be heard crunching on his Lucullan bone, and the waters of the Seine murmured between the Quai and the barges and surged into two gurgling spirals, one at each side of the tillers.

"The trouble with me," said St. Cucuface, "is my appetite," and then, as if justifying something to himself, he added, "But you must agree that entertaining Madame l'Ambassadrice is difficult. I work like an acrobat. I saved her money by asking for the bill, for if she had asked, the amount would have been doubled. Also we are doing her a favor by driving her car to Cannes."

Two black-helmeted motorcycle policemen raced along the Quai.

"They can become rather nasty," said St. Cucuface when they had turned the corner. "Certainly so when you are a Frenchman. You were very fortunate that they didn't take you to the Commissariat and investigate whether it was true that you were an American. It could have been very unpleasant; they care nothing whatsoever for titles."

"But I *am* an American."

"Oh, yes, I had almost forgotten."

*N*ubar Gulbenkian is an international, a decorative fixture of deluxe eating places, and works hard at it. He arrives in a mauve Rolls-Royce, always with at least one attractive woman, and an orchid in his lapel, his beard carefully waved and combed. He makes his entrance and, with old-world manners and large gestures and hearty bellows and flashing eyes, chooses the table, reads the menu with a monocle, selects the wine, waits for the feast. Extremely knowing in the arts of the table, he is not the most welcome guest, and the owners of the places he frequents suffer and shake with mixed feelings. For although he is an advertisement for them, he makes things very difficult. He adds up the bill with the menu in his other hand, to check. He has no taste for waste and thinks nothing of saying, "Now we will start with one portion of sardines grillées divided between us." When he orders other fish he takes his napkin out of his collar and marches out into the kitchen to see that the actual fish he has chosen is in the pan, for there are substitutions made for the tourists. There is one fish in the Mediterranean whose head, when bashed in, resembles another that costs five nouveaux francs more on the menu, but not for Monsieur Gulbenkian. He knows what is on his plate and what string beans and carrots cost at the market. His complaining and his praise alike are bitter to listen to for the maîtres d'hôtel: he thinks, and quite rightly, that the fifteen per cent put on the bill is quite enough by way of tip.

THE
WOMAN
OF MY LIFE

EVELYN HAS LOVELY LEGS, the kind you cannot find in France, simple like all objects of beauty, long and slim; their secure progression on the street is elegance itself, a pleasure to behold. Her hair is blond; her eyes are a marine blue outdoors that changes to deep violet when she is in this room.

She loves rain as I do. Paris is most beautiful in rain, and especially in this lovely month of April. The most remarkable thing about Evelyn is her desire for the mystery of Paris, for the small things that make something what it is, for its very personal language—the right names of objects in the language of the people—for example, the words difficult to know, the precise picturesque expression. This extraordinary creature—normally one would see her in the corridors of the Ritz, at Maxim's, and at the thousand and one nights of boredom of social functions—yet she understands me so well and shares my likes.

Our haunts are the small restaurants where the proprietor cooks and his wife and daughter wait on table. Not necessarily French: there is a Greek one, called Le Vieux Paris, where lamb turns on an upright brass spit in an affair that looks like a tabernacle, with charcoal glowing around it behind filigreed panels, and the excellent meal is a dollar. There are any number of these places all over Paris, the rendezvous of chauffeurs, butchers, plain people. Here things are said worth listening to; there is no protocol, no chichi, no pretense. Here one need not talk, just sit and listen and look. Strange that when one of them is put on canvas, people pay millions for it, and when it is in front of them, alive and humming, they don't see how beautiful it is. Evelyn does. We have a favorite place in the "Street of Shadows," a bistro called the Empty Crate. The kitchen is Lyonnaise, the patronage furniture movers and packers, all heavy men of muscle and security, of solid presence, about a dozen of them.

Their appreciation of Evelyn is that of homage to a queen. They have all given voice to their admiration for her, they have taught her some phrases which are on the edge of being direct, and they are amused like children when she repeats them with her clear voice and school-teacher's face.

They envy me. One of the most rewarding things in love, when one is secure, is the light in other men's eyes when they look at your woman.

We have a word for a woman who flirts back. It is *salope*, and in a playful way I have said it to her often.

She asked what a *salope* was, and I explained. My English stems from a British nanny, and I did not find the right word.

"What you mean," she said after a while, "is 'a bitch.' "

I said that was a little too strong for the French word. So she sent me a book I find most interesting, *The American Language* by H. L. Mencken. In this I discovered a remarkable fact, which is that only in English and American the word which connotes what supposedly is the apotheosis of love is used as a term of abuse, of inflicting damage on someone. I find this most curious—but so is everything about this subject. . . .

Alors, tonight we are going to a new place, a vast establishment on the Boulevard Montparnasse, called the Royal Grand Large, famous for its articulate clientele and the quality of its food, drinks and service at all hours of the day and night. It will be an evening of exploration. A meal there comes to 600 francs—a dollar and a half.

Before she comes I must tell you one more thing about myself. I am terribly shy, and my life is further impeded by a monstrous hurdle, the fact that I cannot lie. This is like being from another planet; it raises the most terrible obstacles. There is silence, of course, but that is akin to lying and seldom protects one.

All this considered, it is fabulous that I have found Evelyn in spite of my handicaps. She is very much like me, outspoken and direct. When we met it was like two people running toward each other through wide-open doors when they had feared them hostilely shut.

The gentle labyrinth that is the soul of woman is the most precious place on earth. To get past its guard—to have a woman's countenance turn toward me with the look of complete trust and of love—to me that is the greatest moment of life. Because from there on is always a descent, I prefer, even if it is juvenile, to remain at the romantic stage, in which the heavens are hung with violins and all is beautiful and stays that way. . . . Old story, that, the story of Paradise.

As I survey the scene now, there are no obstacles that I have not overcome. This is the woman of my life at last, my great love. The fulfillment of the dream.

We walked hand in hand to the Boulevard St. Michel. The Royal Grand Large in Montparnasse is a place of vast dimensions, always alive with agitated clientele, brightly lit, humming with authentic Left Bank atmosphere. Evelyn said, "Let's have a drink," and we went in and stood at the bar, next to where the cashier sat surveying the place and smiling at us through her pince-nez.

Perhaps the only pleasure for a rich man like myself is the very careful spending of money. I was delighted when Evelyn said that she wanted to eat there too, for at the Royal Grand Large in Montparnasse one eats well and at reasonable prices. The Beaujolais in carafes is young, as it should be, and the right temperature.

Restaurant cashiers of this category are very important to the establishment, usually relatives of the owners. The one here was the prototype of all cashiers of that sort. For protection against the drafts of the door, she was wrapped in pullovers, scarfs and wristlets, all a uniform somber palette of colors, to which her face gave no relief. Testimony to her proper status was a wedding ring, long bogged into the flesh of the finger on which it was worn.

Over the woolen protective garments she wore a jacket, tight to bursting, out of the history of dress-making, some thirty years back.

She sat enshrined among the stained-glass effects of lighted liquor bottles on shelves, potted plants, a board with the keys of the wine cellar, the cash register, and a fence of long, pointed metal spikes on which she impaled the stubs which waiters handed her.

She had an assortment of reflexes: a quiet smile of confidence for the cash register; a quick, searching glance for the people who entered and left; and sometimes a greeting with automatic lifting of the lips in a crocodile smile. A face of tolerance for the six headwaiters, a face of

contempt for the waiters, and for the rest a general accusatory inquiry into everything that took place inside the establishment and beyond its plate-glass window at the tables and chairs on the sidewalk. Upon Evelyn the cashier had immediately fastened her eyes, examined her and found her interesting. Between her other preoccupations, her eye returned again and again to Evelyn. There was no waiter for a while, and Madame the cashier screeched, "Marcel"—whereupon a waiter who was busy at another table turned and announced with some impatience that he was busy taking an order. The Royal Grand Large in Montparnasse is a very busy place.

The cashier asked Evelyn and myself what we wanted, and Evelyn said, "A dry Martini; make it two."

The cashier said, "*Oui*, madame, *un* Martini dry." And then she screamed at Marcel, "*Deux* Martini dry."

"Why do they turn everything around?" asked Evelyn. "Why do they say 'Martini dry' when it's 'dry Martini'?"

I have told you how inquiring Evelyn is about things. She asked the cashier.

"Ah—*c'est comme ça*," said the cashier with a trace of annoyance. "That's how it is."

"In America," said Evelyn "a dry Martini is a dry Martini."

"In France, it is 'a Martini dry,'" said the cashier and speared the stubs for the Martinis dry on her fence of spikes.

Evelyn drank and almost choked. "This is terrible," she said. "Did you taste it? It tastes like lacquer and it's sticky."

We called Marcel. "*Un* dry Martini," explained Evelyn, "is made with gin, Gordon's gin, and Noilly Prat vermouth, very dry."

"Yes, yes," said the waiter and took the Martini dry away. The cashier surveyed us coldly; she waved for a maître d'hôtel, and they had a conference on how this should be arranged. The stubs were taken from the spike and went into an empty cigar box.

"Ah, this is it. *Ça*," said Evelyn. "*c'est un* dry Martini." She held it under the nose of the cashier, who lifted the left side of her mouth in the crocodile smile again. She looked at the new stubs, and as she reflected that these dry Martinis cost three times the price of Martini dry she gave an admiring look down our way, folded her hands and watched us drink.

Evelyn wanted two more, and the cashier informed Marcel. "*Deux* dry Martinis," she yelled. Evelyn nodded approval; the battle was won.

The tables were all occupied. After the next Martinis Evelyn announced that she wanted something to eat while waiting, a snack of some kind. She leaned toward the cashier and in her clear French asked whether she could have a *saucisson*.

"But certainly, madame," said the cashier, and again sent her clarion call down the bar. Marcel turned an ear and was informed of the order.

Evelyn smiled at Madame, Madame smiled at Evelyn; this was the fourth Martini. . . . I admire the capability of American women in drinking along with men, but I saw that the pleasant aspect of an economical evening had faded at a five-hundred-franc dry Martini.

The headwaiter announced that he had a table for us. . . . In this region there are people of violent opinions, and the Royal Grand Large in Montparnasse is the scene of an occasional dispute. Therefore the maître d'hôtel of the establishment and his five assistants are in the shape of heavyweight wrestlers. The individual of the group who leads them in work and in combat looks as if someone had pulled the skin off the face of a bulldog and draped it loosely over a stone-shaped skull. With this fleshy drapery, the color of Bel Paese cheese, he manages to smile. He made a deep bow, and, handing us each a menu at the bar, he awaited our pleasure.

"In a moment," said Evelyn. "I am waiting for my *saucisson*." So he stuck the menus under his arm and brought us little knives and forks and plates, and he sent a commandeering look down in the direction from which Marcel was approaching. Madame is watching all this with a continuous performance of her reflexes to cash register, waiters, the maître d'hôtel, and she is busy writing and impaling, for it is the height of business now. Now it comes, on an oval platter, slices of sausage. I took one and ate it—delicious *saucisson d'Arles*.

"But this is not what I ordered," said Evelyn. "I ordered a *saucisson*, not sliced sausages. Please change it. I want a *saucisson*, a small sausage—like a cocktail sausage, a little hot dog. That's simple, isn't it?"

"That is a *saucisson*, madame," said the maître d'hôtel. "You ordered a *saucisson*, here is a *saucisson*." He took some new arrivals to a table.

The cashier spoke. She closed her eyes and pointed her lips, and she held her pencil in her right hand, the sharp end pointing at Evelyn.

"If you will pardon me, madame, you do not speak French properly," she said to Evelyn.

"I beg your pardon," said Evelyn, "and I hate to correct you, but a *saucisson* is a small sausage. Look in the dictionary."

I did not want to correct Evelyn in public, so I said, "Madame, will you be so kind and order a *saucisse* for Madame, and I will finish the *saucisson*."

"Very well, monsieur," said the cashier, and then she turned to Evelyn and snapped, "You should have ordered a *saucisse* if you wanted a small sausage, not a *saucisson*."

"Ah, *alors*." Evelyn rocked her shoulders and put her hands on her hips, to show that she not only spoke French but also knew motions and gestures. "Curious language," said Evelyn.

A storm of words broke from the cashier; she got up and announced to all that people who did not like the way things were in France should go back where they came from—or at least should keep their mouths shut. Especially Americans.

Evelyn reached into the repertoire she had so carefully acquired, the direct words, the colloquialisms, the dictionary of intimacy, and from that she selected the word *"salope"* and flung it at Madame.

Madame issued a terrible cry. The napkins of the maîtres d'hôtel came flying like sea gulls toward us. I received a punch in the nose, for I had taken a protective position in front of Evelyn. We were surrounded on all sides by the brutes in tailcoats.

Suddenly, as in a planned assassination, the five assistant maîtres d'hôtel and the one in charge of them closed in on me. I was flung about, I saw flashes of light alternating with darkness, felt a pain in my jaw, received kicks in my backside, and was suddenly flung through the door. I found myself sprawled on the stony chill of the sidewalk, among wicker furniture and astonished bystanders.

"Let's go back and clean up this place," said Evelyn, but I said, "No, no, there are too many, let's go."

The maîtres d'hôtel and the cashier and the clientele of the Royal Grand Large were glowering at us through the plate-glass doors.

"I can't understand you," said Evelyn, "a man with your name and position—to run from a bunch of headwaiters!"

I could think of nothing to say.

Under a lamp we stopped.

"Poor darling," said Evelyn, trying to straighten out my clothing. She combed my hair and kissed me.

We walked through one of the small streets and came to the place called the Empty Crate, the hangout of the movers and storage people. It was packed tightly, but these kind people, seeing my condition, made room for me, and I got a chair to sit down. Evelyn asked for a napkin and a bowl of water. She told them about what had happened at the Royal Grand Large, and the movers praised her and said that a thing like that must not be allowed to happen—what would people think of France? A punitive expedition should immediately be organized against the Royal Grand Large, to teach them a lesson.

I tried to calm them, but they had in Evelyn their Joan of Arc. "You will lead us," they said. "Come along, Monsieur le Duc," they cried excitedly, and pushed me out into the Rue des Martyres.

I asked them to please go back quietly to the Empty Crate.

"After what they did to my dear Armand?" asked Evelyn.

"En avant!" they shouted and started off. They were more than a match for the maîtres d'hôtel of the Royal Grand Large. "We will teach them," they shouted.

The one with the strongest manner, Jules, the biggest of them, pulled down his sweater and pushed the cap back on his head and said, "You have all heard what has passed—let's punish them good." They all raised their arms with their overdeveloped muscles, two of them put their arms around Evelyn, and they started off, with bulging sleeves and chests, singing and in military step, with Evelyn beside them.

"You go ahead," they said to me. "You lead, Monsieur le Duc, and we follow." I was all for leading them back to the Empty Crate, for I am a man of peace, but the big one took my shoulders and steered me ahead of him across the boulevard.

The cashier saw us approach. She gave a signal of alarm, and the maîtres d'hôtel rushed up to the door, and while two held it closed, a third locked it from the inside. Madame was busy telephoning the police, and in a while there was heard the signal of the squad cars, which goes "Poopaah, poopaah," and the police jumped from them, capes over their arms. The cashier explained our presence, and there were some arguments with the policemen.

"Is it forbidden citizens to walk peacefully on the sidewalk?" asked the

leader of the movers. The police had no taste for a fight with these men. Looking past the movers and talking out of the sides of their mouths, the agents made gentle conciliatory gestures and said things like "Please go home," "Look—this is ridiculous," "After all—*allons—voyons*—let's go!" After a certain amount of time had passed and the movers were dispersed, the police drove away, happy that they had settled the matter without a fight. The warehouse men, who, one by one, had sauntered around the corner very slowly, so as not to lose face, met in the shadows and Jules, the biggest, decided on a new tactic. One of them, he himself, would come to the door all alone, from the other side, where his approach was covered by a storm curtain. He would open the door and hold it for the others to enter. Then each one of them would take on one of the maîtres d'hôtel, and Evelyn would take care of the cashier.

Myself—they left out of all calculations.

I said to Evelyn, "My darling, I know how these things end in France. Please don't go in there again. Let's leave and eat somewhere quietly."

But it was of no avail. The big one had left, running around the block, the plan was in motion, they were like little boys. I saw the beginning of it, but I am not made for things like that. It was dreadful. The interior of the Royal Grand Large disintegrated, the chandeliers swung, broken glass was flying, chairs went through the window.

"Please, Evelyn," I had said, but she said, "Nobody does that to a friend of mine and gets away with it."

"Please," I said, holding onto her. "Let's have a quiet dinner; there's a new Russian restaurant owned by Colonel Renard, a friend of mine—gypsy fiddlers, singing, Evelyn, a lovely restaurant. It's in the Rue Pierre Premier de Serbie. I will order caviar, champagne, anything you want. I implore you—" But she was deaf and like one possessed. She tore herself loose and ran inside the Royal Grand Large. She got hold of the cashier by the hair; the pince-nez fell off and Evelyn stepped on them while the two women pulled each other around.

The cashier screeched, and then came the sound of the squad cars again. Both women were on the floor, battling, and I left the scene. It was not a noble thing to do, but I had good reason not to get mixed up with anything, for I am in difficulties with the police. The wagon which collects all the participants in such goings on, and which is called the "Salad Basket," arrived. Everyone, including Evelyn, was loaded into it and driven off to the station. Evelyn spent the night in the *correctionel*, as it is called.

For two days I looked for her everywhere—at her hairdresser's, at the place she eats breakfast—you know how one looks for a woman, especially the woman of one's life. I filled her room with flowers, I telephoned every half hour. Finally she called; she was out of jail.

"Ah, darling," she said, "I love you."

I said, "Evelyn, I love you. Let's have dinner tonight."

She said, "All right, I'll have dinner tonight with you under one condition."

"And what is that?"

"That we eat at the Royal Grand Large in Montparnasse."

Alas, she is a difficult woman.

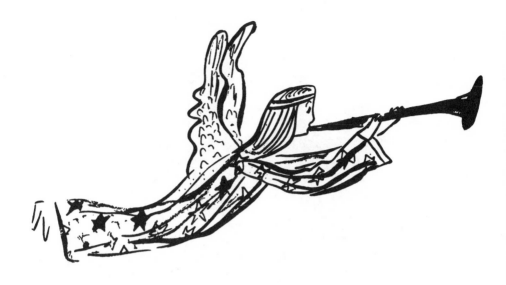

*A*nd the invitations—what will they be like?"

"*Ah, there I shall reduce tradition to nothing. The engraver will inscribe on the finest paper, simply, in gold:*

> *I, Armand, have decided to*
> *enter into marriage with*
> *Evelyn*
> *Will you do us the honor*
> *of assisting at the ceremony?*

"*How elegant— and after the service?*"

I have a horror of wedding breakfasts, of a buffet loaded with things in aspic, hams, turkeys, salads, hard-boiled eggs, and the towering confections of pâtissiers, no matter how artfully constructed. It all leaves you bloated at the worst hour of the afternoon. I shall change that to a feast like the ones in Versailles, a proper dinner of the most careful selection, eaten at leisure; dancing for those who wish; no toasts, no speeches; fountains playing and a band of hunting horns far away in the forest— and let the evening take its course. . . . All this at the Château Lamoury. My house is yours—always.

OF PIGS AND TRUFFLES

THE NEXT DAY the voyage began in earnest and, as it should be, the car was newly washed and in order. Denise was properly dressed, the baggage was in its right place, and I had the route in my head. I set the clock on *"temps de marche"*—an early start is best; it was eight-seventeen. The run would be to Brive la Gaillarde. Normally, in a car like this, I made Cannes in two easy stages, and it could be done in one day, but now I went slowly to look at France. The fields were fresh in the green of spring, it was all orderly, the birds were singing, and nature was celebrating with red, yellow and blue and white flowers and pink blossoms. The day passed and we stopped at the Hôtel de la Truffe Noire in time for dinner.

The hotel itself is nothing extra, but still it is worth a visit. In the kitchen is a chef of the first order, and his specialty is truffles. By way of decoration there is a truffle on all the china.

We arrived there about eight, and I ordered *Truffes sous la cendre*—a manner of cooking them in a jacket of dough under ashes, and when Denise ate them, she looked as if she were eating the ashes. She held a truffle on her fork and she asked, *"Vous aimez ça?"*

I said, "Yes, I like it very much, don't you?"

"Oh, these truffles, *je ne les aime pas trop*," she said, making a face.

"They taste blah blah—I don't know how to say it."

"They are a great delicacy."

"Where do they grow?"

"In the ground, and they are very hard to find. Pigs, special truffle pigs, are used to find them."

"Ah." She said "Ah" the way other people say "Oh" when something unpleasant is told them.

"You don't have to eat them."

"Ah, but if they are so expensive . . ."

"Give them to me and I will order you a *saucisson chaud*."

"*Merci beaucoup*."

The next morning we took a walk around the town and Denise said, "Last night in my room, I thought about the pigs."

"What pigs?"

"The pigs with the truffles. How do they know that they are truffles?"

I had no answer to that, and then she asked how it was that people liked them when they tasted so "blah."

I said that it was an acquired taste.

"What is an acquired taste? To eat things that you don't like?"

"Yes, the first cup of coffee tastes awful, the first oyster is hard to swallow, the first snail, the first dish of tripe, kidney, brains, and also other things. The first cigarette and pipe. . . ."

"But the pigs like the truffles?"

"Yes, they are found mostly in soggy earth. A man on stilts follows the pig, and when the pig has uprooted the truffle, then the man, who has a pole with a nail at the end of it, sticks the pig and the pig cries 'Ouch' and drops the truffle. Every tenth truffle the pig is allowed to keep."

"Poor pig! Are all things that are costly gotten with pain?"

"Yes, most. Diamonds are mined deep underground, pearls are obtained with danger, animals are trapped for fur, and the money to buy things is sometimes as hard to get as the things it buys."

"It is terrible for God to lend you life and then take it away, and make the time between hard for people."

"But just now we are happy."

"We are very happy." Then we rolled on.

"Are you satisfied with yourself?" she asked.

"I wasn't, but now I am. And you?"

"I wasn't and now I am happy also. . . . Oh, what a lovely cemetery. Will you stop, please?"

What a blessing to travel with a companion to whom all is interesting, who is capable of enthusiasm. The words of Goethe, *Geteilte Freude ist doppolte Freude,* are true; likewise that shared sorrow is half sorrow.

I would need a year at the Institut Truffaut to record this happy journey in detail—every hour of it was good. Denise remade the world for me. It was like the music of Mozart. . . . We went to Rome, Venice, Munich, Salzburg and Baden-Baden.

I was enriched by a completely new look at all this, and by a thorough knowledge of all the cemeteries of these places and those in between and of the famous dead buried in them. In order to stretch out the end, I made a turn, avoiding Paris, and entered by way of Versailles and Ville d'Avray, my favorite route. She made the last observations on that route. We passed a stud farm.

"What is that?"

"These are the stables of Monsieur Bussac."

"Who is he?"

"A very rich man."

"Evidently. What is in the stables?"

"Horses."

"How much is a horse?"

"That depends on the horse."

"Well, this kind of horse."

"Oh, ten million francs."

"Who will pay ten million francs for a horse?"

"For a good horse people pay even more."

"And then he puts it in his stable."

"No, it goes to the races."

"Oh, and he makes bets on it and loses."

"Sometimes he wins, because he is Monsieur Bussac and he can buy the best horses. They have a nice life, better than most people."

"How long do they race?"

"Until they are old."

"How old is a horse when it is old?"

"When it's really old, about twenty-five."

"One would think they would get older than people."

"Why?"

"Because they are bigger and they eat only grass."

PERFECT SERVICE

THE BELLS OF NOTRE DAME struck eleven.

"I dream of restaurants sometimes," said Dagobert. "That is perhaps the only thing I miss in my former life—the neighborhood bistro—a place called Chez Armand, very unpretentious, and nothing to brag about by way of kitchen. But it was a refuge for me then, chiefly because there was nobody there who made me suffer. Friends were around me, and the specialty of the house was the *gigot aux flageolets;* the Algerian red wine was served in cloudy glasses, but I found some peace there. Anyway I got away from the family—from my wife's casseroles and the eternal stale smell of domesticity."

The Professor said: "With me restaurants had the opposite effect. I suffered in them—especially in those of the first grand deluxe category."

"I passed the Restaurant Lucas Dubuffet today," said Dagobert. "I inhale the perfume of that kitchen with much pleasure. It's clean—one can look inside—they keep a good table."

"That was my father's favorite eating place," said the Professor. "He had a very small list of restaurants—Maxim's, Le Grand Véfour, a few more three-star places. That's all he ever went to, and he liked Lucas Dubuffet most of all."

"I don't blame him. I could be tempted to go there myself."

"We always went there the first night for dinner whenever my father came to Paris, and also the last night when he left.

"Meals with the family were always a disaster. Toward the end of my father's life they became terrifying, silent sessions. Nobody spoke, for every word somehow provoked my father to outbursts.

"In ordering meals, as in everything else in his life, he decided on what was to be eaten. He had a curious way of ordering—that is, he consulted no one's wishes. He avoided looking at anyone and especially at me. Occasionally he shot a glance at the men taking the order, which was always the same group—the proprietor, the headwaiter and the wine waiter.

"Mostly he ordered the meal past the right side of my face and the wines—because the sommelier usually stood in back of my chair—to the left side of me. I did my best to avoid looking at my father. We were both experts at ignoring each other. I looked at the glasses, the flowers, the silverware, at my mother.

"I also avoided looking at Mr. Chamber, his friend, his steady companion, the one person toward whom my father leaned and with whom he had long whispered conversations.

"Mr. Chamber was a florid man. I had seen him once in his bathing suit in Deauville. He had an immense chest and under it curious girllike legs. Dressed, he was the perfect image of an American executive. You could have put his face on a fifty-dollar savings certificate. Everything connected with my father had a feeling of money about it—except me. Mr. Chamber was a silent, strong man, who had at one time in his youth swum around Manhattan and still believed in long walks, deep breathing and noncompetitive sports. He led the clean life up to five o'clock, when, under the great pressure of his tremendous corporate responsibilities, he started to drink heavily. They both drank well and ate everything the doctor had told them was bad for them. They had contempt for all and everything—labor unions, doctors, the French, me, my mother, the President of the United States, the fact that people could vote, the fact that women had the vote. As for women, there had never been the slightest scandal or even the faintest breath of it, as far as both my father and C. Aubrey Chamber were concerned. That may also have been out of contempt for women. They were both married to gentle, kind and beautiful women, whom they took for granted and treated with a peculiar form of tolerance, a vicious, icy, mostly polite brutality. Every word was loaded with some sort of reproach, insult, or superiority and indifference. It had become chronic; it had always been so ever since I remember having learned to understand speech.

"About the only time I saw them smile together was when some stock they did not own suddenly went down.

"My poor mother suffered in silence. She sat there among the snobbish patronage, attended by the old headwaiters, captains and waiters, all of whom seemed to have a peculiar loathing for their clientele.

"My father was one of the best customers. He said the food was superb, and also the service. I suppose it was.

"The last night we were there was a special occasion. My father asked the proprietor and chef to order the dinner—he wanted something unusual, a bon-voyage dinner on the occasion of his departure for America. I can tell you exactly what we had. It started with everything by way of hors d'oeuvres; then came caviar with blinis, after that a tray of assorted oysters, turtle soup, trout cooked in champagne, followed by capon; then sorbet of wild strawberries; then woodcock, asparagus, and after that goose liver with truffles, soufflé, ice cream, cookies and fruit."

"They left out the cheese," said Dagobert.

"No, no, I forgot the cheese. That is, they came with a wagon with cheeses, a hundred varieties of the best in France, and you could have some if you wanted to, but nobody wanted any. All of the food was eaten in total silence among a décor of flowers and a view of the thick necks of people at other tables which I saw in the tilted mirror overhead.

"Most of the women wore limp hats and dressed in a very special kind of expensive squalor. The men were all heavy, designed for the oversize chairs and banquettes of the room, and all had their special places reserved and always ate at the same tables. In that mirror I could also see the buffet with pyramids of food, the crystal chandeliers, and the obese, unpleasant servitors with bulging eyes, continuously shuffling back and forth and back and forth. I could watch the entry of the arthritic clientele with their grunts and groans, the wine buckets being carried past the obscene faces of most of the men and women who were busily talking about the others in the room . . . the jewels, the hairdos. I also saw the lovely things in this room—the maroon-colored interior edged with gold, the cut-glass partitions to protect the clientele from drafts, the brass fixtures, and the ceiling which looked like old ivory.

"All of it was bright, immaculately dusted and polished, the nearby objects very clearly visible, those in the distance as in a painting. The women were very much like one sees in Renoir or Degas paintings, only doubly lovely. But no matter how much I wanted to turn around,

to look at them directly, to gaze at this or that beautiful face, I could merely watch in the mirror, and even then not openly but only by sweeping casual glances. Here and there I saw a man of a certain age seated with a gem-laden woman of great allure, and the woman would flash an occasional inquiry to me by way of a look, via the mirror. But I am very uncommunicative and not cut out for romance, and I always had to look away. I could not stand the direct saber thrust of love, much as I desired it. I was—I am—an idiot in these matters, afraid to take a step. My hands get moist like a schoolboy's. I worship from afar.

"I sat silent through the whole meal at our table. We were like the French families with their still, straight-sitting, serious children who do not even swing their legs, but sit through these endless meals, and eventually sit on the other side of these same tables with their own children. This restaurant had a tradition. Into the grillwork on the windows the figures 1845 were worked. That is the year it was established.

"Among the details I observed was the serving of wine. The sommelier poured a little of the wine into my father's glass, and then held his bottle with an 'I dare you to complain' look. He had eyes like plover's eggs, which lay in a cinnamon-colored sacking of flesh, and his nose was blue-veined from self-sacrifice in wine tasting. My father was a match for him, however. His arrogance was perfected to the smallest detail. He kept the wine waiter hanging. He tasted the wine slowly, and then, putting the glass back on the table, gave no sign of pleasure, recognition or appreciation, not even a nod of thanks or grunt of assent for its submission to his judgment. The fact that he did not send it back was enough, though, and the sommelier then poured it into the glasses of the people at the table—into Baccarat glasses so fine that when you squeezed them the round top became slightly oval.

417

"A trio played a carefully selected instrumental accompaniment to all this. The chef came to the table. Mr. Chamber nodded and thanked him.

"The cloud of blue smoke overhead, the overheated room, the smell of food—it was enough to make one sick. And still my father sat there, and stared ahead of him, and next to him sat C. Aubrey Chamber, and he also stared. One of my brothers, the middle one of the three who had made good, sat next to me. My mother's unhappy eyes wandered about the scene as mine did. Occasionally people came in, occasionally people paid and went out. The musicians went out for a rest and came back, and the leader of the orchestra stood at our table and began to play for us. My mother smiled pleasantly at him. My father stared. Mr. Chamber handed some money to the fiddler so my father would not be disturbed. The musician bowed and left. The room began to get cool. The service here was really excellent, for although excepting for a few others we were the only party left, the waiters made no motion of clearing off the buffet, or closing up. They stood patiently here and there with arms folded, staring into space.

"The wine waiter never went through the wine-tasting ritual with champagne. It was taken for granted that champagne, like Coca-Cola, was even in quality from bottle to bottle. The waiter merely served as many bottles as he felt were needed. He twisted another cork silently out of a bottle. In one of her few gestures of revolt, my mother always turned the wineglasses at her place upside down at the very beginning of the meal and left only the water glass standing. The music kept playing. The headwaiter came several times and asked if everything was all right, and then backed away.

"We were still waiting when my father moved a little—he made a sound—it was like a sigh. The other guests all had gone by now. We were the last ones left. My mother sat still as always. I looked at my father—his color had changed. I got up. I told my brother to take Mother to the hotel and send the car back for Father. I walked out toward the door. I told the proprietor of the restaurant to call a doctor. I went back. Mr. Chamber sat still next to my father. We waited—my father sometimes fell asleep at the table, as did Mr. Chamber, and they could sit forever. The doctor came and touched my father. He sat down comfortably on the deep upholstery of that restaurant. He took hold of him by both his massive shoulders. My father's head tilted forward a little. He was dead.

"Mr. Chamber was asleep. I don't know whether this happened regularly in this restaurant, but I must say that the service was perfect to the end. Two men came and, taking hold of my father, one on the left and one on the right, sort of walked him out. I felt guilty about being without emotion. A melancholy wave rushed over me.

"I felt a sorrow for all the uselessness of this life, a compassion for all, even the greedy, discontented servitors.

"The proprietor stood in his usual posture and place near the door, with the 'bon soir, monsieur-dames' and the 'merci' expression on his face; his slightly tilted face bore the usual complications of farewell, goodbye and au revoir, and was suited perfectly to the grave adieu. So were the faces of all his maîtres d'hôtel, captains and waiters, who had no need to change any of their miserable expressions, which were in perfect accord with the end, with the departure of the esteemed client.

"It was a play without beginning or end, of figures moving to and fro. It was not without humor. When the croque-morts had come into the room with their black gloves they were for a moment undecided whom to pick up—whether it was C. Aubrey Chamber or my father— for the other looked as dead and gone as did my father. He was drunk and staring. The maître d'hôtel pointed out the one to be removed.

"The limousine had come back and now it stood below and the two men took him down, as if he were a little under the weather. The cloakroom girl, whose name was Mireille, brought his coat and his American businessman's hat and put them into the car. It went off. I went upstairs. Two captains helped Mr. Chamber down the stairs. It was so perfectly done that the doorman was confused and said to me as we loaded Mr. Chamber into a taxi: 'I trust there's nothing wrong with Monsieur Chamber.'

"I said, 'No, no, don't worry, he's all right.'

"Well, my father's battle was over. I went up to tell the headwaiter to add the tips to the bill and send it to the hotel.

"My father had always threatened to cut me out of his will. The will was opened by Mr. Chamber the next day, and either my father had not gotten around to it, or else he hadn't meant to—at any rate, I suddenly had more money than I ever expected to have. We went back to New York for the funeral. My mother died soon after."

"And Mr. C. Aubrey Chamber?"

"Oh, he is still sitting and staring at the same restaurant interiors. One doesn't know if he is alive or dead. At his side is his ever-patient and beautiful dear wife—patiently waiting."

"For him to die?"

"No. Strangely enough she loves him.

"One more thing I must tell you about the perfect service at the Restaurant Lucas Dubuffet. Only after I had signed the bill and said good night to the proprietor and all the maîtres d'hôtel and waiters, only after that was the signal given to clear off and they all went into action to cart off the buffet, remove the linen, put the chairs on the tables and start turning out the lights."

"What was that menu again? Please tell me once more," asked Dagobert.

"Oh, the bon-voyage menu. I know it by heart and will never forget it.

"First: Hors d'oeuvres.

"Then: Caviar de sterlet with blinis.

"After: Assorted oysters served like a wedding cake in a large batch on ice. You chose what you wanted: Les fines claires, those that are boat-shaped, and which I prefer, then those that are flat with a slightly metallic taste, then the Belons, and those from England. My father would eat a dozen of these at least.

"Then: Clear turtle soup.

"Then: Trout cooked in champagne.

"Followed by the specialty of the house: capon cooked à la demi-deuil—in half mourning—an effect produced by slipping thin slices of truffles between the skin and the flesh and this further enhanced by a sauce flavored with morilles. Very good that, I must say. With that a purée of mushrooms.

"By way of a break there was served a sorbet of wild strawberries au Grand Marnier and then we started eating seriously again.

"Flaming woodcock, with its long beak and the skull with its hollow

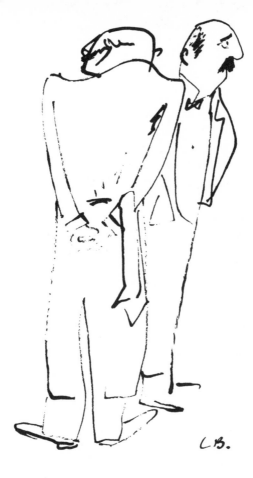

LB.

eyes left on, as well as its gray bird legs, and this accompanied by Egyptian quails, little sparrowlike creatures.

"With this les asperges de France served lukewarm with vinaigrette.

"The médaillons of goose liver with truffles.

"A pause and a change of table linen. They rolled a new tablecloth across, transferring personal belongings, candlesticks, centerpiece, et cetera, the way they make beds in a hospital where they roll the patient from one side to the other. New glasses, new napery, new silverware. Now the third act of the art of eating at table began.

"The soufflé de Grenade à l'Orientale.

"Biscuit glacé aux violettes.

"The tray of petits fours.

"The basket of fruit: nectarines, raisins, hothouse grapes, hothouse peaches, cherries, apricots.

"The tray with liqueurs.

"The fingerbowls.

"The cigars.

"The matches—special kitchen matches."

"You have made me hungry, and again, you have forgotten the cheeses," said Dagobert, who had been pensively picking his teeth while listening. He groaned and, getting up, reached from the edge of his mattress into the baby carriage for the bottle of cheap wine and the crust of bread.

"I have nothing against cheese," said the Professor. "I still have some fine Brie up there. I haven't thrown everything out. I'll hop upstairs. In the icebox there are all kinds of food left, and some wine, and that Brie—"

"Don't bother," said Dagobert. "With an empty stomach one has incredible imagination. I am just starting with that menu all over—we are at the flaming woodcock—" He sniffed pleasantly with closed eyes and held the bottle under his nose.

"Well, a flaming woodcock, I am sorry, I could not supply for you this instant."

"Therefore consider the advantage of the imagination," said Dagobert, blinking and wiping his lips with the back of his hand.

*T*he room was filled with onion and garlic vapor. Dagobert sniffed
with appreciation.

"What is this heavenly soup made of?" he asked Madame Michel.

"Oh, nothing at all. You take an onion, and a little clove of garlic,
and cut them finely and brown them in hot oil. Then you put in small
pieces of leftover meat and ham, then tomatoes, cut up, and a bouquet
of herbs, a little thyme and basil, a laurel leaf. Then you throw in some
rice or a handful of pasta, add a shot of red wine, and you serve it with
grated cheese and bread, very simple. You let it cook slowly on a small
fire before you throw in the rice and the pasta."

"May I have a little more?"

THE TOUR D'ARGENT

As if out of a tunnel, in a humid landscape, far away the bells of Notre Dame were ringing, ringing that melody which seems to say, "We will always be here, we will repeat it eternally."

The Cortis' bedroom faced upon a side street. It was papered in a faded tint of beige, the color of old cigars long exposed to the sun in store windows. A pattern of blue fleur-de-lis was on this paper, which in places hung loose from the wall.

The one window was curtained with violet drapery. On the ceiling were remnants of a stucco décor and from it hung a two-branch gas chandelier. A shaft of light cut through the room like a huge knife. It passed through a cage with two lovebirds, lighting them up green as glass and chattering; it went on through floating gray dust and reached back to a closet stuffed with Gala's many furs. On a dresser were jewels and gloves, and a stand held the intimate garments of both Monsieur and Madame Corti. The bed was held in place by a theatrical trunk used as a night table. The bed, in disorder as was the rest of the room, was filled with pillows and bolsters and out of it hung one small foot attached to the lovely left leg of Gala.

There was a soft knock on the door. Then the door opened and Madame Michel, dressed in her workaday outfit of blue jeans, a blouse, scarf and slippers, came in carrying an immense basket of long-stemmed white roses and tall white branches of blossoming lilacs, all tied with a broad satin ribbon. A stuffed white dove with a card in its beak was attached to the high, looping, wickerwork handle of the basket. Madame Michel placed it near the window and silently left.

The telephone which stood on the trunk close to the bed rang. Next to the telephone was an ashtray. The phone kept ringing. Gala sat up, reached over and picked up the instrument.

"Ah, it's you," she said. "Good morning." The voice talked rapidly. She said: "Speak a little lower." She smiled and said: "I too find you adorable."

Suddenly her head twisted involuntarily to her side, to the wall. Miomo Corti had risen in one quick motion, slapped her face, and gotten out of bed.

He was dressed in an elaborate bathrobe and pajamas. His face was ashen; his eyes looked as if someone with a stylograph had worked endless circular lines around them. His gray hair was in disarray. He kicked the ashtray aside, kicked the phone to the floor and walked around it, looking at it as if it were a hostile creature about to jump up and strike at him. An agitated voice continued out of the phone, "Allo, allo."

Corti bent down to it and shouted, "I don't know who you are, Monsieur, but you are impolite. You awaken us in the middle of the night. I find you disgusting!"

Gala was used to slapping and had no particular reaction to it. It brought color to her cheeks; she looked radiant. Her husband leaned down, picked up the phone and put it back in its cradle.

"Who was it?" Corti yelled. "I want to know!"

She pointed at the large basket of flowers and said, "Your friend, Vittorio Vivanti."

"Why didn't you say so, idiot!" said Corti. "Oh, oh, oh—you're driving me insane." He looked at the flowers and took the card. "You stayed out most of the night, you find him adorable, and he sends you an excessively expensive bouquet of flowers. Now then—explain! What happened?"

He came close, and it was her habit to tilt her head away from him when he did so in order to avoid his loose hand as much as possible.

"What happened?" he screamed, taking her by the shoulders.

"We went to the Tour d'Argent—"

"Of course. He has to show you off. Why couldn't he have taken you to some small place?"

"Well, with his big Rolls-Royce—"

"And?"

"There we ate."

"You left here at ten and you came home after four o'clock in the morning—you couldn't have eaten all this time! Where did you go after dinner? Where did you end up?"

"At his hotel."

"You went to his hotel—to his room? Like a common little whore to a bordel!" He slapped her again.

"But it was the Louis Quatorze."

"The Louis Quatorze, like every other hotel, is a bordel! Ah, no wonder he is grateful and sending you flowers. What did he say on the phone just now?"

"He said how nice it would be if we were in bed together now, and the waiter would be bringing breakfast. He wouldn't be lonesome."

"Were you in bed with him?"

"No."

"The ugly toad. And you said that you found him adorable—"

"Well, he said that he found me adorable as a woman. I was only being polite to him."

Corti moved back and forth at a trot.

"Oh, this is awful! Tell me the truth, don't lie, swear to me—did you go to bed with him?"

"But of course not!"

"I must know—I must be sure—look at me—do you swear?"

"I swear, of course I swear—"

He pulled back the curtain, the light streamed in, she sat in bed; he kneeled on the bed, pulled back her hair, and took her head in his hands; he bent it back and looked at her close.

"Look at me—look into my eyes!"

She did.

"Yes," he said, "I believe you. The eyes don't lie. Oh, that dirty old lecher! You poor innocent child! Just the same, everybody at the Tour d'Argent, and in that hotel every clerk, telephone operator, room waiter and maid takes it for granted that you slept with him, that you are his little whore. Don't laugh, it's terrible. You are so beautiful, so pure, so innocent and so stupid!"

He sat down on the bed dejectedly.

"The old swine. I am sure he tried everything to make you sleep with him. You don't have to tell me, I know. What happened from the moment you left here? I must know everything. You went to the Tour d'Argent, where, of course, Signor Vivanti was greeted by everyone from the owner down and properly taken care of. Go on from there."

"Well, they all know him there—"

"Important client—'*Bon soir*, Your Excellency.' "

"He ordered first, from a beautiful, big menu, and the proprietor himself came to take the order."

"Naturally. Signor Vittorio Vivanti is a very important man."

"We had the best table in the room, overlooking Notre Dame and the Seine, and the cathedral was lit up, and then he said how beautiful it was and how even more beautiful it would be if I went to bed with him after dinner."

"Impossible—the swine—at the start—just like that. What did you say?"

"I said nothing."

"You were shocked."

"No. I was reading the menu because it was the first time I was at the Tour d'Argent and because it was all so beautiful and the first time I could order what I wanted to eat. That is, Signor Vivanti did the ordering. I never had such a meal. Let me tell you what he ordered: first caviar, as much as I wanted, with little pancakes and champagne, and then—"

"Spare me the food. Tell me what he said."

"He talked about going to bed—"

"With the caviar?"

"Yes. He said that was very good for it. He said it several times while they were bringing the caviar and he told me to eat all I wanted. He ate a mountain of it. Then came a lovely soup, Germiny à l'Oseille, and the next course was wonderful, a sole in a white wine sauce, with truffles, mushrooms and little moon-shaped bits of pastry."

"And what did he say?"

"He said he was very lonesome in his big suite at the Louis Quatorze."

"And did it never occur to you to say to this man, 'Monsieur! Unless you change this conversation immediately, I will get up and leave you!' "

"Well, he is much older than I am and you asked me to be nice to him. He wanted me to call him '*tu*' but I addressed him as '*vous*' and 'Monsieur Vivanti' throughout."

"Go on, tell me what he said."

"I had finished eating the fish and then came the owner of the restaurant again and he took me out on the balcony and showed me the scenery and the ship below that was lit up and had just turned around—the *bateau mouche* filled with tourists. The owner of the restaurant asked how everything was, and Monsieur Vivanti said that it was all excellent."

"So then?"

"So then we went back to the table. They had cleared away everything."

"What did he say?"

"Monsieur Vivanti asked me to come home to his hotel with him, after dinner."

"Preposterous; the mentality of this man, to take a young married woman out, the first time, and to ask her at dinner to go to bed with him. To ask anyone that at any time is in the worst bad taste, but at dinner it is awful. But go on. What happened next?"

"Next came the pressed duck. That was the best, and the Tour d'Argent, Monsieur Vivanti explained to me, was the best place in the world to have pressed duck, and we got a card with the number of the duck on it. The duck was presented on a silver platter, it was brown as toast, and then it was taken away, and, Miomo, it's like in church during High Mass, in Notre Dame near the High Altar. There were three fat headwaiters like cardinals, with napkins stuck in their necks. Each one stood in a niche, like in a tabernacle with a light shining down on him, and each one had a duck in front of him, and silverware, and sauce boats, and they sharpened knives, and then they cut up the ducks—that's all they do all night long—and then it's put—that is, the carcass of the duck is put—into silver presses, and they twist and turn a handle and then the blood comes out of a spigot—"

"Will you stop talking about food and come to the point. Vivanti—what about him? What did he say?"

"He said how wonderful it was and how glad he was I enjoyed it all and he said how he would enjoy to go to bed with me—"

"And then?"

"And then came the duck and they served the red wine with it. This was even better than the fish."

"And you just kept on eating, you didn't ever answer him?"

"Well, I said that it was the most wonderful meal I had ever had."

"So what did he say?"

"Well, the same thing."

LB

"So what did you say?"

"I said nothing."

"So what did he say?"

"He said he was very hurt and he wanted to know why I didn't want to go to bed with him. I said, 'I'm sorry, but I can't jump in bed with anyone just because he wants it.'"

"So?"

"They had wonderful soufflé potatoes with the duck. You know, not those you get in other restaurants that are like parchment, or potato chips. These were soft and then there was that wonderful sauce."

"What about Vivanti? What did he say?"

"Just then he couldn't say anything, because the proprietor was back at the table and asked how everything was, and the wine waiter asked how it tasted, and the headwaiter, so Signor Vivanti didn't say anything except 'fine, fine, fine, excellent—very good, thank you.'"

"How discreet."

"It tasted wonderful. He ate and drank and then he wiped some of the fat and sauce off the plate with bread, and ate it, and then he wiped his mouth."

"How vulgar, and you sitting there with him! So what did he say by way of answer when you told him you couldn't jump in bed with just anyone?"

"Yes, he wiped his mouth and took a swallow of wine and then he said that he wasn't 'just anyone—'"

"Oh yes, we know that. Go on."

"He picked his teeth, but very elegantly in back of a napkin that he held in front."

"How chic. Continue!"

"He looked very sad, and ordered some dessert. What would I like, he asked me, and then he told the headwaiter that we would both like some crêpes Suzette. He asked me if I liked that and I said yes, of course, very much. I'd like anything he ordered."

"Except a bed!"

"I will never forget this dinner as long as I live."

"I am sure you never will."

"It was the best meal of my whole life."

"So then?"

"They cleared the table."

"Oh yes, and the discreet seducer from Milano sat silent, perhaps with his hand on your leg, looking down your décolleté."

"No, he was very proper, I must say."

"Oh, the very model of an Italian gentleman. What did he say?"

"He said he was surprised."

"At what?"

"That I was so narrow-minded and did not want to go to bed with him. I said, 'You know, Monsieur Vivanti, the fact that I parade myself on the stage doesn't mean that I sleep with everybody who asks me!' I said that furthermore I was a respectably married woman and loved my husband."

"Did you really say that?"

"Of course. I can't make up things like that, it's the truth."

"So how did he react to that?"

" 'Of course,' he said. He knew and he had great regard for you."

"One never knows one's true friends. Go on. What happened next?"

"So now they made the crêpes Suzette. All at the table on silver platters and everything done by hand in front of us, scraping the orange peel, and the lemon peel, and mixing the butter with orange juice and the liqueurs—"

"Now the waiters and the proprietor were around you again."

"Well, he asked me how I came to meet you, and how I got into this business of which I am a part, and about my beauty and how I got into this flea circus."

"Flea circus? What flea circus?"

"The Relaxez-Vous." Corti slapped her.

"Did you answer him? To that at least?"

"No, I said simply that it was my profession, because I had not learned anything else, and that I owed it all to you."

"So he said?"

" 'Well,' he said, 'well, my darling, carissima, soon you won't have to do it any more,' and then he asked me again to sleep with him."

"Good Lord, it's like listening to a train going over rails, or to an ode by Klopstock."

"What is that?"

"You wouldn't know. It's a German poet I tried reading to stay awake for your return, Gala, all through the night. I fell asleep with it. What about Signor Vivanti?"

"So he painted a picture for me of all he would do for me, the life he would give me if I became his friend."

"That mangy dog, all that the first time he goes out with you. I should have never let you go. Then?"

"Then he asked me if I wanted more crêpes Suzette, and I said yes."

"How could you eat, with this talk going on?"

"Oh, it goes in one ear and out the other."

"What happened next?"

"I said to him, 'I am sorry but I cannot leave Miomo. He is my husband, and he has taught me all I know. My life is to dance, to do my act on the stage.' "

"What did he say to that?"

"Nothing. The waiter came and said, 'Will Monsieur have any more crêpes? Will Madame have any more?' So I ate more, and I ate his too. 'Anyway,' he said, that is, Signor Vivanti said, 'I will make a great actress of you, a star,' and would I sleep with him after. He asked for a cigar and lit it, and for some brandy, and then he started again, looking at me with his bulging eyes, like a frog, and repeating, quack, quack, 'sleep with me.' "

"And you? What did you say?"

"Oh, Miomo, I got a feeling of sickness. I didn't want to listen any more. I got lonesome for this place, for my little stable downstairs. He looked at me again and I said, 'Please don't ask me any more, please stop this conversation. I cannot listen to any more of this talk. I will get sick and you will have to take me home right away.' "

"At last—and of course there was nothing more to eat. What did he say?"

" 'Finish your crêpes Suzette,' he said, and he told the waiter to give me some more champagne. But he was quiet for a second and then he asked me why I didn't want to go to bed with him, when every other girl did. He said that he had stayed an extra day in Paris, just to see the act and to take me out and have dinner with me, and to make plans and that I owed it to him to sleep with him."

"How disgusting! But go on!"

"He said that he could have had dinner with another girl, and then slept with her and had no problems. So I said that I was very sorry, but that he should have taken that other girl and why did he insist on taking me? So he said, because he loved me. I said, 'You come to Paris for a day, you see me, you say you fall in love with me. That isn't love; love is for long years, love is forever.' So he looked very sad and then he sighed and asked for the check. 'I loved you the moment I saw you,' he said. 'Haven't you ever heard of love at first sight?' "

"How romantic. Go on."

"I can't stand anybody looking sad, so I said, 'Monsieur Vivanti, I am sorry. You know it's much easier to say yes to a man than to say no. But I can't go to bed with you or anyone else. I am full of complexes about going to bed with people, or about taking my clothes off. In fact I couldn't do it and have never done it except in public.' "

"What did he say to that?"

"He said, 'Try it with me, it will make no difference to our friendship, nobody will know about it, and I will respect you as before.'

"So I said, 'Please let's talk about something else. Look at the beautiful view.' He called for the check again. The waiter came with the check. Signor Vivanti never looked at it, he didn't add it up. He reached in his pocket and took out a pack of big bills as if they were lottery tickets, and he covered the check with them and pushed it away. Then he gave one to the headwaiter. Then he snapped his fingers and gave another one to the wine waiter, and then they all bowed and pulled chairs, and he went down the elevator and he gave another bill to the doorman and then we got into his big Rolls-Royce and he started again. He said, 'We'll drive to my hotel.' He took my hands and asked me again to sleep with him.

"I said, 'If you had met me at someone's home, or anywhere except at the Relaxez-Vous, would you allow yourself to talk to me this way?'

"So he said that he talked to all women the same way. I asked if he talked to his wife like that also.

"He said, 'No, not to my wife.'

"I said, 'Why not?'

"He said, 'Because she is my wife!' Then he said it was early and did I want to go to see a cabaret, so we went to Monseigneur and that was very nice. And then I had an idea. I wanted to go back to the Indifferent."

Miomo Corti jumped up. "Oh God no, why did you want to do a thing like that for? To go back to that place."

"I just wanted to see the show, to see the girls there."

"So they all know! You go there with this monstrous creature! Did you tell him that you had worked there?"

"Yes, of course. Besides, he bought champagne for everybody, and the Rolls was waiting outside with the chauffeur—very chic, everybody admired it."

"Was the place full?"

"Not at first, but then word got around, and they all came—from the street, from the Sphinx, the Semiramis, the New Paradise. It suddenly was packed and people stood three deep at the bar."

"So what did he say?"

"He couldn't talk about going to bed because everybody sat with us, and the owner of the club said that any time I wanted to come back I would be welcomed with open arms. I had been the greatest attraction since they opened."

"It's getting pretty late now. When did you go to his hotel?"

"Yes, he too said that it was getting late and he would take me to his hotel and that there he had a beautiful apartment with a fine view of Paris."

"What happened next?"

"We were ready to go when the proprietor of the Indifferent said that there was great *ambiance,* and everybody asked me to do one of my numbers."

"Good Lord! The final degradation!"

"So because after all I had to do something for Signor Vivanti and because everybody begged me, the musicians, the girls, and because the director took me by the hand and introduced me to the audience, so suddenly I was there on the stage, and I did 'Tourbillon.' And then there was such applause that I did 'Profound Mirror' and as an encore 'Les Plaisirs Clandestins.' "

Monsieur Corti held his head in both hands. He cried: "But have you gone altogether crazy? Especially 'Les Plaisirs,' my latest creation and not to be shown around—at the Indifferent!" He slapped her three times.

"Well, I thought you wouldn't mind. I only sort of tried it out. Besides it was announced that it would be part of the new show at the Relaxez-Vous, and he gave you credit and also the address."

"How did it go?"

"They went hysterical, but I did not give another encore."

"And the old swine was now excited and wanted to get to bed immediately."

"He said that I was a great artiste."

"Then you went to the hotel?"

"Yes, then we went to the hotel."

"Up to his room! Oh, this is unbearable but go on."

"He was very nice."

"You went—just like that?"

"No. I didn't want to go up at first. I said, 'It's late, please let me go home, I can take a taxi,' but he said, 'Just come up for a moment.' "

"So you are in his room. Go on."

"He showed me the view, he asked me again to please call him Vittorio. Then he asked me to go to bed with him. I said, 'Look, you can call up your other girls, or call the Indifferent. They will send you somebody, anybody you want, but I can't go to bed with you.' "

"What did he say?"

"He said, 'Why not?'

"I said, 'It's impossible because of my husband' and there suddenly I

had to burst out laughing, for I was thinking of you, so Signor Vivanti also laughed, and he asked me what I was laughing at, and I told him how funny it was."

"And he said?"

"He said, 'All women are crazy. Here you refuse my love, and you laugh at your husband. What kind of a brain have women got?'

"I said, 'I have to laugh because it was all so sad.'

"He said, 'Oh, I thought you laughed because you had changed your mind, one never knows with women. I don't understand them, and the older I get, the less I understand them.' I said that I was sorry.

"He said, 'You have ruined my whole evening for me. There is so little in this life to remember with any pleasure, and it is over so quickly.'"

"One must say he has persistence."

"So he said, 'Explain to me why you won't go to bed with me. Here you are in my room, nobody will know.'

"I said, 'But I have explained it to you. I told you that I could go to bed only with somebody I loved.'

" 'Love,' he said, 'what is love?'

"I said, 'Love is when you walk hand in hand in the street, and you see nobody else and it has nothing to do with bed.'

"So he asked if I walked hand in hand with you down the street and saw nothing else.

"So I said, 'Well, I did once.'

"So he said that if it had nothing to do with bed, why not do it?

"But I did not answer. He asked if there was anything I wanted.

"I said yes, that I was very hungry, I wanted something to eat.

"So he said that he was hungry too, but that the room service at the Louis Quatorze was terrible and everything took hours and came up cold even during the day.

"So he said that he knew a place that was still open, a small place, and there we went, and they had something wonderful, a veritable *grand spécialité* of the house, *le jambon Arcadie*, a ham, so light it seems to float on a bed of spinach au gratin—I never ate anything like it—with some mushrooms in cream around it and an Italian dessert with wine."

"So what did he say?"

"I asked him if, because I did not go to bed with him, it was all over, and if any actress or artiste who did not go to bed with the producers, directors, or owners of theaters would be finished.

" 'It has nothing to do with it,' he said. 'Talent is so rare, beauty is so rare—'

"He took my hand, and he said, 'No matter with whom you slept if you have no talent, you will not get there,' and not to worry, he would see to it that I became a star, he would help me because I had beauty and talent."

"*Tiens, tiens,* so he finally gave up."

"He told me that he had to go to Milano by plane today and then he would come back and give a big party at the Relaxez-Vous. I was so sleepy. In the car he said, 'I will be very grateful, always, I will love you always.' He kissed me."

"Of course. Like a father."

"Yes, like a father."

"So what did he say next?"

"He said, 'When do I see you again?'

"I said, 'You are a very important man, Monsieur Vivanti, and as you say all the girls want to sleep in your bed, so don't waste another evening on me.' He leaned back in his corner of the car and he said, 'Such

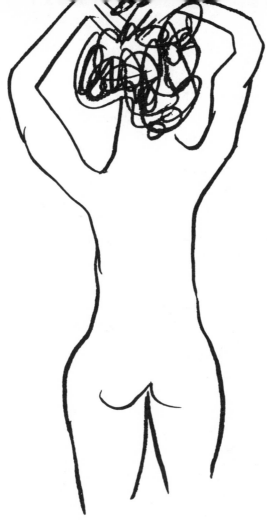

a thing has never happened to me before.'

"So we were again in front of the hotel, and he held me by the arm.

"He said again, 'Come up just for a moment.'

"But I said, 'I have seen the view from your lovely apartment and I thank you for a wonderful evening, but I am dead of fatigue. Please let me go.' But he said, 'Just a minute. Come up just for a minute. I have a surprise for you.' So I said, 'But you promise!'

" 'Yes,' he said, 'I promise. I have a present for you. Just come for a minute,' and we went up the elevator."

"*Bon Dieu*, is this never coming to an end?"

"He wanted to give me something."

"So you go to his room a second time. What happens now?"

"When we were there he opened a bottle of champagne and then he turned on the television, but there wasn't any. The Eiffel Tower was all violet in the morning light. He picked up some telegrams; he said it would be wonderful if I were as crazy about him as he was about me. Then he said I would lose you all your friends if I behaved with them as I did with him."

"Touching, his concern for me."

"Then he asked me to go to bed with him, for the last time. I shook my head. Then he said that most probably I wasn't any good in bed anyway, and I said I was certain I wouldn't be. So he said he wanted to get a little sleep, his plane was leaving early, and he said his chauffeur would take me home."

"And what did he give you?"

"He forgot to give it to me.

"I said good night and that I was sorry for having ruined his evening. He said maybe it was better so, but he looked very tired. He started to put things away in his suitcase, put some papers into folders, and he looked around for things to put in his pockets and it all made me feel terrible. Then he took me down and put me in his car and told his chauffeur to take me home. I sat in the car alone and I had to cry because life is so sad. 'I will call you tomorrow morning and give Miomo my best,' he said.

"I said, 'Forgive me.'

"He said, 'Of course,' so the car drove on. At the Place de l'Alma, the chauffeur stopped the car and he said, 'Madame, excuse me, but may I ask you a great favor?' "

"No, not the chauffeur also!"

"So I said, 'What is it?'

"He said, 'I am a married man. My wife is insanely jealous and she poisons my life. She does not believe that every night Signor Vivanti rolls from one place to the other, all night long, from one restaurant to another, from Maxim's to the Tour d'Argent to the Elephant Blanc, to the Left Bank, to the Right Bank, to night clubs, to parties, to private houses until four or five in the morning. She thinks I am out with other women, and so tonight I put her into the baggage trunk of the car, and took her along, so that she finds out for herself, and now I would like to let her out, if you don't mind.'

"So I said, 'Of course, let her out immediately.'

"So he opened the trunk of the car, and his little wife came out and stretched herself, and she thanked me, and sat in front with him, and she

put her arms around his neck while he was driving, and she said that she forgave him. And that is all."

As she talked Gala was busy feeding her two small birds, who cracked sunflower seeds with their parrot jaws. Outside in the street the crash of little boys' voices was heard as they came rushing out of school. Gala stood against the sunlighted window, her lithe figure silhouetted, and Miomo Corti studied her. He said, "I too forgive you, Gala." But she did not hear it. There was the sound of the bells for the full midday concert from the towers of Notre Dame.

As it is now, so it was then, only more so—a setting like the scenery for a Viennese operetta. A place in which, a plot in which nothing violent would happen. The décor was in pastel colors, gay and simple and immediately understood. In it people walked about in lovely costumes.

There was music everywhere. Men in uniforms, women who were elegant. Peasant women in beautifully embroidered silks. The emperor had a villa close by and a joke was told about Francis Joseph, who was a serious man.

He had invited the Danny Kaye of those days, a comedian named Giradi, to cheer him up. They sat opposite each other and there was silence and then the emperor said: "Why don't you say something funny?"

Giradi replied: "What could you say that's funny when you lunch with the emperor?"

Attributions

I. Behind the Scenes

ADIEU TO THE OLD RITZ—*Town and Country*, December 1950

MONSIEUR VICTOR—*Life Class*, The Viking Press, 1938; *Hotel Bemelmans*, The Viking Press, 1946

"THE PROBLEM OF SEATING PEOPLE . . ."—*Holiday*, February 1953

GRAPES FOR MONSIEUR CAPE—*Life Class*, The Viking Press, 1938; *Hotel Bemelmans*, The Viking Press, 1946

HERR OTTO BRAUHAUS—*Life Class*, The Viking Press, 1938; *Hotel Bemelmans*, The Viking Press, 1946

BEAU MAXIME—*Life Class*, The Viking Press, 1938; *Hotel Bemelmans*, The Viking Press, 1946

THE EDUCATION OF A WAITER—*Life Class*, The Viking Press, 1938; *Hotel Bemelmans*, The Viking Press, 1946

DINNER OUT—*Life Class*, The Viking Press, 1938; *Hotel Bemelmans*, The Viking Press, 1946

OLD LUCHOW—*Life Class*, The Viking Press, 1938; *Hotel Bemelmans*, The Viking Press, 1946

ART AT THE HOTEL SPLENDIDE—*Hotel Splendide*, The Viking Press, 1941; *Hotel Bemelmans*, The Viking Press, 1946

THE BRAVE COMMIS—*Life Class*, The Viking Press, 1938; *Hotel Bemelmans*, The Viking Press, 1946

"THE ARMY IS LIKE A MOTHER . . ."—*My War with the United States*, The Viking Press, 1937; *The World of Bemelmans*, The Viking Press, 1955

THE BUTTERMACHINE—*My War with the United States*, The Viking Press, 1937; *The World of Bemelmans*, The Viking Press, 1955

NO TROUBLE AT ALL—*Small Beer*, The Viking Press, 1939; *Hotel Bemelmans*, The Viking Press, 1946; *The World of Bemelmans*, The Viking Press, 1955

AFFAIR—*Life Class*, The Viking Press, 1938; *Hotel Bemelmans*, The Viking Press, 1946

"ALL MAÎTRES D'HÔTEL LOVE TO EAT . . ."—*Life Class*, The Viking Press, 1938; *Hotel Bemelmans*, The Viking Press, 1946

COMING OUT—*Life Class*, The Viking Press, 1938; *Hotel Bemelmans*, The Viking Press, 1946

"MY FIRST VISIT TO PARIS . . ."—*Holiday*, January 1954

THEODORE AND "THE BLUE DANUBE"—*Small Beer*, The Viking Press, 1939; *The World of Bemelmans*, The Viking Press, 1955

"MOST SWINDLES IN AUSTRIA . . ."—*Holiday*, August 1962

THE KITCHEN OF THE GOLDEN BASKET—*The Golden Basket*, The Viking Press, 1936

LADY MENDL'S CHEF—*Father, Dear Father*, The Viking Press, 1953

THE SURVIVORS—*The Best of Times*, Simon and Schuster, 1948

MONSIEUR ALBERT OF MAXIM's—*The Best of Times*, Simon and Schuster, 1948

ON INNKEEPING—*Holiday*, February 1953

THE CHEF I ALMOST HIRED—*My Life in Art*, Harper & Brothers, 1958

MONSIEUR DUMAINE—*Town and Country*, January 1959

MONSIEUR SOULÉ—*Holiday*, February 1953

II. At Table

DOWN WHERE THE WÜRZBURGER FLOWS—*The World of Bemelmans*, The Viking Press, 1955

GRANDFATHER AND THE ZIPPERL—*Life Class*, The Viking Press, 1938; *Hotel Bemelmans*, The Viking Press, 1946

"AMONG THE BIRDS THAT MAKE GOOD EATING . . ."—*The High World*, Harper & Brothers, 1954

FILET DE SOLE COLBERT—*Life Class*, The Viking Press, 1938; *Hotel Bemelmans*, The Viking Press, 1946

THE S.S. MESIAS—*The Donkey Inside*, The Viking Press, 1941; *The World of Bemelmans*, The Viking Press, 1955

THE DAY WITH HUNGER—*The Donkey Inside*, The Viking Press, 1941; *The World of Bemelmans*, The Viking Press, 1955

APPLES—*Now I Lay Me Down to Sleep*, The Viking Press, 1944

VACATION—*I Love You, I Love You, I Love You*, The Viking Press, 1942; *The World of Bemelmans*, The Viking Press, 1955.

YOU SHALL HAVE MUSIC—*To the One I Love the Best*, The Viking Press, 1955

"WHAT HAS HAPPENED TO THE FAMOUS VINTAGES . . ."—*The Best of Times*, Simon and Schuster, 1948

LES SAUCISSONS D'ARLES—*The Best of Times*, Simon and Schuster, 1948

BAKED CLAMS CHEZ GEORGES—*The Best of Times*, Simon and Schuster, 1948

THE TREASURED CLIENT—*The Best of Times*, Simon and Schuster, 1948

TO BE A GOURMET—*Holiday*, February 1953

"PRINCES, GENERALS, DEEP-SEA CAPTAINS . . ."—*Town and Country*, August 1958

THE SPAGHETTI TRAIN—*Father, Dear Father*, The Viking Press, 1953

POULETS DE BRESSE—*How to Travel Incognito*, The Viking Press, 1953

LADY MENDL'S DINING ROOM—*To the One I Love the Best*, The Viking Press, 1955

LUNCH WITH BOSY—Unpublished manuscript

LUCHOW'S—*Luchow's German Cookbook* by Leonard Jan Mitchell, Introduction by Ludwig Bemelmans, Doubleday & Company, 1952

"LADY MENDL LIKED DOGS AND PEOPLE SLIM . . ."—*Father, Dear Father*, The Viking Press, 1953

AMONG THE ARABS—*Holiday*, October 1953

CAVIAR—*Playboy*, January 1961

AT THE MÉDITERRANÉE—*How to Travel Incognito*, The Viking Press, 1952

RECIPE FOR COCKLES OR CLAMS—*Town and Country*, September 1959

TEXAS LEGEND—*McCalls*, August 1959

"SECOND DOOR TO YOUR RIGHT . . ."—*To the One I Love the Best*, The Viking Press, 1955

THE BEST WAY TO SEE CUBA—*Holiday*, December 1957

CHEZ RENÉ—*On Board Noah's Ark*, The Viking Press, 1962

THE BEST WAY TO SEE RIO—*Holiday*, December 1958

SHIPOWNER—*On Board Noah's Ark*, The Viking Press, 1962

THE ISLAND OF PORQUEROLLES—Unpublished manuscript, 1961

TONI AND ROCCO—*On Board Noah's Ark*, The Viking Press, 1962

THE SOUL OF AUSTRIA—*Holiday*, August 1962

HOW I TOOK THE CURE—*Holiday*, June 1959

LETTER TO A RESTAURATEUR—Unpublished correspondence, 1962

THE FRENCH TRAIN—Unpublished journal, 1962

HOTEL DE PARIS, MONTE CARLO—Unpublished journal, 1962

L'OUSTAU DE BAUMANIÈRE—Unpublished journal, 1962

THE FIRST CHERRIES—Unpublished journal, 1962

III. Fancies

THE ELEPHANT CUTLET—*My War with the United States*, The Viking Press, 1937; *The World of Bemelmans*, The Viking Press, 1955

CHRISTMAS IN TYROL—*The High World*, Harper & Brothers, 1954

GLOW WINE—*The High World*, Harper & Brothers, 1954

ABOUT CLOUDS AND LEBKUCHEN—*Hansi*, The Viking Press, 1934

WEDDING IN TYROL—*The Eye of God*, The Viking Press, 1949

SCHWEINEREI—*The Blue Danube*, The Viking Press, 1945

TALES OF THE SOUTH AMERICAN GENERAL—*Now I Lay Me Down to Sleep*, The Viking Press, 1944

PEPITO—*Madeline and the Bad Hat*, The Viking Press, 1957

GERMINY A L'OSEILLE—*To the One I Love the Best*, The Viking Press, 1955

ROMANOFF'S FOR LUNCH—*Dirty Eddie*, The Viking Press, 1947

ROMANOFF'S—TWO VIEWS—*To the One I Love the Best*, The Viking Press, 1955; *Dirty Eddie*, The Viking Press, 1947

THE COMMISSARY—*Dirty Eddie*, The Viking Press, 1947

SERVANT TROUBLE—*Dirty Eddie*, The Viking Press, 1947

SNOWY NIGHT IN MALIBU—*Dirty Eddie*, The Viking Press, 1947

COME RAIN, COME SHINE—*Dirty Eddie*, The Viking Press, 1947

MOCAMBO—*Dirty Eddie*, The Viking Press, 1947

HUNGER DREAM—*Father, Dear Father*, The Viking Press, 1953

GUTEN APPETIT—*Are You Hungry Are You Cold*, The World Publishing Company, 1960

TWELVE LITTLE GIRLS—*Madeline*, The Viking Press, 1939

MADAME L'AMBASSADRICE—*How to Travel Incognito*, The Viking Press, 1952

THE INTERNATIONAL—*On Board Noah's Ark*, The Viking Press, 1962

THE WOMAN OF MY LIFE—*The Woman of My Life*, The Viking Press, 1957

WEDDING BREAKFAST—*The Woman of My Life*, The Viking Press, 1957

OF PIGS AND TRUFFLES—*The Woman of My Life*, The Viking Press, 1957

PERFECT SERVICE—*The Street Where the Heart Lies*, The World Publishing Company, 1963

HEAVENLY SOUP—*The Street Where the Heart Lies*, The World Publishing Company, 1963

THE TOUR D'ARGENT—*The Street Where the Heart Lies*, The World Publishing Company, 1963

WHEN YOU LUNCH WITH THE EMPEROR—*My Life in Art*, Harper & Brothers, 1958

Permissions

Eclipse Fever by Walter Abish
352 PAGES; *036-5; $15.95

The American Boy's Handy Book by Daniel C. Beard
472 PAGES; 449-0; $12.95

The Book of Camp-Lore & Wood Craft
by Daniel C. Beard
288 PAGES; 352-0; $12.95

The American Girl's Handy Book by Lina & Adelia Beard
496 PAGES; 666-3; $12.95

The Field & Forest Handy Book by Daniel C. Beard
448 PAGES; *165-5; $14.95

Borstal Boy by Brendan Behan
400 PAGES; *105-1; $16.95

La Bonne Table by Ludwig Bemelmans
448 PAGES; 808-9; $17.95

The Best of Beston by Henry Beston
208 PAGES; *104-3; $16.95

The Decline and Fall of Practically Everybody
by Will Cuppy
240 PAGES; 377-1; $15.95

How to Attract the Wombat by Will Cuppy
176 PAGES; *156-6; $14.95

How to Tell Your Friends from the Apes by Will Cuppy
160 PAGES; *297-X; $15.95

The Geography of the Imagination by Guy Davenport
384 PAGES; *080-2; $19.95

Aubrey's Brief Lives by Oliver Lawson Dick (ed.)
408 PAGES; *063-2; $20.95

Fauna and Family by Gerald Durrell
240 PAGES; *441-7; $15.95

Fillets of Plaice by Gerald Durrell
192 PAGES; *354-2; $15.95

Bear
by Marian Engel
128 PAGES; 667-1; $13.95

The Kitchen Book & the Cook Book
by Nicolas Freeling
360 PAGES; 862-5; $17.95

Bright Stars, Dark Trees, Clear Water by Wayne Grady
336 PAGES; *019-5; $16.95

On Eagle Pond
by Donald Hall
272 PAGES; *560-X; $16.95

String Too Short to Be Saved
by Donald Hall
176 PAGES; *554-5; $14.95

Swimmer in the Secret Sea by William Kotzwinkle
96 PAGES; 356-8; $9.95

As I Walked Out One Midsummer Morning
by Laurie Lee
216 PAGES; *392-5; $15.95

Cider With Rosie by Laurie Lee
224 PAGES; 355-1; $15.95

A Moment of War by Laurie Lee
144 PAGES; *516-2; $15.95

Ring of Bright Water by Gavin Maxwell
344 PAGES; *400-X; $18.95

Images and Shadows by Iris Origo
288 PAGES; *103-5; $16.95

War in Val d'Orcia by Iris Origo
256 PAGES; 476-8; $15.95

Giving Up the Gun by Noel Perrin
136 PAGES; 773-2; $12.95

Hamlet's Mill
by Giorgio de Santillana & Hertha von Dechend
576 PAGES; 215-3; $21.95

The Maine Reader by Charles & Samuella Shain (eds.)
544 PAGES; *078-0; $19.95

The Philosopher's Diet by Richard Watson
128 PAGES; *084-5; $14.95

The Philosopher's Demise by Richard Watson
128 PAGES; *227-9; $15.95

NB: *The* ISBN *prefix for titles with an asterisk is 1-56792. The prefix for all others is 0-87923.*